D0556171

LAW OF THE SEA
IN A NUTSHELL

Second Edition

By

LOUIS B. SOHN (1914–2006)

Late Bemis Professor of International Law Emeritus,
Harvard Law School
Late Woodruff Professor of International Law,
University of Georgia School of Law
Late Distinguished Research Professor,
The George Washington University Law School

KRISTEN GUSTAFSON JURAS

Assistant Professor,
University of Montana School of Law

JOHN E. NOYES

Roger J. Traynor Professor of Law,
California Western School of Law

ERIK FRANCKX

President, Department of International and European Law
Director, Center for International Law
Professor, Vrije Universiteit Brussel

WEST®

A Thomson Reuters business

Mat #40498719

Nutshell Series, In a Nutshell and the Nutshell Logo are trademarks registered in the U.S. Patent and Trademark Office.

COPYRIGHT © 1984 WEST PUBLISHING CO.
© 2010 Thomson Reuters

    610 Opperman Drive
    St. Paul, MN 55123
    1–800–313–9378

Printed in the United States of America

ISBN: 978–0–314–16941–9

PREFACE AND DEDICATION

Much has changed in the law of the sea in the quarter century since the 1984 publication of the first edition of Law of the Sea in a Nutshell, by Louis B. Sohn and Kristen Gustafson Juras. The goal of this second edition nevertheless remains the same as that of the first edition: to provide a comprehensive and accessible introduction for students and professionals to the rules, concepts, institutions, and processes underlying the international law of the sea. Some aspects of European law, U.S. law, and other national law are analyzed to illustrate how countries implement their international legal obligations and address oceans issues, but the primary focus is on international law.

The authors of this second edition dedicate it to the memory of their colleague and mentor, Louis B. Sohn (1914–2006), who greatly influenced modern international law. Louis Sohn participated in the 1945 San Francisco drafting conference that established the United Nations and, during 1969–1971, worked as the first Counselor on International Law at the U.S. Department of State. His vision, dedication, vast knowledge, and skill made him instrumental in the development of the modern law of the sea. In his capacity as a U.S. delegate to the Third United Nations Conference on the Law of the Sea from 1974 to 1982, he was one of the primary architects of the dispute settlement provisions of the 1982 Law of the Sea Convention. Louis Sohn also contributed significantly to many other areas of international law, including human rights, international environmental law, international organizations, arms control and disarmament, and dispute settlement. Those active in the International Law Section of the American Bar Association, the American Society of International Law, and the American Branch of the International Law Association know about his dedication to and leadership of those organizations. Louis Sohn also served as a reporter for the American Law Institute's Restatement (Third) of the Foreign Relations Law of the United States. In his distinguished career as a scholar and teacher at Harvard Law School, the University of Georgia School of Law (where he taught Kristen Gustafson Juras and Erik Franckx), and The George Washington University Law School, he encouraged many of his students to pursue careers in international law. We are immensely grateful for his tireless and persistent efforts to mold a better international legal system for future generations.

The authors are grateful as well to many other colleagues, far too numerous to mention, who have supported their work and influenced their views about the law of the sea. William Aceves, Craig Allen, Caitlyn Antrim, Coalter Lathrop, and Steven Smith were particularly helpful with issues related to this volume. Andres Haladay, Jamie Howard, Amy Lord, Omar Nassar, Emily Von Jentzen, Linda

Weathers, Bobbi Weaver, Shanshan Xue, and Xiping Zhou provided essential research support, and the technical support of Wendy Owens, Diane Sopko, and Joyce Stallworth was invaluable.

KRISTEN GUSTAFSON JURAS
Missoula

JOHN E. NOYES
San Diego

ERIK FRANCKX
Brussels

ABOUT THE AUTHORS

Professor Kristen Gustafson Juras is the coauthor, with Louis B. Sohn, of the first edition of Law of the Sea in a Nutshell (1984). She teaches property, business, tax, and commercial classes at the University of Montana School of Law and has taught classes on the law of the sea at the Marco Polo Institute of Xiamen University in Xiamen, China. Professor Juras has been active in the Jessup International Moot Court Competition as a judge and coach, and has participated in the drafting of the American Bar Association's White Paper on International Environmental Issues and the Rule of Law. Prior to teaching, Professor Juras practiced for more than twenty years, including the representation of clients in international transactions.

Professor John E. Noyes is the Roger J. Traynor Professor of Law at California Western School of Law. He has also taught international law or law of the sea classes at the University of Connecticut School of Law, Roger Williams University School of Law, Suffolk University Law School, Wake Forest University School of Law, Victoria University (Wellington) in New Zealand, and the University of San Diego Institute of International and Comparative Law. His books include International Law Cases and Commentary (3d ed. 2006) (with Mark W. Janis) and Cases and Materials on the International Law of the Sea (2004) (with Louis B. Sohn), and he has written numerous other publications about the international law of the sea and international dispute settlement. Professor Noyes is the President of the American Branch of the International Law Association and the former Chair of the American Bar Association's Law of the Sea Committee, and he has been an American Branch, ILA representative on three International Law Association law of the sea committees.

Professor Erik Franckx is President of the Department of International and European Law and Director of the Center for International Law at the Vrije Universiteit Brussel (V.U.B.). Professor Franckx teaches at several other institutions, including Vesalius College (V.U.B.), the Université Libre de Bruxelles, the Brussels School of International Studies (University of Kent at Canterbury), the Program on International Legal Cooperation (Institute of European Studies, V.U.B.), and the Université Paris–Sorbonne Abu Dhabi. He has been appointed by Belgium as a member of the Permanent Court of Arbitration, The Hague, The Netherlands; as an expert in marine scientific research for use in special arbitration under the 1982 United Nations Convention on the Law of the Sea; as a legal expert in the Advisory Body of Experts of the Law of the Sea of the Intergovernmental Oceanographic Commission of the United Nations Educational, Scientific and Cultural Organization; and as an expert in maritime boundary delimitation to the International Hydrographic Organization. Professor Franckx is the author of numerous writings on the international law of the sea.

OUTLINE

TABLE OF CASES

References are to Pages

TABLE OF CASES

TABLE OF CASES

LOS CONVENTION TABLE

TABLE OF TREATIES

Short Title	**Full Title and Citation**
1910 United States–Great Britain Boundary Treaty	Treaty Concerning the Boundary Line of Passamaquoddy Bay (May 21, 1910), 36 Stat. 2477, T.S. No. 551
1911 Fur Seal Convention	Convention Between the United States and Other Powers Providing for the Preservation and Protection of Fur Seals (July 7, 1911), 37 Stat. 1542, T.S. No. 564
1919 Treaty of Peace with Germany	Treaty of Peace between the Allied and Associated Powers and Germany (June 28, 1919), 225 Consol. T.S. 188
1923 Statute on the International Régime of Maritime Ports	Convention and Statute on the International Régime of Maritime Ports, and Protocol of Signature thereto (Dec. 9, 1923), 58 L.N.T.S. 285
1924 United States–United Kingdom Anti–Smuggling Convention	Convention for the Prevention of Smuggling of Intoxicating Liquors (Jan. 23, 1924), 43 Stat. 1761, T.S. No. 685
1926 Convention to Suppress the Slave Trade and Slavery	Convention to Suppress the Slave Trade and Slavery (Sept. 25, 1926), 46 Stat. 2183, T.S. No. 778, 60 L.N.T.S. 253
1936 Montreux Straits Convention	Convention Concerning the Regime of the Straits, with Annexes and Protocol (July 20, 1936), 173 L.N.T.S. 213
1944 Chicago Convention on International Civil Aviation	Convention on International Civil Aviation (Dec. 7, 1944), 61 Stat. 1180, T.I.A.S. No. 1591, 15 U.N.T.S. 295

TABLE OF TREATIES

TABLE OF TREATIES

Short Title	Full Title and Citation
1961 Single Convention on Narcotic Drugs	Single Convention on Narcotic Drugs (Mar. 30, 1961), 18 U.S.T. 1407, 520 U.N.T.S. 204
1962 Convention on Liability for Operators of Nuclear Ships	Convention on the Liability of Operators of Nuclear Ships (May 25, 1962), 57 Am. J. Intl. L. 268 (1963)
1963 Convention on Civil Liability for Nuclear Damage	Vienna Convention on Civil Liability for Nuclear Damage (May 21, 1963), 1063 U.N.T.S. 265
1963 Limited Test Ban Treaty	Treaty Banning Nuclear Weapon Tests in the Atmosphere, in Outer Space and Under Water (Aug. 5, 1963), 14 U.S.T. 1313, 480 U.N.T.S. 43
1963 Convention on Offences and Certain Other Acts Committed on Board Aircraft	Convention on Offences and Certain Other Acts Committed on Board Aircraft (Sept. 14, 1963), 20 U.S.T. 2941, 704 U.N.T.S. 219
1964 Sweden–United States Agreement Relating to the Use of Swedish Ports and Waters by the N.S. Savannah	Exchange of Notes Constituting an Agreement Between the United States and Sweden Relating to the Use of Swedish Ports and Waters by the N.S. Savannah (July 6, 1964), 529 U.N.T.S. 287
1965 Maritime Traffic Convention	Convention on Facilitation of International Maritime Traffic (Apr. 9, 1965), 18 U.S.T. 411, 591 U.N.T.S. 265
1965 Denmark–Norway Continental Shelf Boundary Agreement	Agreement Between Denmark and Norway Relating to the Delimitation of the Continental Shelf (Dec. 8, 1965), 634 U.N.T.S. 76

Short Title	Full Title and Citation
1972 Convention on the Prevention of Marine Pollution by Dumping of Wastes and Other Matter	Convention on the Prevention of Marine Pollution by Dumping of Wastes and Other Matter (Dec. 29, 1972), 26 U.S.T. 2403, 1046 U.N.T.S. 120
1973 Protocol Relating to Intervention on the High Seas in Cases of Pollution by Substances Other than Oil	Protocol Relating to Intervention on the High Seas in Cases of Pollution by Substances Other than Oil, 1973 (Feb. 11, 1973), 34 U.S.T. 3407, 1313 U.N.T.S. 4
1973 Convention on Trade in Endangered Species of Wild Fauna and Flora (CITES)	Convention on International Trade in Endangered Species of Wild Fauna and Flora (Mar. 3, 1973), 27 U.S.T. 1087, 993 U.N.T.S. 243
1973 Convention for the Prevention of Pollution from Ships, as modified by the 1978 Protocol (MARPOL)	International Convention for the Prevention of Pollution by Ships (Nov. 2, 1973), 1340 U.N.T.S. 184, amended by Protocol of 1978 Relating to the International Convention for the Prevention of Pollution from Ships, 1973 (Feb. 17, 1978), 1340 U.N.T.S. 61
1973 Internationally Protected Persons Convention	Convention on the Prevention and Punishment of Crimes against Internationally Protected Persons, Including Diplomatic Agents (Dec. 14, 1973), 28 U.S.T. 1975, 1035 U.N.T.S. 167
1974 Japan–South Korea Joint Development Zone Agreement	Agreement Concerning Joint Development of the Southern Part of the Continental Shelf (Jan. 30, 1974), 1225 U.N.T.S. 103

TABLE OF TREATIES

Short Title	Full Title and Citation
1992 Convention on the Protection of the Marine Environment of the Baltic Sea Area (HELCOM)	Convention on the Protection of the Marine Environment of the Baltic Sea Area (Apr. 9, 1992), 2099 U.N.T.S. 195
1992 Protocol on Cooperation in Combating Pollution of the Black Sea Marine Environment by Oil and Other Harmful Substances in Emergency Situations	Protocol on Cooperation in Combating Pollution of the Black Sea Marine Environment by Oil and Other Harmful Substances in Emergency Situations (Apr. 21, 1992), 1764 U.N.T.S. 24
1992 Protocol on the Protection of the Black Sea Marine Environment Against Pollution by Dumping	Protocol on the Protection of the Black Sea Marine Environment Against Pollution by Dumping (Apr. 21, 1992), 1764 U.N.T.S. 27
1992 United Nations Framework Convention on Climate Change	United Nations Framework Convention on Climate Change (May 9, 1992), 1771 U.N.T.S. 107
1992 Convention on Biological Diversity	Convention on Biological Diversity (June 5, 1992), 1760 U.N.T.S. 79
1992 Convention for the Protection of the Marine Environment of the North–East Atlantic (OSPAR)	Convention for the Protection of the Marine Environment of the North–East Atlantic (Sept. 22, 1992), 32 Intl. Leg. Materials 1069 (1993)
1992 Fund Convention	Protocol of 1992 to Amend the International Convention for the Establishment of an International Fund for Compensation for Oil Pollution Damage of 18 December 1971 (Nov. 27, 1992), 1953 U.N.T.S. 373

TABLE OF TREATIES

ILLUSTRATIONS AND TABLES

LAW OF THE SEA
IN A NUTSHELL

Second Edition

CHAPTER 1

INTRODUCTION

From the early times when sailors and fishermen first ventured into the sea, two principles traditionally governed the law of the sea: the right of the coastal state to control a narrow strip along the coast, and the freedoms of navigation and fishing in the high seas beyond that coastal area. Some states made attempts to appropriate vast areas of the sea. For example, centuries ago Rome and later Venice claimed dominion over the Mediterranean, and Great Britain over the North Sea. In the sixteenth and early seventeenth centuries, Portugal and Spain claimed control over the seas connecting America, Africa, and southern Asia. See Thomas Weymyss Fulton, The Sovereignty of the Sea 1–22 (1911; reprinted 2002). In the "battle of the books" in the seventeenth century the Dutchman Hugo Grotius (de Groot) advanced the concept of the freedom of the sea, debating the issue with the Englishman John Selden, who advocated "closed seas." Grotius's views prevailed, reinforced in the eighteenth and nineteenth centuries by British sea power, which was exercised to keep the oceans open for trade and fishing. On the high seas, a vessel was generally subject only to the authority of the state in which it was registered, known as the "flag state." For 300 years there were only occasional challenges to the freedoms of the high seas, and the rules governing the exercise of these freedoms (especially the freedoms of navigation and fishing) were generally accepted as customary international law. See Ruth Lapidoth, Freedom of Navigation— Its Legal History and Its Normative Basis, 6 J. Mar. L. & Com. 259 (1975).

In the twentieth century the international law codification movement addressed both traditional and new law of the sea issues. The League of Nations in 1930 and then the United Nations in its 1958 and 1960 First and Second United Nations Conferences on the Law of the Sea (UNCLOS I and UNCLOS II) tried to solve the recurrent issue of the breadth of the territorial sea under the control of coastal states. These efforts proved unsuccessful, but UNCLOS I resulted in the codification of many other rules governing the territorial sea and the high seas in the 1958 High Seas Convention, the 1958 Fishing on the High Seas Convention, and the 1958 Territorial Sea Convention. A fourth convention, the 1958 Continental Shelf Convention, added new rules relating to the oil-rich continental shelf, the submerged part of the land territory over which coastal states, led by the United States, started claiming jurisdiction in the 1940s.

The new treaties soon proved largely inadequate, due to the rapid increase in the use of the oceans and in the exploitation of its resources. Fishing ceased to be a local enterprise, as large factory ships and vast fleets of smaller ships started roaming the oceans, severely depleting the resources of one area after another. Mammoth oil tankers began carrying tremendous quantities of oil across the oceans, and several horrendous oil spills made the people of the world conscious of the dangers of pollution of their beaches and fishing grounds. The marine environment could no longer cope with the assault from many directions: dumping of wastes from land, oil pollution from ships, and additional oil pollution from drilling on the continental shelf. Technology developed to the point that even resources on the deep seabed, some 5,000 meters (over two and a half miles) below the surface of the sea, became accessible, and a new regime became necessary for governing the potential exploitation of billions of tons of polymetallic nodules, potato-sized lumps containing manganese, copper, nickel, and cobalt.

Consequently, in the late 1960s, the world was faced with a nightmare of conflicts over maritime rights. Not only did disparate views arise between developed and developing countries, coastal and land-locked states, and large and small maritime powers, but also within these groups. The only logical solution was the establishment of a new international legal regime, a code of international law for the oceans. Therefore, the states arranged for the Third United Nations Law of the Sea Conference (UNCLOS III). Over a period of nine years, 1973–1982, UNCLOS III hammered out a convention on the law of the sea, a complex document of some 400 articles (approximately 300 in the main text and 100 in annexes), containing provisions on fifteen major topics. The geographical area covered is tremendous, comprising more than seventy percent of the surface of the earth. In the final division of spoils, the coastal states were able to obtain jurisdiction (as a rule, diminishing in proportion to distance from land) over the resources and uses of approximately one-third of the ocean area. The 1982 United Nations Convention on the Law of the Sea (referred to in this text as the LOS Convention) set out the rights and responsibilities of coastal states and other states in the following maritime zones:

– internal waters, such as ports, located inside a coastal state's baseline (usually its coastline);

– the territorial sea, extending up to twelve nautical miles[1] from the baseline, over which a coastal state has sovereignty (subject to the right of other states to sail their vessels through the territorial sea in innocent passage);

– the contiguous zone, located outside the territorial sea and extending up to twenty-four nautical miles from the baseline, in which the coastal state may prevent violations of its fiscal, customs, immigration, and sanitary laws;

– the exclusive economic zone, located outside the territorial sea and extending up to 200 nautical miles from the baseline, in which the coastal state has sovereign rights or jurisdiction over natural

1. A nautical mile is 1852 meters, as compared to a land or statute mile of 1609.34 meters. As used in this text, "mile" generally refers to a nautical mile. In illustrations and tables, nautical mile is abbreviated as "M."

resources and specified economic uses, and in which other states enjoy specified high seas freedoms;

– a continental shelf, in general extending as far as the exclusive economic zone and in some cases beyond it, comprising the seabed and subsoil of the natural prolongation of a coastal state's land territory, and over which the coastal state has sovereign rights to exploit the natural resources found there.

The LOS Convention also contains separate provisions concerning archipelagic states and the rights and responsibilities of coastal states in straits near their shores. In addition, the LOS Convention established a legal regime governing mineral resources in the Area, which is the seabed and subsoil beyond the limits of national jurisdiction. For the various maritime zones, the LOS Convention developed many new rules, more precise than in the past, to control navigation, fishing, and exploitation of the other resources of the sea, and to protect the marine environment from pollution.

More than 120 states signed the LOS Convention in December 1982 at Montego Bay, Jamaica, and a dozen other countries signed it soon thereafter. One country—the United States—was conspicuously absent. In 1981 the Reagan administration expressed some doubts about the compromises previous U.S. administrations had reached with other countries, especially the developing countries, and finally decided that the LOS Convention was not acceptable to it. In particular, the Reagan administration opposed some provisions relating to deep seabed mining as contrary to its philosophy and ideologically alien. Nevertheless, it indicated that it would regard practically all the other provisions, especially those relating to international navigation and the rights and duties of coastal states, as customary international law and as such binding on all states, whether parties to the LOS Convention or not. In April 1983 President Reagan proclaimed a 200–mile wide exclusive economic zone, in terms consistent with the LOS Convention, and promised that the United States, subject to reciprocity, would respect similar zones established by other states. Exec. Procl. No. 5030, 48 Fed. Reg. 10,605 (1983), 22 Intl. Leg. Materials 465 (1983).

In November 1993 the LOS Convention received its sixtieth ratification, thus allowing the Convention to enter into force, in accordance with its terms, one year later. In July 1994 negotiation of a Part XI Implementation Agreement, proposed by the U.N. Secretary–General, was concluded. This Agreement, which is applied with the LOS Convention as a single instrument, modified the Convention's provisions concerning deep seabed mining to which the Reagan administration had objected. These modifications prompted many industrialized states to accept the Convention, as modified by the Implementation Agreement. As of July 15, 2009, there were 159 parties to the Convention, including, with the exception of the United States, the major developed states.

The practice of the United States, a major maritime power with an extensive coastline, has and likely will continue to influence the international law of the sea, and U.S. measures concerning the law of the sea are noted throughout this text. Although the United States is not a party to the LOS Convention, it has accepted many of the dozens of other international treaties that address specific law of the sea issues and that complement the LOS Convention. In addition, U.S. administrations have continued to promote the LOS Convention itself. The Clinton administration signed the 1994 Implementation Agreement and sent it, together with the 1982 LOS Convention, to the Senate, recommending that the Senate give its advice and consent to U.S. acceptance of the modified Convention. Sen. Treaty Doc. No. 103–39 (1994). The George W. Bush administration also urged U.S. acceptance of the Convention. 2001 Digest of U.S. Practice in International Law 676, 683; President's Statement on Advancing U.S. Interests in the World's Oceans, May 15, 2007, 46 Intl. Leg. Materials 890 (2007). In 2004 and again in 2007, the Senate Foreign Relations Committee recommended that the U.S. Senate give its advice and consent to U.S. acceptance of the LOS Convention as modified by the 1994 Implementation Agreement. The Obama administration also supports U.S. acceptance. As of July 15, 2009, however, the full Senate had not voted on the matter.

Meanwhile, U.S. policy is "to act in a manner consistent with" the LOS Convention's "provisions relating to traditional uses of the oceans and to encourage other countries to do likewise." Presidential Letter of Transmittal of the Law of the Sea Convention, Oct. 6, 1994, Sen. Treaty Doc. No. 103–39, at iii (1994). As we shall see throughout this book, the United States has incorporated many rules found in the LOS Convention, along with many other law of the sea treaties, into its legislation and executive branch proclamations. The LOS Convention also has shaped, and in many respects provides the best evidence of, customary international law, which U.S. courts may apply in accordance with the rules articulated by the U.S. Supreme Court in The Paquete Habana, 175 U.S. 677, 700 (1900) ("International law is part of our law, and must be ascertained and administered by the courts of justice of appropriate jurisdiction, as often as questions of right depending upon it are duly presented for their determination. For this purpose, where there is no treaty, and no controlling executive or legislative act or judicial decision, resort must be had to the customs and usages of civilized nations[.]"), and The Charming Betsy, 6 U.S. 64, 118 (1804) ("[A]n act of congress ought never to be construed to violate the law of nations if any other possible construction remains[.]").

The LOS Convention established new international institutions, which are fully operational. These include the International Tribunal for the Law of the Sea (http://www.itlos.org), the International Seabed Authority (http://www.isa.org.jm), and the Commission on the Limits of the Continental Shelf (http://www.un.org/Depts/los/clcs_new/clcs_

home.htm). Other specialized and regional international organizations, many of which predate UNC-LOS III and the LOS Convention, engage in a wide range of study, advice-giving, treaty-making, and policy-making functions concerning oceans matters. Global intergovernmental organizations involved with the law of the sea include the United Nations Environment Programme (UNEP) (http://www.unep.org), the International Maritime Organization (IMO) (http://www.imo.org), the Food and Agriculture Organization (FAO) (http://www.fao.org), the International Labor Organization (ILO) (http://www.ilo.org), and the United Nations Conference on Trade and Development (UNCTAD)(http://www.unctad.org). Nongovernmental organizations (NGOs) have become increasingly involved in education and lobbying concerning oceans issues, and some NGOs participate in the work of international organizations.

Although the law of the sea still reflects the traditional tension between the rights of coastal states to exercise authority near their shores and the rights of other states to use the oceans freely, broader perspectives have evolved on many oceans issues. Marine pollution and the depletion of living resources are matters of regional and global concern. The 1972 United Nations Conference on the Human Environment in Stockholm, the 1992 United Nations Conference on Environment and Development in Rio de Janeiro, and the 2002 World Summit on Sustainable Development in Johannesburg have led to the development of widely accepted treaties, broad declarations of principles, and increased attention to the interconnected nature of the marine ecosystem. Individuals and states have increasingly recognized that the law of the sea addresses human rights, including the rights of laborers on board ships, slaves, crew members detained in foreign ports, and those claiming property interests in marine resources. Numerous treaties and cooperative measures developed by states and international organizations have tackled threats to maritime security. The marine environment, the depletion of fish stocks and other living resources, human rights, and maritime security are among the many oceans issues that concern the international community as a whole.

A wide range of forums interpret and apply traditional and new rules about the law of the sea. Many oceans issues arise before national courts, agencies, and military services; this book highlights many applications of the international law of the sea by U.S. and other forums. Law of the sea issues are also addressed in diplomatic correspondence and interstate negotiations. In addition, international organizations and international courts and tribunals interpret and apply the law of the sea. It is important to understand the process dimension of this body of law, as well as its substantive rules.

This book first explores traditional concepts that continue to influence the modern law of the sea: high seas freedoms (Chapter 2), the nationality of vessels (Chapter 3), and the duties and jurisdiction of flag states with respect to vessels of their nationality (Chapter 4). Flag state jurisdiction has been one central mechanism for implementing law of the sea rules. Coastal zones also remain essential to an understanding of the modern law of the sea, and the next two chapters address foundational concepts concerning such zones: the baseline for determining zones of national jurisdiction (Chapter 5) and boundaries of maritime jurisdiction between adjacent and opposite states (Chapter 6). The book then examines the rights and responsibilities of coastal states and other states in various coastal zones, including internal waters and ports (Chapter 7), the territorial sea and contiguous zone (Chapter 8), the exclusive economic zone (Chapter 9), and the continental shelf (Chapter 10). Chapter 11 explores the law applicable to the deep seabed beyond the limits of national jurisdiction, particularly its mineral resources. Chapters 12–14 build on concepts introduced in earlier chapters. Chapter 12 addresses marine pollution, Chapter 13 the conservation of high seas living resources, and Chapter 14 maritime terrorism and security. Chapter 15 discusses how oceans disputes are settled, and Chapter 16 explores future challenges facing the oceans.

Illustration 1: Zones of National Jurisdiction

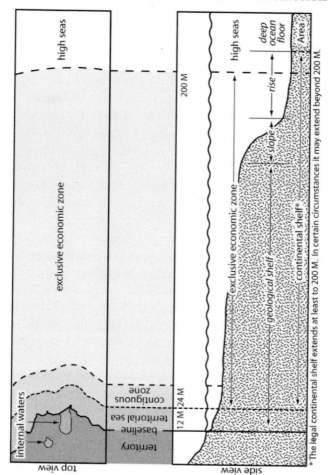

CHAPTER 2

THE HIGH SEAS AND HIGH SEAS FREEDOMS

A. INTRODUCTION

The high seas are an international common space available for lawful uses by all states and their citizens. No state may appropriate any part of the high seas or otherwise subject it to that state's sovereignty. LOS Convention, Article 89; 1958 High Seas Convention, Article 2. The legal framework governing the use of those areas of the oceans that are not subject to coastal state sovereignty has traditionally depended on the "freedom of the high seas," which is based on two core principles. First, a ship of any state may freely navigate and engage in lawful activities on the oceans, without interference from other states. Second, the state of the ship's nationality has exclusive jurisdiction over the ship on the high seas; with few exceptions, no other state may exercise jurisdiction over that ship. Nationality of vessels and jurisdiction over vessels are addressed in Chapters 3 and 4.

In this Chapter we first discuss efforts to define the "high seas" (Section B), and then turn to the fundamental concept of freedom of the high seas (Section C). Section D addresses traditional limita-

13

tions on the exercise of high seas freedoms, and Section E examines the duty to render assistance to those in distress on the high seas.

B. DEFINITION OF "HIGH SEAS"

Article 1 of the 1958 High Seas Convention defined "high seas" as "all parts of the sea that are not included in the territorial sea or in the internal waters of a state." In contrast, the LOS Convention does not specifically define the term "high seas." The term certainly includes the water column outside any zone of national jurisdiction. In drafting the LOS Convention, however, a dispute arose as to whether the high seas also included the exclusive economic zone (EEZ). The new regime of the EEZ, as codified in Part V of the LOS Convention, extended coastal state jurisdiction and sovereign rights over certain resource-related activities in an area beyond the territorial sea, up to 200 nautical miles from the coastal state's baseline. The extension of coastal state rights over the newly created EEZ had the effect of bringing significant portions of the high seas under a new form of coastal state authority. To protect their exercise of historical high seas freedoms within the EEZ, many maritime countries, including the United States, took the position that the EEZ was a part of the high seas, subject to special rights of the coastal states. Other countries took the position that the EEZ is not a part of the high seas, but rather is a special zone of the coastal state subject to the freedom of navigation and certain other high seas freedoms. Reports

of the United States Delegation to the Third United
Nations Conference on the Law of the Sea 148–149,
174–175 (Myron H. Nordquist & Choon-ho Park
eds., 1983).

As finally adopted, the LOS Convention does not
define the EEZ to be either a part of the territorial
sea or a part of the high seas. As discussed in more
detail in the following Sections and Chapter 9, the
delineation of the exact scope of high seas freedoms
in the EEZ of another state is an area of on-going
development in international law. For a discussion
of some of these tensions, see Jon M. Van Dyke,
Balancing Navigational Freedom with Environmental and Security Concerns, 2003 Colo. J. Intl. Envtl.
L. & Policy 19; George V. Galdorisi, Military Activities in the Exclusive Economic Zone: Preventing
Uncertainty and Defusing Conflict, 32 Cal. W. Intl.
L.J. 253 (2002).

C. HIGH SEAS FREEDOMS

The freedom of the high seas has been a basic
precept of the law of the sea since the seventeenth
century (see Chapter 1). All states, both coastal and
land-locked, have the right to exercise the freedom
of the high seas, which includes, inter alia:

(1) the freedom of navigation;

(2) the freedom of overflight;

(3) the freedom of fishing;

(4) the freedom to lay submarine cables and pipelines;

(5) the freedom to construct artificial islands, installations and structures; and

(6) the freedom of scientific research.

The first four of these freedoms are expressly mentioned in Article 2 of the 1958 High Seas Convention; the last two were added in Article 87(1) of the LOS Convention.

All high seas freedoms apply in the waters that do not constitute the internal waters, territorial sea, or exclusive economic zone (EEZ) of a state, or the archipelagic waters of an archipelagic state. LOS Convention, Article 86; see also 1958 High Seas Convention, Article 1. Within the EEZ of other states, a foreign vessel may exercise the freedoms of navigation, of overflight, and of laying submarine cables and pipeline, along with "other internationally lawful uses of the sea related to these freedoms." LOS Convention, Article 58(1). A foreign vessel may only do so, however, with due regard to the rights and duties of the coastal state and in compliance with the laws and regulations of the coastal state, insofar as those laws and regulations are compatible with international law. Id. at Article 58(3). Foreign states and vessels may not exercise, within the EEZ of another state, the freedom to construct artificial installations, the freedom to fish, or the freedom to conduct marine research. Id. at Article 58(1). As discussed in Chapter 9, these activities are subject to the regulation of the coastal state.

The exercise by a coastal state of its rights regarding the continental shelf, which may extend beyond the EEZ in certain situations, "must not infringe or result in any unjustifiable interference with navigation and other rights and freedoms of other States as provided for" in the LOS Convention. Id. at Article 78(2). For further discussion of the continental shelf, see Chapter 10.

As discussed in more detail in Section D, the exercise by any state of the freedom of the high seas is subject to important limits, including due regard for the interests of other states, refraining from any acts that unreasonably interfere with the use of the high seas by nationals of other states, and compliance with applicable treaties and other rules of international law. Furthermore, the high seas are reserved for peaceful purposes.

1.   Freedom of Navigation

Every state, whether coastal or land-locked, has the right to sail ships flying its flag on the high seas. LOS Convention, Article 90; 1958 High Seas Convention, Article 4. However, due consideration for the interests of passengers, crews, and other states requires that ships on the high seas observe rules relating to the safety of navigation, the protection of life at sea, and the prevention, reduction, and control of pollution of the marine environment. The flag state traditionally has the primary duty to regulate its ships in these regards. See Chapter 4.

"Freedom of navigation" is based on the concept that ships sailing under the flag of any state have the right to navigate across the high seas without interference from another sovereign. On the high seas, subject to certain exceptions discussed below, the flag state alone has the right to exercise jurisdiction over ships sailing under its flag. This principle of non-interference in the navigation of a ship of another nationality applies not only on the high seas, but also restricts coastal states from interfering with a foreign ship's innocent passage through its territorial and archipelagic waters (LOS Convention, Articles 24, 54), or transit passage through straits (id. at Article 44). The regimes of innocent, archipelagic, and transit passage are discussed in Chapter 8.

The freedom of navigation is not without certain limitations and responsibilities. The greatest freedom of navigation is enjoyed by warships and ships owned or operated by states for noncommercial purposes. These ships, when on the high seas, have complete immunity from the jurisdiction of any state other than the flag state. LOS Convention, Articles 95–96; 1958 High Seas Convention, Articles 8(1), 9. Article 29 of the LOS Convention defines a warship as "a ship belonging to the armed forces of a State bearing the external marks distinguishing such ships of its nationality, under the command of an officer duly commissioned by the government of the State and whose name appears in the appropriate service list or its equivalent, and manned by a crew which is under regular armed forces discipline." See also 1958 High Seas Convention, Article 8(2).

As discussed in more detail in Chapter 4, ships, other than warships and government-owned or operated ships involved in noncommercial activities, may be stopped and boarded on the high seas by a warship or law enforcement vessel of another country if there is reasonable cause to suspect that it is engaged in either piracy or the slave trade. LOS Convention, Article 110; 1958 High Seas Convention, Article 22. A warship or law enforcement vessel may also stop and board any ship that is "stateless," as well as any ship that is of the same nationality as the warship or law enforcement vessel. LOS Convention, Article 110; 1958 High Seas Convention, Article 22. If a ship is engaged in unauthorized broadcasting on the high seas, a warship of a state where the transmissions are received or where interference with authorized transmissions is suffered may stop and board the vessel. Additionally, a warship of the nationality of either the ship engaged in unauthorized broadcasting or of any person engaged in the broadcasting may stop and board the vessel. LOS Convention, Articles 109, 110(1)(c). Chapter 4 notes examples of other bilateral and multilateral treaties that also authorize a warship or law enforcement ship of one contracting party to stop and board a ship flying the flag of another contracting party.

If the suspicions giving rise to the stopping and boarding of a foreign vessel prove to be unfounded, and consequently the boarding was not justified, international law requires that the vessel be compensated for any loss resulting from the boarding. LOS Convention, Article 110(3); 1958 High Seas Convention, Article 22(3). See also Chapter 4 for a discussion of what, if any, actions a warship may take against a vessel or its crew if the suspicions giving rise to the stopping and boarding are justified.

2. *Freedom of Overflight*

As the development and use of aircraft expanded in the twentieth century, the principle of freedom of navigation of the high seas correspondingly expanded to include the freedom of overflight in the airspace above the high seas. "Freedom of overflight" means that all states have the right for both their civilian and state-owned or operated airplanes to overfly the high seas, without interference from or regulation by other states. Although Article 39(3) of the LOS Convention governs the overflight of straits, it enunciates the generally accepted principle that in exercising the freedom of overflight, civil aircraft must observe the Rules of the Air enacted by the International Civil Aviation Organization (ICAO) under the auspices of Article 12 of the 1944 Chicago Convention on International Civil Aviation. The 1944 Chicago Convention is the primary international agreement relating to international civil aviation. It also relates to state aircraft in certain important respects, including the obligation that each state, in regulating its state aircraft, must require such aircraft to operate at all times with due regard for the safety of navigation of civil aircraft. Similarly, Article 39(3) of the LOS Convention provides that state aircraft will normally comply with ICAO safety measures and will at all times operate with due regard for the safety of navigation.

The United States and other countries have established "air defense identification zones" (ADIZs), sometimes extending far offshore. ADIZ regulations generally require foreign and domestic aircraft intending to enter the ADIZ to file flight plans and to provide periodic position reports. For U.S. ADIZ regulations, see 14 C.F.R. §§ 99.1 et seq. The purpose in establishing ADIZs is to prevent surprise attacks or threats to national security, and to ensure the safety of international air traffic. Several states, including the United States, have extended ADIZs beyond their territorial sea and into areas where the freedom of overflight may be exercised. There is controversy as to whether such ADIZs are legal under international law, particularly as they apply beyond the territorial sea to aircraft not intending to enter the airspace over the coastal state's territory. Restatement (Third) of U.S. Foreign Relations Law § 521 n.2 (1987). U.S. military sources assert that if a foreign aircraft "is merely passing through the ADIZ" outside the territorial sea, and is not seeking to enter territorial airspace, then "the aircraft need not, as a matter of law, abide by the coastal State's conditions. As a matter of comity and safety, however, most usually do." John Astley III &

Michael N. Schmitt, The Law of the Sea and Naval Operations, 42 A.F. L. Rev. 119, 137–138 (1997). See also Andrew S. Williams, The Interception of Civil Aircraft over the High Seas in the Global War on Terror, 59 A.F. L. Rev. 73 (2007); Kay Hailbronner, Freedom of the Air and the Convention on the Law of the Sea, 77 Am. J. Intl. L. 490, 517–518 (1983); Elizabeth Cuadra, Student Author, Air Defense Identification Zones: Creeping Jurisdiction in the Airspace, 18 Va. J. Intl. L. 485 (1978).

The United States maintains that the freedom of overflight may be freely exercised over the EEZs of other states. While conducting a surveillance mission over the EEZ of the People's Republic of China in April 2001, a U.S. military plane collided mid-air with a Chinese military plane that was monitoring the U.S. aircraft. The Chinese government protested as unlawful the use of the overflight for purposes of military surveillance, asserting that such activity failed to give "due regard" to the sovereign rights of China in its EEZ as required under Article 58 of the LOS Convention. The United States responded that its activities did not exhibit lack of due regard for China's rights, in that they did not interfere with any of the activities over which China has jurisdiction in the EEZ, such as fishing. See 2001 Digest of U.S. Practice in International Law 703–711.

3. Freedom of Fishing

All states have the right to fish on the high seas, subject to their treaty obligations and the rights and duties of coastal states. LOS Convention, Article 116; 1958 High Seas Convention, Article 2; 1958 Fishing on the High Seas Convention, Article 1. When Grotius propounded the principle of open seas (see Chapter 1), he was convinced that fisheries were an inexhaustible resource, and that "[i]f a man were to enjoin other people from fishing, he would not escape the reproach of monstrous greed." Hugo Grotius, The Freedom of the Seas 38 (1633, Ralph van Deman Magoffin trans. & James Brown Scott ed., 1916; reprinted 2001). Modern international law no longer views fisheries as inexhaustible. As noted by the International Court of Justice in the Fisheries Jurisdiction Case (United Kingdom v. Iceland), "the former *laissez-faire* treatment of the living resources of the sea in the high seas has been replaced by a recognition of a duty to have due regard to the rights of other States and the needs of conservation for the benefit of all." 1974 I.C.J. 3, 31.

As negotiators began drafting the LOS Convention, they were aware that unregulated fishing in the high seas had resulted in the over-exploitation and depletion of several fish stocks. Their concerns regarding fishery resources were a primary force behind the adoption of the EEZ regime, which grants the coastal state primary responsibility for

management and conversation of fisheries in its
EEZ. LOS Convention, Article 56. Modern international law also recognizes the obligation of all
states, especially those whose nationals fish in the
high seas, to take measures for the conservation
and management of the living resources of the high
seas, and to ensure that their nationals comply with
these measures. Where appropriate, such measures
may be taken in cooperation with other states. Id.
at Articles 87(1)(e), 117–118; 1958 Fishing on the
High Seas Convention, Articles 1(2), 4. Chapter 13
addresses the obligations of states with regard to
the conservation and management of the living
resources in the high seas.

4. *Freedom to Lay Submarine Cables and Pipelines*

The first transatlantic telegraph cable was laid in
1866. By the year 2000, more than 370,000 kilometers of submarine fiber-optic cable had been laid
across the ocean floors, enough to circle the globe
almost ten times. By 2008 this figure had tripled.
Submarine cables transport a significant portion of
today's telecommunications. Scott Coffen–Smout &
Glen J. Herbert, Submarine Cables: A Challenge for
Ocean Management, 24 Marine Policy 441, 441–442
(2000); International Cable Protection Committee,
The Voyage that Changed the World (2008), available at http://www.iscpc.org/.

All states are entitled to lay submarine cables and
pipelines on the continental shelf and on the seabed
underlying the high seas, subject to provisions of

the LOS Convention. LOS Convention, Articles 79, 87(1)(c), 112; see also 1958 High Seas Convention, Article 26. Subject to its rights to explore and exploit its continental shelf and to prevent pollution from pipelines, the coastal state may not impede the laying or maintenance of submarine cables or pipelines. However, delineation of the course for the laying of pipelines (but not cables) on the continental shelf is subject to the consent of the coastal state. LOS Convention, Article 79; see also 1958 High Seas Convention, Article 26; 1958 Continental Shelf Convention, Article 4.

As evidenced by the adoption of the 1884 Convention for the Protection of Submarine Cables, states have long recognized the need to protect submarine cables from damage that may result from competing uses of the high seas. Every state must adopt laws and regulations necessary to punish its ships or nationals who willfully or through culpable negligence break or injure a submarine cable or pipeline, unless caused with the objective of saving lives or ships. LOS Convention, Article 113; 1958 High Seas Convention, Article 27. Every state must also adopt laws and regulations to cause its nationals who own submarine cables or pipelines to bear the costs of repairs incurred if, in laying or repairing cables or pipelines, those owners injure another cable or pipeline. LOS Convention, Article 114; 1958 High Seas Convention, Article 28. Where ships have sacrificed an anchor, net, or fishing gear to reasonably avoid injury to a cable or pipeline, states must adopt laws and regulations to ensure that the ship owners are indemnified for those costs by the cable or pipeline owner. LOS Convention, Article 115; 1958 High Seas Convention, Article 29.

5. *Freedom to Construct Artificial Islands*

Artificial islands and similar structures are commonly used as deepwater ports and oil drilling rigs. Additional purposes have included use as broadcasting facilities, fish processing facilities, and gambling resorts. On the high seas, all states enjoy the freedom to construct artificial islands and other installations permitted under international law, subject to rules pertaining to the continental shelf. LOS Convention, Article 87(1)(d). As discussed in more detail in Chapter 9, Section K, in the EEZ and on the continental shelf, the coastal state has the exclusive right to construct and regulate the construction, operation, and use of any artificial islands or installations. Id. at Articles 60, 80. Article 147 of the LOS Convention governs the construction and operation of artificial islands for purposes of deep seabed mining activities in the Area, which is the seabed and subsoil beyond national jurisdiction. See generally Chapter 11.

6. *Freedom of Scientific Research*

Although the freedom of scientific research was not explicitly recognized in the 1958 High Seas Convention, scientific activities in the oceans have taken place since the nineteenth century. The world as a whole has benefitted from scientists being able, without impediment, to study the circulation of ocean waters, the biology of the sea floor and the water column, the movement of continents, and other geological activity on the sea floor. One of the most controversial issues at the Third United Nations Conference on the Law of the Sea, however, was the extent to which this freedom should be limited in the newly created EEZ and on the continental shelf. Some coastal states feared that marine scientific research could be used to appropriate coastal state resources or to gain sensitive information that could endanger coastal state security.

All states as well as competent international organizations have the right to conduct research in the water column beyond the limits of the EEZ of coastal states. LOS Convention, Article 257. States and competent international organizations may also conduct scientific research in the seabed and subsoil of the continental shelf beyond the EEZ, except in those areas that the coastal state publicly designates as areas "in which exploitation or detailed exploratory operations focused on those areas are occurring or will occur within a reasonable period of time." Id. at Article 246(6). See Chapter 9, Section J, for a discussion of the rights of the coastal state and noncoastal states to conduct marine scientific research within the EEZ, and Chapter 11, Section F, for a discussion of marine scientific research in the Area.

In the conduct of marine scientific research the following principles apply:

(1) marine research is to be conducted exclusively for peaceful purposes;

(2) such research may not unjustifiably interfere with other legitimate uses of the sea and in turn is to be duly respected by other users;

(3) such research may not constitute the legal basis for any claim to any part of the marine environment or its resources;

(4) such research may deploy and use any type of scientific research installations or equipment, subject to specified conditions.

LOS Convention, Articles 240–241, 258–262.

7. *Other Freedoms*

The freedom of the high seas comprises, *"inter alia,"* the six freedoms explicitly listed in Article 87 of the LOS Convention. The use of the term *"inter alia"* suggests that the list of freedoms is not exclusive. 3 United Nations Convention on the Law of the Sea 1982: A Commentary ¶ 87.9(i) n.26 (Myron H. Nordquist, Neal R. Grandy, Satya N. Nandan & Shabtai Rosenne eds., 1995). Additional freedoms may include, for example, the launching of satellites or the conduct of military exercises. The exercise of such other freedoms, like all high seas freedoms, is subject to the limitations discussed in the following Sections.

D. LIMITATIONS ON THE EXERCISE OF HIGH SEAS FREEDOMS

The exercise of high seas freedoms is subject to important constraints. The concept of freedom of the seas is not a license to conduct war, obliterate living resources, pollute the environment, or unreasonably interfere with lawful uses of the high seas by vessels of other states.

1. Due Regard to Interests of Other States

The high seas freedoms must be exercised by all states with due regard to the interests of other states in their exercise of the freedom of the high seas. LOS Convention, Article 87(2). In the Fisheries Jurisdiction Case (United Kingdom v. Iceland), the International Court of Justice observed that the 1958 High Seas Convention was declaratory of "established principles of international law," including the principle that states, in exercising their high seas freedom, must give "reasonable regard" to the rights of other states. The Court ruled that Iceland's unilateral actions in asserting exclusive fishing rights over certain areas in which the United Kingdom had historically exercised its freedom to fish infringed the "reasonable regard" principle. 1974 I.C.J. 3, 22, 29.

The drafters of the LOS Convention chose to use the term "due regard" in Article 87(2) to replace the "reasonable regard" language used in its predecessor, Article 2 of the 1958 High Seas Convention, after use of the term "due consideration" was considered and rejected. 3 United Nations Convention on the Law of the Sea 1982: A Commentary ¶ 87.9(i) n.32 (Myron H. Nordquist, Neal R. Grandy, Satya N. Nandan & Shabtai Rosenne eds., 1995). The International Law Association (American Branch) Law of the Sea Committee has proposed the following definition for "due regard":

"Due regard," as used in the 1982 LOS Convention, art. 87, is a qualification of the rights of states in exercising the freedoms of the high seas. "Due regard" requires all states, in exercising their high seas freedoms, to be aware of and consider the interests of other states in using the high seas, and to refrain from activities that interfere with the exercise by other states of the freedom of the high seas. States are bound to refrain from any acts that might adversely affect the use of the high seas by nationals of other states. Article 87 recognizes that all states have the right to exercise high seas freedoms, and balances consideration for the rights and interests of all states in this regard.

Reprinted in George K. Walker, Defining Terms in the 1982 Law of the Sea Convention IV: The Last Round of Definitions Proposed by the International Law Association (American Branch) Law of the Sea Committee, 36 Cal. W. Intl. L.J. 133, 174 (2005).

In the Nuclear Tests Cases, Australia and New Zealand brought a proceeding before the International Court of Justice, seeking to stop French nuclear atmospheric weapons testing in the Pacific. Australia and New Zealand asserted, among other arguments, that the conduct of the nuclear tests infringed on and unreasonably interfered with Australia's and New Zealand's freedom of the high seas, primarily their freedom of fishing. Although the Court entered an interim order requiring France to avoid nuclear tests, 1973 I.C.J. 99, in 1974 the Court dismissed the cases after determining that while the matter was pending, France made binding commitments not to undertake further atmospheric tests. 1974 I.C.J. 253, 272 (Australia v. France); 1974 I.C.J. 457, 478 (New Zealand v. France). When France commenced underground (versus under water or atmospheric) nuclear tests on Pacific atolls in the mid–1990s, New Zealand again asserted that the nuclear tests violated, among other rights, the right of New Zealand to exercise its high seas freedoms, but the International Court of Justice determined it did not have jurisdiction over France to examine the claim. 1995 I.C.J. 288. See Barbara Kwiatkowska, New Zealand v. France Nuclear Tests: The Dismissed Case of Lasting Significance, 37 Va. J. Intl. L. 107 (1996).

A common practice among states is the declaration of a temporary warning area on the high seas advising other states of the conduct of government activities, such as military exercises, missile testing, or space vehicle recovery operations, that may be hazardous to navigation or overflight. Foreign vessels are not required to remain outside of the warning zones. In January 1984 the United States issued a notice that U.S. naval forces were operating in the Persian Gulf, and warned aircraft and ships to identify themselves before approaching within five miles of a U.S. naval vessel. The notice, however, did not prohibit transit through the warning zone. When Iran protested the notice as violating international law, the United States responded as follows:

> The procedures adopted by the United States are well established and fully recognized in international practice on and over international waters and straits such as the Persian Gulf, Strait of Hormuz, and the Gulf of Oman. The United States has made clear they will be implemented in a manner that does not impede valid exercises of the freedom of navigation and overflight and of the right of transit passage. Accordingly, the United States cannot accept the assertions by the Government of Iran that these procedures do not comport with international law. The United States will continue to exercise its rights and rejects the protest of the Government of Iran.

Reproduced at M. Nash Leich, Contemporary Practice of the United States Relating to International Law, 78 Am. J. Intl. L. 884, 884–885 (1984). See also Robin R. Churchill & A. Vaughan Lowe, The Law of the Sea 270–277 (3d ed. 1999); Jon M. Van Dyke, Military Exclusion and Warning Zones on the High Seas, in Freedom for the Seas in the 21st Century 445 (Jon M. Van Dyke, Durwood Zaelke & Grant Hewison eds., 1993).

Another use that has been protested as violating the "due regard" principle is the disposal of radioactive waste on the high seas, which is the topic of several treaties, including the 1972 Convention on the Prevention of Marine Pollution by Dumping of Wastes and Other Matter. See Chapter 12, Section E.

States may negotiate treaties to specify the conduct they will engage in to insure that they fulfill their "due regard" obligation. For example, the United States and the Soviet Union entered into the 1972 Agreement for the Prevention of Incidents on and Over the High Seas to establish procedures for state aircraft of one party when approaching warships of the other party on the high seas.

All states also must exercise their high seas freedoms with due regard for rights under the LOS Convention "with respect to activities in the Area." LOS Convention, Article 87(2). See Chapter 11.

2.   *Peaceful Purposes*

Article 88 of the LOS Convention provides that the "high seas shall be reserved for peaceful purposes." Article 301 of the LOS Convention further requires that states, in exercising their rights and duties under the LOS Convention, shall refrain from any threat or use of force in violation of the U.N. Charter. Although these provisions do not prevent all uses of the high seas by naval forces, use of vessels to carry out an act of aggression in violation of Article 2(4) of the U.N. Charter is not permissible.

The LOS Convention neither defines "peaceful purposes" nor identifies the types of military uses of the oceans that are permissible. The United States and many other countries have taken the view that military activities that are consistent with the U.N. Charter are not prohibited on the high seas and that a naval presence is necessary to preserve the peaceful uses of the high seas. See Scott C. Truver, The Law of the Sea and the Military Use of the Oceans in 2010, 45 La. L. Rev. 1221 (1985); Boleslaw A. Boczek, The Peaceful Purposes Clauses: A Reappraisal after the Entry into Effect of the Law of the Sea Convention in the Post–Cold War Era, 13 Ocean Y.B. 404 (1998).

When the United States had grounds to believe in 1962 that the Soviet Union was constructing missile sites in Cuba, President John F. Kennedy authorized, as a measure to preserve the peace and security of the United States, a quarantine for the purpose of inspecting and intercepting cargoes containing materials suspected to be used in constructing the missile sites. Ships not carrying prohibited cargoes were allowed to proceed. See Marjorie M. Whiteman, 4 Digest of International Law 523–529 (1965). For a history of the use of blockades and embargoes on the high seas, see Ronald S. McClain, The Coastal Fishing Vessel Exemption From Capture and Targeting: An Example and Analysis of the Origin and Evolution of Customary International Law, 45 Naval L. Rev. 77, 112–118 (1998).

During the 1982 conflict between Argentina and the United Kingdom regarding the Falkland Islands (Islas Malvinas), both the United Kingdom and Argentina established maritime "exclusion zones." The United Kingdom and Argentina expressed their intent to fire on certain foreign vessels entering or transiting the exclusion zones. Unlike the "warning zones" discussed above, exclusion zones impede or prohibit entry of a vessel into the zone. Commercial and fishing vessels of neutral countries were seized or attacked both within and outside of these exclusion zones. See, for example, the claim brought by the owners of a commercial vessel injured outside of Argentina's exclusion zone in Amerada Hess Shipping Corp. v. Argentine Republic, 830 F.2d 421 (2d Cir. 1987), rev'd, 488 U.S. 428 (1989). The legality of exclusion zones has been much debated. See W.J. Fenrick, The Exclusion Zone Device in the Law of Naval Warfare, 24 Can. Y.B. Intl. L. 91 (1986); G.P. Politakis, Waging War at Sea: The Legality of War Zones, 38 Neth. Intl. L. Rev. 125 (1991).

In 1990, after Iraq's invasion of Kuwait, the U.N. Security Council, which is authorized under the U.N. Charter to adopt legally binding decisions to prevent threats to international peace and security, passed Resolution 661. This Resolution forbade U.N. member states from providing certain goods to Iraq or Kuwait, exporting from those countries, or making economic or financial resources available to them. UN Doc. S/RES/661 (1990). The Security Council subsequently adopted Resolution 665, which called on member states "to use such measures commensurate to the specific circumstances as may be necessary under the authority of the Security Council to halt all inward and outward shipping in order to inspect and verify their cargoes and destinations and to insure strict implementation of the provisions related to such shipping laid down in Resolution 661." UN Doc. S/RES/665 (1990). By the end of the conflict, the international coalition forces responsible for enforcing the Resolutions had conducted over 7,500 challenges to ships, boarded 965, and diverted 51 vessels. Lawrence Freedman & Efraim Karsh, The Gulf Conflict, 1990–1991: Diplomacy and War in the New World Order 153 (1992). For further discussion of military interceptions of vessels relating to the Iraq–Kuwait crisis, see Lois E. Fielding, Maritime Interception: Centerpiece of Economic Sanctions in the New World Order, 53 La. L. Rev. 1191 (1993).

3.   *Other Rules of International Law*

The exercise of the freedom of the high seas is subject not only to the provisions of the LOS Convention, but also to conditions imposed by "other rules of international law." LOS Convention, Article 87(1). There is some uncertainty as to which "other" rules of international law apply in interpreting Article 87. When two states are involved in war, the law of armed conflict applies to transactions between the belligerent states occurring on the high seas, as well as to neutral vessels. Boleslaw A. Boczek, Peaceful Purposes Provisions of the

United Nations Convention on the Law of the Sea, 20 Ocean Dev. & Intl. L. 359, 367–368, 371–372 (1989). An important recent effort to articulate the modern law of naval warfare is the San Remo Manual on International Law Applicable to Armed Conflicts at Sea, prepared under the auspices of the International Institute of Humanitarian Law (Louise Doswald–Beck ed., 1995).

Although many commentators would limit the phrase "other rules of international law" to the law of armed conflict, several argue that the term should not be interpreted so restrictively, and, where the context so requires, rules of international law in addition to the law of armed conflict may apply. See John E. Noyes, Commentary to Definitions for the 1982 Law of the Sea Convention and the Importance of Context: "Ships" and Other Matters, 33 Cal. W. Intl. L.J. 310, 311–314 (2003). See also the Preface to the LOS Convention, which affirms that "matters not regulated by this Convention continue to be governed by the rules and principles of general international law," and LOS Convention, Article 311.

E. DUTY TO RENDER ASSISTANCE

Each state has an obligation to require that the masters of ships flying its flag render assistance to persons in distress on the high seas, in so far as possible without causing serious danger to the ship, crew, or passengers. LOS Convention, Article 98(1); 1989 Salvage Convention, Article 10; 1974 Safety of

Life at Sea Convention (SOLAS), Chapter V; 1958 High Seas Convention, Article 12(1). The duty to render assistance has been incorporated into numerous maritime treaties, and is applicable regardless of the nationality or status of the persons in peril. Many states have codified the duty of masters of ships flying their flags to render assistance at sea, with criminal sanctions for failing to do so. See, e.g., 46 U.S.C. § 2304.

A ship master's duty encompasses several obligations: (1) to render assistance to persons found at sea whose lives are in danger of being lost; (2) to proceed to assist in responding to distress calls that come to the attention of the ship master insofar as such action may be reasonably expected of the ship master; and (3) to render assistance to a ship, its crew, and its passengers after a collision, informing the distressed vessel, if possible, of the name of the rescuing ship, its registry, and the nearest port at which it will call following the rescue. LOS Convention, Article 98(1). Although it is generally recognized that the duty to render assistance includes an obligation to disembark the rescued persons, the details of disembarkation (which generally occurs at the nearest port of call) and the obligations of states to accept the rescued persons have only recently begun to be clarified in applicable treaties, particularly when the rescued persons are refugees.

As a parallel to the obligation of a ship master to render assistance, Article 98(2) of the LOS Convention requires every coastal state to promote the establishment, operation, and maintenance of an adequate and effective search and rescue service in its waters, and to cooperate with neighboring states for this purpose. The 1979 Maritime Search and Rescue Convention, which entered into force in 1985, obligates states to provide search and rescue plans in the area of their coasts, and to cooperate with neighboring states in establishing and implementing coordinated search and rescue plans. Revisions to the Maritime Search and Rescue Convention adopted in 1998 clarify the obligations and roles of contracting governments, emphasize the importance of regional cooperation, and better coordinate maritime and aeronautical activities. Concurrently with the 1998 revisions to the Maritime Search and Rescue Convention, the International Maritime Organization and the International Civil Aviation Organization jointly developed the International Aeronautical and Maritime Search and Rescue (IAMSAR) Manual.

The 1974 Safety of Life at Sea Convention (SOLAS) includes provisions obligating ship masters to proceed to the assistance of those in distress and obligating the governments of contracting parties to ensure that all ships are adequately equipped and manned from a safety point of view. Under a 1988 amendment to the 1974 Safety of Life at Sea Convention, the Global Maritime Distress and Safety System (GMDSS) was implemented in phases between 1993 and 1999. All passenger ships and all cargo ships of 300 gross tons or more on international voyages are required to carry search and rescue transponders that will send automatic distress signals, as well as satellite emergency position-indicating radio beacons to assist in locating vessels in distress. For discussion of the effectiveness of the GMDSS and its use in fulfilling the duties to render assistance and provide effective search and rescue plans, see Arthur Alan Severance, Student Author, The Duty to Render Assistance in the Satellite Age, 36 Cal. W. Intl. L.J. 377 (2006).

The 1970s and 1980s saw an increase in the use of vessels as a means of escape for refugees seeking asylum in other countries. Often these vessels were overcrowded and not equipped or supplied for lengthy sea voyages, resulting in many incidents requiring rescue at sea. Ship masters began to face difficulties in disembarking refugees rescued at sea, as states began to refuse to accept the refugees or to guarantee their resettlement. Ships incurred significant expenses in caring for the refugees on board and in the delays incurred in diverting to assist in the rescue and delivering the refugees to a port that would accept and accommodate the refugees. Concerned that ship masters were becoming reluctant to render assistance to these refugees, in December 1978, the U.N. High Commissioner for Refugees and the Inter–Governmental Maritime Consultative Organization (now the International Maritime Organization (IMO)) issued a joint appeal to governments, shipowners, and ship masters to continue the rescue of refugees on the high seas. 1978 Digest of U.S. Practice in International Law 340–349. In 1983, the U.N. High Commissioner for Refugees issued Guidelines for Disembarkation of Refugees, which explain in some detail established procedures that should be followed whenever refugees are rescued at sea. The Guidelines are reprinted in Erastus C. Benedict, 6C Benedict on Admiralty, Doc. No. 13–8 (Frank L. Wiswall ed., 7th rev. ed., 2001).

In August 2001, the master of the Norwegian merchant vessel *M/V Tampa* diverted the ship from its scheduled course to rescue more than 400 people from an Indonesian ferry that was sinking. Most of the rescued persons were fleeing the Taliban regime in Afghanistan. When the *Tampa* sought to disembark the refugees at a port on Christmas Island, the government of Australia refused to allow disembarkation. This incident caused renewed concern and discussion regarding the duty to render assistance at sea, including the obligation of states to assist in disembarkation of the rescued persons. See Symposium, Australia's Tampa Incident: The Convergence of International and Domestic Refugee Law in the Pacific Rim, 12 Pac. Rim. L. & Policy J. 1 (2002).

After the *Tampa* incident, the IMO developed amendments to both the 1974 Safety of Life at Sea Convention (SOLAS) and the 1979 Maritime Search and Rescue Convention. These amendments were adopted in 2004 and entered into force on July 1, 2006. Among other matters, the amendments specify that contracting states are obligated to assist ship masters in delivering persons rescued at sea to a place of safety. In 2004, the IMO adopted Guidelines on the Treatment of Persons Rescued at Sea to provide further guidance to states in fulfilling their obligations under international law to provide a place of safety to persons rescued at sea. MSC Res. 167(78) app. P 1, MSC Doc. 78/26/Add.2 Annex 34 (2004). See Barbara Miltner, Irregular Maritime Migration: Refugee Protection Issues in Rescue and Interception, 30 Fordham Intl. L.J. 75 (2006).

CHAPTER 3

NATIONALITY OF VESSELS

A. INTRODUCTION

The concept of the "nationality" of a vessel is central to an understanding of the rights and duties of states vis-à-vis vessels. This concept and reasons for its significance are discussed in Section B of this Chapter. Section C addresses the right of states to confer nationality on a ship, along with limitations on that right. Section D concerns vessel documentation and registration and their links to the concept of nationality. Finally, Section E explores the question of what is a ship or vessel.

B. THE CONCEPT OF NATIONALITY OF VESSELS

The term "nationality" has long been used to define the legal relationship between a state and a ship that is authorized by the state to fly its flag. It is used in both the 1958 High Seas Convention, Articles 5–6, and the LOS Convention, Articles 91–92. Several national laws and international agreements refer to the "registration" or "documentation" of a ship rather than its nationality in describing the special relationship between a ship and the state under whose flag it sails (the "flag state"). Discussions in the International Law Commission in 1951 reflected concern that the use of the term "nationality" in reference to ships was misleading as it implied similarity to the term's use in defining the legal relationship between a state and its citizens. UN Doc. A/CN.4/42 (1951); 1951–1 Y.B. Intl. L. Commn. 328–329. Nonetheless, the term has continued to be the one most often employed in describing the relationship between a ship and its flag state. It is important to realize, however, that in spite of their common names, the legal relationship ascribed to the nationality of ships does differ from that arising from the nationality of natural or juridical persons.

The concept of nationality of ships has developed over the centuries on lines parallel to those of the concept of freedom of the high seas. As stated by the Permanent Court of International Justice:

A corollary of the principle of the freedom of the seas is that a ship on the high seas is assimilated to the territory of the State the flag of which it flies, for, just as in its own territory, that State exercises its authority upon it, and no other State may do so.

The S.S. Lotus, P.C.I.J., Ser. A, No. 10, 25 (1927).

Absence of nationality practically precludes a ship from engaging in international trade or commerce or navigation on the high seas. Any state may board and assert its jurisdiction over a stateless ship on the high seas. LOS Convention, Article 110(1)(d);

United States v. Marino–Garcia, 679 F.2d 1373, 1382–1383 (11th Cir. 1982). A stateless vessel is not able to benefit from treaties on which rights to enter foreign ports are normally based. See, for example, 1956 United States–Netherlands Treaty of Friendship, Commerce and Navigation, Article 19(2). It is the flag state that protects the interests of vessels flying its flag. After Iranian air attacks in 1987, the United States reflagged several Kuwaiti oil tankers as U.S. vessels in an effort to protect them. See Report of U.S. Secretary of Defense Caspar W. Weinberger to Congress on Security Arrangements in the Persian Gulf, 26 Intl. Leg. Materials 1433 (1987). Furthermore, in international forums it is the flag state that is generally authorized to bring claims on behalf of a vessel's owners and crew members, even though the owners or crew members are not nationals of the flag state. M/V Saiga (No. 2) Case (Saint Vincent and the Grenadines v. Guinea), ITLOS Case No. 2, ¶¶ 103–109 (1999). The interpretative declaration that the European Community and its member states deposited when signing the 1995 Fish Stocks Convention, and repeated when ratifying that Convention, emphasized the significance of flag state jurisdiction:

> The European Community and its Member States understand that the term "States whose nationals fish on the high seas" shall not provide any new grounds for jurisdiction based on the nationality of persons involved in fishing on the high seas rather than on the principle of flag State jurisdiction.

Available at http://www.un.org/Depts/los. For further discussion of stateless vessels, see Chapter 4, Section C.3.

Each state has the right to confer its nationality on a ship, though only after World War I was it recognized that a land-locked state may also have ships sailing under its flag. LOS Convention, Article 90; 1958 High Seas Convention, Article 4; 1919 Treaty of Peace with Germany, Article 273. International organizations, such as the United Nations and its agencies, may sail vessels under their flags. LOS Convention, Article 93; 1958 High Seas Convention, Article 7. Ordinarily a state confers its nationality on a ship by registering the ship, authorizing it to fly its flag, and issuing documents evidencing the ship's nationality.

A ship may fly the flag of one state only. LOS Convention, Article 92(1); 1958 High Seas Convention, Article 6(1). If a ship flies more than one flag, it is rendered stateless. LOS Convention, Article 92(2); 1958 High Seas Convention, Article 6(2); United States v. Passos–Paternina, 918 F.2d 979, 981–982 (1st Cir. 1990). See Section D regarding certain dual registration procedures for bareboat charters.

C. THE RIGHT OF STATES TO CONFER NATIONALITY ON A SHIP

1. General Principle

In the Muscat Dhows Case (France v. Great Britain), the Permanent Court of Arbitration pronounced the generally accepted principle that "it belongs to every sovereign to decide to whom he will accord the right to fly his flag and to prescribe the rules governing such grants." The Hague Court Reports 93, 96 (James Brown Scott ed., 1916; reprinted 2004), available at http://www.pca-cpa.org. The U.S. Supreme Court reiterated this principle, stating that "[e]ach state under international law may determine for itself the conditions on which it will grant its nationality to a merchant ship." Lauritzen v. Larsen, 345 U.S. 571, 584 (1953). The European Court of Justice has also observed "that under international law a vessel has the nationality of the State in which it is registered and that it is for that State to determine in the exercise of its sovereign powers the conditions for the grant of such nationality." Commission v. Ireland, Case C–280/89, 1992 E.C.R. I–6185, ¶ 24. Numerous treaties and international agreements have incorporated this principle. For instance, the 1956 United States–Netherlands Treaty of Friendship, Commerce and Navigation provides in Article 19(1) that "[v]essels under the flag of either Party, and carrying the papers required by its laws in proof of nationality, shall be deemed to be vessels of that Party both on the high seas and within the ports, places and waters of the other Party."

2. Limitations

International law has developed certain limitations on a state's unilateral right to confer its nationality on a ship. One such limitation is the principle generally prohibiting a state from granting its nationality to a ship already authorized to fly the flag of another state, except pursuant to arrangements for transferring the ship from one state's registry to another. LOS Convention, Article 92(1); 1958 High Seas Convention, Article 6(1). When Honduras enacted a law providing that a vessel in the service of an individual residing in Honduras would be considered Honduran, the United States protested that the imposition of Honduran nationality on a ship flying the U.S. flag would violate this international principle. Consequently, Honduras did not enforce the law. 1909 U.S. Foreign Relations 367–375. See also 46 U.S.C. § 12103(a), which makes only those ships not registered under the laws of a foreign state eligible for U.S. documentation.

If a coastal state confiscates a foreign flag vessel for violating the coastal state's laws, the confiscation changes the ownership of the vessel but does not automatically change its nationality. Tomimaru Case (Japan v. Russia), ITLOS Case No. 15, ¶ 70 (2007).

See also the discussion of certain dual registration procedures for bareboat charters in Section D.

3. *Genuine Link*

A second limitation on the prerogative of a state to confer its nationality on ships is the requirement of a "genuine link" between a ship and its flag state. LOS Convention, Article 91(1); 1958 High Seas Convention, Article 5(1). The principle of a genuine link arises from the long-standing practice of states to confer nationality on a ship only if certain conditions reflecting a connection between the flag state and its ships exist. These conditions vary among states, but often include one or more of the following criteria: (1) ownership by nationals; (2) national officers; (3) national crew; and (4) national build. See Report by the UNCTAD Secretariat, Conditions for Registration of Ships, UN Doc. TD/B/AC.34/2 (1982). The requirement of a sufficient connection between a flag state and its ships is premised on the belief that a state can carry out its obligation to exercise effective control over its ships only if such a link exists.

After World War II, many shipowners transferred their ships to the registries of countries such as Panama, Liberia, and Honduras in order to avoid increasingly restrictive (and costly) national laws regulating labor and wages, technical and safety standards, pollution control, and similar matters. The new host countries did not impose the requirements of national ownership or control, national crews or officers, or national build, and permitted easy access to and transfer from their shipping registries on payment of modest fees and taxes. For a detailed history of the flight from national flags to "flag of convenience" registries, also referred to as "open registries," see Boleslaw Adam Boczek, Flags of Convenience 26–63 (1962).

To address the increased use of "flags of convenience" or "open registries," the 1958 High Seas Convention incorporated the "genuine link" requirement into Article 5(1). This requirement also appears in Article 91(1) of the LOS Convention. The terminology was borrowed from a 1955 decision of the International Court of Justice holding that because of the absence of a "genuine link" between an individual claiming Liechtenstein nationality and Liechtenstein, Guatemala could refuse to recognize Liechtenstein's grant of nationality to the individual. Nottebohm Case (Liechtenstein v. Guatemala), 1955 I.C.J. 4.

The delegates to the First United Nations Conference on the Law of the Sea refrained from defining genuine link, though early drafts of the International Law Commission had attempted to do so (relying primarily on the criteria of national ownership and national officers). See UN Doc. A/CN.4/42 (1951); 1951–1 Y.B. Intl. L. Commn. 330–332. The delegates also eliminated a provision that would have enabled states other than the flag state to withhold recognition of a ship's nationality if they considered that no genuine link existed between the state and the ship. Marjorie M. Whiteman, 9 Digest of International Law 14–15 (1968).

As in the 1958 High Seas Convention, "genuine link" is not defined in the LOS Convention. Under Article 94(6) of the LOS Convention, if one state has "clear grounds to believe that proper jurisdiction and control with respect to a ship have not been exercised" by the flag state, it may report the facts to the flag state, which then has an obligation to "investigate the matter and, if appropriate, take any action necessary to remedy the situation." Nothing in the LOS Convention permits a state that questions the existence of a genuine link to disregard the jurisdiction of the flag state over the ship. This principle was affirmed in the M/V Saiga (No. 2) Case (Saint Vincent and the Grenadines v. Guinea), ITLOS Case No. 2, ¶¶ 80–86 (1999), discussed in Section D.

In 1981, the Committee on Shipping of the U.N. Conference on Trade and Development (UNCTAD) adopted a resolution recommending that "the present régime of open registries be gradually transformed into one of normal registries by a process of tightening the conditions under which open-registry countries retain or accept vessels on their registers." Res. 43 (S–III) (1981), in Report of the Committee on Shipping, UNCTAD Trade and Development Board Official Records, 23d Sess., Supp. No. 3, UN Doc. TD/C.4/227, 19 (1981). Several countries objected to this resolution as an intrusion on the sovereign right of every state to determine its own registration requirements, although they acknowledged that this right was subject to various obligations, especially with respect to the safety of ships and the protection of the marine environment. UN Doc. TD/B/904, 5–6 (1982).

The UNCTAD discussions culminated in the drafting of the 1986 Registration Convention. Article 7 of the Registration Convention allows the genuine link requirement to be met through the participation of nationals in either the ownership or manning of a vessel. The Convention does not specify minimum levels of national ownership, but allows states to determine the participation in a manner sufficient to permit the flag state to exercise effective control. Id. at Article 8. Similarly, each state may determine rules applicable to the manning of its vessels, subject to the principle that a "satisfactory part" of the officers and crew shall be nationals or permanent residents of the flag state. Id. at Article 9. As of June 1, 2009, the Convention had received insufficient support to enter into force. For discussion of the 1986 Registration Convention, see Moira L. McConnell, Business as Usual: An Evaluation of the 1986 United Nations Convention on Conditions for Registration of Ships, 18 J. Mar. L. & Com. 435 (1987).

In 2002 the Commission of the European Communities brought an action for a declaration by the European Court of Justice that the Netherlands' statutory requirements for registering and managing a ship in that state violated European Community law. The Netherlands' registration law required a ship to be owned by at least two-thirds natural persons or companies having European Community or European Economic Area nationality. The Netherlands asserted that the ship-registration measures were justified by its obligations to establish a genuine link and to exercise effective control and jurisdiction over ships flying the Netherlands' flag, as required by LOS Convention Articles 91(1) and 94(1). The court, in an opinion that found the Netherlands' requirements inconsistent with European Community law (namely the freedoms of movement and establishment), concluded that Articles 91(1) and 94(1) did not obligate the Netherlands to adopt the restrictive nationality requirements it had enacted. Commission v. Netherlands, Case C–299/02, 2004 E.C.R. I–9761, ¶ 23; see also Alvin Kan, International Decision: Commission v. Netherlands, 99 Am. J. Intl. L. 867 (2005).

In sum, the meaning of the "genuine link" limitation today is indeterminate. Although the general purpose of the genuine link requirement "is to secure more effective implementation of the duties of the flag state," M/V Saiga (No. 2) Case, ITLOS Case No. 2, ¶ 83 (1999), that goal is addressed in detail in Article 94 of the LOS Convention, as discussed in Chapter 4, and is not made concrete in the "genuine link" concept. In addition, as noted above, nothing in the LOS Convention authorizes a nonflag state to challenge the nationality of a vessel on the grounds that the vessel lacks a genuine link with the flag state, and no body of accepted international practice has evolved to make the meaning of "genuine link" more determinate. In his recent study of the genuine link requirement prepared for the International Transport Workers' Federation, a respected scholar concluded "[t]here is no single or obligatory criterion by which the genuineness of a link is to be established. A state has a discretion as to how it ensures that the link between a ship having its nationality and itself is genuine ...." Robin R. Churchill (with Christopher Hedley), The Meaning of the "Genuine Link" Requirement in Relation to the Nationality of Ships 70 (Oct. 2000), available at http://www.oceanlaw.net/projects/ consultancy/pdf/ITF–Oct2000.pdf.

As more countries, including such land-locked states as Mongolia, have offered open registries, the registration by owners of vessels under flags of convenience has continued to expand. In 2003, approximately fifty percent of the world's ocean fleet (by tonnage) was registered in "flag of convenience" countries, with Panama and Liberia accounting for sixty-six percent of the open-registry fleet. See U.N. Secretary–General Report of the Consultative Group on Flag State Implementation 44–45, UN Doc. A/59/63 (2004). As discussed in the Report, the failure of some open-registry states to regulate ships effectively has been cited as a major concern in enforcing international law regulating ship safety, labor conditions, protection of the marine environment, and, most recently, fishery management and conservation.

Several solutions have been proposed and implemented to address these concerns. First, several international guidelines and conventions have been developed that more clearly delineate flag state obligations. A second response has been to create incentives for open-registry states to accept various international conventions or to implement their requirements. Third, port states have exercised increasing jurisdiction over foreign flag vessels entering their ports, a development recognized and coordinated in treaties. Fourth, some legal instruments authorize states to regulate directly the conduct of their citizens, even when those individuals seek to register and operate a vessel under a foreign flag. Fifth, efforts have been made to provide financial assistance to less developed countries, to enable them more effectively to carry out port state inspections and flag state obligations. For further discussion of these efforts, see Chapters 4, 7, 12, and 13. Despite these efforts, the challenges posed by the system of open registry remain significant.

4.   *U.S. Ownership and Manning Requirements*

Under 46 U.S.C. § 12103, a vessel of at least five net tons may be documented in the United States if it is not registered under the laws of a foreign country, and if it is owned by: (1) an individual U.S. citizen; (2) an entity, such as a trust or a joint venture, all of whose members are U.S. citizens; (3) a partnership whose general partners are U.S. citizens and whose controlling interest is owned by U.S. citizens; (4) a U.S. corporation whose chief executive officer and chairman of the board are U.S.

citizens and no more of whose directors are non-citizens than a minority of the number necessary to constitute a quorum; or (5) the government (federal, state, or local). Additional requirements may apply for certain types of licenses (known as endorsements). For example, vessels obtaining a fishery endorsement or domestic coastwise trade endorsement must generally be built in the United States, and a fishery endorsement requires ownership of the vessel by individual U.S. citizens or by entities at least seventy-five percent of whose interests are owned by U.S. citizens. Id. at § 12113. In addition, all vessels documented by the United States (other than those with only a recreational endorsement or unmanned barges operating outside of the territorial waters of the United States) must be placed under the command of a U.S. citizen. Id. at § 12131. The master, chief engineer, radio officer, and officer in charge of deck watch or engineering watch must also be U.S. citizens. Id. at § 8103(a). Generally, at least seventy-five percent of the crew of a U.S. vessel must be U.S. citizens, and the balance of the crew must be resident aliens lawfully admitted to the United States. Id. at § 8103(b). If a U.S. vessel has received a construction or operation subsidy, one hundred percent of the crew must be U.S. citizens (ninety percent if a passenger vessel). Id. at § 8103(c)–(d). For discussion of U.S. registration and documentation requirements, see Michael P. Drzal & Phyllis D. Carnilla, Documentation of Vessels: The Fog Lifts, 13 J. Mar. L. & Com. 261 (1982); Constantine G.

Papavizas, New Developments in U.S. Flag Vessel
Financing and Citizenship Requirements, 24 Tul.
Mar. L.J. 205 (1999); Constantine G. Papavizas,
U.S. Flag Vessel Financing and Citizenship Requirements Update, 32 Tul. Mar. L.J. 35 (2007).
Vessels smaller than five net tons may also be U.S.
vessels, but they are typically licensed under the
laws of the individual U.S. states, rather than documented pursuant to federal statute.

D. DOCUMENTATION AND REGISTRATION

Each state that authorizes a ship to fly its flag
must maintain a register of ships containing the
name and description of each ship so authorized.
LOS Convention, Article 94(2); 1986 Registration
Convention, Article 11. The state must also issue
documents to ships verifying such authorization.
LOS Convention, Article 91(2); 1986 Registration
Convention, Article 5(3); 1958 High Seas Convention, Article 5(2). Neither the LOS Convention nor
the 1958 High Seas Convention requires the flag
state to maintain information regarding the ownership of the vessel. Article 6 of the 1986 Registration
Convention requires states to maintain information
regarding the owners of ships, and to take such
measures as are necessary to ensure that the owners and operators of a ship can be easily identified
by persons having a legitimate interest in obtaining
such information. As noted in Section C.3, the 1986
Registration Convention had not entered into force

as of June 1, 2009. There have been some recent national and international efforts to require disclosure of vessel ownership in attempts to reduce maritime terrorism and illegal fishing, though the effectiveness of such measures has been questioned. See 1993 FAO Flag State Compliance Agreement, Article VI(1)(d); J. Bennett Fox, Jr., Vessel Ownership and Terrorism: Requiring Disclosure of Beneficial Ownership is Not the Answer, 4 Loy. Mar. L.J. 92 (2005).

The flag symbolizes the nationality of a ship, but in the event of a discrepancy between a ship's flag and its documents, the documents generally control the question of nationality. In The Merritt, 84 U.S. 582, 586 (1873), the U.S. Supreme Court stated that "[t]he documents a vessel carries furnish the only evidence of her nationality." See also 46 U.S.C. § 12134, which provides that a certificate of documentation issued under U.S. shipping laws is "conclusive evidence of nationality for international purposes, but not in any proceeding conducted under the laws of the United States," nor is it "conclusive evidence of ownership in any proceeding in which ownership is in issue."

In October 1997 Guinea seized the M/V Saiga for alleged violations of Guinea's laws. The vessel (owned by a Cypriot company, managed by a Scottish company, manned by a Ukrainian crew, and chartered to a Swiss company) had been provisionally registered in Saint Vincent and the Grenadines, but the provisional registration had expired at the time of the vessel's arrest. In the first case before the International Tribunal for the Law of the Sea, Saint Vincent and the Grenadines pursued a variety of claims related to the alleged illegality of Guinea's arrest of the *Saiga*. Guinea argued that the claims of Saint Vincent and the Grenadines were inadmissible, due to the lack of a valid Vincentian registration at the time of the arrest. The Tribunal did not find the lack of registration on the day of arrest dispositive regarding the issue of the ship's nationality. In ruling that the claims of Saint Vincent and the Grenadines were admissible, the Tribunal considered additional evidence, including the "consistent conduct of Saint Vincent and the Grenadines" in asserting its jurisdiction over the vessel in question and the delay of Guinea in raising the issue of nationality until well after the proceedings had begun. M/V Saiga (No. 2) Case (Saint Vincent and the Grenadines v. Guinea), ITLOS Case No. 2, ¶¶ 67–73 (1999). In his separate opinion, Vice–President Wolfrum disagreed that consistent conduct by Saint Vincent and the Grenadines could support the conclusion that the *Saiga* retained Vincentian nationality, noting that documentation provided the means "most traditionally upheld to prove the registration and/or nationality of a particular ship." Id. at Sep. Op. Wolfrum, ¶ 22. Vice–President Wolfrum did, however, concur that the claims of Saint Vincent and the Grenadines were admissible, on the grounds of estoppel and acquiescence by Guinea. In a subsequent article regarding the case, Judge Treves noted that "the Tribunal had in mind the distinction between nationality and proof of nationality, which makes it possible to substitute elements indicating nationality for the missing registration." Tullio Treves, Flags of Convenience Before the Law of the Sea Tribunal, 6 San Diego Intl. L.J. 179, 186 (2004).

In another case before the International Tribunal for the Law of the Sea, the provisional registration of the *Grand Prince*, a ship registered in Belize, had expired at the time of its arrest by France in the exclusive economic zone of the French Southern and Antarctic Territories. In contrast to the *Saiga* case, the Tribunal determined that Belize did not consistently treat the *Grand Prince* as a vessel of its nationality after its arrest, noting that at one point in the proceedings Belize had informed France that the *Grand Prince* had been de-registered. The Tribunal concluded that "the documentary evidence submitted by the Applicant fails to establish that Belize was the flag state of the vessel when the application was made." Grand Prince Case (Belize v. France), ITLOS Case No. 8, ¶ 93 (2001). See Chapter 15, Section D for discussion of the "prompt release" procedure at issue in this case.

Once a ship is registered under the laws of a particular country, it may not change its flag during voyage or while in a port of call unless pursuant to a real change in registry or transfer of ownership. LOS Convention, Article 92(1); 1958 High Seas Convention, Article 6(1). A state may give a temporary authorization for a ship to fly its flag, which often occurs to permit ships purchased abroad to be delivered to the purchaser's country. See, for example, 46 U.S.C. § 12115. Another use of a temporary registration is pursuant to a bareboat charter, which is defined at Article 2 of the 1986 Registration Convention as the lease of a ship pursuant to which complete possession and control of the ship, including the right to appoint its master and crew, is granted to the lessee (charterer). Article 12 of the 1986 Registration Convention allows a state to "grant registration and the right to fly its flag to a ship bareboat chartered-in by a charterer in that State, for the period of the charter." Many countries have adopted dual registration procedures for bareboat charterers, whereby the owner's original registration is suspended during the temporary registration by the bareboat charterer, but remains effective for certain purposes, such as the recording of mortgages against the ship. At the end of the charter, the registration of the ship reverts to the original flag state. See generally Richard M.F. Coles & Nigel P. Ready, Ship Registration: Law and Practice, Ch. 3 (2002); Ademun–Odeke, An Examination of Bareboat Charter Registries and Flag of Convenience Registries in International Law, 36 Ocean Dev. & Intl. L. 339 (2005).

The adoption of "provisional" or temporary registration procedures by several countries, particularly those classified as open registries, has raised concerns. The registration issues presented in the *Saiga* and *Grand Prince* cases arose from provisional registrations. In his separate opinion in the *Saiga* case, President Mensah of the International Tribunal for the Law of the Sea noted that Saint Vincent and the Grenadines' twelve-month provisional registration period "provides scope for abuse by unscrupulous shipowners who may wish to operate sub-standard ships, for it makes possible for them to switch such ships between flags on consecutive 'provisional registrations' for one year at a time." M/V Saiga (No. 2) Case (Saint Vincent and the Grenadines v. Guinea), ITLOS Case No. 2, Sep. Op. Mensah, ¶ 22 (1999). Provisional registration and open registries facilitate "flag hopping," which is the practice of repeated and rapid changes of a vessel's flag for the purposes of circumventing international legal requirements regarding ship safety, labor conditions, protection of the marine environment, and fishery management and conservation.

E. SHIPS OR VESSELS

For purposes of the LOS Convention, other treaties, many national laws, and this text, the terms "ship" and "vessel" are synonymous. Early definitions excluded vessels that were not capable of self-propulsion. Gilbert Gidel, 1 Le droit international public de la mer 70 (1932). Today, the term "ship" or "vessel" is defined in numerous ways, according to the purposes of the instrument defining the term.

The LOS Convention does not provide a general definition of "ship" or "vessel," although Article 29 does provide a definition for a "warship." See Chapter 2, Section C.1. Similarly, after preparatory efforts at the International Law Commission to draft a general definition failed, the 1958 High Seas Convention does not define "ship" or "vessel." Although several commentators argue that a single definition of "ship" or "vessel" for purposes of the LOS Convention is preferable, many others believe that in view of the encompassing nature of the LOS Convention, it is more appropriate to define the term "ship" or "vessel" in light of the purposes of particular provisions. For contrasting views, see George K. Walker, Definitions for the 1982 Law of the Sea Convention (Revised Tentative Draft No. 1., Feb. 10, 2003), 33 Cal. W. Intl. L.J. 196, 217–218 (2003); John E. Noyes, Definitions for the 1982 Law of the Sea Convention and the Importance of Context: "Ships" and Other Matters, 33 Cal. W. Intl. L.J. 310, 316–322 (2003). The latter position favoring context-based definitions is supported by current state practice, as evidenced by the differing definitions of "ship" or "vessel" contained in national legislation as well as international conventions, varying in accordance with the specific purposes of the laws. For example, Article 2(4) of the 1973 Convention for the Prevention of Pollution from Ships, as modified by the 1978 Protocol (MARPOL), includes, among other types of craft, "fixed or floating platforms" in the definition of "ship." In contrast, Article 2 of the 1986 Registration Convention more narrowly defines "ship" to include "any self-propelled sea-going vessel used in international seaborne trade for the transport of goods, passengers, or both with the exception of vessels of less than 500 gross registered tons."

The U.S. Code generally describes the term "vessel" to mean "every description of watercraft or other artificial contrivance used, or capable of being used, as a means of transportation on water." 1 U.S.C. § 3. In Stewart v. Dutra Construction Co., 543 U.S. 481 (2005), the U.S. Supreme Court reviewed this statutory definition to determine whether a large platform dredge that was not capable of self-propulsion, but that was towed by a tug to various locations to remove silt, was a "vessel in navigation" for purposes of the Longshore Harbor Workers' Compensation Act, 33 U.S.C. §§ 901 et seq. The Supreme Court, after a comprehensive discussion of statutory and case law, ruled that the dredge was a vessel, stating that the definition encompasses "any watercraft practically capable of maritime transportation, regardless of its primary purpose or state of transit at a particular moment." 543 U.S. at 497. See also In re Complaint of Sedco, Inc., 543 F.Supp. 561 (S.D. Tex. 1982), vacated in part on other grounds, 610 F.Supp. 306 (S.D. Tex. 1984), rev'd on other grounds, 767 F.2d 1140 (5th Cir. 1985), in which the court determined that a semi-submersible drilling rig that was anchored while in use, but which navigated across the oceans from site to site, was a vessel, thus allowing the owner of the rig to assert the limited liability protection afforded to vessel owners under the Limitation of Liability Act, 46 U.S.C. §§ 30505 et seq.

The general definition of "vessel" found at 1 U.S.C. § 3 does not apply if another statute has provided a more specific definition. For example, in implementing regulations for preventing collisions at sea, "vessel" is defined at 33 U.S.C. § 1601 to include "nondisplacement craft and seaplanes."

When Denmark proposed the construction of a bridge over a strait leading to the Baltic Sea, Finland brought a proceeding before the International Court of Justice, arguing that the sixty-five meter height of the proposed bridge would interfere with the passage of certain Finnish-manufactured oil rigs and drilling ships through the strait, in violation of international law. Denmark responded that such structures are not ships, and thus are not entitled to transit passage through straits. Without examining whether oil rigs were ships, the International Court of Justice denied Finland's request for provisional relief. Case Concerning Passage through the Great Belt (Finland v. Denmark), 1991 I.C.J. 12. The case was subsequently settled and discontinued prior to a decision on the merits. 1992 I.C.J. 348.

CHAPTER 4

DUTIES AND JURISDICTION OF THE FLAG STATE AND EXCEPTIONS TO FLAG STATE JURISDICTION

A. INTRODUCTION

As a corollary to the principle that the flag state has exclusive jurisdiction over ships flying its flag on the high seas, international law creates a corresponding obligation requiring the flag state to effectively regulate and enforce administrative, technical, social, and safety matters relating to its ships, in accordance with generally accepted international regulations. This Chapter addresses the duties of flag states in Section B, and principles applicable to the exercise of flag state jurisdiction in Section C.

International law recognizes certain instances where a government vessel of one state may exercise jurisdiction on the high seas over foreign non-government vessels, most often pursuant to treaties or in the context of facts giving rise to a reasonable belief that the foreign vessel is committing certain specific violations of international law. These exceptions to the principle of exclusive flag state jurisdiction on the high seas are the topic of Section D of this Chapter. As discussed more fully in Chapters 7–10, when a foreign vessel enters the waters of a coastal state, the coastal state may exercise limited jurisdiction over such foreign vessel.

B. DUTIES OF THE FLAG STATE

Each state has a duty under international law to "effectively exercise its jurisdiction and control in administrative, technical and social matters over ships flying its flag." LOS Convention, Article 94(1); 1958 High Seas Convention, Article 5(1). Article 94 of the LOS Convention further specifies that each flag state has the obligation to:

(1) Maintain a register of ships authorized to fly its flag;

(2) Govern the internal affairs of the ship regarding administrative, technical, and social matters;

(3) Ensure safety at sea with regard to the construction, equipment, and seaworthiness of ships, labor conditions and the training of crews, the maintenance of communications, and the prevention of collisions;

(4) Ensure that each ship is surveyed by a qualified surveyor of ships and has on board appropriate charts, nautical publications, and navigational equipment;

(5) Ensure that each ship is manned by a qualified master, officers, and crew; and

(6) Ensure that the master, officers, and, to the appropriate extent, crew are fully conversant with

and are required to observe applicable international regulations regarding the safety of life at sea, the prevention of collisions, the prevention, reduction, and control of marine pollution, and the maintenance of radio communications.

The LOS Convention contemplates that every flag state will adopt domestic legislation to ensure that its duties under Article 94 are implemented and enforced. Article 94(5) requires such legislation to conform to "generally accepted" international regulations, procedures, and practices, which are embodied in a growing number of international conventions regarding safety at sea, prevention of collisions, pollution control, maritime traffic, maritime communications, and related matters. Many of these conventions have become generally accepted and therefore must be taken into account by parties to the LOS Convention when implementing legislation to fulfill their obligations under Article 94, even if they have not ratified a particular convention. For discussion of the term "generally accepted," see Bernard H. Oxman, The Duty to Respect Generally Accepted International Standards, 24 N.Y.U. J. Intl. L. & Pol. 109 (1991).

Although several international organizations have worked to draft and implement international agreements and regulations regarding "administrative, technical and social matters concerning the ship," the International Maritime Organization (IMO), formerly the Intergovernmental Maritime Consultative Organization, has been particularly influential. The IMO was established as a specialized agency of the United Nations pursuant to the 1948 Convention on the Intergovernmental Maritime Consultative Organization, which entered into force in 1958. As of June 1, 2009, 169 states were parties to the IMO Convention. The IMO's primary purposes are to adopt measures to improve the safety and security of international shipping and to prevent marine pollution from ships. The IMO has also introduced important measures regarding liability and compensation for damages, including pollution, caused by ships. Some widely-accepted IMO conventions include the 1966 Convention on Load Lines, the 1972 Convention on the Prevention of Collisions at Sea, the 1973 Convention for the Prevention of Pollution from Ships, as modified by the 1978 Protocol (MARPOL), the 1974 Safety of Life at Sea Convention (SOLAS), the 1978 Convention on Standards of Training, Certification and Watchkeeping for Seafarers, and the 1988 Convention for the Suppression of Unlawful Acts Against the Safety of Maritime Navigation. For a complete listing of IMO conventions and their status, see http://www.imo.org.

The International Labor Organization has adopted numerous conventions relating to the working and living conditions of seamen. Most recently, it adopted the 2006 Maritime Labour Convention, which consolidates into a single instrument matters previously addressed in more than sixty conventions, including minimum requirements for seafarers to work on ships, conditions of employment, appropriate accommodations (including recreational facilities and food), medical care, and social security protection. In addition to incorporating binding general principles and mandatory regulations, it also proposes nonmandatory recommendations and guidelines. Although compliance and enforcement are primarily the responsibility of the flag state, port states are also given inspection authority.

C. FLAG STATE JURISDICTION

1. General Principles

Pursuant to Article 92(1) of the LOS Convention, the flag state has exclusive jurisdiction over its ships on the high seas, except where the flag state has consented to the exercise of jurisdiction by other states under an international treaty, or as otherwise provided in the LOS Convention (see Section D).

Though the notion that a ship is a floating part of the flag state's territory is generally recognized as fiction, the law of the flag state is applied "on the pragmatic basis that there must be some law on shipboard, that it cannot change at every change of waters, and no experience shows a better rule than that of the state that owns her." Lauritzen v. Larsen, 345 U.S. 571, 585 (1953). However, the U.S. Supreme Court has also noted that a flag state's jurisdiction over a vessel "partakes more of the characteristics of personal than of territorial sovereignty," and on this basis refused to apply the National Prohibition Act to U.S. ships outside of

U.S. territorial waters. Cunard S.S. Co. v. Mellon, 262 U.S. 100, 123 (1923). Similarly, in Lam Mow v. Nagle, 24 F.2d 316 (9th Cir. 1928), the court held that a person born aboard a U.S. ship was not born in the United States and not entitled to U.S. citizenship.

2. *Collisions at Sea and the Distinction between Jurisdiction to Prescribe and Jurisdiction to Enforce*

In the Case of the S.S. Lotus (France v. Turkey), a French and Turkish vessel collided on the high seas, resulting in harm to Turkish citizens. 1927 P.C.I.J. Ser. A, No. 10. Turkey initiated a criminal action against the French officer. France argued that it alone had jurisdiction over this officer with respect to conduct occurring on the French vessel on the high seas. The Permanent Court of International Justice concluded that "there is no rule of law in regard to collision cases to the effect that criminal proceedings are exclusively within the jurisdiction of the state whose flag is flown." Id. at 25. Although Turkish laws could apply to this accident, i.e., Turkey had "jurisdiction to prescribe," the Court also emphasized traditional limitations on the exercise of "jurisdiction to enforce" on the high seas. (For a general discussion of the various categories of state jurisdiction under international law, see Restatement (Third) of U.S. Foreign Relations Law §§ 401 et seq. (1987).) According to the Court, "[i]n virtue of the principle of the freedom of the seas ... no State may exercise any kind of jurisdiction over foreign vessels upon [the high seas]. Thus, if a war vessel, happening to be at a spot where a collision occurs between a vessel flying its flag and a foreign vessel, were to send on board the latter an officer to make investigations or take evidence, such an act would undoubtedly be contrary to international law." Id. at 20. In the *Lotus* case, Turkey obtained custody of the French vessel's officer only after the French vessel entered Turkish port; Turkey did not interfere with the French vessel on the high seas.

The Court's decision in the *Lotus* case to allow a nonflag state to apply its laws to prosecute the officer of a foreign flag vessel involved in a collision could result in delays in maritime transport as well as conflicts among states. Several international agreements have provided exclusive jurisdiction in the event of collisions to the flag state of the vessel alleged to be responsible for the collision or to the state of nationality of the accused. See, for example, LOS Convention, Article 97; 1952 Convention on Penal Jurisdiction in Matters of Collision; 1958 High Seas Convention, Article 11. For discussion of the development of international law regarding collisions at sea and U.S. legislation waiving sovereign immunity where government vessels are involved in collisions, see J. Michael Lennon, The Law of Collision and the United States Navy, 50 Buff. L. Rev. 981 (2002).

3. *Stateless Vessels*

A ship that is not registered in any country is stateless, although the temporary expiration of a registration may not necessarily result in statelessness if the flag state takes timely steps to restore the registration or otherwise acknowledge the nationality of the vessel. M/V Saiga (No. 2) Case (Saint Vincent and the Grenadines v. Guinea), IT-LOS Case No. 2, ¶¶ 67–73 (1999) (discussed at Chapter 3, Section D). A ship flying the flags of more than one state, using them according to convenience, is treated as a stateless ship and may not claim the nationality of either flag state. LOS Convention, Article 92(2); 1958 High Seas Convention, Article 6(2).

Where there are reasonable grounds to believe that a vessel is stateless, a warship (as defined in LOS Convention, Article 29) may board the stateless vessel on the high seas and inspect the vessel's documentation. LOS Convention, Article 110(1)(d); United States v. Marino–Garcia, 679 F.2d 1373, 1382–1383 (11th Cir. 1982). Reasonable grounds include the failure to fly a flag, displaying more than one flag, changing flags while en route, and inconsistency between a vessel's flag and its documentation. Upon boarding, the government officials may request documentation of the vessel's registration, and, if provided, may confirm the validity of the documents with the purported flag state. If a valid registration is confirmed, the boarding vessel may exercise no further jurisdiction over the vessel, unless authorized by the flag state or otherwise under international law. If reasonable suspicion remains after the document inspection, the boarding party "may proceed to a further examination on board the ship, which must be carried out with all possible consideration." LOS Convention, Article 110(2). If the suspicions are unfounded and the boarding was unjustified, the ship is entitled to compensation for any damages sustained as a result of the boarding. Id. at Article 110(3).

If it is determined after a lawful boarding that a vessel is stateless, the question arises as to what extent, if any, the boarding warship may exercise further jurisdiction. As noted in one respected treatise:

> Ships without nationality are in a curious position. Their "statelessness" will not, of itself, entitle each and every State to assert jurisdiction over them, for there is not in every case any recognised basis upon which jurisdiction could be asserted over stateless ships on the high seas.... It has been held, for example, ... that such ships enjoy the protection of no State, the implication being that if jurisdiction were asserted no State would be competent to complain of a violation of international law. Widely accepted as this view is, it ignores the possibility of diplomatic protection being exercised by the national State of the individuals on such stateless ships. The better view appears to be that there is a need for some jurisdictional nexus in order that a State may

extend its laws to those on board a stateless ship and enforce the laws against them.

Robin R. Churchill & A.Vaughan Lowe, The Law of the Sea 214 (3d ed. 1999). See also Andrew W. Anderson, Jurisdiction over Stateless Vessels on the High Seas, 13 J. Mar. L. & Com. 323 (1982); Deirdre M. Warner–Kramer & Krista Canty, Stateless Fishing Vessels: The Current International Regime and a New Approach, 5 Ocean & Coastal L.J. 227 (2000).

The United States extends its jurisdiction under the Maritime Drug Enforcement Act to "vessel[s] without nationality." 46 U.S.C. § 70502(c). U.S. courts have frequently been called on to determine whether a vessel is stateless for purposes of the Act. See, e.g., United States v. Martinez–Hidalgo, 993 F.2d 1052, 1055 (3d Cir. 1993) (jurisdiction extended over flagless vessel that failed to provide evidence of its claimed registration with Columbia); United States v. Juda, 46 F.3d 961, 965 (9th Cir. 1995) (jurisdiction extended over vessel not registered in any state). Once a vessel has been determined to be stateless, courts must determine whether the United States can exercise further jurisdiction over the vessel or its crew. In United States v. Marino–Garcia, 679 F.2d 1373 (11th Cir. 1982), the court upheld the extension of U.S. jurisdiction to the foreign crew and officers of a stateless vessel even in the absence of evidence that the illicit drugs discovered on board were intended for distribution in the United States. After noting that stateless vessels are "international pariahs," the court concluded:

> [I]nternational law permits any nation to subject stateless vessels on the high seas to its jurisdiction. Such jurisdiction neither violates the law of nations nor results in impermissible interference with another sovereign nation's affairs. We further conclude that there need not be proof of a nexus between the stateless vessel and the country seeking to effectuate jurisdiction. Jurisdiction exists solely as a consequence of the vessel's status as stateless. Such status makes the vessel subject to action by all nations proscribing certain activities aboard stateless vessels and subjects those persons aboard to prosecution for violating the proscriptions.

Id. at 1383. Notwithstanding the pronouncement of the Marino–Garcia court that those on board the vessel could, by virtue of its stateless status, be subject to prosecution, a state's authority at international law to try alleged drug traffickers should depend on links between those individuals and the state accusing them of a crime under its laws. It is questionable whether drug trafficking has been recognized as an offense, such as slavery, piracy, or genocide, that any state may punish under the principle of universal jurisdiction. United States v. James–Robinson, 515 F.Supp. 1340, 1344 n.6 (S.D. Fla. 1981); Restatement (Third) of U.S. Foreign Relations Law § 404 (1987); Anne H. Geraghty, Universal Jurisdiction and Drug Trafficking: A Tool for Fighting One of the World's Most Pervasive Problems, 16 Fla. J. Intl. L. 371 (2004).

D. EXCEPTIONS TO FLAG STATE JURISDICTION

International law recognizes several exceptions to the exclusive jurisdiction of a flag state over its vessels on the high seas. Generally, the exceptions may be exercised only by a warship or authorized government vessel, and the authority granted over a foreign vessel is most commonly limited to the "right of visit," i.e., to board and inspect the foreign vessel's registration, following the same procedures noted in Section C with respect to stateless vessels. Most of the exceptions giving rise to the exercise of jurisdiction by a state other than the flag state arise when a vessel is engaged in unlawful activities, and serve the purpose of monitoring or enforcing the vessel's compliance with international law or flag state treaty obligations.

The exceptions to flag state jurisdiction discussed below do not apply to warships and government vessels used for noncommercial service on the high seas; these vessels have complete immunity from interference by states other than the flag state. LOS Convention, Articles 95, 96; 1958 High Seas Convention, Article 9. Governments have increasingly used government vessels to engage in trade. In Berizzi Brothers Co. v. Steamship Pesaro, 271 U.S. 562, 574 (1926), the Supreme Court held that government commercial ships "have the same immunity as war ships." In Mexico v. Hoffman, 324 U.S. 30 (1945), however, the Supreme Court denied immunity from jurisdiction to a commercial ship owned but not possessed by the Mexican government. The U.S. Department of State adopted in 1952 a policy of not asserting immunity in claims against government-owned or operated commercial ships. 26 Dept. St. Bull. 984 (1952). The Foreign Sovereign Immunity Act allows actions against foreign governments arising from specified commercial activities, including the assertion of maritime liens. 28 U.S.C. §§ 1605(a)(2), 1605(b). For discussion of the application of the Foreign Sovereign Immunity Act in connection with foreign government vessels, see William R. Dorsey, III, Reflections on the Foreign Sovereign Immunities Act After Twenty Years, 28 J. Mar. L. & Com. 257 (1997). Many other countries also refuse to grant sovereign immunity to state-owned commercial vessels. Id. at 258.

1. Treaty–Based Exceptions

A flag state may by treaty authorize another state to exercise jurisdiction over the flag state's vessels. LOS Convention, Article 92(1); 1958 High Seas Convention, Article 6(1). For example, Article V of the 1992 North Pacific Salmon Treaty allows authorized officials of parties to board and investigate the vessels flying the flag of other parties for purposes of enforcing the treaty, and to arrest and seize any violating vessels. Other common arrangements for such cooperation relate to illicit drug traffic, illegal immigration, and terrorist threats. See, for example, 1997 United States–Haiti Illicit Maritime Drug Traffic Agreement, Article 14; 2004 United States–Marshall Islands Agreement Concerning Cooperation to Suppress the Proliferation of Weapons of Mass Destruction, Articles 4–5. In the absence of a treaty, where reasonable grounds exist to believe that a foreign vessel is engaged in illegal activities, the United States has adopted a practice of seeking the consent of the flag state to board that vessel. See, for example, United States v. Green, 671 F.2d 46, 50 (1st Cir.), cert. denied, 457 U.S. 1135 (1982).

2. *Piracy*

Pirates fundamentally disrupt the legal order of the oceans. Pirates prevent vessels of all states from exercising the freedom of navigation and other high seas freedoms. Furthermore, when pirates are in charge of a vessel, the flag state cannot exercise its jurisdiction and control over the vessel. For these reasons the pirate has historically been condemned as an enemy of all humankind. Many authorities have regarded piracy as a violation of international law and have asserted that any state may exercise jurisdiction over pirates. See, e.g., United States v. Smith, 18 U.S. 153 (1820).

International law has long recognized a general duty of all countries to cooperate in the repression of piracy. LOS Convention, Article 100; 1958 High Seas Convention, Article 14. Where there are reasonable grounds to believe that a vessel (other than a warship or noncommercial government vessel) is engaged in piracy, a warship may board the vessel on the high seas. LOS Convention, Article 110(1)(a); 1958 High Seas Convention, Article 22(1)(a). In addition to this right to visit, a ship engaged in piracy on the high seas may be seized by a warship or government vessel of any state. However, where such a seizure has been effected without adequate grounds, the seizing state is liable for damages to the flag state. LOS Convention, Articles 105–107; 1958 High Seas Convention, Articles 19–21.

Despite the universal condemnation of piracy, there has been debate about what constitutes piracy under customary international law. Most courts and commentators agree that an act of violence (other than an act of war) committed at sea is a necessary element of piracy. In re Piracy Jure Gentium, Great Britain, Judicial Committee of the Privy Council, 1934 App. Cas. 586, 598, reprinted in 3 Brit Intl. L. Cases 836, 842 (1965). Some courts and commentators have required an intent to commit robbery or otherwise achieve private gains, thus excluding acts motivated by a political purpose, such as acts of anti-government insurgents. In The Ambrose Light, 25 F. 408, 412–413 (S.D.N.Y. 1885), the U.S. district court ruled that only those insurgents who had been recognized as belligerents by their own government or by another government would be exempt from acts of piracy. Other issues include whether government-owned vessels may engage in piracy and whether piracy is limited to acts committed by or through the use of one vessel against another vessel. For example, in 1961 the *Santa Maria*, a Portuguese passenger ship, was overtaken by a group of armed men who had boarded at a port of call. The U.S. government did not consider the incident an act of piracy, because another ship was not involved. Marjorie M. Whiteman, 4 Digest of International Law 665–666 (1965).

Several of these issues were brought to the forefront in 1985 when the Italian-flag cruise ship *Achille Lauro* was seized by members of the Palestine Liberation Front who had boarded the ship in Genoa, posing as tourists. They held the ship's crew and passengers hostage, and threatened to kill the passengers unless Israel released fifty Palestinian prisoners. The hijackers shot and threw overboard one American passenger. Although widely acknowledged as an act of terrorism, considerable debate arose as to whether the incident could be properly characterized as an act of piracy, subjecting the *Achille Lauro* to the jurisdiction of any warship while on the high seas. As a result of the *Achille Lauro* incident, the International Maritime Organization initiated efforts that culminated in the drafting and adoption of the 1988 Convention for the Suppression of Unlawful Acts Against the Safety of Maritime Navigation. See generally Malvina Halberstam, Terrorism on the High Seas: The Achille Lauro, Piracy and the IMO Convention on Maritime Safety, 82 Am. J. Intl. L. 269 (1988). Issues of jurisdiction relating to maritime terrorism are discussed further in Chapter 14.

Article 101 of the LOS Convention, like Article 15 of the 1958 High Seas Convention, defines piracy to include "any illegal acts of violence or detention, or any act of depredation, committed for private ends by the crew or the passengers of a private ship or aircraft," and directed against another ship or aircraft (or persons or property on board) either "on the high seas" or "in a place outside the jurisdiction of any State." According to Article 58, the provisions of the LOS Convention regarding piracy apply in the exclusive economic zone, to the extent that they are not incompatible with either the Convention's exclusive economic zone provisions or any applicable coastal state laws, and subject to the further requirement of giving due regard to the coastal state's rights.

The United Nations has become concerned with piracy in recent years. In 2002 the U.N. General Assembly adopted a resolution urging all states and relevant international bodies to cooperate in preventing and combating piracy and armed robbery at sea by adopting measures to assist with preventing, reporting, and investigating incidents, and to bring the alleged perpetrators to justice, in accordance with international law. UN Doc. A/RES/57/141 (2002). As an example of such cooperation, see the 2004 Regional Cooperation Agreement on Combating Piracy and Armed Robbery against Ships in Asia.

Pirate attacks off the coast of Somalia in East Africa have been a particular concern in recent years. The International Maritime Bureau's Piracy

Reporting Centre, an arm of the International Chamber of Commerce, reported 111 attacks off Somalia in 2008 of commercial ships and ships providing humanitarian aid to Somalia. These attacks resulted in forty-two hijackings, with the hijacked vessels held for ransom and 815 crew members held hostage. As of May 12, 2009, the number of 2009 attacks in the region had surpassed the total number for 2008, and successful hijackings were on a pace to exceed the 2008 total. See Pirate Attacks off Somalia Already Surpass 2008 Figures (May 12, 2009), available at http://www.icc-ccs.org.

In June 2008 the U.N. Security Council, concerned about these attacks, approved a binding decision providing that, for a period of six months, states cooperating with Somalia's transitional government could "[e]nter the territorial waters of Somalia for the purpose of repressing acts of piracy and armed robbery at sea, in a manner consistent with such action permitted on the high seas with respect to piracy under relevant international law," using "all necessary means to repress" the piratical acts. UN Doc. S/RES/1816 (2008). In December 2008 the Security Council extended similar authority for another twelve months. UN Doc. S/RES/1851 (2008). Besides these restrictions in time, other limitations apply. The Security Council resolutions apply only to the coast of Somalia and not to the coasts of any other states in the neighborhood, and the resolutions explicitly disclaim any relevance with respect to the generation of customary international law. These resolutions find their legal basis in the prior authorization of the Somali Transitional Federal Government to allow anti-piracy actions in the Somali territorial sea, and are therefore not as revolutionary as they may appear at first glance. Tullio Treves, Piracy, Law of the Sea, and Use of Force: Developments off the Coast of Somalia, 20 Eur. J. Intl. L. 399, 406–408 (2009).

Other responses to the upsurge in pirate attacks off East Africa have included: trials of pirates in various countries, including in Kenya pursuant to agreements with the European Union, as mentioned below, and the United States; increased deployment of naval vessels of various states; and increased private security measures and rerouting of ships. After the Assembly of the International Maritime Organization (IMO) called for governments to conclude a regional piracy agreement (IMO Res. A.1002(25) (2007)), a high-level meeting adopted a Code of Conduct Concerning the Repression of Piracy and Armed Robbery Against Ships in the Western Indian Ocean and the Gulf of Aden on January 29, 2009. Djibouti Meeting Resolution 1, Annex, available at http://www.fco.gov.uk/resources/en/pdf/pdf9/piracy-djibouti-meeting. The Djibouti Resolution also urged governments to consult further within two years, with the goal of concluding a binding agreement. Id. at ¶ 2(2). In addition, the IMO issued two piracy-related circulars in June 2009. One circular, addressed to governments, sets out a number of recommendations for preventing and suppressing acts of piracy and armed robbery against ships. IMO Doc. MSC.1/Circ.1333 (2009). A second circular, addressed to shipowners, ship operators, masters, and crews, contains additional guidelines on the same subject focusing on evasive and defensive practices. IMO Doc. MSC.1/Circ.1334 (2009). See also International Expert Group, Piracy off the Somali Coast: Final Report (Nov. 2008), available at http://www.imcsnet.org/imcs/docs/somalia_piracy_intl_experts_report_consolidated.pdf.

Responses of the European Union (EU) to the upsurge of piracy illustrate the non-static nature of the division of competence between the EU and its member states, as mentioned in Chapter 9, Section H, as well as how in practice member states transfer competence to the EU. The EU first established a coordination cell in support of military activities already undertaken by its member states in response to the pirate attacks off East Africa. See Council Joint Action 2008/749/CFSP, 2008 O.J.L. 252, 39, Article 2(1). This cell was repealed when Operation Atalanta was launched on December 8, 2008. See Council Decision 2008/918/CFSP, 2008 O.J.L 330, 19, Article 2. Operation Atalanta is an EU military operation in an area up to 500 miles off the coast of Somalia and neighboring countries in support of the above-mentioned U.N. Security Council resolutions, as well as in support of another resolution calling for the protection of vessels delivering food aid to Somalia. UN Doc. S/RES/1814 (2008); see Council Joint Action 2008/851/CFSP, 2008 O.J.L. 301, 33, Article 1. The mandate of Operation Atalanta includes the use of force as well as the authority to seize vessels and arrest, detain, and transfer persons. Id. at Article 2(d)–(e). The internal European legal basis for Operation Atalanta is to be found in new provisions on a common European foreign and security policy (Articles 14, 25(3), and 28(3) of the 1992 Treaty on European Union). These provisions did not even exist when, in 1984, the European Community (EC) signed the LOS Convention and submitted a declaration specifying EC competences. The common European foreign and security policy, i.e., the second pillar of the EU, was introduced with the 1992 Treaty of European Union establishing the EU. Yet the competence to conduct Operation Atalanta also cannot be found in the declaration submitted at the time of the EC's formal confirmation of the LOS Convention in 1998, despite the creation of the EU with its common foreign and security policy in the interim between signing and confirmation. (For the text of the EC declarations, see http://www.un.org/Depts/los/convention_agreements/convention_declarations. htm#European Community.) This is because a European security and defense policy only became an integral part of the EU's common foreign and security policy in 1999, after the EU incorporated the tasks of the Western European Union, an intergovernmental defense and security organization. Only then did the EU receive a proper military capability, an indispensable condition for fighting piracy. This military capability and Operation Atalanta suggest that EU member states have now granted the EU competence with respect to maritime security operations. This new competence should therefore be added to the competences included in the EC declaration filed at the time of confirmation, which is said to be "subject to continuous development." Id. at ¶ 8. However, the criminal prosecution of pirates remains beyond EU competence.

The external legal bases for Operation Atalanta are the high seas piracy provisions of the LOS Convention and, with respect to the territorial sea, the consent of the coastal state. See, e.g., Council Joint Action 2008/851/CFSP, 2008 O.J.L. 301, 33, Articles 1(1), 12 (the latter article indicating that the EU apparently considered it superfluous to invoke the relevant Security Council resolutions). The EU Council has approved two agreements concerning anti-piracy measures, one concluded on December 31, 2008, with Somalia, and the second concluded January 5, 2009, with Djibouti. See Council Decision 2009/29/CFSP, 2009 O.J.L. 10, 27; Council Decision 2009/88/CFSP, 2009 O.J.L. 33, 41. In addition, the EU and Kenya addressed criminal prosecution issues in a March 6, 2009 agreement, with Kenya acknowledging as a general principle that it would investigate and prosecute persons detained during Operation Atalanta. See Council Decision 2009/293/CFSP, 2009 O.J.L. 79, 47.

3. *Slave Trade*

Although, as noted in Exodus and other books of the Bible, slavery has been practiced since the beginning of recorded history, customary international law today prohibits slavery and the slave trade. Slavery is now regarded as a violation of jus cogens, so that a treaty purporting to authorize the practice would be void. Recognition of the slave trade as an illegal act did not begin until the nineteenth century. In Le Louis, 2 Dods. 210 (1817), a British government vessel seized a French ship on the high seas, alleging that the French ship was engaged in the slave trade and subject to seizure under international law. Sir William Scott (later Lord Stowell) held that the British ship was not justified in seizing the French ship under international law at that time. Chief Justice Marshall came to the same conclusion. The Antelope, 23 U.S. 66, 116–125 (1825). But in United States v. The Schooner La Jeune Eugenie, 26 Fed. Case No. 15,551 (Cir. Ct. Mass. 1822), Justice Story concluded that the slave trade did violate international law, citing several bilateral and multilateral treaties prohibiting slavery, as well as the domestic laws of several countries outlawing the slave trade.

The Convention to Suppress the Slave Trade and Slavery was adopted in 1926 under the direction of the League of Nations, and the Supplementary Convention on the Abolition of Slavery was adopted in 1956. Article 7 of the latter Convention defines the "slave trade" to include:

> all acts involved in the capture, acquisition or disposal of a person with intent to reduce him to slavery; all acts involved in the acquisition of a slave with a view to selling or exchanging him; all acts of disposal by sale or exchange of a person

acquired with a view to being sold or exchanged; and, in general, every act of trade or transport in slaves by whatever means of conveyance.

Article 4 of the Universal Declaration of Human Rights, which the U.N. General Assembly adopted in 1948, declares that slavery and the slave trade shall be prohibited in all their forms. GA Res. 217(III), UN GAOR, 3d Sess., Supp. No. 13, UN Doc. A/810 (1948). For discussion of the development of the prohibition of slavery into customary international law, see Renee Colette Redman, Freedom: Beyond the United States: The League of Nations and the Right to be Free from Enslavement: The First Human Right to be Recognized as Customary International Law, 70 Chi.-Kent. L. Rev. 759 (1994). For discussion of the development of rules against the maritime slave trade, see Louis B. Sohn, Peacetime Use of Force on the High Seas, in The Law of Naval Operations 38, 39–59 (Vol. 64, International Law Studies; Horace B. Robertson, Jr. ed., 1991).

Both the LOS Convention and the 1958 High Seas Convention recognize the obligation of the flag state to take measures to prevent and punish the transport of slaves in ships authorized to fly its flag. LOS Convention, Article 99; 1958 High Seas Convention, Article 13. A warship on the high seas may board any foreign nongovernment vessel if there are reasonable grounds to believe that such vessel is engaged in the slave trade. LOS Convention, Article 110(1)(b); 1958 High Seas Convention, Article 22(1)(b). On boarding, officials from the warship may proceed to verify the ship's registration. If the ship's registration is confirmed, it is the flag state that has jurisdiction over the ship and its crew. The boarding warship may not exercise further jurisdiction by seizing the vessel or its crew, unless authorized by special agreement or by the consent of the flag state. However, if the boarding party determines that the vessel is stateless, the warship may seize the vessel. A crew member engaged in the slave trade may be prosecuted by any state, pursuant to the principle of universal jurisdiction. Restatement (Third) of U.S. Foreign Relations Law § 404 (1987). Furthermore, if a slave takes refuge on board any ship, the slave "shall *ipso facto* be free." LOS Convention, Article 99; 1958 High Seas Convention, Article 13.

Slavery exists today in the form of trafficking in persons, including "the recruitment, transportation, transfer, harbouring or receipt of persons, by means of the threat or use of force or other forms of coercion, of abduction, of fraud, of deception" for the purpose of "sexual exploitation, forced labour or services, slavery or practices similar to slavery, servitude or the removal of organs." 2000 Trafficking in Persons Protocol to the Convention Against Transnational Organized Crime, Article 3. This widely accepted Protocol requires states parties to criminalize such acts, to take national and international cooperative measures to prevent trafficking in persons, and, when appropriate, to assist and protect victims. The 2005 Council of Europe Convention on Action against Trafficking in Human

Beings, which entered into force in February 2008, establishes more specific victim protection, international cooperation, and monitoring provisions. See generally Suzanne Miers, Slavery in the Twentieth Century: The Evolution of a Global Problem (2003); A. Yasmine Rassam, International Law and Contemporary Forms of Slavery: An Economic and Social Rights–Based Approach, 23 Penn St. Intl. L. Rev. 809 (2005).

4. *Unauthorized Broadcasting*

Article 109(1) of the LOS Convention requires all states to cooperate in the suppression of unauthorized broadcasting from the high seas. Unauthorized broadcasting is defined in Article 109(2) as "the transmission of sound radio or television broadcasts from a ship or installation on the high seas intended for reception by the general public contrary to international regulations, but excluding the transmission of distress calls." When reasonable grounds exist for suspecting that a foreign ship is engaged in unauthorized broadcasting, the ship may be boarded by a warship of a state having jurisdiction over that illegal activity. Id. at Article 110(1)(c). Such jurisdiction may be exercised by the flag state (or state of registry if it concerns an installation), the state of which the person engaged in unauthorized broadcasting is a national, "any State where the transmissions can be received," or "any State where authorized radio communication is suffering interference." Id. at Article 109(3). Although the practice of unauthorized commercial broadcasting from foreign ships on the high seas has greatly diminished or disappeared, Article 109 remains available to address such matters as the broadcasting of propaganda from ships on the high seas. See J.C. Woodliffe, The Demise of Unauthorized Broadcasting from Ships in International Waters?, 1 Intl. J. Estuarine & Coastal L. 402 (1986).

5. *Drug Trafficking*

All states are under a duty to cooperate in suppressing illicit drug trafficking. LOS Convention, Article 108; 1961 Single Convention on Narcotic Drugs, Article 35. Neither of these conventions authorizes the warship of a foreign state to board, search, or seize a vessel suspected of engaging in illicit drug trade; such jurisdiction is reserved to the flag state. However, as discussed in Section C, a country may, through domestic legislation, authorize its warships to board and seize a stateless vessel engaged in drug trafficking. Article 17 of the 1988 Convention against Illicit Traffic in Narcotic Drugs encourages states to enter into bilateral and regional agreements relating to the suppression of illegal drug trafficking. In the absence of such a treaty, Article 17 of the 1988 Convention requires a party with reasonable grounds to suspect that a vessel is engaged in illicit traffic to request authorization from the flag state before boarding or taking other appropriate measures. On receiving such a request, the flag state, if a party to the 1988 Convention, has a duty to cooperate.

Several states have entered bilateral agreements for the suppression of drug trafficking. Some treaties allow law enforcement officials of one state party to board a vessel flying the flag or claiming registration of another state party without prior approval, if reasonable grounds exist to suspect that the vessel is engaged in illicit drug trafficking. See, for example, the 1997 United States–Haiti Illicit Maritime Drug Traffic Agreement, Article 14. Other treaties require the consent of the flag state prior to stopping and boarding a vessel suspected of illegal drug trafficking. See, for example, the 2000 United States–Honduras Implementing Agreement Concerning Cooperation for the Suppression of Illicit Maritime Traffic in Narcotic Drugs and Psychotropic Substances, Article VI(1). For discussion of the varying levels of authority for nonflag state action provided in the U.S. Model Maritime Agreement, which has served as the framework for several bilateral treaties, see Joseph E. Kramek, Bilateral Maritime Counter–Drug and Immigrant Interdiction Agreements: Is This the World of the Future?, 31 U. Miami Inter–Am. L. Rev. 121 (2000).

For discussion of the exercise of U.S. jurisdiction over stateless vessels under the Maritime Drug Enforcement Act, see Section C.

6. *Hot Pursuit*

Another exception to the exclusive right of a flag state to exercise jurisdiction over its ships on the high seas is the "right of hot pursuit." A coastal

state may engage in pursuit of a foreign ship beyond its coastal waters if the state has reason to
believe the ship has violated its laws. The pursuit
must commence when the foreign ship is within the
coastal state's waters, and within a short time after
the violation by the foreign vessel, and must continue without interruption. With regard to violations
occurring within the coastal state's contiguous zone
or exclusive economic zone, the violation must pertain to the laws of the coastal state applicable in
such waters. The right of hot pursuit also applies to
violations of a coastal state's lawful regulation of its
continental shelf, including safety zones around
continental shelf installations. The right of hot pursuit may be exercised only by warships or authorized government vessels or aircraft of the coastal
state, and may only be commenced after a visual or
auditory signal to stop has been given in a manner
that enables it to be seen or heard by the foreign
ship. The right of hot pursuit ceases as soon as the
ship pursued enters the territorial waters of another state. Where a ship has been stopped or arrested
outside the territorial sea in circumstances that do
not justify the exercise of the right of hot pursuit, it
must be compensated for any loss or damage that
may have been sustained. LOS Convention, Article
111; 1958 High Seas Convention, Article 23. See
generally Nicholas M. Poulantzas, The Right of Hot
Pursuit in International Law (2d ed. 2002); Robert
C. Reuland, The Customary Right of Hot Pursuit
Onto the High Seas: Annotations to Article 111 of

the Law of the Sea Convention, 33 Va. J. Intl. L. 557 (1993).

In October 1997, the *M/V Saiga*, an oil tanker registered in the Saint Vincent and Grenadines, supplied fuel oil to three fishing vessels licensed by Guinea to fish in its 200–mile exclusive economic zone. The next day Guinean patrol boats pursued, fired on, boarded, and arrested the *Saiga* outside of Guinea's exclusive economic zone, wounding two persons on board. Guinea seized the *Saiga* and its cargo and prosecuted its master for customs violations. Saint Vincent and the Grenadines sought damages in a proceeding before the International Tribunal for the Law of the Sea, arguing that Guinea had not lawfully exercised the right of hot pursuit. The Tribunal noted that "the conditions for the exercise of the right of hot pursuit under article 111 of the Convention are cumulative; each of them has to be satisfied for the pursuit to be legitimate under the Convention." M/V Saiga (No. 2) Case (Saint Vincent and the Grenadines v. Guinea), ITLOS Case No. 2, ¶ 146 (1999). The Tribunal determined that Guinea had not met several requirements of Article 111, including lack of a reasonable basis to believe that a violation of its laws pertaining to its contiguous or exclusive economic zone had occurred, failure to give the required visual or auditory signals to stop prior to engaging in the pursuit, and interruption of the pursuit. Id. at ¶ 147. The Tribunal also found that Guinea had used excessive and unreasonable force in stopping and arresting the *Saiga*, id. at ¶¶ 155–159, and awarded damages.

7. Vessel of Same Nationality as Warship

Another exception justifying interference by a warship with a foreign ship on the high seas is where the warship has reason to suspect that, though flying a foreign flag, the ship has the same nationality as the warship. LOS Convention, Article 110(1)(e); 1958 High Seas Convention, Article 22(1)(c). In United States v. Ricardo, 619 F.2d 1124, 1130 n.4 (5th Cir. 1980), the court acknowledged the authority of a U.S. Coast Guard ship to board a vessel that it reasonably believed to be of U.S. nationality. The court stated that "[f]ailure to fly its flag or exhibit its nationality, the presence of American interpreters, and the proximity to and bearing towards the U.S. coast generate ample suspicion that the [ship] may have been of American registry."

CHAPTER 5

THE BASELINE FOR DETERMINING ZONES OF NATIONAL JURISDICTION

A. INTRODUCTION

Three types of delimitations are involved in determining the zones of a coastal state's maritime jurisdiction. This Chapter addresses the first type—the "baseline" from which the breadth of a coastal state's various maritime jurisdictions is measured. The second type of delimitation determines the outer limit of each zone of maritime jurisdiction; it is discussed in Chapters 8 (territorial sea and contiguous zone), 9 (exclusive economic zone), and 10 (continental shelf). The final type of delimitation, discussed in Chapter 6, determines the boundaries of maritime jurisdiction between states with adjacent or opposite coasts.

Although the determination of a boundary by a state is often a unilateral act, the boundary's validity with regard to other states depends on international law. The International Court of Justice acknowledged the applicability of this principle to maritime boundaries in the Fisheries Case (United Kingdom v. Norway), stating that "[t]he delimitation of the sea areas has always an international aspect; it cannot be dependent merely upon the will of the coastal State as expressed in its municipal law." 1951 I.C.J. 116, 132.

As noted throughout this Chapter, several U.S. Supreme Court decisions rely on rules of international law, both to determine the baseline from which U.S. state and federal zones of jurisdiction are measured, and to ascertain the existence of "historic waters" along the U.S. coast. The Submerged Lands Act of 1953, 43 U.S.C. §§ 1301 et seq., confirms a U.S. state's title to the seabed and coastal waters (including the natural resources therein) extending three miles from its coastline. Id. at § 1311. The Act allows an extended boundary of up to three marine leagues (nine miles) into the Gulf of Mexico, id. at § 1301(b), if such boundary "was so provided by [the state's] constitution or laws prior to or at the time such State became a member of the Union, or if it has been heretofore approved by Congress." Id. at § 1312. Texas and Florida have established maritime boundaries of three marine leagues into the Gulf of Mexico. The maritime boundaries of Louisiana, Mississippi, and Alabama have been limited to three miles. United States v. Louisiana, 363 U.S. 1 (1960); United States v. Florida, 363 U.S. 121 (1960). For discussion of the delimitation of U.S. state maritime boundaries, including the establishment of baselines for purposes of determining the breadth of coastal U.S. state waters, see generally Gerard J. Mangone,

Marine Boundaries: States and the United States, 21 Intl. J. Marine & Coastal L. 121 (2006).

After a discussion of the use of the low-water line as the normal baseline (Section B), this Chapter addresses several geographical and physical features that affect the baseline, including: bays (Section C); rivers (Section D); islands (Section E); low-tide elevations (Section F); and harbor works and roadsteads (Section G). Sections H and I examine special rules concerning the use of straight baselines and archipelagic baselines. Finally, in Section J we introduce the concept of historical waters and their effect on baselines.

Illustration 2: Baseline Map

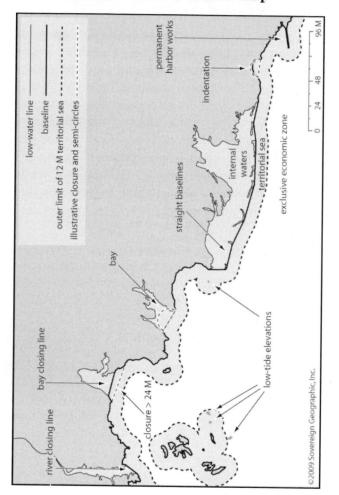

B. NORMAL BASELINE: THE LOW–WATER LINE

The normal baseline for measuring the breadth of the territorial sea and of all the other zones of a coastal state's maritime jurisdiction is "the low-water line along the coast as marked on large-scale charts officially recognized by the coastal State." LOS Convention, Article 5; 1958 Territorial Sea Convention, Article 3. In the many geographical circumstances where internal waters (such as rivers) border a coastal state's territorial sea, the line of demarcation between the internal waters and the territorial sea forms the baseline for measuring the zones of maritime jurisdiction. LOS Convention, Articles 9, 10; 1958 Territorial Sea Convention, Articles 7, 13.

Waters on the landward side of the baseline form part of the internal waters of the coastal state. LOS Convention, Article 8; 1958 Territorial Sea Convention, Article 5(1). However, a different rule applies to archipelagic states, as discussed in Section I.

In the Fisheries Case (United Kingdom v. Norway), the International Court of Justice found that "for the purpose of measuring the breadth of the territorial sea, it is the low-water mark as opposed to the high-water mark, or the mean between the two tides, which has generally been adopted in the practice of States. This criterion is the most favorable to the coastal State and clearly shows the character of territorial waters as appurtenant to the

land territory." 1951 I.C.J. 116, 128. In United
States v. California, the United States asserted that
the low-water line should be determined by averag-
ing all of the low tides; California asserted that only
the lower low tides should be taken into account.
The Court agreed with the latter view, noting that
only the lower low-water line was marked on the
U.S. Coast and Geodetic Survey's charts. 381 U.S.
139, 175–176 (1965).

Although the normal "low-water line" rule for
establishing baselines is seemingly straightforward,
its application is far from simple. "Low-water
marks" are not constant; they shift from day to day
and season to season. Irregularities in coastal configurations add to the complexity of determining the
appropriate low-water line. Neither the 1958 Territorial Sea Convention nor the LOS Convention pre-
scribes the method to be used by coastal states in
determining the low-water mark. A state may em-
ploy any method available, but must publish the
low-water lines on officially recognized, large-scale
charts so that navigators will be aware of them. For
discussion of the many geographical methods of
determining low-water lines, see P.B. Beazley, Maritime Limits and Baselines: A Guide to Their Delineation (3d ed. 1987); D.P. O'Connell, 1 The International Law of the Sea 170–183 (1982); Michael W.
Reed, 3 Shore and Sea Boundaries 177–185 (2000).
Many countries now rely on global positioning systems (GPS) to aid in the establishment of the low-
water line. See also the work of the International

Hydrographic Organization, whose website is http://
www.iho-ohi.net/english/home/.

C. BAYS

The waters of a bay are internal waters of a
coastal state if the bay possesses prescribed geographical characteristics. First, it must be a well-
marked indentation in the coast that is more than a
mere curvature. Under Article 10(2) of the LOS
Convention and Article 7(2) of the 1958 Territorial
Sea Convention, this requirement is met when a
bay's area is as large as or larger than that of the
semi-circle whose diameter is a line drawn across its
mouth. See Illustration 2 above. In determining
whether a body of water was a bay subject to
Alaska's jurisdiction under the 1953 Submerged
Lands Act, the U.S. Supreme Court expanded on
the "well-marked indentation" requirement. The
Court stated that "a body of water must possess
physical features that would allow a mariner look-
ing at navigational charts that do not depict bay
closing lines nonetheless to perceive the bay's limits, and hence to avoid illegal encroachment into
inland waters." Alaska v. United States, 545 U.S.
75, 94 (2005) (noting that "the test is what mari-
ners see, not what litigators invent").

A second requirement of a bay is that the closing
line between the bay's natural entrance points may
not exceed twenty-four nautical miles. If the closing
line exceeds twenty-four miles, a straight baseline
of twenty-four miles may be drawn within the bay

in such a manner as to enclose the maximum area of water that is possible within a line of that length. LOS Convention, Article 10; 1958 Territorial Sea Convention, Article 7. As depicted in Illustration 3, Cook Inlet is an example of a bay whose mouth exceeds twenty-four miles. In United States v. Alaska, 422 U.S. 184, 185–186 (1975), both Alaska and the federal government agreed that waters lying within a twenty-four-mile line in the inland portion of Cook Inlet constituted internal waters.

Illustration 3: Cook Inlet

In addition, international law recognizes "historic" bays that, based on previous usage, have been considered internal waters even though they do not satisfy the above geographical criteria for a bay. Historic waters, including historic bays, are discussed in Section J.

An early landmark in the development of the law of bays was the North Atlantic Fisheries Case (Great Britain v. United States), decided by the Permanent Court of Arbitration in 1910. 11 Rep. Intl. Arb. Awards 173. The case involved in part the interpretation of the term "bay" as used in the 1818 United States–Great Britain Fisheries Convention. Id. at 195–200. The United States requested the arbitral tribunal to apply a mathematical rule for defining bays, limiting bays to a six-, ten-, or twelve-mile closing line. In defending its position, the United States relied on state practice as evidenced by numerous treaties providing that the mouth of a bay could be no more than ten miles wide, such as the 1882 North Sea Fisheries Convention, Article 2(2). In construing the 1818 Convention, the tribunal found the parties had intended to use the term "bay" in its "popular sense," and found no generally applicable mathematical closing rule of international law. The tribunal named a range of geographical and nongeographical considerations relevant to determining a "bay." Relevant geographical factors included the purported bay's penetration inland relative to the width of its mouth and the proximity of the bay to the navigational routes of the high seas. The tribunal identified as nongeographical factors the defense needs and the economic importance of the enclosed waters to the local population, and "other circumstances not possible to enumerate in general." 11 Rep. Intl. Arb. Awards 173, 199. Since this general formulation left "room for doubts and differences in practice," however, the tribunal recommended that the parties adopt (with some exceptions) a ten-mile closing line for bays, a length that Great Britain had adopted in treaties with other countries. Id. at 199–200. The International Court of Justice also rejected the ten-mile limit as a rule of international law in the Fisheries Case (United Kingdom v. Norway), 1951 I.C.J. 116, 131.

Departing from an International Law Commission proposal that a closing line of fifteen miles be adopted as a compromise between the ten-mile rule and the twenty-four-mile rule supported by states claiming a twelve-mile territorial sea (1956–2 Y.B. Intl. L. Commn. 268–269), the 1958 Geneva Conference approved a twenty-four-mile line. 3 UNCLOS I Off. Rec. 144–146 (1958). The twenty-four mile rule is carried over into the LOS Convention, Article 10.

The source of the semi-circle rule, noted at the beginning of this Section C, is the Report of the Committee of Experts on Technical Questions Concerning the Territorial Sea, annexed to UN Doc. A/CN.4/61/Add. 1 (1953), 1953–2 Y.B. Intl. L. Commn. 75, 77. In applying the semi-circle test, the closing line is drawn between the natural entrance points of the bay. In computing the area within an asserted bay, islands within the indentation are included as if they were part of the water area. LOS

Convention, Article 10(3); 1958 Territorial Sea Convention, Article 7(3).

In United States v. Louisiana, 394 U.S. 11 (1969), the U.S. Supreme Court applied the 1958 Territorial Sea Convention rules in deciding several issues concerning bays and their baselines under the 1953 Submerged Lands Act. One question presented to the Court was "to what extent indentations within or tributary to another indentation can be included in the latter for purposes of the semicircle test." Id. at 48. The United States argued that inner indentations should be included for the semi-circle test only if they could reasonably be considered part of the single, outer indentation; indentations separated from another indentation by a line of islands or linked only by narrow passages could not be considered. The Court included an inner bay separated from a larger bay only by a string of islands across the mouth of the inner bay in applying the semi-circle test. The Court did not, however, include an inner bay that was linked to a larger indentation only by a narrow channel. Id. at 48–51.

A second issue presented in United States v. Louisiana was the effect of islands in the mouth of the bay. The Supreme Court held that the closing line of the bay should be drawn between appropriate points on the low-water lines of the islands. The Court rejected Louisiana's argument that lines connecting islands in the mouth of a bay should not be drawn landward of a direct line between the headlands of a bay. Id. at 55–60. For another application of these principles, see United States v. California (Decree), 432 U.S. 40, 41 (1977).

Another issue raised in United States v. Louisiana was whether the headland for determining the bay closing line could be situated on an island in close proximity to the mainland at the entrance of the bay. The Court noted that although generally islands are not headlands of a bay but only create multiple mouths, there may be instances where islands are such an integral part of the coast that they may be used as a headland from which the closing line is drawn. Whether an island constitutes an integral part of the coast depends on such factors as the island's size, its distance from the shore, its shape, and its relationship to the configuration of the coast, as well as the depth and utility of the intervening waters between the island and the mainland. 394 U.S. at 66. See also United States v. Maine, 469 U.S. 504, 517–518 (1985), in which the U.S. Supreme Court allowed Long Island to be used as the headland for determining the closing line of a bay. The resulting indentation formed by Long Island Sound and Block Island Sound satisfied the requirements of a juridical bay as set forth in Article 7(2) of the 1958 Territorial Sea Convention. Id. at 519.

In United States v. California, 381 U.S. 139 (1965), California asserted that the Santa Barbara Channel constituted a "fictitious bay," because the openings at both ends of the channel and between the islands fringing the seaward side of the channel were less than twenty-four miles. The Supreme

Court agreed with the federal government's position that the channel was not a bay entitled to status as inland waters, but rather was a strait connecting two areas of open sea. Id. at 170–172.

Article 10 of the LOS Convention and Article 7 of the 1958 Territorial Sea Convention do not apply to bays bounded by more than one country. A 1957 study identified forty-eight such bays in the world. R.H. Kennedy, A Brief Geographical and Hydrographical Study of Bays and Estuaries the Coasts of Which Belong to Different States, UN Doc. A/CONF.13/15 (1957), 1 UNCLOS I Off. Rec. 198. The rule with respect to such bays is not clear. One view is that each state bordering the bay has a belt of territorial waters, and the remainder is open to navigation by vessels of third states under the high seas freedom of navigation. According to another view, the bay is divided among the bordering states according to principles applicable to states with adjacent or opposite coasts (see Chapter 6).

Yet another view was set forth in El Salvador v. Nicaragua, decided in 1917 by the Central American Court of Justice, 11 Am. J. Intl. L. 674 (1917). In that case, the Court found on the basis of special historic and geographic facts that the Gulf of Fonseca, which is bordered by El Salvador and Nicaragua at its headlands and by Honduras at its base, was held, as against the rest of the world, in community by the three states, except for an exclusive territorial belt accorded each state off its coast. Id. at 711. Under this theory, one coastal state cannot alter, deliver to, or share with another the use and enjoy-

ment of the common waters without the consent of
the other states that hold a common interest in the
bay waters. In 1986, El Salvador and Honduras
requested a chamber of the International Court of
Justice to reconsider the legal status of the Gulf of
Fonseca. The Court allowed Nicaragua to intervene.
Consistent with the 1917 decision, the International
Court of Justice concluded that the Gulf of Fonseca
is a historic bay "the subject of [a] condominium or
co-ownership" by El Salvador, Nicaragua, and Honduras, except for a three-mile territorial sea owned
exclusively by each state along its coast. Land,
Island and Maritime Frontier Dispute (El Salva-
dor/Honduras, with Nicaragua intervening), 1992
I.C.J. 351, ¶¶ 412, 432(1). The Court also noted that
"there are notoriously no agreed and codified general rules" governing multi-state historic bays. Id. at
¶ 384. At the least, though, all states involved must
consent to a condominium status. After the Soviet
Union dissolved, for example, Latvia wanted the
Gulf of Riga to be a condominium, but Estonia
refused, and the bay bordered by these two states
was later delimited according to the principles described in Chapter 6. See generally A. Gioia, The
Law of Multinational Bays and the Case of the Gulf
of Fonseca, 24 Neth. Y.B. Intl. L. 81 (1993).

Good treatises on bays include Leo J. Bouchez,
The Regime of Bays in International Law (1964),
Mitchell P. Strohl, The International Law of Bays
(1963), and Gayl S. Westerman, The Juridical Bay
(1987). For further material on the technical aspects of bay closing lines, see Aaron L. Shalowitz, 1

Shore and Sea Boundaries 31–44, 218–225 (1962), updated in Michael W. Reed, 3 Shore and Sea Boundaries 223–310 (2000).

D. RIVERS

Where a river flows directly into the sea, the baseline is a straight line across the mouth of the river between points on the low-water line of its banks. LOS Convention, Article 9; 1958 Territorial Sea Convention, Article 13. Where a river flows into an estuary, the 1956 preparatory work of the International Law Commission proposed that the rules governing bays apply, since estuaries most commonly form a bay. 1956–2 Y.B. Intl. L. Commn. 253, 271–272. Although the provision was not incorporated into the 1958 Territorial Sea Convention, the United States has adopted this principle. On this basis the United States, the United Kingdom, and the Netherlands in 1961 objected to Argentina's and Uruguay's use of a straight line (exceeding twenty-four miles in length) across the mouth of the Rio de la Plata in fixing the baseline from which to measure maritime zones. Marjorie M. Whiteman, 4 Digest of International Law 342–343 (1965). See also the recommendations of the Special Master noted in United States v. California, which adopt this rule, 381 U.S. 139, 144–145 n.6 (1965), and the objection of the United States and Guyana to Venezuela's claim of a 98.9 mile straight line across the Orinoco River estuary. U.S. Dept. of State, Pub. No. 21, Limits in the Sea Series: Straight Baselines—Venezuela, (1970), available at http://www.law.fsu.edu/

library/collection/LimitsinSeas/numerical.html,
which includes a map depicting the straight line.

Where a river at its entrance to the sea forms a
delta that is highly unstable, the coastal state may
draw straight lines from appropriate points across
the most seaward low-water lines of the delta. The
baselines so drawn shall remain effective in spite of
subsequent regressions of the delta until changed
by the coastal state in accordance with the LOS
Convention. LOS Convention, Article 7(2). This provision was incorporated to protect the interests of
deltaic countries such as Bangladesh whose shore-
lines are characterized by continual fluvial erosion
and sedimentation. 1978 Digest of U.S. Practice in
International Law 942–943. In the United States,
this provision may apply to the Mississippi delta,
but the United States has not chosen to adopt this
method. United States v. Louisiana, 394 U.S. 11,
72–73 (1969).

E. ISLANDS

All islands are entitled to a territorial sea, exclusive economic zone, and continental shelf. An island
is "a naturally-formed area of land, surrounded by
water, which is above water at high tide." LOS
Convention, Article 121; 1958 Territorial Sea Convention, Article 10. Artificial islands or installations
are not islands that are entitled to a territorial sea,
exclusive economic zone, or continental shelf, nor
may they be considered in determining baselines.
LOS Convention, Articles 11, 60(8); United States v.

California, 447 U.S. 1, 4 n.3 (1980). However, a coastal state may establish a safety zone around artificial islands or installations in which it may prescribe appropriate measures to ensure the safety of navigation and of the artificial islands or installations. LOS Convention, Article 60(4)–(5). See generally Nikos Papadakis, The International Legal Regime of Artificial Islands (1977). Rocks that cannot sustain human habitation or economic life have only a territorial sea. LOS Convention, Article 121(3).

The presence of an island or a small group of islands in close proximity to the mainland raises the question whether the baseline should depart from the low-water line of the mainland to encompass such islands, in which case the waters so embraced are internal waters. A distinction must be made between a fringe of islands and the presence of one or a few scattered islands off the coast. Where they are sufficient in number to constitute a fringe of islands that are closely linked to the land, straight baselines may be drawn, as discussed in detail in Section H. LOS Convention, Article 7; 1958 Territorial Sea Convention, Article 4; Fisheries Case (United Kingdom v. Norway), 1951 I.C.J. 116. Where one or more islands not constituting a "fringe of islands" are immediately proximate to the mainland, it has been suggested that an exception may be made to the normal low-water line baseline, and the coastal state may draw the baseline to encompass such islands. 1953–2 Y.B. Intl. L. Commn. 57, 65–66. This proposal was based on a draft prepared by

the Second Subcommittee of the Territorial Waters
Commission at the 1930 Hague Conference. See
Acts of the Conference for the Codification of International Law, LN Pub. 1930.V.16, 206. The Director
of the Coast and Geodetic Survey, U.S. Department
of Commerce, has stated that "[t]he coast line
should not depart from the mainland to embrace
offshore islands, except where such islands either
form a portico to the mainland ... or they form an
integral part of a land form." Memorandum of April
18, 1961, excerpted in Aaron L. Shalowitz, 1 Shore
and Sea Boundaries 161 n.125 (1962).

Several cases have considered the characteristics
of islands that may be considered an integral part of
the mainland for purposes of drawing baselines. In
The Anna, 165 Eng. Rep. 809, 815 (1805), Lord
Stowell concluded that "a number of little mud
islands composed of earth and trees drifted down"
by the Mississippi River, incapable of supporting
life, "are the natural appendage of the coast on
which they border." They therefore served as the
baseline from which the limits of the territorial sea
were to be measured. In Louisiana v. Mississippi,
the Supreme Court found that St. Bernard Peninsula, a land formation consisting in large part of
uninhabited mud islands, formed an integral part of
the coast of Louisiana. 202 U.S. 1, 45–47 (1906). See
also the discussion in Section C of United States v.
Louisiana, 394 U.S. 11 (1969), and United States v.
Maine, 469 U.S. 504 (1985), in which the U.S.
Supreme Court ruled that certain islands were suf-

ficiently integral to the coast to serve as headlands for drawing bay closing lines.

F. LOW–TIDE ELEVATIONS

A low-tide elevation is a naturally formed area of land surrounded by and above water at low tide, but submerged at high tide. Low-tide elevations situated wholly or partly within the distance of the territorial sea from the mainland or an island may be used as the baseline for measuring the breadth of the territorial sea. Low-tide elevations situated wholly beyond that distance have no territorial sea of their own. LOS Convention, Article 13; 1958 Territorial Sea Convention, Article 11. See Illustration 2. These provisions prevent a coastal state from "leap frogging" from low-tide elevation to low-tide elevation, in order to extend its baseline far from shore. Maritime Delimitation and Territorial Questions (Qatar v. Bahrain), 2001 I.C.J. 40, ¶ 207.

In the case of islands situated on atolls or of islands having fringing reefs, the baseline is the seaward low-water line of the reef. LOS Convention, Article 6.

G. HARBOR WORKS AND ROADSTEADS

For the purpose of measuring the breadth of zones of maritime jurisdiction, including the territorial sea, the outermost permanent harbor works that form an integral part of the harbor system are regarded as forming part of the coast. Offshore installations and artificial islands are not considered as permanent harbor works. LOS Convention, Article 11; 1958 Territorial Sea Convention, Article 8. The U.S. Supreme Court has stated that "harbor works" connote "structures" and "installations" that are "part of the land," that in some sense enclose and shelter the waters within, and that are "connected with the coast." Therefore, "dredged channels leading to ports and harbors" are not "harbor works." United States v. Louisiana, 394 U.S. 11, 36–38 (1969).

In United States v. California, the Supreme Court found certain jetties, breakwaters, and other artificial structures to be part of the coastline for baseline purposes. 432 U.S. 40, 41–42 (1977). The Court, however, refused such treatment to piers that were not coast protective works and to an artificial island used to service offshore oil facilities. United States v. California, 447 U.S. 1, 8 (1980). In United States v. Alaska, 503 U.S. 569 (1992), the Supreme Court upheld the authority of the Secretary of the Army, acting through the Army Corps of Engineers, to condition the grant of a permit for the construction of port facilities for the city of Nome on a disclaimer by Alaska of rights to additional submerged lands resulting from the seaward extension of the baseline caused by the construction of the port.

In 2009 the International Court of Justice considered Romania's use of the seaward end of the 7.5-kilometer (4.66-mile) Sulina dike for purposes of determining its maritime boundary with Ukraine. Romania had previously notified the United Nations of its use of the seaward end of the dike as a basepoint for drawing the baseline for its territorial sea; Ukraine did not contest the use of the basepoint for this purpose. The Court stressed that the determination of baselines for measuring the breadth of maritime zones and the identification of basepoints for delimitation purposes between states are two different issues. Because the dike did not serve any direct role in port activities, and thus could not be regarded as "permanent harbour works which form an integral part of the harbour system" under Article 11 of the LOS Convention, the Court concluded that the seaward end of the dike was not an appropriate basepoint for purposes of delimitation. However, the Court did use the landward end of the dike as a relevant basepoint in delimiting the maritime boundary between the two states. Maritime Delimitation of the Black Sea (Romania v. Ukraine), 2009 I.C.J. ___, ¶¶ 130–141.

Roadsteads are places at a distance from the coast used for the loading, unloading, and anchoring of ships. Roadsteads situated wholly or partially outside the outer limit of the territorial sea are included in the territorial sea. LOS Convention, Article 12; 1958 Territorial Sea Convention, Article 9. As they are considered a part of the territorial sea and not of the internal waters, their delimitation does not influence the baseline from which the areas of coastal jurisdiction are measured. See Myres S. McDougal & William T. Burke, The Public Order of the Oceans 423–437 (1962). Deepwater ports established under the Deepwater Port Act of 1974, 33 U.S.C. §§ 1501 et seq., do not affect the baseline. Concerning deepwater ports, see also Chapter 9, Section J.

H. STRAIGHT BASELINES

"In localities where the coastline is deeply indented and cut into, or if there is a fringe of islands along the coast in its immediate vicinity, the method of straight baselines joining appropriate points may be employed in drawing the baseline" from which the breadth of maritime zones of jurisdiction, including the territorial sea, is measured. LOS Convention, Article 7(1); 1958 Territorial Sea Convention, Article 4(1). This provision is based on the Fisheries Case (United Kingdom v. Norway), in which the International Court of Justice recognized the validity of the straight baseline method employed by Norway, as depicted in Illustration 4. The Court noted that although the method of following the low-water mark of the coast "in all its sinuosities ... may be applied without difficulty to an ordinary coast, which is not too broken, ... where a coast is deeply indented and cut into ... or where it is bordered by an archipelago" a more practical method must be applied. 1951 I.C.J. 116, 128–129.

The Court imposed certain limitations on the use of straight baselines. They "must not depart to any appreciable extent from the general direction of the coast," and the "areas lying within these lines" must be "sufficiently closely linked to the land domain to be subject to the regime of internal waters." In addition, account should be taken of "certain economic interests peculiar to a region, the reality and importance of which are clearly evidenced by a long usage," in determining the appropriateness of straight baselines in a particular area. Id. at 133. These concepts were incorporated in Article 4(2) and (4) of the 1958 Territorial Sea Convention and in Article 7(3) and (5) of the LOS Convention. The Court stated that the allowable length of a straight baseline is not limited by rules of international law, as the United Kingdom had urged. 1951 I.C.J. at 128–129. While the two conventions cited above contain no limitations on the length of straight baselines of mainland states, Article 47(2) of the LOS Convention establishes a basic limit of 100 nautical miles on the length of archipelagic baselines. See Section I.

Illustration 4: Norway's Straight Baselines

There is a rising concern that many states have applied straight baselines in a manner not allowed by international law, resulting in the enclosure of internal waters previously regarded as territorial waters or international straits. Since 1951, approximately seventy-five states have drawn straight baselines along at least part of their coasts. One treatise examines the straight baseline claims of more than thirty states, and concludes that only six of them substantially comply with international law. Nonconforming claims include the use of straight baselines drawn along nonindented coasts (for example, Australia and Cuba); use of straight baselines to enclose a single island or small group of islands not constituting a "fringe" (for example, France and Vietnam); use of straight baselines to enclose nonjuridical bays (for example, Colombia's Caribbean coast); and use of archipelagic straight baselines by states that are not archipelagic states (for example, Ecuador and Spain). W. Michael Reisman & Gayl S. Westerman, Straight Baselines in International Maritime Boundary Delimitation, Ch. 5 (1992).

When a coastal state proclaims a straight baseline that other states regard as illegal, those states may file diplomatic protests, indicating their refusal to recognize the straight baselines. When Egypt used straight baselines to establish its maritime boundaries, the United States submitted the following protest:

The United States observes that ... the Egyptian coastline in all seas is generally smooth and gently undulating, and is neither deeply indented and cut into nor fringed with islands along its coast. Hence, in localities where neither criteria is met, the method of straight baselines may not be used; rather, in those areas the low water line, as depicted on official charts, must be used.

1991–1999 Digest of U.S. Practice in International Law 1580–1581.

Under its Freedom of Navigation Program, the United States also demonstrates its objections to excessive claims arising from the inappropriate use of straight baselines by sending its warships into the contested waters. U.S. Dept. of State, Pub. No. 112, Limits in the Seas: United States Responses to Excessive Maritime Claims 6–8 (1992); William J. Aceves, The Freedom of Navigation Program: Study of the Relationship between Law and Politics, 19 Hastings Intl. & Comp. L. Rev. 259 (1996). A state could also choose to challenge excessive straight baseline claims through the dispute resolution provisions of the LOS Convention, discussed at Chapter 15. See John E. Noyes, The International Tribunal for the Law of the Sea, 32 Cornell Intl. L.J. 109, 154–158 (1998). In the Case Concerning Maritime Delimitation and Territorial Questions (Qatar v. Bahrain), the International Court of Justice, noting that the straight baseline provisions of the LOS Convention "must be applied restrictively," found that Bahrain was not entitled to draw straight baselines connecting various maritime features lying off the eastern coast of its main islands. The Court observed that Bahrain's main islands were not part of a "deeply indented" coast, nor could they be characterized as a "fringe of islands." 2001 I.C.J. 40, ¶¶ 211–215.

Straight baselines may not be drawn to and from low-tide elevations, unless lighthouses or similar installations that are permanently above sea level have been built on them. LOS Convention, Article 7(4); 1958 Territorial Sea Convention, Article 4(3). The LOS Convention has excepted from this limitation baselines to and from low-tide elevations, where such baselines have received general international recognition. Article 7(4). In the dispute between Eritrea and Yemen regarding its maritime boundaries, the arbitral tribunal did not allow Eritrea to use a low-tide elevation as a basepoint for its straight baseline, because it failed to meet the requirements of Article 7(4) of the LOS Convention. See W. Michael Reisman, International Decision: Eritrea–Yemen Arbitration (Award, Phase II: Maritime Delimitation), 94 Am. J. Intl. L. 721 (2000).

Where a delta or another natural condition causes the coastline to be highly unstable, the appropriate points from which the straight baselines are drawn may be selected along the farthest seaward extent of the low-water line and shall remain effective until changed by the coastal state. LOS Convention, Article 7(2). See also Section C.

A state may not apply the system of straight baselines in such a manner as to cut off the territorial sea of another state from the high seas or an exclusive economic zone. LOS Convention, Article 7(6); 1958 Territorial Sea Convention, Article 4(5). See also LOS Convention, Article 47(6) (concerning archipelagic waters) and Section I.

Where the establishment of a straight baseline encloses as internal waters areas that had not previously been considered as such, the coastal state must grant the right of innocent passage through those waters. LOS Convention, Article 8(2). The right of innocent passage is discussed in Chapter 8, Section D.

The United States has refrained from using straight baselines, even where permissible under international law. In United States v. California, California claimed certain waters shoreward of a straight baseline running from Point Conception around the seaward side of relevant islands to Point Loma as inland waters, although the U.S. government had consistently used the normal baseline method. The U.S. Supreme Court found that the decision to use straight baselines "is one that rests with the Federal Government, and not with the individual States." 381 U.S. 139, 168 (1965). The general effect of the federal government's refusal to use straight baselines is to limit the seaward boundaries of U.S. states under the 1953 Submerged Lands Act, causing more offshore oil and gas leases to fall outside of the U.S. states' waters and under federal control.

In United States v. Alaska, 521 U.S. 1 (1997), Alaska argued that the United States should be required to draw straight baselines around a fringe of Arctic barrier islands, resulting in the enclosure of Stefansson Sound and other Arctic waters as "inland" waters subject to Alaska's jurisdiction and control under the Submerged Lands Act. Alaska based its argument on its assertion that the United States had practiced, between the early 1900s and 1971, a consistent policy of enclosing as inland waters areas between the mainland and a group or fringe of islands where no entrance (either between the islands or between an island and the mainland) exceeded ten miles. The Court determined that the evidence did not establish a fully consistent U.S. practice in applying the ten-mile rule in drawing closing lines around fringing islands. Absent a "firm and consistent" application of the ten-mile rule, the normal baseline rules of the 1958 Territorial Sea Convention applied. Id. at 20–21. See David J. Bederman, International Decision: United States v. Alaska, 92 Am. J. Intl. L. 82 (1998).

I. ARCHIPELAGIC BASELINES

An archipelagic state is a state, such as the Philippines, whose territory consists wholly of one or more archipelagoes. LOS Convention, Article 46(a). An archipelago is "a group of islands, including parts of islands, interconnecting waters and other natural features which are so closely interrelated that such islands, waters and other natural features form an intrinsic geographical, economic and political entity, or which historically have been regarded as such." Id. at Article 46(b). An archipelagic state may include islands lying outside the archipelago (to which baselines may not be drawn), but may not possess any continental mainland territory.

An archipelagic state may "draw straight archipelagic baselines joining the outermost points of the outermost islands" and measure its territorial sea from these baselines, provided that the baselines do not exceed 100 nautical miles (with some exceptions) and that the areas thus encompassed include the main islands. The area enclosed by the straight baselines must have a ratio of water area to land area between one-to-one and nine-to-one. Id. at Article 47(1)–(2). The ratio requirement prevents an island state, such as the United Kingdom, that is comprised of significantly greater land area than water area, from qualifying as an archipelagic state. Archipelagic baselines enclose "archipelagic waters;" baselines of the types considered in the other Sections in this Chapter (such as a baseline across a juridical bay located on one of the archipelagic state's islands) enclose the internal waters of archipelagic states. For discussion of rights of passage through archipelagic waters, see Chapter 8, Section F.

Archipelagic baselines are subject to certain limitations. The baselines shall not depart to any appreciable extent from the general configuration of the archipelago. Such baselines shall not be drawn to and from low-tide elevations, unless lighthouses or similar installations that are permanently above sea level have been built on them or where a low-tide elevation is situated wholly or partly within the territorial sea of the nearest island. The system of straight baselines shall not be applied in such a manner as to cut off from the high seas or the exclusive economic zone the territorial sea of another state. If a part of the archipelagic waters lies between two parts of a neighboring state, that state has the right to continue to exercise all rights it has traditionally exercised in such waters. Id. at Article 47(3)–(6).

The United States had in the past objected to the right of archipelagic states to draw straight baselines. The U.S. position had been that the baselines for measuring the territorial sea and other maritime zones were to be drawn around each island. See 1978 Digest of U.S. Practice in International Law 943. In connection with the issuance of the U.S. proclamation of an exclusive economic zone in March 1983, however, the President stated that the Law of the Sea Convention "fairly balances the interests of all states . . . relating to the traditional uses of the oceans—such as navigation and overflight," and that the United States stood ready to accept and act in accordance with this balance. He announced that in this respect "the United States will recognize the rights of other states in the waters off their coasts, as reflected in the Convention, so long as the rights and freedoms of the United States and others under international law are recognized by such coastal states." 22 Intl. Leg. Materials 461, 464 (1983). The United States has thus recognized the rights of archipelagic states under the Convention, provided they observe the provisions of the LOS Convention relating to the right of archipelagic sea lanes passage. For example, in 1986 the United States accepted the archipelagic claims of Indonesia on the condition that its claim would be applied in full conformity with international law, including the right of transit passage through archipelagic waters used as international straits. When Indonesia subsequently closed portions of its archipelagic waters normally used as an international strait for the purpose of conducting military exercises, the United States protested. Marian Nash Leich, Contemporary Practice of the United States Relating to International Law, 83 Am. J. Intl. L. 558, 559–561 (1989).

If a state possesses an archipelago away from its continental mass, it is not entitled to the special treatment accorded an archipelagic state. Archipelagic baselines may not be drawn by states that do not qualify as archipelagic states. For example, the United States is not an archipelagic state even though the archipelago of Hawaii is part of the United States, nor may the United States use straight baselines to connect the Hawaiian islands to each other or to the U.S. mainland. The United States has objected to the claims of several states, including Denmark, Ecuador, and Spain, that have established straight baselines around their islands in a manner simulating an archipelagic state. U.S. Dept. of State, Pub. No. 112, Limits in the Seas: United States Responses to Excessive Maritime Claims 48–49 (1992).

J. HISTORIC INLAND WATERS, INCLUDING HISTORIC BAYS

The International Court of Justice has defined "historic waters" as internal waters that "would not have that character were it not for the existence of an historic title." Fisheries Case (United Kingdom v. Norway), 1951 I.C.J. 116, 130. Because historic waters are internal waters, the baseline is drawn to enclose historic waters. Three factors are considered in determining whether a state has acquired historic title in coastal waters: (1) the state must exercise sovereign authority over the area; (2) such authority must have been exercised regularly for a considerable time; and (3) other states must acquiesce in such exercise of authority. U.N. Secretariat, Juridical Regime of Historic Waters, Including Historic Bays, UN Doc. A/CN.4/143 (1962), 1962–2 Y.B. Intl. L. Commn. 1, 13–21; Alabama and Mississippi Boundary Case, 470 U.S. 93, 102 (1985). See also U.N. Secretariat, Historic Bays, UN Doc. A/CONF.13/1 (1957), 1 UNCLOS I, Off. Rec. 1 (UN Pub. No. 58.V.4, Vol. I).

As with straight baselines, the United States has sometimes challenged other states' assertions of historic bays by sailing its military vessels into such disputed waters. For example, after Libya asserted historic title to the Gulf of Sidra, the United States protested by sending its warships into the Gulf. Yehuda Z. Blum, The Gulf of Sidra Incident, 80 Am. J. Intl. L. 668 (1986). For discussion of historic title claims to which the United States has objected, see U.S. Dept. of State, Pub. No. 112, Limits in the Seas: United States Responses to Excessive Maritime Claims 8–21 (1992).

In Louisiana v. United States, Louisiana argued that regulation of navigation over certain coastal waters had given rise to historic title over the waters as inland waters. The U.S. Supreme Court held that the exercise of authority necessary to establish historic title must be commensurate in scope with the nature of the title claimed, and that the regulation of innocent passage characterized the waters at most as territorial sea rather than inland waters. 394 U.S. 11, 24–26 (1969). In the same case, the United States contended that the activities of Louisiana should not be considered in determining the existence of historic title. The Court stated that even where the United States disclaims historic title, a case could arise where sufficient state activities established historic title prior to any disclaimer by the United States. Louisiana, however, did not prove the existence of such activities. Id. at 75–78.

In United States v. Alaska, Alaska claimed historic title to Cook Inlet on the basis of federal and Alaskan regulation of fish and wildlife. The U.S. Supreme Court found that the enforcement of fish and wildlife regulations was insufficient in scope to establish historic title to Cook Inlet as inland waters. 422 U.S. 184, 196–197 (1975). Other bays that the U.S. Supreme Court has ruled are not historic bays include Santa Monica Bay and San Pedro Bay in California (United States v. California, 381 U.S. 139, 172–175 (1965)), Florida Bay (United States v. Florida, 420 U.S. 531, 533 (1975)), and Nantucket Sound (Massachusetts Boundary Case, 475 U.S. 89, 94–103 (1986)). The Supreme Court has found the Mississippi Sound (Alabama and Mississippi Boundary Case, 470 U.S. 93, 101 (1985)), Long Island

Sound (Rhode Island and New York Boundary Case, 469 U.S. 504, 509 (1985)), and Vineyard Sound (Massachusetts Boundary Case, 475 U.S. 89, 91 n.2 (1986)) to be historic waters.

For a listing of historic bays around the world, see Marjorie M. Whiteman, 4 Digest of International Law 233–242 (1965).

K. THE IMPACT OF CLIMATE CHANGE ON BASELINES

Climate change and a corresponding rise in ocean levels may affect baselines and hence the delimitation of offshore zones. Since the baseline is normally drawn following the ambulatory low-water line, even a small rise in ocean levels will cause a regression of the normal baseline. Other significant changes will result, for example, if low-tide elevations previously used as basepoints (see Section F) become totally submerged, or if rising ocean levels cause an island to become uninhabitable or unable to sustain economic life, thus resulting in the loss of the island's exclusive economic zone. Sea level rise could result in coastal zones no longer extending as far into deep, resource-rich waters as they previously had, and coastal zones associated with a submerged island would disappear completely. Reacting to the potential impact of climate change, some scholars have suggested that existing international law be changed, in order to fix baselines in their current locations. See David D. Caron, Climate

Change, Sea Level Rise and the Coming Uncertainty in Oceanic Boundaries: A Proposal to Avoid Conflict, in Maritime Boundary Disputes, Settlement Processes, and the Law of the Sea 1 (Seoung-Yong Hong & Jon M. Van Dyke eds., 2009).

CHAPTER 6

BOUNDARIES OF MARITIME JURISDICTION BETWEEN ADJACENT AND OPPOSITE STATES

A. INTRODUCTION

This Chapter addresses the international rules governing the delimitation of maritime boundaries between adjacent or opposite states. Chapter 5 addresses the delimitation of the baseline from which the breadth of a coastal state's various maritime jurisdictions is measured. The determination of the outer limit of each zone of maritime jurisdiction is discussed in Chapters 8 (territorial sea and contiguous zone), 9 (exclusive economic zone), and 10 (continental shelf).

Prior to the mid-twentieth century, most maritime boundary disputes involved the delimitation of the territorial sea, generally extending from three to twelve miles beyond the states' baselines. Certain commonly applied methods of delimiting the territorial sea were incorporated into both the 1958 Territorial Sea Convention and the LOS Convention, and have become customary international law. The delimitation of the territorial sea is discussed in Section B.

As coastal states asserted jurisdiction over exclusive economic zones and continental shelves extending up to 200 miles or more beyond their coasts, it became more difficult to resolve boundary disputes due to the much larger geographical areas and resources at stake. As discussed in Section C, there is no single method of delimitation that must be applied in resolving these boundary disputes. Although numerous exclusive economic zone and continental shelf boundary disputes have been resolved, many others have not, resulting in international tensions and uncertainty in the disputed areas.

As illustrated by the cases discussed below, the International Court of Justice and other international tribunals have played an important role in resolving boundary disputes. Article 298 of the LOS Convention contains special provisions for resolving boundary disputes among parties to the Convention. These provisions are discussed in Section C.4 and in Chapter 15, Section C.

The United States generally relies on rules of international law not only in determining the baseline from which U.S. state and federal zones of jurisdiction are measured as noted in Chapter 5, but also in resolving the lateral seaward boundaries between U.S. states. See, e.g., Texas v. Louisiana, 426 U.S. 465, 468–70 (1976); New Hampshire v. Maine, 434 U.S. 1, 3 (1977). Canada has also relied on international law rules in resolving maritime delimitation disputes between its provinces. See John H. Currie, Maritime Boundary Delimitation in a Federal Domestic Setting: The Newfoundland and Labrador v. Nova Scotia Arbitration, 17 Leiden J. Intl. L. 155 (2004).

B. TERRITORIAL SEA

Unless otherwise agreed between them, where the coasts of two states are opposite or adjacent to each other, neither state is entitled to extend its territorial sea beyond the median line every point of which is equidistant from the nearest points on the baseline from which the breadth of the territorial sea is measured. However, this rule does not apply where historic title or other special circumstances require a different delimitation. LOS Convention, Article 15; 1958 Territorial Sea Convention, Article 12.

Several early treaties between adjacent and opposite states used the equidistance method, primarily in situations of opposite coasts. See, e.g., 1846 United States–Great Britain Boundary Treaty, Article 1 (establishing boundary in the Juan de Fuca Straits); 1910 United States–Great Britain Boundary Treaty, Article 1 (establishing boundary in Passamaquoddy Bay). In 1953, a Committee of Experts consulted by the International Law Commission recommended the equidistance method, provided that where the presence of special circumstances led to an inequitable solution, a boundary be drawn by agreement. 1953–2 Y.B. Intl. L. Commn. 77, 79. Concerning methods of drawing equidistance boundaries, see S. Whittemore Boggs, International Boundaries 176–

192 (1940); Leonard Legault & Blair Hankey, Method, Oppositeness and Adjacency, and Proportionality in Maritime Boundary Delimitation, in 1 International Maritime Boundaries 203, 206–211 (Jonathan I. Charney & Lewis M. Alexander eds., 1993).

On the basis of the report of the Committee of Experts, the International Law Commission agreed quickly on applying the median line between opposite states, unless another boundary is justified by special circumstances. It encountered more difficulties with respect to the boundary line between two adjacent states. Before settling on the equidistance-special circumstances combination, the Commission explored alternatives. For instance, it considered a boundary drawn perpendicular to the general direction of the coast, a method applied in the 1909 award of the Permanent Court of Arbitration regarding the Norwegian–Swedish maritime boundary. Grisbådarna Case, 1 The Hague Court Reports 121, 129 (James Brown Scott ed., 1916; reprinted 2004), available at http://www.pca-cpa.org/. The Committee of Experts consulted by the Commission found that this rule involved the difficulty of choosing an arbitrary stretch of coast to determine "the general direction of the coast." UN Doc. A/3159 (1956); 1956–2 Y.B. Intl. L. Commn. 253, 272. The Commission also found impracticable a line drawn at right angles to the coast where the land frontier reaches the sea, which could cause the line to meet the coast at another point in the presence of a curvature of the coast. Id. The Commission rejected as well a boundary that represented the continuance of the land frontier boundary, finding such a proposal impracticable where the land boundary meets the coast at an acute angle. Similarly, the Commission found that a line tracing the geographical parallel passing through the point at which the land frontier meets the coast would not be appropriate in all cases. Id.

The equidistance principle cannot be applied if the presence of special circumstances requires another boundary in order to reach an equitable solution. "Equidistance" and "special circumstances" are two integral components of a single rule. 1977 France–United Kingdom Continental Shelf Arbitration, 18 Rep. Intl. Arb. Awards 3, 44–45, 18 Intl. Leg. Materials 397, 421 (1979). In its final draft on the regime of territorial waters, the International Law Commission noted as possible "special circumstances" the presence of islands or navigable channels near the baseline and an exceptional configuration of the coast. 1956–2 Y.B. Intl. L. Commn. 253, 300. In negotiating the 1975 Treaty of Osimo, Italy and Yugoslavia took into account the shallow depth of the territorial sea near the northern coast of Italy to deviate from an equidistant line so that large ships entering and departing from Italian ports would not be required to pass through Yugoslavian waters. See Rep. No. 8–7(2), 2 International Maritime Boundaries 1639–1649 (Jonathan I. Charney & Lewis M. Alexander eds., 1993).

The International Court of Justice has acknowledged the existence of historic title, including historic fishing rights "founded on the vital needs of the population and attested by very ancient and peaceful usage," as a factor that may "legitimately be taken into account in drawing a line." Fisheries Case (United Kingdom v. Norway), 1951 I.C.J. 116, 142. See also the Grisbådarna Case, 1 The Hague Court Reports 121, 130–131 (James Brown Scott ed., 1916; reprinted 2004), available at http://www. pca-cpa.org/; Continental Shelf Case (Tunisia/Libya), 1982 I.C.J. 18, ¶¶ 97–102.

In 1999 an arbitral tribunal, for which the International Bureau of the Permanent Court of Arbitration served as the registry, determined the maritime boundaries between the opposite states of Eritrea and Yemen in the Red Sea. Although most of the maritime boundary delimited the exclusive economic zone and continental shelf between Eritrea and Yemen, in one area islands belonging to Eritrea and islands belonging to Yemen were situated four to five miles apart, resulting in overlapping territorial seas. Yemen argued that the tribunal, rather than drawing a boundary between these Eritrean and Yemeni islands, should disregard the Eritrean islands on the grounds that they were uninhabited small rocks located outside of Eritrea's twelve-mile territorial sea. The tribunal, however, treated these rocks as islands entitled to their own territorial sea under Article 121 of the LOS Convention. Because of their location within twenty-four miles of Eritrea's mainland baseline, the territorial sea generated by these Eritrean islands intersected with Eritrea's territorial sea, thus generating a continuous band of territorial sea. Applying Article 15 of the LOS Convention, the tribunal drew an equidistant median line between the Eritrean islands and the Yemeni islands. The tribunal also concluded that neither historic title nor other special circumstances required a variance from the equidistant median line. Eritrea/Yemen Arbitration (Second Phase: Maritime Delimitation, Dec. 17, 1999), 40 Intl. Leg. Materials 983, ¶¶ 154–159 (2001).

C. CONTINENTAL SHELF AND EEZ

1. *General Rule: Delimitation by Agreement*

The delimitation of the exclusive economic zone (EEZ) and continental shelf between adjacent or opposite states shall be determined by agreement. LOS Convention Articles 74, 83; 1958 Continental Shelf Convention, Article 6. In the North Sea Continental Shelf Cases (Federal Republic of Germany/Denmark; Federal Republic of Germany/Netherlands), 1969 I.C.J. 3, ¶ 83, the International Court of Justice stated that under international law:

[T]he parties are under an obligation to enter into negotiations with a view to arriving at an agreement, and not merely to go through a formal process of negotiation as a sort of prior condition for the automatic application of a certain method of delimitation in the absence of an agreement; they are under an obligation so to conduct themselves that the negotiations are meaningful, which will not be the case when either of them insists upon its own position without contemplating any modification of it.

Articles 74 and 83 of the LOS Convention do not provide specific guidance as to the method of delimitation to be applied in negotiating an agreement. However, such agreements are to be based on international law, as referred to in Article 38 of the Statute of the International Court of Justice, with the purpose of achieving an equitable solution. The decisions of international courts and tribunals, one of the sources of law referred to in Article 38 of the Court's Statute, have played an important role in shaping what states consider to be reasonable negotiating positions. See Section C.2 for discussion of several important cases.

In an effort to analyze the practice of states in the delimitation of the EEZ and continental shelf by agreement, several scholars have compiled and reviewed maritime boundary treaties. Important works include Yoshifumi Tanaka, Predictability and Flexibility in the Law of Maritime Delimitation (2006), and the multi-volume International Maritime Boundaries (Jonathan I. Charney, Lewis M. Alexander, David A. Colson & Robert W. Smith eds., 1993, 1998, 2002, 2005). These studies indicate that a significant percentage of states with opposite coasts rely on the equidistance principle in determining their maritime boundaries, with adjustments for special circumstances. The equidistance-special circumstances rule is used less frequently in maritime boundary agreements between adjacent states. The Division for Ocean Affairs and the Law of the Sea, Office of Legal Affairs, United Nations Secretariat has also compiled maritime boundary treaties at http://www.un.org/Depts/los/ LEGISLATIONANDTREATIES.

It is possible, in applying Articles 74 and 83 of the LOS Convention, that the boundary established for the EEZ between adjacent or opposite states may vary from the boundary established for the continental shelf between those same states. As a practical matter, many states have entered into agreements to establish a single maritime boundary for the delimitation of their EEZ and continental shelf boundaries. See, for example, the 1994 Finland–Sweden Delimitation Agreement; Erik Franckx, Finland and Sweden Complete Their Maritime Boundary in the Baltic Sea, 27 Ocean Dev. & Intl. L. 291 (1996). Similarly, in submitting boundary disputes to various international tribunals and courts, many countries have requested the delimitation of a single maritime boundary for the various maritime zones involved in the dispute. When asked by Qatar and Bahrain to determine a single maritime boundary between their respective maritime areas of seabed, subsoil, and superjacent waters, the International Court of Justice observed:

> [T]he concept of a single maritime boundary does not stem from multilateral treaty law but from State practice, and ... finds its explanation in the wish of States to establish one uninterrupted boundary line delimiting the various—partially coincident—zones of maritime jurisdiction appertaining to them.

Maritime Delimitation and Territorial Questions Between Qatar and Bahrain (Qatar v. Bahrain), 2001 I.C.J. 40, ¶ 173. Not all treaties, however, establish a single maritime boundary. See, for example, the 1982 Australia–Papua New Guinea Torres Strait Maritime Boundaries Agreement, which establishes separate boundaries for purposes of the seabed and fisheries, as well as a protected zone in which inhabitants are allowed to carry out traditional activities. H. Burmester, The Torres Strait Treaty: Ocean Boundary Delimitation by Agreement, 76 Am. J. Intl. L. 321 (1982).

The United States has entered into agreements with other countries concerning many U.S. maritime boundaries. The 1976 Fishery Conservation and Management Act authorized the U.S. Secretary of State to "initiate and conduct negotiations with any adjacent or opposite foreign nation to establish the boundaries of the EEZ of the United States in relation to any such nation." 16 U.S.C. § 1822(d). Relying on this statutory authority, in 1977 and 1978 the U.S. government negotiated and executed maritime boundary agreements with Cuba, Mexico, and Venezuela, establishing a single boundary line for both the EEZ and continental shelf. In various forms, the U.S. administration agreed to abide provisionally by the maritime delimitation treaties until such time as they entered into force. When the treaties were transmitted to the U.S. Senate in 1979 for ratification, the Senate Foreign Relations Committee questioned the legality under U.S. law of establishing maritime boundaries on a provisional basis by means of executive agreements. S. Exec. Rep. No. 96–49, 4 (1980); Marian L. Nash, U.S. Maritime Boundaries with Mexico, Cuba, and Venezuela, 75 Am. J. Intl. L. 161 (1981). Any concerns about the legality under U.S. law of the maritime delimitation agreement with Venezuela were soon laid to rest, as the United States–Venezuela treaty was ratified in 1980. The United States–Mexico treaty was not ratified until 1997 (followed in 2000 by a treaty delimiting the continental shelf between Mexico and the United States beyond 200 miles). The United States–Cuba treaty has not yet been ratified, but has been renewed on a provisional basis every two years by an exchange of formal notes. U.S. Dept. of State, Pub. No. 110, Limits in the Seas: Maritime Boundary—Cuba–United States (1990).

In addition to the maritime boundary agreements discussed above, since 1976 the United States has entered maritime boundary treaties with the Cook Islands, New Zealand, Niue, the Soviet Union, and the United Kingdom. For a compilation of U.S. treaties deposited with the United Nations, see http://www.un.org/Depts/los/LEGISLATIONAND TREATIES/ STATEFILES/USA. The United States has several unresolved maritime boundary issues, including portions of the boundary with Canada in the straits of Juan De Fuca and the U.S.–Canadian boundary in the Beaufort Sea.

According to the LOS Convention, pending agreement on maritime EEZ and continental shelf boundaries, the states concerned must "make every effort" to enter into provisional agreements and must not "jeopardize or hamper the reaching of the final agreement." Articles 74, 83. The duty to "make every effort" promotes the adoption of interim measures pending a final agreement. The duty "not to jeopardize the reaching of" a final agreement limits the activities of states with respect to the area in dispute. See Rainer Lagoni, Interim Measures Pending Maritime Delimitation Agreements, 78 Am. J. Intl. L. 345 (1984).

Beginning in the 1960s, states began to include in maritime boundary agreements provisions addressing the exploitation of "straddling" petroleum or mineral deposits that may be discovered after the treaty enters into force. For example, Article 4 of the 1965 Denmark–Norway Continental Shelf Boundary Agreement provides:

> If it is found that natural resources on or below the seabed extend to both sides of the boundary between the contracting parties' continental shelf, so that resources which are found in one party's area could wholly or in part be extracted from the other party's area, agreement on the exploitation of these natural resources shall be concluded at the request of one of the contracting parties.

Other agreements provide more detailed procedures for allocating resources discovered after the treaty enters into force. See generally David Colson, The Legal Regime of Maritime Boundary Agreements, 1

International Maritime Boundaries 41, 54–60 (Jonathan I. Charney & Lewis M. Alexander eds., 1993).

As states began to negotiate boundaries relating to their EEZs and continental shelves, the existence of known or potential natural resources in areas of overlapping claims gave rise to several disputes. Various types of arrangements have been developed to resolve these disputes. Some agreements delimit a maritime boundary and provide for joint development of common deposits located near the boundary. For example, the 1969 Qatar–Abu Dhabi Agreement establishes a maritime boundary and grants equal ownership rights to both states in a petroleum deposit that straddles it. A concessionaire licensed by Abu Dhabi administers and develops the petroleum deposit, and the revenues are divided equally between the two states. See also the joint management provisions relating to the conservation and management of fisheries in a protected zone established in the 1982 Australia–Papua New Guinea Torres Strait Maritime Boundaries Agreement. H. Burmester, The Torres Strait Treaty: Ocean Boundary Delimitation by Agreement, 76 Am. J. Intl. L. 321 (1982). Disputes concerning living resources are often treated in an agreement separate from the boundary agreement. See, e.g., 1988 Sweden–U.S.S.R. Agreement on Mutual Fishery Relations in the Baltic Sea.

Other agreements, rather than designating a boundary in disputed areas, establish boundaries of a joint development zone to which both states are granted rights of development. For example, the

1974 Japan–South Korea Joint Development Zone Agreement provides for exploitation of continental shelf mineral resources in a designated joint development zone through joint ventures in which both states or their licensees participate. Joint development zones have also been established regarding living resources, marine scientific research, and environmental regulation. See, for example, the 1993 Colombia–Jamaica Maritime Delimitation Treaty. See generally Barbara Kwiatkowska, Economic and Environmental Considerations in Maritime Boundary Delimitations, 1 International Maritime Boundaries 75 (Jonathan I. Charney & Lewis M. Alexander eds., 1993).

2. *Rules to be Applied in the Absence of Agreement and the Role of International Courts and Arbitral Tribunals*

Principles to be applied to delimitation of the continental shelf and the EEZ in the absence of agreement have been a source of great controversy. Article 6 of the 1958 Continental Shelf Convention provides that in the absence of agreement, and unless another boundary is justified by special circumstances, the continental shelf boundary shall be the median line between opposite states, and an equidistant line between adjacent states. During the Third United Nations Conference on the Law of the Sea, an early draft provided that the delimitation of the EEZ and continental shelf between adjacent or opposite States "shall be effected by agreement in accordance with equitable principles, employing, where appropriate, the median or equidistance line, and taking account of all the relevant circumstances." UN Doc. A/CONF.62/W.P. 10/Rev.1, 51, 57 (1979). A later proposed version of Articles 74 and 83 of the LOS Convention provided that the delimitation of the EEZ and continental shelf between states with opposite or adjacent coasts "shall be effected by agreement on the basis of international law ... in order to achieve an equitable solution." When this text was first presented in 1981, some states, including the United States, expressed reservations about this formula. See 2 United Nations Convention on the Law of the Sea 1982: A Commentary ¶¶ 83.17–83.18 (Satya N. Nandan & Shabtai Rosenne eds., 1993).

As finally adopted, LOS Convention Articles 74 and 83 provide that delimitation of the EEZ and the continental shelf between states with opposite or adjacent coasts "shall be effected by agreement on the basis of international law, as referred to in article 38 of the Statute of the International Court of Justice, in order to achieve an equitable solution." Article 38 of the Statute of the Court includes, as sources of international law, both international judicial decisions ("as subsidiary means for the determination of rules of law") and "international custom, as evidence of a general practice accepted as law." Although state practice as evidenced by numerous agreements concluded since 1958 is relevant in determining the international law applicable to maritime boundaries, this practice does not seem to be very instructive and, thus, is less influential than the adjudications. While the Court and arbitration tribunals are required to apply the law, coastal states have greater latitude when fashioning voluntary settlements. That may account, in part, for the diversity of these boundary settlements.... Developments in the jurisprudence strongly influence the course of interstate negotiations and the resulting delimitation agreements.

Jonathan I. Charney, Progress in International Maritime Delimitation Law, 88 Am. J. Intl. L. 227, 228 (1994).

In this and the following Subsection, we discuss several important decisions that have influenced the development of appropriate methods to apply in the delimitation of maritime boundaries. Although we note several arbitral decisions, we focus on the influential jurisprudence of the International Court of Justice.

One of the first major decisions is the North Sea Continental Shelf Cases (Federal Republic of Germany/Denmark; Federal Republic of Germany/Netherlands), 1969 I.C.J. 3. Although the 1958 Continental Shelf Convention did not apply because the Federal Republic of Germany was not a party to it, Denmark and the Netherlands argued that the equidistance-special circumstances rule as set forth in the 1958 Convention had become a rule of customary international law applicable to continental shelf delimitations between adjacent states. The court rejected this argument. Id. at ¶ 69. The distortions caused by certain coastal configurations, which may produce an acceptable effect within territorial waters, are magnified in the context of a continental shelf delimitation, resulting in an inequitable boundary. Id. at ¶¶ 59, 89. The Court found that there is no single obligatory method of delimitation of the continental shelf, id. at ¶ 90, and that "delimitation is to be effected by agreement in accordance with equitable principles, and taking account of all the relevant circumstances." Id. at ¶ 101. Relevant circumstances included such factors as:

(1) "the general configuration of the coasts of the Parties, as well as the presence of any special or unusual features;"

(2) "so far as known or readily ascertainable, the physical and geological structure, and natural resources, of the continental shelf areas involved;"

(3) "the element of a reasonable degree of proportionality," taking into account "the extent of the continental shelf areas appertaining to the coastal State and the length of its coast measured in the general direction of the coastline;" and

(4) "any other actual or potential continental shelf delimitations between adjacent States in the same region."

Id.

The Court also noted that the delimitation should "leave as much as possible to each Party all those parts of the continental shelf that constitute a natural prolongation of its land territory into and under the sea, without encroachment on the natural prolongation of the land territory of the other." Id. However, as discussed in more detail in Chapter 10, under Article 76 of the LOS Convention all states are allowed a 200-nautical-mile continental shelf, even if it extends beyond the state's geological continental shelf. As a result of this development of a "juridical" (versus geological) continental shelf, the "natural prolongation" criterion of the North Sea Continental Shelf Cases would only appear to apply where the geological continental shelf extends beyond the 200-nautical-mile juridical limit. Libya–Malta Continental Shelf Case, 1985 I.C.J. 13, ¶ 39.

The Court was not asked to draw the boundary for the parties, but to enunciate the applicable principles. After the Court's judgment, the parties entered into an agreement on the delimitation of their continental shelves. See 1971 Protocol between Denmark, the Federal Republic of Germany and the Netherlands; 1971 Federal Republic of Germany–Denmark North Sea Continental Shelf Delimitation Treaty; 1971 Federal Republic of Germany–Netherlands North Sea Continental Shelf Delimitation Treaty. Illustration 5 depicts the equidistant lines proposed by the Netherlands and Denmark, and the boundaries ultimately negotiated between the parties. The negotiated boundaries took into account existing Danish oil and gas concessions, leaving them on the Danish side of the boundary.

Illustration 5: North Sea
Continental Shelf Cases

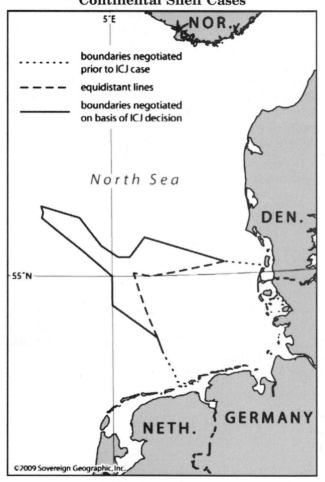

In 1982, the International Court of Justice applied the "equitable principles" rule to determine the rules applicable to the delimitation of the boundary of the continental shelf between the adjacent states of Tunisia and Libya. Continental Shelf Case (Tunisia/Libya), 1982 I.C.J. 3, ¶ 2. Each state urged the Court, in accordance with the North Sea Continental Shelf Cases, to leave to it "all those parts of the continental shelf that constitute a natural prolongation of its land territory into and under the sea." 1969 I.C.J. 3, ¶ 101. Libya argued that the natural prolongation of its land territory ran in a northerly direction; Tunisia argued that the natural prolongation of its land territory ran eastward. 1982 I.C.J. at ¶ 15.

The Court clarified its 1969 North Sea Continental Shelf Cases pronouncement on natural prolongation by stating that it "did not regard an equitable delimitation and a determination of the limits of 'natural prolongation' as synonymous." Id. at ¶ 44. After rejecting the arguments of the parties relating to geological features such as plate tectonics and the allegedly northward thrust of the African continent, the Court proceeded to apply the equitable principles rule, noting that an "equitable result" is the predominant purpose, and that equitable principles are subordinate to that goal. Id. at ¶ 70. The Court also stated:

It is clear that what is reasonable and equitable must depend on its particular circumstances. There can be no doubt that it is virtually impossible to achieve an equitable solution in any delimitation without taking into account the particular relevant circumstances which characterize the area.

Id. at ¶ 72.

In order to achieve "an overall equitable result" the Court treated the continental shelf near the coasts of the parties differently from the area farther offshore. By adopting two different delimitation methods, the Court felt it could avoid the distorting effects of certain coastal configurations that might be appropriately taken into account in delimiting a boundary close to shore. Id. at ¶ 114.

In the first area, closer to the parties' coasts, the Court determined that the appropriate delimitation was a line running perpendicular from the coast in a northeasterly direction. See Illustration 6, points A to B. The Court noted as relevant factors the parties' prior conduct in observing this line in granting oil and gas concessions, the line's perpendicularity to the coast, and its general prolongation of the land boundary between the parties. Id. at ¶¶ 117–121, 133. Farther from the coast, the Court considered two important factors that required an adjustment in the line: the marked change in the direction of Tunisia's coastline at the Gulf of Gabes and the presence of the Kerkennah Islands off the Tunisian coast. Not wanting to give full weight to the Kerkennah Islands, the Court bisected the area between the Tunisian coast and the islands (Illustration 6, points D to E) and applied a boundary line parallel to this bisecting line, causing an eastward shifting of the line of delimitation (Illustration 6, points B to C). Id. at ¶¶ 122–129, 133. Finally, the Court determined that the ratio of the continental shelf areas appertaining to each party as a result of the application of the above methods was roughly proportionate to the ratio of the lengths of the parties' coasts. Id. at ¶ 131.

Some dissenting judges criticized the majority's opinion as "stray[ing] into subjectivism" and as "*ex aequo et bono.*" 1982 I.C.J. 156 (Diss. Op. Gros), 157 (Diss. Op. Oda). A decision ex aequo et bono is a decision that rests purely in the discretion of the Court. Such a decision need not be based on any legal rules or principles, but the parties must explicitly authorize the Court to use this ex aequo et bono reasoning. The majority of the Court emphasized that its decision was not ex aequo et bono, and that while there were admittedly no "rigid rules" as to the exact weight to be applied to the various factors, its application of equitable principles was "very far from being an exercise of discretion or conciliation." 1982 I.C.J. 3, ¶ 71.

Illustration 6:
Tunisia/Libya Case

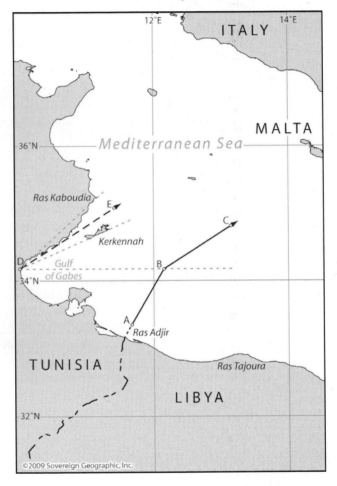

By Special Agreement dated March 29, 1979, Canada and the United States submitted their boundary dispute in the Gulf of Maine to the International Court of Justice. Gulf of Maine Case (Canada/United States), 1984 I.C.J. 246. The case is distinguishable from prior maritime boundary cases in several respects. First, rather than requesting the enunciation of applicable rules and principles, the parties asked the Court to actually draw the maritime boundary in the disputed area. Second, the parties requested the delimitation of a single line of demarcation to determine the maritime boundary for both the continental shelf and the exclusive fishery zone between the two countries. Third, the parties restricted the Court's discretion by specifying the area in which the delimitation line had to end. Fourth, at the request of the parties as allowed under Article 26 of its Statute, the Court for the first time in its history formed a special chamber to hear the case. The Chamber was composed of a judge from Canada, a judge from the United States, and three of the Court's judges whom the parties agreed should serve on the Chamber.

Both parties agreed that the "fundamental norm" required a delimitation in accordance with equitable principles, taking into account the relevant circumstances in the area, to produce an equitable solution. Id. at ¶ 99. However, they differed as to the appropriate equitable principles and relevant circumstances to be considered. The United States urged a boundary perpendicular to the general direction of the coast in the area, with some adjustments to avoid dividing certain fishing banks. Canada proposed an equidistant line without reference to certain U.S. geological features that the United States considered as relevant circumstances, including the Cape Cod Peninsula, Nantucket Island, and Martha's Vineyard. Both countries argued various geological, historic, economic, and social factors as equitable criteria in support of their respective positions. Id. at ¶¶ 12–13.

The Chamber did not adopt the positions of either party. It fragmented the boundary line into three segments. In the first segment commencing near the coast (points A to B in Illustration 7), it divided the overlapping claims of the two countries into as equal areas as possible. Id. at ¶ 213. In the second segment (points B to C in Illustration 7), it made adjustments to a median line to take into account the greater length of the U.S. coast and the location of Canada's Seal Island. Id. at ¶¶ 222–223. In the important third segment of the boundary (points C to D in Illustration 7), which crosses the fishery-rich Georges Banks, the Chamber noted that in the open ocean there was no appropriate geographical reference in drawing the boundary, outside of the actual shores of the Gulf. It seemed obvious to the Chamber "that the only kind of practical method which can be considered for this purpose is, once again, a geometrical method," and that "the most appropriate is that recommended above all by its simplicity, namely in this instance the drawing of a perpendicular to the closing line of the Gulf." Id. at ¶ 224.

Finally, having established a proposed boundary, the Chamber then reviewed it to determine whether the result was "intrinsically equitable, in the light of all the circumstances which may be taken into account." Id. at ¶ 230. After rejecting the U.S. appeal to consider the historic presence of U.S. nationals in the Georges Bank area and Canada's request to consider the socio-economic aspects of maintaining fishing patterns vital to Canadian coastal communities, id. at ¶¶ 233–234, the Chamber concluded that the proposed line "produced an equitable overall result." Id. at ¶ 241. See generally Jan Schneider, The First ICJ Chamber Experiment: The Gulf of Maine Case: The Nature of an Equitable Result, 79 Am. J. Intl. L. 539 (1985).

Illustration 7:
Gulf of Maine Case

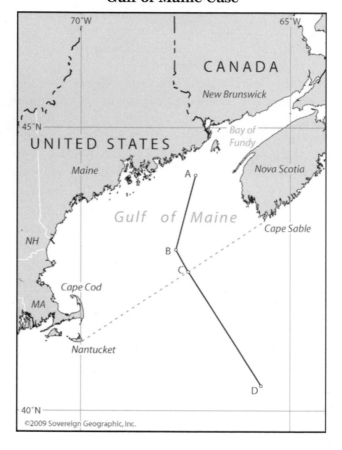

Following the North Sea Continental Shelf, Tunisia–Libya, and Gulf of Maine cases, the law of maritime delimitation of zones beyond the territorial sea was far from clear. As noted by Presiding Judge Gilbert Guillaume of the International Court of Justice in a speech delivered to the Sixth Committee of the General Assembly of the United Nations, "case law and treaty law had become so unpredictable that there was extensive debate on whether there still existed a law of delimitations or whether, in the name of equity, we were not ending up with arbitrary solutions." ICJ Press Release (Oct. 31, 2001), available at http://www.icj-cij.org/presscom/.

The Libya–Malta Continental Shelf Case, 1985 I.C.J. 13, marked a significant turning point in the jurisprudence governing maritime boundary delimitations. First, with regard to the continental shelf, the International Court of Justice noted that Article 76 of the LOS Convention had departed from a strict geological concept of the continental shelf by allowing a state to claim a continental shelf of up to 200 nautical miles "whatever the geological characteristics of the corresponding sea-bed and subsoil." Id. at ¶ 39. In view of this development, the Court determined that there is "no reason to ascribe any role to geological or geophysical factors within that distance" in determining the delimitation of the continental shelf, id., thus pounding a nail in the coffin of natural prolongation.

In a second important development, the Court found it appropriate in this case involving states with opposite coasts to begin its analysis by examining an equidistant median line, as depicted in Illustration 8. Id. at ¶¶ 43, 62. After taking into account "relevant factors," including the general configuration of the coasts of Libya and Malta, the significantly greater length of Libya's coast, and the proportionality of each country's coast to the area of its continental shelf, the Court then made an adjustment by moving the boundary north of the median line, granting a greater area of continental shelf to Libya, in order to achieve an equitable result. Id. at ¶¶ 71, 79.

Illustration 8:
Libya/Malta Case

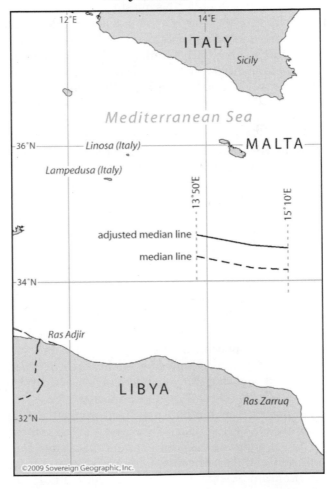

In the Libya–Malta case, the Court rejected the notion that the equidistance method must always be used or is the only "permissible point of departure." Id. at ¶ 43. However, in subsequent decisions the Court and other tribunals have generally followed this method of beginning with an equidistant line, then modifying it to take into account relevant circumstances. It is, however, the "equitable result" that is predominant; the methodology used, whether starting with an equidistant line or applying another principle, must achieve that goal. More recently, the Court has stated that the equidistance-special circumstances rule, applicable to territorial sea maritime boundary delimitations, and the equitable principles-relevant circumstances rule "are closely interrelated." Maritime Delimitation and Territorial Questions between Qatar and Bahrain (Qatar v. Bahrain), 2001 I.C.J. 40, ¶ 231.

In 1993 the International Court of Justice applied the methodology of beginning with an equidistant line, subject to correction for relevant circumstances, to determine a single maritime boundary delimiting the continental shelf and fishery zones between the opposite coasts of Greenland and Jan Mayen. Maritime Delimitation in the Area between Greenland and Jan Mayen (Denmark v. Norway), 1993 I.C.J. 38, ¶¶ 54–56. In yet another significant development, the method has been applied in the delimitation of boundaries between states whose coasts are adjacent. See, for example, Maritime Delimitation and Territorial Questions between Qatar and Bahrain (Qatar v. Bahrain), 2001 I.C.J. 40; Case Concerning the Land and Maritime Boundary Between Cameroon and Nigeria (Cameroon v. Nigeria; Equatorial Guinea intervening), 2002 I.C.J. 303. Furthermore, the Cameroon–Nigeria case was the first in which the Court found no relevant circumstances that required the adjustment of the equidistant line. Id. at ¶¶ 305–306. See also Maritime Delimitation in the Black Sea (Romania v. Ukraine), 2009 I.C.J. ___, in which the Court concluded that an equidistant line without adjustment achieved an equitable result. Yet in some cases, the extreme instability of the coastal geography or other circumstances may preclude the use of an equidistant line. See Territorial and Maritime Dispute between Nicaragua and Honduras in the Caribbean Sea (Nicaragua v. Honduras), 2007 I.C.J. ___, ¶¶ 272–283.

3. Special and Relevant Circumstances

In determining when to adjust an initial equidistant line to take into account special or relevant circumstances in order to achieve an equitable solution, the International Court of Justice and other international tribunals have given the most significance to geographical factors such as the configuration and relative lengths of the parties' coasts and the presence of islands. For a general discussion of the juridical development of the role of special and relevant circumstances, see Malcolm D. Evans, Relevant Circumstances and Maritime Delimitation (1989). For a detailed account of geography in maritime delimitation, see Prosper Weil, Geographic Considerations in Maritime Delimitation, in 1 International Maritime Boundaries 115 (Jonathan I. Charney & Lewis M. Alexander eds., 1993).

In the Tunisia–Libya Continental Shelf Case, the International Court of Justice indicated that the actual or potential delimitation of maritime boundaries between other states in the area is a relevant circumstance. 1982 I.C.J. 3, ¶ 81. Another relevant circumstance may be the conduct of the parties. For example, the conduct of Libya and Tunisia in issuing oil exploration concessions in certain areas, tacitly respected by both parties, "constitute[s] a circumstance of great relevance for the delimitations." Id. at ¶ 96. But the Court did not consider conduct of the parties concerning oil concessions as a relevant circumstance requiring adjustment of an equidistant line in the Cameroon–Nigeria Maritime Boundary Case, 2002 I.C.J. 303, ¶¶ 304–305.

Courts and tribunals have been less willing to give effect to nongeological factors such as economic considerations and historic use. In rejecting Tunisia's argument in the Tunisia–Libya Continental Shelf Case that it must take into consideration Tunisia's poverty vis-à-vis Libya, the International Court of Justice explained that economic considerations "are virtually extraneous factors since they are variables which unpredictable national fortune or calamity, as the case may be, might at any time cause to tilt the scale one way or the other." 1982 I.C.J. 3, ¶ 106.

In the Gulf of Maine case, the United States urged that consideration be given as a relevant circumstance to its continuous and historical presence in the Georges Bank, including the harvesting, conservation, and management of its fisheries. 1984

I.C.J. 246, ¶ 233. Canada urged the Chamber to consider the economic devastation that Canadian nationals would experience if they were deprived of access to the Georges Bank. Id. at ¶ 234. The Chamber stated that the "respective scales of activities connected with fishing—or navigation, defence or, for that matter, petroleum exploration and exploitation—cannot be taken into account as a relevant circumstance or, if the term is preferred, as an equitable criterion to be applied in determining the delimitation line" unless the result would "entail catastrophic repercussions for the livelihood and economic well-being of the population of the countries concerned." Id. at ¶ 237.

In contrast, the Court did consider the economic importance of the migratory capelin fishery in the southern boundary area in determining the maritime boundary between Greenland and Jan Mayen, and shifted the boundary eastward from a median line to assure that both Denmark and Norway would have equitable access to this fishery. 1993 I.C.J. 38, ¶¶ 73–76. However, the Court disregarded other socio-economic factors, including the populations of Greenland and Jan Mayen. Id. at ¶¶ 79–80. See Barbara Kwiatkowska, Economic and Environmental Considerations in Maritime Boundary Delimitations, in 1 International Maritime Boundaries 75 (Jonathan I. Charney & Lewis M. Alexander eds., 1993).

4. Conciliation

States may choose to resolve their maritime boundary disputes through a nonbinding process of conciliation. After establishing by agreement the EEZ boundary between the Norwegian island of Jan Mayen and Iceland, Iceland and Norway agreed to establish a conciliation commission to formulate a nonbinding recommendation regarding the continental shelf boundary between the two countries. 1980 Iceland–Norway Fishery Agreement, Article 9. In its 1981 report to the governments of Iceland and Norway, the conciliation commission recommended that the continental shelf boundary be coterminous with the previously established EEZ boundary, and that Iceland and Norway enter a joint development agreement for the exploration and exploitation of an area straddling the proposed boundary with potential hydrocarbon production. Conciliation Commission on the Shelf Area between Iceland and Jan Mayen, Report and Recommendations to the Governments of Iceland and Norway, 20 Intl. Leg. Materials 797 (1981). The governments of Iceland and Norway accepted and adopted the conciliation commission's recommendations, as reflected in the 1981 Iceland–Norway Continental Shelf Agreement. This was the first instance that a conciliation commission was used to establish a maritime boundary. See generally R.R. Churchill, Maritime Delimitation in the Jan Mayen Area, 9 Marine Policy 16 (1985).

Articles 279–296 of the LOS Convention provide general procedures for third-party settlement of disputes arising among parties to the Convention, but Article 298 contains special provisions for boundary disputes. It permits a party to the Convention to file a declaration to exempt boundary disputes arising prior to the entry into force of the Convention from the mandatory dispute settlement procedures. However, if such a declaration is made, a boundary dispute arising subsequent to the entry into force of the Convention must be submitted to a conciliation commission. Although the report of the conciliation commission is not binding on the parties, the Convention requires that they negotiate an agreement on the basis of the report, and if they cannot agree, that they shall, by mutual consent, submit the dispute to a third-party procedure entailing a binding decision.

As of July 15, 2009, only twenty-two of the 159 parties to the LOS Convention had invoked the Article 298 opt-out provisions with regard to boundary disputes. As a result, international tribunals, rather than conciliation commissions, may hear most boundary disputes between states that are parties to the LOS Convention when just one state initiates a proceeding. Arbitral tribunals constituted under Annex VII of the LOS Convention—which are, as explained further in Chapter 15, Section C, the "default" forum authorized to hear cases under the LOS Convention when two states do not agree on the same forum—have decided several recent maritime boundary delimitation disputes. See the 2006 Arbitration between Barbados and Trinidad and Tobago and the 2007 Arbitration between Guyana and Suriname, both available at http://www. pca-cpa.org. The Permanent Court of Arbitration acted as registry for both cases. Unless more states opt out under Article 298 from the application of the LOS Convention's provisions for binding third-party dispute settlement, it is likely that arbitral tribunals will hear more delimitation disputes in the future. See Chapter 15 for additional discussion of the dispute resolution mechanisms of the LOS Convention.

CHAPTER 7

INTERNAL WATERS
AND PORTS

A. INTRODUCTION

Internal waters are the waters landward of the baseline of the territorial sea, such as lakes, rivers, bays, and ports. LOS Convention, Article 8; 1958 Territorial Sea Convention, Article 5. See Chapter 5 with regard to the determination of the baseline. A port is "a place where ships are in the habit of coming for the purpose of loading or unloading, embarking or disembarking." The Möwe, 1915 P. 1, 15; 2 Lloyds Prize Cas. 70.

Section B of this Chapter summarizes the juridical status of internal waters. In Section C we examine the question of access to foreign ports by merchant vessels, nuclear-powered ships, warships, and vessels in distress. Section D concerns the allocation of jurisdiction between coastal states and flag states when a foreign vessel is in internal waters. Section E addresses "enlarged port state jurisdiction," which port states exercise to help enforce international rules governing pollution, vessel safety, labor standards, and fishery conservation measures. Section F briefly notes the issue of deepwater ports.

B. SOVEREIGNTY OVER INTERNAL WATERS

Subject to the provisions of applicable treaties and other rules of international law, a coastal state has sovereignty over its internal waters and ports, as if they were part of its land territory. Similarly, an archipelagic state has sovereignty over the internal waters of the archipelago (as distinguished from archipelagic waters). LOS Convention, Article 50. Foreign flag vessels have no right of innocent passage through internal waters, whereas such vessels enjoy this right in the territorial sea (as discussed in Chapter 8). However, if the use of straight baselines has the effect of enclosing as internal waters areas not previously considered as such, a right of innocent passage exists in those waters. LOS Convention, Article 8(2); 1958 Territorial Sea Convention, Article 5(2).

C. FREEDOM OF ACCESS TO PORTS

The dependence of states on sea trade raises the issue of access of foreign merchant vessels to ports. Approximately ninety percent of the world's trade by volume is transported by sea. U.N. Conference on Trade and Development (UNCTAD), Transport Newsletter No. 38 (4th Quarter 2007/1st Quarter 2008), 14, UNCTAD/SDTE/TLB/MISC/2008/1. Global seaborne trade has grown steadily in the 21st century, surpassing 8.0 billion tons of loaded goods in 2007. UNCTAD, Review of Maritime Transport 2008, at 5, UN Doc. UNCTAD/RMT/2008, E.08.-

II.D.26 (2008). The use of ports by foreign vessels is an essential link in seaborne trade.

1. *Access to Ports Established by Treaties*

The 1923 Statute on the International Régime of Maritime Ports, drafted under the auspices of the Transit Committee of the League of Nations, was an important early effort to formulate a regime governing access to ports by foreign merchant vessels. Article 2 of the 1923 Statute provides for access to ports and equality of treatment for foreign merchant vessels (other than fishing vessels), on the condition of reciprocity. As of June 1, 2009, approximately forty states had ratified or succeeded to the treaty (including Germany, Japan, and the United Kingdom, but excluding the United States).

The LOS Convention does not specifically provide a right of access to ports. However, Articles 17 and 18(1)(b) of the LOS Convention recognize a right of innocent passage through the territorial sea in order to enter or depart from internal waters. Article 25(2) of the LOS Convention further provides that the coastal state has the right to take the necessary steps to prevent the breach by a ship proceeding to its ports or internal waters of any conditions to which admission of those ships is subject.

The right of access to ports is most commonly established in bilateral friendship, commerce, and navigation treaties that grant reciprocal access to ports between the contracting parties. For instance, Article 13(1) of the 1961 United States–Belgium

Treaty of Friendship, Establishment and Navigation provides:

Vessels of either Contracting Party shall have liberty, on equal terms with vessels of the other Party and on equal terms with vessels of any third country, to come with their cargoes to all ports, places and waters of such other Party open to foreign commerce and navigation. Such vessels and cargoes shall in the ports, places and waters of such other Party be accorded in all respects national treatment and most-favored-nation treatment.

International trade law has also promoted the freedom of access to ports by foreign vessels. Article V(2) of the General Agreement on Tariffs and Trade (GATT) provides that "[t]here shall be freedom of transit through the territory of each contracting party . . . for traffic in transit to or from the territory of other contracting parties. No distinction shall be made which is based on the flag of vessels . . . or on any circumstances relating to the ownership of . . . vessels." When Chile closed its ports to Spanish fishing vessels as a result of a dispute over Chilean regulation of swordfish stocks, the European Community filed a complaint with the World Trade Organization, alleging a violation by Chile of the free transit provisions of Article V of GATT. See Request from Permanent Delegation of European Communities, Chile—Measures Affecting the Transit and Importation of Swordfish, WT/DS193/1 (Dec. 12, 2000). Chile and the European Community subsequently agreed to submit a case to a Special

Chamber of the International Tribunal for the Law of the Sea concerning the European Community's alleged violations of certain fishery provisions of the LOS Convention. Case Concerning the Conservation and Sustainable Exploitation of Swordfish Stocks in the South–Eastern Pacific Ocean (Chile/European Community), ITLOS Case No. 7, Order 2000/3 (Dec. 20, 2000). Chile and the European Community have provisionally resolved the dispute by agreement. See John Shamsey, ITLOS vs. Goliath: The International Tribunal for the Law of the Sea Stands Tall with the Appellate Body in the Chilean–EU Swordfish Dispute, 12 Transnatl. L. & Contemp. Probs. 513 (2002).

The treaties establishing access to ports typically set forth general, rather than specific, parameters governing port access. Commonly, the right of access is limited to those ports normally open to foreign trade; access to military or strategic ports may be restricted. 1923 Statute on the International Régime of Maritime Ports, Article 1. Most treaties grant freedom of access on the basis of equality with national vessels and most-favored-nation vessels, subject to reciprocity. However, land-locked states may not be denied freedom of access to ports solely because of their inability to reciprocate. LOS Convention, Article 131; 1958 High Seas Convention, Article 3; Protocol to the 1923 Statute on the International Régime of Maritime Ports, ¶ 4. As discussed at Section C.3, access to ports is also regularly conditioned on compliance with coastal state and international laws governing port operations, customs, security, safety, and environmental matters.

A right of access to port generally does not encompass any right of foreign vessels to engage in coastal trade or national fisheries. See, for example, Articles 9 and 14 of the 1923 Statute on the International Régime of Maritime Ports, excluding, respectively, the coastal trade and fishing from the treaty's application.

2.   *Access to Ports in the Absence of Treaties*

Absent a treaty providing for access to ports, the issue of whether the principle exists under customary international law has been subject to debate. One international arbitral tribunal has stated that "[a]ccording to a great principle of international law, ports of every state must be open to foreign vessels and can only be closed when the vital interests of a State so require." Saudi Arabia v. Arabian American Oil Company (ARAMCO), Award of Aug. 23, 1938, 27 Intl. L. Rep. 117, 212 (1963). The American Law Institute has also adopted the position that under customary international law, "in time of peace, commercial ports must be left open to international traffic." Restatement (Third) of U.S. Foreign Relations Law § 513 n.3 (1987).

Most legal writers have concluded that customary international law does not require a state to open its ports to foreign vessels. As noted by one commentator, "[w]hile there is a presumption that ports are open unless a state indicates otherwise, it is a presumption only and not a legal obligation." Louise de La Fayette, Access to Ports in International Law, 11 Intl. J. Mar. & Coastal L. 1, 22 (1996). This view is based on the precept that a coastal state's internal waters are, like its land territory, subject to its sovereign control. As expressed by the International Court of Justice in the Case Concerning Military and Paramilitary Activities in and against Nicaragua (Nicaragua v. United States), 1986 I.C.J. 14, ¶ 212:

> The basic legal concept of State sovereignty in customary international law, expressed in, *inter alia*, Article 2, paragraph 1, of the United Nations Charter, extends to the internal waters and territorial sea of every State and to the air space above its territory.

The International Court of Justice further acknowledged the right of the coastal state "by virtue of its sovereignty" to "regulate access to its ports," id. at ¶ 213, as well as the "customary right of innocent passage in territorial waters" enjoyed by foreign vessels "for the purpose of entering or leaving internal waters." Id. at ¶ 214. The Court concluded that hindering access by one state to the ports of another state "prejudices both the sovereignty of the coastal State over its internal waters, and the right of free access enjoyed by foreign ships." Id. Although the Court ruled that one country cannot interfere with freedom of access to another country's ports, the Court did not specifically address whether and under what circumstances the freedom of access to ports exists under customary international law.

For a summary of authorities for and against the existence of the principle of freedom of access as a matter of customary international law, see Vasilios Tasikas, The Regime of Maritime Port Access: A Relook at Contemporary International and United States Law, 5 Loy. Mar. L.J. 1 (2007).

3. Restrictions on Port Access

A coastal state may condition a foreign ship's access to port on compliance with laws and regulations governing the conduct of the business of the port. Such laws and regulations may not discriminate against or among foreign vessels. 1923 Statute on the International Régime of Maritime Ports, Article 3. Such regulations may include, for instance: arrival and departure procedures, 46 U.S.C. §§ 60101–60109; tonnage duties, 46 U.S.C. §§ 60301–60312; and pilotage, 46 U.S.C. §§ 8501–8503.

To facilitate maritime traffic, the 1965 Maritime Traffic Convention and its amendments establish mandatory standards and recommended practices with respect to documents that may be required to be submitted upon port entrance. Pursuant to the Convention, the International Maritime Organization has developed standardized shipping documents, including cargo declarations, crew lists, and passenger lists, as well as methods for delivering the data electronically. As of June 1, 2009, 114 states were parties to the Convention. Several other widely adopted conventions, including the 1966 Load Lines Convention, the 1973 Convention for the Prevention of Pollution from Ships and its 1978 Protocol (MARPOL), and the 1974 Safety of Life at Sea Convention and its amendments (SOLAS), provide for standard certificates relating to loading regulations, pollution-prevention standards, safety standards, and tonnage. The certificates issued to a vessel pursuant to these conventions must be accepted at ports of parties to the conventions as evidence that the foreign vessel complies with applicable requirements.

States have historically restricted access to ports for national security reasons. See, for example, U.S. Executive Order No. 1613 issued September 23, 1912, prohibiting entrance to certain strategic ports by foreign commercial and noncommercial vessels without prior authorization. Marjorie M. Whiteman, 4 Digest of International Law 408 (1965). Article 18 of the 1923 Statute on the International Régime of Maritime Ports specifically excludes its application in time of war with regard to the rights and duties of belligerents and neutrals. Article 16 of that Statute permits "[m]easures of a general or particular character which a Contracting State is obliged to take in case of an emergency affecting the safety of the State or the vital interests of the country" that temporarily prohibit free access to ports and equality of treatment. See also the Orinoco Steamship Co. Case (United States v. Venezuela, 1903), 9 Rep. Intl. Arb. Awards 180, 203–204 ("the right to open and close, as a sovereign on its own territory, certain harbors, ports and rivers" cannot be denied "when used ... in defense of the very existence of the Government" against revolutionary forces).

Numerous national and international steps have recently been taken to combat the threats posed to national security by maritime terrorism. These measures include adoption of the International Ship and Port Facility Security Code (ISPS Code) under the 2002 amendments to the 1974 Safety of Life at Sea Convention (SOLAS). The ISPS Code and related SOLAS amendments require most ships involved in the sea-going trade to be fitted with automatic information and recording systems. A ship that complies with the ISPS Code and other security requirements of SOLAS is issued an International Ship Security Certificate. Ships that have not been issued an International Ship Security Certificate or otherwise fail to comply with the ISPS Code may be denied entrance to ports of states parties. The United States has implemented the ISPS Code and other SOLAS maritime security measures through the 2002 Maritime Transportation Security Act. Section 102 of the Act allows the United States to prescribe conditions of entry to vessels arriving from a foreign port that fails to maintain effective antiterrorism measures, and to deny entry if such conditions are not met. 46 U.S.C. § 70110. These and other national and international efforts to prevent maritime terrorism are discussed in more detail in Chapter 14.

The U.N. Security Council has the authority, under Chapter VII of the U.N. Charter, to make recommendations or decisions to preserve international peace and security. In response to the 1990 invasion of Kuwait by Iraq, the U.N. Security Council issued Resolution 670. Although not characterized as a binding decision, the Resolution "called upon" all member states to deny Iraqi ships "entrance to their ports except in circumstances recognized under international law as necessary to safeguard human life." UN Doc. S/RES/670, ¶ 8 (1990). See Section C.6. In 2004, the U.N. Security Council adopted Resolution 1540, a binding decision requiring all member states to "take and enforce effective measures to establish domestic controls to prevent" the proliferation of weapons of mass destruction, including "appropriate laws and regulations to control export, transit, trans-shipment and re-export." UN Doc. S/RES/1540, ¶ 3 (2004). For discussion of the issues surrounding the decision-making authority of the U.N. Security Council, see Stefan Talmon, The Security Council as World Legislature, 99 Am. J. Intl. L. 175 (2005).

Several multilateral treaties regarding the conservation of fisheries place port restrictions on fishing vessels that fail to comply with fishery regulations. Although these restrictions may not deny such vessels access to port, the vessels' ability to land or transship their cargoes of fish may be denied. For example, Article 23(3) of the 1995 Fish Stocks Convention provides that "states may adopt regulations empowering the relevant national authorities to prohibit landings and transshipments where it has been established that the catch has been taken in a manner which undermines the effectiveness of sub-regional, regional or global conservation and management measures on the high seas." For an analysis of port access measures adopted under various multilateral fishery treaties, see Rosemary Gail Rayfuse, Non–Flag State Enforcement in High Seas Fisheries (2004). See Chapter 13 for further discussion of the conservation of high seas fisheries.

Article 211(3) of the LOS Convention confirms the principle that states may condition port entrance on compliance with national laws adopted to prevent, reduce, or control pollution of the marine environment, subject to the requirement that the state give public notice of such requirements and communicate them to the International Maritime Organization. The United States has enacted several laws, including the 1972 Port and Waterways Safety Act, Pub. L. No. 92–340, 86 Stat. 424 (1972), and the 1978 Port and Tanker Safety Act, Pub. L. No. 95–474, 92 Stat. 1471 (1978), that condition port access on compliance by foreign vessels with various requirements intended to prevent, reduce, or control pollution. See, for example, 46 U.S.C. §§ 3701–3719, requiring, among other measures, that foreign vessels transporting oil or hazardous materials comply with strict equipment, manning, and construction requirements prior to operating in U.S. navigable waters or transferring oil or hazardous material in U.S. ports. In 2003, the European Union banned single-hulled tankers carrying heavy grade oil from entering any ports of its member states. Regulation (EC) No. 1726/2003, 2003 O.J.L. 249, 1, available at http://eur-lex.europa.eu/. See Chapter 12 for a more detailed discussion of national and international laws governing the marine environment.

In Ray v. Atlantic Richfield Co., 435 U.S. 151 (1978), the U.S. Supreme Court held that the 1972 Ports and Waterways Safety Act intended to create uniform national standards for the design and construction of tankers, and thus preempted the higher standards legislated by the state of Washington. Similarly, in United States v. Locke, 529 U.S. 89 (2000), the Supreme Court ruled that the 1990 Oil Pollution Act preempted regulations adopted by Washington's Office of Marine Safety that established standards to prevent oil spills, including crew training and manning requirements. In its opinion, the Supreme Court noted the concern raised by governments of several countries that:

> "[L]egislation by the State of Washington on tanker personnel, equipment and operations would cause inconsistency between the regulatory regime of the US Government and that of an individual State of the US. Differing regimes in different parts of the US would create uncertainty and confusion. This would also set an unwelcome precedent for other Federally administered countries."

Id. at 98, quoting Note Verbale from the Royal Danish Embassy to the U.S. Department of State.

4. Access to Ports by Nuclear–Powered Ships

Article 27 of the 1962 Convention on Liability for Operators of Nuclear Ships (which had not entered into force as of June 1, 2009) recognizes the right of states to deny access to its ports of commercial nuclear-powered vessels. Commercial nuclear-powered vessels were owned and operated by the United States, Germany, Japan, and Russia. Many states refused access to these vessels absent an agreement establishing, among other conditions, strict liability for any damages caused by a nuclear incident and a waiver of the defense of sovereign immunity. See, for example, the 1964 United States–Sweden Agreement relating to the Use of Swedish Ports and Waters by the N.S. Savannah; 1972 Brazil–Germany Agreement concerning the Entry of Nuclear Ships into Brazilian Waters. Today's nuclear-powered vessels consist primarily of warships. CRS Report for Congress, Navy Nuclear–Powered Surface Ships: Background, Issues, and Options for Congress 1–2 (2008).

5. Access to Ports by Warships

There is no right of access to ports for foreign warships under customary international law. Article 13 of the 1923 Statute on the International Régime of Maritime Ports specifically excludes warships from the treaty's application. Many bilateral treaties establishing the right of access to ports exclude warships from their application. See 1961 United States–Belgium Treaty of Friendship, Establishment and Navigation, Article 12(3). See also the Permanent Court of International Justice advisory opinion construing a treaty that allowed Polish vessels access to Danzig's port for "imports and exports" to exclude warships. Access to, or Anchorage in, the Port of Danzig, of Polish War Vessels, Advisory Opinion, 1931 P.C.I.J. Ser. A/B No. 43, 128–129. Customary international law requires advance notice and coastal state consent prior to the entrance of a foreign warship into port. In addition, a foreign warship must refrain from certain activities while the warship is in port, such as deployment of helicopters from the warship.

Several countries have banned either nuclear-powered warships or warships carrying nuclear weapons, or both, from their ports. Michael C. Pugh, The ANZUS Crisis: Nuclear Visiting and Deterrence 62–64 (1989). Several countries with nuclear capabilities, including the United States, the United Kingdom, and France, neither confirm nor deny the presence of nuclear weapons on their warships for security reasons. This policy has resulted in the denial of such warships' entrance into the ports of countries that ban nuclear weapons within their territory. When New Zealand refused to allow a U.S. warship to enter its ports in 1985, the United States asserted a breach by New Zealand of its obligations under the 1951 Australia–New Zealand–United States Security Treaty and suspended application of the treaty between the United States and New Zealand. For discussion of the dispute, see id.; J.C. Woodliffe, Port Visits by Nuclear

Armed Vessels: Recent State Practice, 35 Intl. & Comp. L.Q. 730, 731 (1986).

It is U.S. policy to pay claims arising from incidents involving nuclear-powered warships (other than as a result of combat or civil resurrection). 42 U.S.C. § 2211. As of June 1, 2009, no reported claims had been asserted or paid under this policy.

6. Entrance into Ports and Places of Refuge as a Result of Distress or Force Majeure

A ship in distress is one that faces an "urgent necessity" based on "a well grounded apprehension of the loss of vessel and cargo, or of the lives of the crew." The New York, 16 U.S. 59, 68 (1818). The burden of proving the requisite necessity rests with the vessel or person claiming distress. The Eleanor, 1809 Edwards' Admiralty Reports 135, 165.

Historically, bilateral friendship, commerce, and navigation treaties have provided for entrance to ports of one contracting party by ships in distress that fly the flag of the other contracting party. For instance, Article 14 of the 1961 United States–Belgium Treaty of Friendship, Establishment and Navigation provides:

If a vessel of either Contracting Party runs aground or is wrecked on the coasts of the other Party, or if it is in distress and must put into a port of the other Party, the latter Party shall extend to the vessel as well as to the crew, the passengers, the personal property of the crew and passengers, and to the cargo of the vessel, the same protection and assistance as would have been extended to a vessel under its own flag in like circumstances . . . .

Several national and international courts have recognized the existence, at customary international law, of the right of a ship in distress to enter into a port. See, for example, Kate A. Hoff Claim (United States v. Mexico), 4 Rep. Intl. Arb. Awards (1929); Aldo E. Chircop, The Customary Law of Refuge for Ships in Distress, in Places of Refuge for Ships: Emerging Environmental Concerns of a Maritime Custom 163, 185–189 (Aldo E. Chircop & Olof Linden eds., 2006). The principle derives largely from humanitarian law, which obligates states to render assistance to those whose lives are in peril. See Chapter 2, Section E regarding the duty to render assistance on the high seas.

Current state practice indicates that the right of entrance to ships in distress is not absolute; entrance may be conditioned or refused to protect important national interests of the coastal state. In considering under what circumstances a damaged Chinese vessel could enter Dutch territorial waters for emergency repairs, a Netherlands court allowed the Netherlands to condition access on the posting of a bond or other security for recovery of any damages that might result from the ship's entry. Guangzhou Ocean Shipping Co. v. Minister of Transport, Public Works and Water Management, 27 Neth. Y.B. Intl. L. 354 (1996). In December 2000, the Cypriot oil tanker *Castor* developed a significant crack along its main deck while transporting gasoline in the Mediterranean Sea. Eight Mediterranean countries subsequently refused the *Castor*'s request for entrance into their ports to make necessary repairs, due to their concern over environmental pollution. In November 2002, the oil tanker *Prestige* suffered a fractured hull approximately thirty miles off the coast of Spain. Spain denied access to its ports and required the tanker to be towed out to sea, where the ship and its cargo of approximately 77,000 tons of fuel oil sank, resulting in an oil spill that harmed fisheries and caused environmental damage to the coasts of France and Spain.

In response to these and other incidents, the International Maritime Organization adopted Guidelines on Places of Refuge for Ships in Need of Assistance, IMO Doc. A/23/RES/949 (2004). The nonbinding Guidelines provide a framework of factors for coastal states, ship masters, and salvors to consider in deciding whether and where to provide refuge for a "ship in need of assistance," defined as "a ship in a situation, apart from one requiring rescue of persons on board, that could give rise to loss of the vessel or an environmental or navigational hazard." Id. at ¶ 1.18. For discussion of the Guidelines, see Aldo E. Chircop, The IMO Guidelines on Places of Refuge for Ships in Need of Assistance, in Places of Refuge for Ships: Emerging Environmental Concerns of a Maritime Custom 35 (Aldo E. Chircop & Olof Linden eds., 2006). See also Chapter 2, Section E for discussion of the refusal by Australia to allow the Norwegian vessel *M/V Tampa* into its ports to disembark Indonesian refugees it had rescued from a sinking ferry, and the international response to the incident.

D. COASTAL AND FLAG STATE JURISDICTION OVER VESSELS WHILE IN INTERNAL WATERS

1. *Conflict of Laws Principles*

When a foreign vessel is located within the internal waters of a coastal state, events involving the vessel may occur that have a significant relationship to both the flag state and the coastal state. As in all conflict of laws situations, several issues must be addressed. What rules determine whether the coastal state or flag state may lawfully exercise enforcement or judicial jurisdiction? Is jurisdiction over a particular matter concurrent or exclusive? Should the laws of the coastal state or flag state apply?

The decisions of national and international tribunals and the application of bilateral and multilateral treaties have not resulted in a fully uniform approach to resolving these issues. In determining which of potentially conflicting laws to apply, courts and tribunals have adopted varying approaches, including the application of the law of the territory in which an incident occurs, application of the law of a flag state if the issue relates to the internal affairs of a vessel, an inquiry into legislative intent as to the appropriate law to apply, and application of a multi-factor balancing test.

2. *Exercise of Jurisdiction by the Coastal State over Foreign Vessels and the Peace of the Port Doctrine*

As a general principle, most states recognize that if a foreign merchant ship voluntarily enters the ports or internal waters of a coastal state, the vessel subjects itself fully to the administrative, civil, and criminal jurisdiction of that state, unless otherwise agreed by treaty between the coastal state and the flag state. Wildenhus' Case, 120 U.S. 1, 11 (1887). As a general rule, every foreign ship, including warships, must comply in port or internal waters with the laws and regulations of the coastal state relating to navigation, safety, health, and port administration.

The coastal state may as a matter of international comity or public policy "choose to forego the exertion of its jurisdiction or to exert the same only in a limited way, but this is a matter resting solely in its discretion." Cunard S.S. Co. v. Mellon, 262 U.S. 100, 124 (1922). Most countries, including the United States, generally do not exert their jurisdiction over a ship's internal matters that do not involve the "peace or dignity" of the coastal state or the "tranquility of the port." Wildenhus' Case, 120 U.S. 1, 12 (1887). As a matter of international comity, "all matters of discipline and all things done on board which affec[t] only the vessel or those belonging to her, and [do] not involve the peace or dignity of the country, or the tranquility of the port, should be left by the local government to be dealt with" by the flag state. Id. at 18.

Numerous bilateral agreements reflect this principle. For instance, the 1951 United States–United Kingdom Consular Convention provides in Article 22(2):

[T]he administrative and police authorities of the territory should not, except at the request or with the consent of the consular officer,

(a) concern themselves with any matter taking place on board the vessel unless for the preservation of peace and order or in the interests of public health or safety, or

(b) institute prosecutions in respect of crimes or offenses committed on board the vessel unless they are of a serious character or involve the tranquillity of the port or unless they are committed by or against persons other than the crew.

In applying the peace of the port doctrine, the U.S. Supreme Court has noted that "it may not be easy at all times" to classify a particular act involving a foreign vessel or its crew as a matter that rises to the level of disturbing the peace of the port. Wildenhus' Case, 120 U.S. 1, 18 (1887). Serious crimes, such as a felonious homicide involving foreign crewmen on a foreign vessel while docked at a U.S. port, are generally considered to be matters that disturb the peace of the port. Id. In a 1985 incident, the United States asserted jurisdiction to investigate reports of the severe beating and drugging of a foreign sailor who may have been attempting to seek asylum in the United States while on board a Soviet ship docked in U.S. internal waters.

Marian Nash Leich, Contemporary Practice of the United States Relating to International Law, 80 Am. J. Intl. L. 612, 622–627 (1986).

Many countries take the position that the application of the peace of the port doctrine is within the discretion of the coastal state. Under this viewpoint, a coastal state may choose to extend jurisdiction to some matters relating to the internal affairs of the ships although such matters do not necessarily disturb the peace of the port. For example, in Cunard S.S. Co. v. Mellon, 262 U.S. 100 (1922), the U.S. Supreme Court found a congressional intent that the alcohol prohibition statutes were to be applied everywhere within the jurisdiction of the United States, including on board foreign vessels in U.S. ports. Other countries have determined that the peace of the port doctrine is not discretionary, but must be applied as a rule of customary international law. For example, when Italy arrested and prosecuted a Greek sailor on a Cypriot vessel located in an Italian harbor for drug possession, the Italian court ruled that the possession of drugs on the foreign vessel by the foreign sailor did not interfere with the peace of the port, and the flag state alone had authority to exercise criminal jurisdiction. State v. Jannopulos (Court of Naples, 1974), 1 Ital. Y.B. Intl. L. 268 (1975).

Some statutes, such as the Seamen's Act of 1915 governing the payment of seamen's wages, specifically state that they apply to foreign vessels while in U.S. waters. 46 U.S.C. § 10313. Absent a clear statement of congressional intent to apply a U.S.

law concerning internal management to foreign vessels while in U.S. waters, it has been the practice of U.S. courts not to apply U.S. law to foreign vessels concerning such matters. See, for example, Benz v. Compania Naviera Hidalgo, S.A., 353 U.S. 138 (1957) (Labor Management Relations Act not applicable to the internal labor relations of a foreign ship and its foreign crew while in a U.S. port absent a clear statement of congressional intent to that effect); McCulloch v. Sociedad Nacional de Marineros de Honduras, 372 U.S. 10 (1963) (National Labor Relations Act not intended to be applied to foreign vessels employing foreign seamen).

Recently, the U.S. Supreme Court was faced with the issue of whether the Americans with Disabilities Act (ADA), 42 U.S.C. §§ 12181 et seq., applied to a foreign vessel whose base of operations was located within the United States and whose passengers were primarily U.S. citizens. Spector v. Norwegian Cruise Line Ltd., 545 U.S. 119 (2005). Following the rationale of the Benz and McCulloch cases discussed above, the court of appeals dismissed the ADA claims due to the absence of a clear statement of congressional intent to apply the ADA to foreign ships. 356 F.3d 641 (5th Cir. 2004). The U.S. Supreme Court reversed the Fifth Circuit's ruling that the ADA is not applicable, in any respect, to foreign vessels, characterizing the Fifth Circuit's application of the Benz and McCulloch "clear statement" rule as overly broad. A majority of the Supreme Court ruled that under principles of statutory construction, defendant's cruise ships, which did a significant amount of business from U.S. ports and with U.S. passengers, were forms of "public accommodations" and "public transportation" intended to be regulated under the ADA. However, where certain ADA provisions, such as those requiring barrier removals for wheelchair accessibility, would result in non-compliance by a foreign vessel with its international obligations, including the 1974 Safety of Life at Sea Convention, the Court ruled that such modifications would not be "readily achievable" and thus not required by the ADA. The plurality opinion authored by Justice Kennedy more broadly concluded that as a matter of international comity, the ADA should not apply to foreign vessels to the extent its application interfered with the internal affairs of a foreign vessel. Id. at 133. The plurality opinion construed several of the claims raised by plaintiffs, including charging higher fares for disabled patrons and requiring that they travel with a companion, as involving the relationship between the foreign cruise ship and its passengers, rather than its internal affairs. For that reason, those claims were not precluded. For an analysis of the fractured opinion rendered by the Court as to the parameters and applicability of the internal affairs rule, see Duncan B. Hollis, International Decision: Spector v. Norwegian Cruise Line Ltd., 99 Am. J. Intl. L. 881 (2005).

The Jones Act of 1920 broadly provides that any seaman who is injured or dies in the course of his employment may maintain an action for damages in U.S. courts. 46 U.S.C. § 30104. With an exception for certain claims relating to injuries suffered while engaged in oil or mineral exploration or extraction activities in the territorial waters of other countries, id. at § 30105, the statute would, on its face, allow a foreign seaman injured on a foreign vessel in foreign waters to bring a claim for injuries in U.S. courts. The U.S. courts have not applied the "peace of the port" doctrine or the "internal affairs" rule in determining whether U.S. jurisdiction over a crewman's personal injury claim under the Jones Act is appropriate. Instead, U.S. courts have developed a separate "balancing of contacts" test, with the intent of limiting the applicability of the Jones Act "only to areas and transactions in which American law would be considered operative under prevalent doctrines of international law." Lauritzen v. Larsen, 345 U.S. 571, 577 (1953). The relevant factors include: (1) the place of the wrongful act; (2) the law of the flag state; (3) the allegiance or domicile of the injured party; (4) the allegiance of the defendant; (5) the place of contract; (6) the inaccessibility of a foreign forum; (7) the law of the forum; and (8) the location of the defendant's base of operations. Id. at 582–89; Hellenic Lines v. Rhoditis, 398 U.S. 306, 309 (1970). The fact that an injury occurs while a foreign vessel is in a U.S. port is insufficient of itself to confer jurisdiction on U.S. courts. See, for instance, Katelouzos v. The S.S. Othem, 184 F.Supp. 526 (E.D. Va. 1960); Rodriguez v. Orion Schiffahrts–Gesellschaft Reith & Co., 348 F.Supp. 777 (S.D.N.Y. 1972). In Lauritzen, the U.S. Supreme Court refused to apply the Jones Act in an action brought by a foreign seaman injured on a foreign ship in the territorial waters of a foreign state. In Rhoditis, the Jones Act was held applicable where a foreign national injured in a U.S. port aboard a foreign vessel brought suit against a foreign employer residing in the United States whose base of shipping operations was in the United States. Even where sufficient contacts exist, a U.S. court may decline jurisdiction on the principle of forum non conveniens.

For discussion of the choice-of-law rules that U.S. courts have used in various maritime settings, see Symeon C. Symeonides, Cruising in American Waters: Spector, Maritime Conflicts, and Choice of Law, 37 J. Mar. L. & Com. 491 (2006).

3. *Jurisdiction of Coastal State over Persons Seeking Asylum aboard Foreign Vessels While in Its Ports*

Where a person, before boarding a ship, has committed a crime in the territory of a foreign state, that person is not entitled to asylum aboard the ship after it has entered a port or internal waters of a third state. In the Eisler case, Poland protested the arrest of Eisler, a Polish national, by British authorities on board a Polish vessel while in a British port. The United States had requested Eisler's arrest and extradition for a crime committed in the United States. In its reply to Poland, the British government, after citing numerous instances of arrest by local authorities of persons seeking refuge on foreign vessels, concluded:

The absence of any right to grant asylum on board merchant ships, and consequently the right of the coastal authority to arrest a person on board, either for an offence committed by him on shore or in virtue of a request for his extradition under an extradition treaty with another country in which he has committed an offence, springs from the principle of international law, universally recognised by the authorities, that a merchant ship in the ports or roadsteads of another country falls under the jurisdiction of the coastal state.

The British government further stated that the right of the coastal state to act did not depend on a prior request for assistance by the vessel's captain or the flag state's consular officer. Marjorie M. Whiteman, 9 Digest of International Law 135–136 (1968).

4. Coastal State Jurisdiction over Distressed Vessels Seeking Refuge

As noted in Section C.6, customary international law has historically recognized a right of a vessel in distress to access the ports or internal waters of a coastal state, although such right is not absolute. When a foreign vessel has entered the ports or internal waters of a coastal state due to distress or force majeure, the principles of coastal state jurisdiction discussed above generally do not apply, and the foreign ship is immune from coastal state jurisdiction. For example, such vessels are not subject to coastal state customs laws. Kate A. Hoff Claim

(United States v. Mexico), 4 Rep. Intl. Arb. Awards 444 (1929). Some states have narrowly applied the exemption from immunity enjoyed by foreign distressed vessels. For example, although a Canadian court recognized that a foreign vessel entering Canadian waters in distress was exempt from penalties or forfeitures that it may have incurred if it had entered voluntarily, the vessel was nonetheless subject to Canadian customs laws to the extent it was required to report the contents of its cargo. Cashin v. Canada, 1935 Ex. C.R. 103.

As discussed in Section E, Articles 218 and 220 of the LOS Convention allow port states to investigate and enforce certain violations of pollution laws committed by foreign vessels that have "voluntarily" entered their ports or offshore terminals. These investigation and enforcement provisions do not apply to vessels in distress that have entered a port involuntarily. However, a port state may prevent a distressed vessel from leaving until it has been repaired if the vessel is in violation of international rules and standards relating to seaworthiness and poses a threat to the marine environment. Id. at Article 219.

Principles of state responsibility may render the flag state liable for damages caused to a coastal state by its flag ships that seek a place of refuge. See Gotthard Mark Gauci, Places of Refuge: Compensation for Damage Perspective, in Places of Refuge for Ships: Emerging Environmental Concerns of a Maritime Custom 299, 318–320 (Aldo E. Chircop & Olof Linden eds., 2006).

5. *Coastal State Jurisdiction over Foreign Warships*

While a foreign warship or government noncommercial ship is in the internal waters of a coastal state, the coastal state cannot extend its criminal jurisdiction over such ships. In The Schooner Exchange v. McFaddon, 11 U.S. 116 (1812), plaintiffs commenced proceedings to obtain possession of a ship while it was in a U.S. port. The ship was previously owned by them, but had been seized by the French government and converted into a French warship. The Supreme Court deferred to the "principle of public law, that national ships of war, entering the port of a friendly power open for their reception, are to be considered as exempted by the consent of that power from its jurisdiction." Id. at 145–146. More recently, the Netherlands Supreme Court ruled that a U.S. warship that had damaged a Dutch harbor was immune from jurisdiction of the coastal state. United States v. Havenschap Delfzijl/Eemshaven (1999), noted in 32 Neth. Y.B. Intl. L. 240 (2001).

In 1990, the U.S. government had arranged with the Brazilian government for a visit to a Brazilian port by the nuclear-powered warship *U.S.S. Greenling*. After its arrival, a Brazilian environmental group sought a ruling from a Brazilian federal court to require the immediate departure of the naval vessel from Brazilian waters. Although the first judge to consider the issue denied the request, on reconsideration a second judge ordered departure of the U.S. naval vessel from Brazilian waters. The U.S. government filed a protest with the Brazilian government, stating its position that U.S. warships are not subject to local jurisdiction while in port. 1989–1990 Digest of U.S. Practice in International Law 476–477.

As discussed at Chapter 4, Section D, government vessels used for commercial purposes generally are not immune from the jurisdiction of the coastal state.

6. Jurisdiction of the Flag State over Vessels in Foreign Ports or Internal Waters

Where the coastal state declines to assert jurisdiction over an offense occurring on a foreign vessel while in its ports or internal waters, "it is the duty of the courts of the flag state to apply to offenses committed by its citizens on vessels flying its flag, its own statutes." United States v. Flores, 289 U.S. 137, 158–159 (1933). In that case, a U.S. citizen murdered another U.S. citizen while aboard a U.S. merchant vessel docked at a river port 250 miles inland in the Belgian Congo. The Belgian authorities did not take any steps to punish the crime, and the Supreme Court upheld U.S. jurisdiction on the principle that a merchant vessel is deemed "to be part of the territory" of the United States.

In United States v. Reagan, 453 F.2d 165 (6th Cir. 1971), a crew member of U.S. nationality was accused of killing another crew member of U.S.

nationality on a U.S. vessel in a German harbor. The defendant had been taken into custody by German authorities and was committed to a German mental institution. He was subsequently released. The court held that these "preliminary proceedings" did not constitute an assertion of jurisdiction sufficient "to oust the jurisdiction of the flag sovereign." Id. at 171.

In National Labor Relations Board v. Dredge Operators, Inc., 19 F.3d 206 (5th Cir. 1994), the U.S. National Labor Relations Board appointed the National Maritime Union as the representative of a U.S. flag vessel's crew. The Union sought to initiate collective bargaining with the ship's owner on behalf of the crew. The ship's owner refused to negotiate, asserting that the National Labor Relations Board did not have jurisdiction because the U.S. vessel was performing long-term dredging operations in Hong Kong territorial waters. The court noted "the well-established rule of international law that the law of the flag state ordinarily governs the internal affairs of a ship," id. at 211, as well as the principle that a U.S. flag vessel is considered "American territory." Id. at 212. The court upheld the jurisdiction of the National Labor Relations Board to order collective bargaining negotiations. Although the ship's owner raised the potential conflict between U.S. and Hong Kong labor laws, the court concluded that Hong Kong had not required representation by a different union nor had Hong Kong required full compliance by the U.S. vessel

with its laws requiring preferential treatment of
Hong Kong crew members.

E. ENLARGED PORT STATE JURISDICTION

In an effort to enforce international treaties and
standards governing, among other matters, pollution, vessel safety, labor standards, and fishery conservation measures, the LOS Convention and other
treaties allow port states to inspect foreign vessels
while in port. If violations are discovered, the port
state may undertake certain enforcement procedures including, if necessary, detention of violating
vessels.

The LOS Convention authorizes a port state to
undertake investigations and institute proceedings
in respect of discharges from a ship "voluntarily
within a port or at an offshore terminal" in violation of applicable international rules and standards.
This rule applies to discharges that have occurred
not only "within the territorial sea or the exclusive
economic zone of that state," but also "outside the
internal waters, territorial sea, or exclusive economic zone of the State." Articles 218(1), 220(1). If the
discharge has occurred in the coastal waters of
another state, proceedings may be instituted in the
port state only on request of that coastal state, the
flag state, or a state damaged or threatened by the
discharge. If the state that has requested the initi-
ation of the proceedings in the port state so asks,
the proceedings may be transferred to it. Even if

the proceedings were not instituted at the request of the flag state, it may request suspension and initiate its own proceedings. However, a port state that has instituted the original proceedings need not suspend them if they relate to a case of major damage to the port state, or if the flag state in question "has repeatedly disregarded its obligations to enforce effectively the applicable international rules and standards in respect of violations committed by its vessels." Id. at Articles 218(2)–(4), 228. To mitigate the high cost of holding violating vessels in port, the ship must be permitted to proceed after posting a bond or providing other appropriate financial security. Id. at Article 220(7); see also id. at Articles 228, 292.

LOS Convention Article 219 further allows port states to detain a foreign vessel that is in violation of applicable international rules and standards relating to seaworthiness and threatens damage to the marine environment. An unseaworthy vessel may proceed to the nearest appropriate repair yard. Upon repair, the port state must allow the vessel to continue immediately. The port state must comply with "safeguard" provisions intended to prevent discrimination and to protect the interests of the vessels and flag states. Id. at Articles 223–233.

In United States v. Royal Caribbean Cruises Ltd., 11 F. Supp. 2d 1358 (S.D. Fla. 1998), a U.S. Coast Guard airplane witnessed a discharge by a foreign vessel, the *Nordic Empress* cruise ship, while in Bahamian waters on February 1, 1993. When the *Nordic Empress* arrived several days later at its destination port of Miami, Florida, a U.S. Coast Guard official asked to see the Oil Record Book required to be maintained under the 1973 Convention for the Prevention of Pollution from Ships, as modified by 1978 Protocol (MARPOL). The oil record book did not disclose the reported discharge. The United States referred the matter to Liberia, the flag state, which undertook an investigation but failed to initiate any enforcement proceedings against the vessel or its owner. In 1998, the United States brought criminal charges against the vessel's owner under 18 U.S.C. § 1001, alleging that the vessel's owner had made materially false statements to the U.S. Coast Guard by providing it with an oil record book that failed to disclose the discharge in Bahamian waters. The vessel's owner argued that both MARPOL and customary international law reflecting provisions of the LOS Convention prohibited the exercise of jurisdiction by the United States, because neither the flag state nor the Bahamas had requested port state enforcement proceedings. The court concluded that the criminal indictment was not based on the discharge of oil in Bahamian waters, but on a knowing presentation of a false statement to U.S. officials while in a U.S. port, a violation of U.S. criminal law. As a result, the case fell within the jurisdiction of the United States.

Numerous other international measures encourage port states to exercise limited enforcement jurisdiction over the pollution, safety, and social standards of foreign merchant vessels entering their ports. Articles 5 and 6 of the 1973 Convention for the Prevention of Pollution from Ships, as modified by the 1978 Protocol (MARPOL), contain provisions authorizing a port state to inspect a foreign vessel in its internal waters or ports to ensure compliance with international construction and design standards as well as anti-pollution obligations. The International Maritime Organization has adopted "Procedures for the Control of Ships" setting forth guidelines for port states as to their powers of inspection and detention of foreign merchant vessels under the 1974 Safety of Life at Sea Convention (SOLAS) and the 1966 Load Lines Convention. IMO Doc. A.787(19); IMO Doc. A.882(21). As noted at Section C.3, the ISPS Code amendments to the 1974 Safety of Life at Sea Convention (SOLAS) provide for port state control measures regarding maritime security and other matters. The 1976 Minimum Standards in Merchant Ships Convention, adopted by the International Labor Organization, authorizes contracting port states to inspect foreign merchant vessels, regardless of whether the flag state has ratified the Convention, and to take remedial measures if the vessel does not meet labor conditions specified in the Convention. See also the port state inspection provisions of Article V(4) of the 2006 Maritime Labour Convention, discussed in Chapter 4, Section B. As discussed in Chapter 13, the 1995 Fish Stocks Convention and several other regional and bilateral fishery conservation treaties provide for expanded port state jurisdiction with respect to certain fishing violations.

Many countries have entered into regional Memoranda of Understanding (MOUs) establishing regimes for coordinated implementation of port state control measures. See, for example, the 1982 Paris Memorandum of Understanding on Port State Control; 1996 Caribbean Memorandum of Understanding on Port State Control. Their purpose is to enhance, through port state inspections and enforcement proceedings, compliance by all vessels with international standards governing pollution, safety, seamen's living and working conditions, and other matters. Each MOU agreement identifies the relevant conventions to be enforced by that particular MOU. The governing documents also establish rules for inspection and detention procedures, and provide for the exchange of information with regard to inspection results. Most MOUs establish targets for the inspection of a minimum number or percentage of vessels visiting member state ports. For example, the 1982 Paris Memorandum of Understanding on Port State Control encourages each state party to inspect twenty-five percent of all vessels that enter its ports. In 2008 the twenty-seven members of the Paris MOU inspected 24,647 vessels, resulting in 1,220 detentions. 2008 Paris MOU Annual Report, available at http://www.parismou.org. For discussion of MOUs, see Ted L. McDorman, Regional Port State Control Agreements: Some Issues of International Law, 5 Ocean & Coastal L.J. 207 (2000).

F.   DEEPWATER PORTS

For discussion of a coastal state's jurisdiction over deepwater ports constructed in its territorial sea or exclusive economic zone, see Chapter 9, Section K.

CHAPTER 8

THE TERRITORIAL SEA, STRAITS, ARCHIPELAGIC WATERS, AND CONTIGUOUS ZONE

A. INTRODUCTION

The territorial sea, a narrow band of water extending seaward from a coastal state's baseline, is a long-standing feature of the law of the sea. Sections B and C address, respectively, a coastal state's sovereignty over its territorial sea and the breadth of the territorial sea. Section D examines an important limitation on the coastal state's exclusive authority in its territorial sea—the right of foreign vessels to engage in innocent passage—and the extent of a coastal state's jurisdiction over vessels passing through its territorial sea.

Special rules have developed with regard to certain categories of waters near shore. Section E discusses the regime of transit passage through straits, and Section F analyzes the laws governing archipelagic waters and archipelagic sea lanes passage. Section G concerns the contiguous zone, which lies beyond the territorial sea.

Section H highlights the allocation of authority between the federal government and the states of the United States in the U.S. territorial sea. Section I introduces the general international law concerning shipwrecks and underwater cultural heritage, which are most commonly located in the territorial sea and contiguous zone.

B.   COASTAL STATE SOVEREIGNTY OVER THE TERRITORIAL SEA

Subject to the right of innocent passage through the territorial sea and to special passage rights through straits and archipelagic waters, the coastal state has the same sovereignty over its territorial sea, and over the air space, seabed, and subsoil thereof, as it has with respect to its land territory. LOS Convention, Article 2; 1958 Territorial Sea Convention, Articles 1, 2.

Prior to the Second World War, the sovereignty of the coastal state over its territorial sea was contested, as some courts (especially French ones) and writers had characterized the territorial sea as part of the high seas subject to special rights for the coastal states. See Lassa Oppenheim, 1 International Law 487 (Hersch Lauterpacht ed., 8th ed. 1955). The sovereignty of a coastal state over its territorial sea has since been accepted as customary international law, and is recognized by the 1958 Territorial Sea Convention, Articles 1–2, and the LOS Convention, Article 2.

C. BREADTH OF THE TERRITORIAL SEA

Every state has the right to establish the breadth of its territorial sea up to a limit not exceeding twelve nautical miles, measured from the baseline as determined in accordance with the principles discussed in Chapter 5. LOS Convention, Article 3. The territorial sea extends not only around the primary land territory of a coastal state, but also around any islands owned by it. Id. at Article 121. Although rocks that cannot sustain human habitation or economic life of their own have no exclusive economic zone or continental shelf, they are entitled to a territorial sea. Id. at Article 121(3).

States historically exercised offshore jurisdiction for different purposes, including security, fishing regulation, and customs and immigration control. Several states maintained zones of varying breadths for varying purposes. When practice began to consolidate around one territorial sea of uniform breadth, a three-mile limit—associated with the range of a cannon—became common. In the twentieth century, many states extended the breadth of their territorial sea, first to six miles and later to twelve miles, though in some instances claims were made of up to 200 miles. Several major maritime countries, including the United States, strongly opposed extended claims of territorial sea jurisdiction as an intrusion on the freedoms of the high seas. See U.S. Notes of July 2, 1948 to the Governments of Peru, Chile, and Argentina, Marjorie M. Whiteman, 4 Digest of International Law 793, 796, 798 (1965).

The International Law Commission reported in 1956 that there was no uniform practice regarding the breadth of the territorial sea, but stated that "international law does not permit that limit to be extended beyond 12 miles." 1956–2 Y.B. Intl. L. Commn. 253, 265–266. After much debate between proponents of a three-mile limit to the territorial sea and proponents of an extended territorial sea, the First United Nations Conference on the Law of the Sea failed to establish a uniform limit to the breadth of the territorial sea. The 1960 Conference (UNCLOS II) also failed to agree on the limit. Marjorie M. Whiteman, 4 Digest of International Law 91–137 (1965).

An increasing number of states extended their claims of a territorial sea in the 1960s and 1970s from three miles up to as much as 200 miles. See, for instance, Ecuador's Decree of 1966 establishing a 200–mile territorial sea, National Legislation and Treaties Relating to the Law of the Sea, UN Doc. ST/LEG/SER.B/15, 78–79 (1970). The need for a uniform limit to the breadth of the territorial sea was again the subject of much debate in the Third United Nations Conference on the Law of the Sea. UNCLOS III finally accepted a limit of twelve nautical miles. LOS Convention, Article 3.

Although the United States initially resisted the extension of the territorial sea beyond three miles, in 1988 President Reagan extended the U.S. territorial sea to twelve miles from its baselines. Exec. Procl. 5928, 54 Fed. Reg. 777 (Jan. 9, 1989). Very few states claim a territorial sea of less than twelve miles. Some states claim varied widths of territorial sea. For example, as of June 1, 2009, Turkey claimed a territorial sea of six miles in the Aegean Sea, and twelve miles in the Black and Mediterranean Seas. After the LOS Convention entered into force in 1994, several countries, such as Argentina, reduced their claims to a territorial sea to twelve miles. However, a few countries continue to assert territorial seas that exceed twelve miles. For a summary of national territorial sea claims as of May 28, 2008, see UN Division for Ocean Affairs and the Law of the Sea, Summary of National Claims to Maritime Zones, available at http://www.un.org/Depts/los/LEGISLATIONANDTREATIES/claims.htm. See also J. Ashley Roach & Robert W. Smith, United States Responses to Excessive Maritime Claims 147–162 (2d ed. 1996). See Chapter 5, Section H regarding the practice of some states to use straight baselines that result in a seaward extension of their territorial sea claims.

D. THE RIGHT OF INNOCENT PASSAGE

1. General Rules Governing Innocent Passage

An exception to the complete control of a coastal state over its territorial sea is the right of ships of all states to innocent passage through the territorial sea of any coastal state. LOS Convention, Article 17; 1958 Territorial Sea Convention, Article 14. Where the use of a straight baseline has the effect of "enclosing as internal waters areas which had not previously been considered as such, a right of innocent passage" exists in those waters. LOS Convention, Article 8(2). Passage means navigation through the territorial sea for the purpose of either traversing that sea without entering internal waters, or proceeding to or from internal waters. Passage must be continuous and expeditious, but a ship may stop and anchor if this is incidental to ordinary navigation, is rendered necessary by force majeure, or is required in order to assist persons, ships, or aircraft in danger or distress. Id. at Article 18(2); 1958 Territorial Sea Convention, Article 14(3).

Passage is innocent "so long as it is not prejudicial to the peace, good order or security of the coastal State." LOS Convention, Article 19(1); 1958 Territorial Sea Convention, Article 14(4). The coastal state has the right to determine whether passage is innocent, and may take the necessary steps in its territorial sea to prevent passage that is not innocent. LOS Convention, Article 25(1). Article 19(2) of the LOS Convention provides a specific list of activities that render passage noninnocent if engaged in by foreign vessels in territorial waters:

(a) any threat or use of force against the sovereignty, territorial integrity or political independence of the coastal State, or in any other manner in violation of the principles of international law embodied in the Charter of the United Nations;

(b) any exercise or practice with weapons of any kind;

(c) any act aimed at collecting information to the prejudice of the defense or security of the coastal state;

(d) any act of propaganda aimed at affecting the defence or security of the coastal State;

(e) the launching, landing or taking on board of any aircraft;

(f) the launching, landing or taking on board of any military device;

(g) the loading or unloading of any commodity, currency or person contrary to the customs, fiscal, immigration or sanitary laws and regulations of the coastal State;

(h) any act of wilful and serious pollution contrary to [the LOS] Convention;

(i) any fishing activities;

(j) the carrying out of research or survey activities;

(k) any act aimed at interfering with any systems of communication or any other facilities or installations of the coastal State; or

(*l*) any other activity not having a direct bearing on passage.

The specific list of noninnocent activities was intended to produce a more objective definition than provided in Article 14(4) of the 1958 Territorial Sea Convention, thus reducing the discretion of coastal states in determining whether passage is innocent. The United States takes the position that this list is exhaustive, and that a coastal state may not treat passage as noninnocent if a foreign vessel is not engaging in any of the above activities. See, for example, 1989 United States–U.S.S.R. Uniform Interpretation of Rules of International Law Governing Innocent Passage, Article 3. Not all states adhere to this position, invoking instead the open-ended language of Article 19(1) of the LOS Convention, quoted above.

The coastal state may not hamper the innocent passage of foreign ships through its territorial sea except in accordance with the provisions of international law. LOS Convention, Article 24(1); 1958 Territorial Sea Convention, Article 15(1). In the case of ships proceeding to internal waters or ports, the coastal state also has the right to prevent any breach of the conditions to which admission of those ships is subject. LOS Convention, Article 25(2); 1958 Territorial Sea Convention, Article 16(2). See Chapters 7 and 14 for a more detailed discussion of conditions to port access, including compliance with maritime security measures.

The coastal state may suspend temporarily in specified areas of its territorial sea the innocent passage of ships if such suspension is essential for the protection of its security, including suspension in areas where the coastal state is conducting weapons exercises. Suspension may take effect only after due publication and may not be discriminatory. LOS Convention, Article 25(3); 1958 Territorial Sea

Convention, Article 16(3). In 1995, France issued a notice of suspension of navigation in the territorial waters surrounding the Mururoa and Fangataufa Atolls in the South Pacific for approximately one year to allow it to conduct nuclear testing. Several states objected to the prolonged suspension. When a Greenpeace vessel entered the territorial sea in which innocent passage had been suspended, French authorities arrested the crew and seized the vessel. For discussion of this incident and several other instances in which innocent passage has been suspended by various states, see Donald R. Rothwell, Innocent Passage in the Territorial Sea: The UNCLOS Regime and Asia Pacific State Practice, in Navigational Rights and Freedoms and the New Law of the Sea 74 (Donald R. Rothwell & Sam Bateman eds., 2000).

The coastal state may adopt laws and regulations relating to innocent passage through the territorial sea with regard to certain specified subjects, so long as such laws and regulations are not discriminatory and are in conformity with the provisions of the LOS Convention and other rules of international law. LOS Convention, Articles 21(1), 24(1)(b). Furthermore, the coastal state regulations may not "have the practical effect of denying or impairing the right of innocent passage." Id. at Article 24(1)(a). The laws and regulations may pertain to: the safety of navigation and the regulation of maritime traffic; the protection of navigational aids and other installations; the protection of cables and pipelines; the conservation of living resources; the enforcement of fisheries regulations; the preservation of the environment of the coastal state and the prevention, reduction, and control of pollution of this environment; marine scientific research; and the enforcement of customs, fiscal, immigration, and sanitary regulations. Id. at Article 21(1). Foreign ships must comply with these regulations. Id. at Article 21(4). These coastal state laws and regulations may not apply to the design, construction, manning, or equipment of foreign ships unless such laws and regulations implement generally accepted international rules and standards. Id. at Article 21(2).

The coastal state may establish sea lanes and traffic separation schemes for passage through its territorial sea, where they are necessary to ensure the safety of navigation. The coastal state is required to take into account the recommendations of the International Maritime Organization (IMO), any channels customarily used for international navigation, the special characteristics of particular ships and channels, and the density of traffic. Id. at Article 22. Under the supervision of the IMO and taking into account widely adopted international conventions, including the 1972 Convention on the Prevention of Collisions at Sea and the 1974 Safety of Life at Sea Convention (SOLAS), almost all coastal states have implemented shipping routes, traffic separation schemes, and vessel traffic services to control navigation of vessels within internal and territorial waters. Foreign ships exercising their right of innocent passage must comply with these traffic regulations, as well as with international regulations relating to the prevention of collisions at sea. LOS Convention, Articles 21(4), 22(1).

Pursuant to the 1973 Convention for the Prevention of Pollution from Ships, as modified by the 1978 Protocol (MARPOL), the IMO has the authority to classify a sea area as a "particularly sensitive sea area," in which specialized ship routing or other traffic measures may be adopted to protect and preserve the area and its living resources. For example, upon application by Australia, the IMO recognized the waters surrounding the Great Barrier Reef as a "particularly sensitive sea area," resulting in a compulsory pilotage program for all vessels exercising their right of innocent passage through these waters. See generally IMO, Revised Guidelines for the Identification and Designation of Particularly Sensitive Sea Areas, IMO Doc. A/24/RES/982 (2006). As of June 1, 2009, the IMO had designated twelve particularly sensitive sea areas, including the Florida Keys and the Hawaii Papahanaumokuakea Marine National Monument. For discussion of area-based management tools, see Chapter 12, Section I.

More recently, several coastal states have established systems requiring the monitoring of foreign vessels transiting their territorial waters for various purposes. For example, European Union Directive 2002/59 requires member states to implement national legislation establishing uniform reporting and monitoring requirements "with a view to enhancing the safety and efficiency of maritime traffic, improving the response of authorities to incidents, accidents or potentially dangerous situations at sea, including search and rescue operations, and contributing to a better prevention and detection of pollution by ships." Directive (EC) No. 2002/59, Article 1, 2002 O.J.L. 208, 10 at 12, available at http://eurlex.europa.eu/. In addition to mandating that member states implement IMO-approved ship reporting systems and ship routing systems, the directive also requires member states to monitor compliance with vessel traffic systems in their territorial seas. These vessel traffic systems, which each member state operates on the basis of IMO guidelines, apply both to European Community and non-European Community vessels, including non-European Community vessels outside the territorial sea if they intend to call at a European Community port. If not bound for a European Community port, a non-European Community vessel need comply with such systems only "wherever possible." Id. at Article 8, 2002 O.J.L. 208 at 15.

The United States, with the approval of the IMO, has adopted mandatory ship reporting systems in some of its territorial waters. The goals of these systems include reduction of the threat of ship collisions with endangered northern right whales, 33 C.F.R. § 169.100, and protection of ecologically fragile areas, such as the coral reefs of the Papahanaumokuakea Marine National Monument, formerly known as the Northwestern Hawaiian Islands National Monument. 50 C.F.R. § 404.4.

2. Innocent Passage of Warships

The International Court of Justice addressed the issue of whether a warship is entitled to exercise the right of innocent passage in the Corfu Channel Case (United Kingdom v. Albania), 1949 I.C.J. 4. Albania fired on British warships passing through the Corfu Channel, a strait located within its territorial waters, asserting that the foreign warships could not travel through its territorial waters without prior notification and permission. Id. at 27. The Court found it unnecessary to consider the question of the innocent passage of warships through the territorial sea in general, id. at 30, but in addressing the particular matter of the Corfu Channel, stated that it was "generally recognized and in accordance with international custom that States in time of peace have a right to send their warships through straits used for international navigation between two parts of the high seas without the previous authorization of a coastal State, provided that the passage is innocent." Id. at 28.

The right of a warship to pass through the territorial waters of another state remains a matter of controversy. Several countries have taken the position that passage of a foreign warship through territorial waters is inherently prejudicial to the security of the coastal state, and thus cannot be innocent. Many coastal states have enacted national legislation requiring prior notification or approval. 1981–1988 Digest of U.S. Practice in International

Law 1844–1854. In negotiations at the First and Second United Nations Conferences on the Law of the Sea, several proposals requiring previous notification or authorization for the innocent passage of a warship through the territorial sea were discussed. The proposed measures encountered strong opposition from many maritime states, including the United States, and were not adopted. See Marjorie M. Whiteman, 4 Digest of International Law 404–417 (1965); Reports of the United States Delegation to the Third United Nations Conference on the Law of the Sea 95 (Myron Nordquist & Choon-ho Park eds., 1983). In ratifying the LOS Convention, several states, including Algeria, China, and Yemen, made declarations clarifying their position that prior notification or approval is required before a foreign warship may enter or pass through their territorial seas. Several countries objected to these declarations. See George K. Walker, Professionals' Definitions and States' Interpretative Declarations (Understandings, Statements, or Declarations) for the 1982 Law of the Sea Convention, 21 Emory Intl. L. Rev. 461, 522–534 (2007).

The United States adheres to the position that no prior notification or approval is required for warships engaged in innocent passage, and consistently objects to such requirements. 1981–1988 Digest of U.S. Practice in International Law 1844–1854. When the former Soviet Union enacted legislation in 1983 limiting passage of foreign warships through its territorial sea to a few designated sea lane routes, the United States objected. See Erik

Franckx, The U.S.S.R. Position on the Issue of Innocent Passage of Warships through Foreign Territorial Waters, 18 J. Mar. L. & Com. 33 (1987). Pursuant to its Freedom of Navigation Program, in which the United States exercises its navigational freedoms by sending its warships into waters over which other countries assert excessive maritime claims, several U.S. warships traversed "continuously and expeditiously" through Soviet territorial waters in the Black Sea, outside of the authorized sea lanes. In 1986 and 1988, "bumping" incidents occurred between U.S. and Soviet warships. In 1989, the United States and Soviet Union reached an understanding acknowledging the right of innocent passage of warships, and the Soviet Union subsequently modified its restrictions. 1989 United States–U.S.S.R. Uniform Interpretation of Rules of International Law Governing Innocent Passage, Article 3. See Erik Franckx, Innocent Passage of Warships: Recent Developments in U.S.–Soviet Relations, 14 Marine Policy 484 (1990); John W. Rolph, Freedom of Navigation and the Black Sea Bumping Incident: How "Innocent" Must Innocent Passage Be?, 135 Mil. L. Rev. 137 (1992).

As noted in Section D.1, a vessel exercising its right of innocent passage may not engage in certain specified activities, including any threat or use of force, weapons exercises, and the launching or landing of aircraft or military devices. LOS Convention, Article 19(2). By listing these activities, the LOS Convention implicitly recognizes a right of innocent passage for warships. For the definition of warship, see LOS Convention, Article 29, discussed at Chapter 2, Section C.1.

Submarines and other underwater vehicles passing through the territorial sea must navigate on the surface and show their flag. Id. at Article 20; 1958 Territorial Sea Convention, Article 14(6).

The coastal state may require a warship to leave the territorial sea immediately if the warship does not comply with the applicable laws and regulations of the coastal state and disregards any request for compliance. LOS Convention, Article 30; 1958 Territorial Sea Convention, Article 23.

3. *Innocent Passage of Vessels Transporting Dangerous Substances and Nuclear–Powered Vessels*

The LOS Convention allows tankers, nuclearpowered ships, and ships carrying nuclear or other inherently dangerous or noxious substances to engage in innocent passage through territorial waters. However, due to the pollution and safety risks posed by these vessels, a coastal state may require such ships to confine their passage to identified sea lanes. LOS Convention, Article 22(2). These ships also must carry documents and observe special precautionary measures as prescribed for them by international agreements. Id. at Article 23.

Several conventions and regulations address the transport of hazardous goods generally, including the 1965 International Maritime Dangerous Goods

Code adopted by the IMO (which became mandatory in 2004 for parties to the 1974 Safety of Life at Sea Convention) and the 1989 Basel Convention on the Transboundary Movement of Hazardous Wastes and Their Disposal. With regard to nuclear and radioactive wastes, since 1961 the International Atomic Energy Agency (IAEA) has published and regularly updated advisory regulations for the safe transport of these materials. See, for example, IAEA Regulations for the Safe Transport of Radioactive Material, No. TS–R–1 (2005). These regulations promote uniformity for both national and international transport safety. The IAEA Regulations also served as a basis for the Code for the Safe Carriage of Irradiated Nuclear Fuel, Plutonium and High–Level Radioactive Waste in Flasks on Board Ships, adopted by the IMO in 1993. IMO Doc. A/18/RES/748 (1993). In 2001 the 1993 Code became mandatory for parties to the 1974 Safety of Life at Sea Convention (SOLAS). See also the 1979 Convention on the Protection of Nuclear Material.

Although the LOS Convention does not specifically allow coastal states to suspend innocent passage for nuclear-powered ships or ships carrying nuclear or radioactive materials, several countries—including Djibouti, Malaysia, Oman, Pakistan, and Yemen—require prior notice or permission before these ships may enter their territorial waters. See U.S. Dept. of State, Pub. No. 36, Limits in the Seas: National Claims to Maritime Jurisdictions 42, 96, 117, 118, 174 (Robert W. Smith ed., 6th rev. ed. 2000). Several states cite their obligation to protect the marine environment as a basis for restricting innocent passage of these ships, as well as the evolving "precautionary principle" discussed in Chapter 12. See generally Jon van Dyke, Applying the Precautionary Principle to Ocean Shipments of Radioactive Materials, 27 Ocean Dev. & Intl. L. 379 (1996). The United States adheres to the position that no prior notification or approval is required for nuclear-powered ships or ships carrying nuclear materials engaged in innocent passage through the territorial seas of other states, and consistently objects to such requirements. 1981–1988 Digest of U.S. Practice in International Law 1854–1859.

4. *Coastal State Exercise of Criminal and Civil Jurisdiction over Foreign Vessels in the Territorial Sea*

A coastal state's right to exercise criminal jurisdiction over foreign vessels passing through its territorial sea—whether such passage is innocent or not—is limited. With regard to a crime committed before a foreign vessel enters the territorial sea, a coastal state is prohibited from exercising criminal jurisdiction where a foreign vessel proceeding from a foreign port is only passing through its territorial sea without entering internal waters. An exemption from this limitation applies to certain environmental violations or violations occurring within the coastal state's exclusive economic zone. LOS Convention, Article 27(5); 1958 Territorial Sea Convention, Article 19(5).

With regard to a crime committed on board a foreign vessel while passing through the territorial sea, the coastal state "should not" exercise criminal jurisdiction for the purpose of arresting a person on board the ship or of conducting any investigation unless one of the following exceptions applies:

(a) if the consequences of the crime extend to the coastal State;

(b) if the crime is of a kind to disturb the peace of the country or the good order of the territorial sea;

(c) if the assistance of the local authorities has been requested by the master of the ship or by a diplomatic agent or consular officer of the flag State; or

(d) if such measures are necessary for the suppression of illicit traffic in narcotic drugs or psychotropic substances.

LOS Convention, Article 27(1); see also 1958 Territorial Sea Convention, Article 19(1).

The above provisions do not affect the right of the coastal state to take any steps authorized by its laws for the purpose of an arrest or investigation on board a foreign ship in connection with a crime committed during the ship's sojourn in the state's internal waters. LOS Convention, Article 27(2); 1958 Territorial Sea Convention, Article 19(2). See also the discussion of enlarged port state jurisdiction at Chapter 7, Section E.

Similarly, the coastal state should not exercise its civil jurisdiction over foreign ships passing through its territorial sea in relation to a person on board the ship. The coastal state may not levy execution against or arrest the ship for the purpose of any civil proceedings, save only in respect of obligations or liabilities assumed or incurred by the ship itself in the course or for the purpose of its voyage through the waters of the coastal state. However, a coastal state may levy execution against or arrest for civil proceedings a foreign ship lying in the territorial sea or passing through the territorial sea after leaving the coastal state's internal waters. LOS Convention, Article 28; 1958 Territorial Sea Convention, Article 20.

5. No Right of Innocent Passage by Aircraft through Air Space above the Territorial Sea

The sovereignty of the coastal state in the air space above its territorial sea is not subject to any right of innocent passage except when so provided by international agreement. Most coastal states have granted rights to overfly their territorial sea as part of their agreement to overflight of their territory generally. 1944 Chicago Convention on International Civil Aviation, Articles 2, 5; 1944 International Air Services Transit Agreement, Article 1. Military and other state aircraft are not covered by these agreements and enjoy overflight or landing rights only by special agreement. See generally Kay Hailbronner, Freedom of the Air and the Convention on the Law of the Sea, 77 Am. J. Intl. L. 490 (1983).

E. TRANSIT PASSAGE THROUGH STRAITS

In 1949, the International Court of Justice confirmed that under customary international law ships of all countries, including warships in time of peace, have the right to navigate through international straits without the prior permission of the coastal state, even if the strait lies partially or wholly within the coastal state's territorial sea, as long as such passage is innocent. Corfu Channel Case (United Kingdom v. Albania), 1949 I.C.J. 4, 28. The Court identified two criteria in determining whether the right of passage applies to a particular strait: the strait must connect one part of the high seas with another, and there must be some usage of the strait for international navigation. Id. at 28–29. For discussion of the on-going debate as to the volume of usage that must occur to satisfy the second criterion, see Donald R. Rothwell, The Canadian–U.S. Northwest Passage Dispute: A Reassessment, 26 Cornell Intl. L.J. 331, 354–355 (1993).

Using the Corfu Channel Case criteria as a framework, the 1958 Territorial Sea Convention incorporated a right of innocent passage "through straits which are used for international navigation between one part of the high seas and another part of the high seas or the territorial sea of a foreign State." Article 16(4). Although this provision was included in the regime governing innocent passage through territorial seas, it differed significantly from territorial sea innocent passage in that a coastal state had no right to suspend the right of passage through straits. Id.

In negotiating the LOS Convention, many maritime countries, including the United States, were vitally concerned that the proposed extension of the territorial sea to twelve miles would cause more than 100 international straits with a width of less than twenty-four miles to fall within the extended territorial seas of the states bordering those straits. These maritime states were unwilling to accept the extension of the breadth of the territorial sea to twelve miles without a guarantee of unimpeded passage through international straits. The regime of innocent passage as established for territorial seas was considered inadequate because, among other reasons, the coastal state could suspend innocent passage in certain situations. For a statement of the U.S. position, see 1976 Digest of U.S. Practice in International Law 341–342. To address these concerns, the LOS Convention established a comprehensive regime governing transit passage through straits, separate from the regime of innocent passage applicable to territorial seas. LOS Convention, Articles 34–45. See generally John Norton Moore, The Regime of Straits and the Third United Nations Conference on the Law of the Sea, 74 Am. J. Intl. L. 77 (1980).

Transit passage means navigation or overflight for the purpose of continuous and expeditious transit of a strait between one area of the high seas or exclusive economic zone and another area of the high seas or exclusive economic zone. LOS Convention, Article 38(2). The right of transit passage applies even in narrow straits that lie entirely within the territorial seas of states bordering the strait. Ships and aircraft exercising the right of transit passage must proceed without delay and refrain from any activities other than those incidental to their normal modes of passage, unless rendered necessary by force majeure or by distress. Id. at Article 39. Unlike innocent passage through territorial seas, transit passage through straits extends to aircraft, and submarines are permitted to navigate in their "normal mode," i.e., under water. Id. at Article 39(1)(c).

States bordering straits may not hamper transit passage and do not have the right to suspend transit passage. Id. at Article 44. When Denmark proposed building a bridge between two Danish islands across a strait between the Baltic and North Seas, Finland sought provisional relief from the International Court of Justice on the basis that the bridge would impede the transit of large drilling ships and oil rigs constructed and assembled in Finland. Denmark argued that the right of transit passage did not apply to such vessels, that alternative routes were available, and that disassembly or other modifications of the vessels would enable the vessels to pass under the proposed bridge. Case Concerning Passage through the Great Belt (Finland v. Denmark), 1991 I.C.J. 12. The case was discontinued and the bridge was built after Denmark paid Finland approximately US$15 million in settlement. 1992 I.C.J. 348. See Martti Koskenniemi, Case Concerning Passage Through the Great Belt, 27 Ocean Dev. & Intl. L. 255 (1996).

A state's regulatory authority over transit passage through a strait that it borders is more limited than a coastal state's regulatory authority over innocent passage through its territorial sea. A state bordering on a strait may put into effect international standards and regulations regarding pollution control; it may regulate fishing activities; and it may enact customs, fiscal, immigration, and sanitary regulations. LOS Convention, Article 42. The more extensive subject matters that a coastal state may regulate with regard to innocent passage are discussed at Section D.1. The bordering state's regulation of transit passage may not discriminate against foreign ships or have the practical effect of impeding transit passage. Id. at Article 42(2). In the territorial sea a coastal state may unilaterally establish sea lanes and traffic separation schemes, subject to the requirement that it take into account the recommendations of the International Maritime Organization (IMO). Id. at Article 22(3). However, in international straits the designation of sea lanes or traffic separation schemes requires concurrent action by all states bordering the strait and adoption by the IMO. Id. at Article 41(3)–(4).

The LOS Convention excepts a few types of straits from the transit passage regime. One exception applies where a strait is located between an island of the bordering state and its mainland, and there exists an equally convenient route through the high seas or exclusive economic zone seaward of the island. Id. at Article 38. An example of this type of strait is the Strait of Messina located between Italy and the island of Sicily. A second exception to transit passage exists when a strait originating in the high seas or an exclusive economic zone "dead-ends" into the territorial sea of a coastal state. Id. at Article 45. For discussion of the applicability of this exception, see Jonathan E. Fink, The Gulf of Aqaba and the Strait of Tiran: The Practice of "Freedom of Navigation" after the Egyptian–Israeli Peace Treaty, 42 Naval L. Rev. 121 (1995). With regard to these two types of straits, the regime of innocent passage, rather than transit passage, applies, with one significant limitation: the coastal state may not suspend innocent passage. LOS Convention, Article 45.

Furthermore, a right of transit passage does not exist where a strait is wide enough to allow navigation through a high seas or exclusive economic zone route in its middle, so long as the high seas or exclusive economic zone route is of similar convenience with respect to navigational and hydrographic characteristics. Id. at Article 36. The principles governing freedom of navigation apply to such high seas or exclusive economic zone routes through straits, as discussed in Chapter 2, Section C.1.

Finally, the LOS Convention does not affect the legal regime of straits in which passage is regulated by special international conventions of long standing, such as the 1936 Montreux Straits Convention concerning the regime of the straits leading to the Black Sea. LOS Convention, Article 35(c).

States bordering a strait and states whose vessels use the strait are required to cooperate in establishing and maintaining navigational safety through straits and in preventing pollution from ships within straits. Id. at Article 43. Article 43 contemplates that states whose vessels use straits will assist states bordering the straits with the burden of ensuring safe navigation and environmental protection. See generally Satya N. Nandan, The Management of Straits Used for International Navigation: International Cooperation in Malacca and Singapore Straits, in Current Maritime Issues and the International Maritime Organization 27 (Myron H. Nordquist & John Norton Moore eds., 1999). The first effort to implement Article 43 is the 2007 Cooperative Mechanism Between the Littoral States and User States on Safety of Navigation and Environmental Protection in the Straits of Malacca and Singapore. IMO Doc. SGP 2.1/1 (2007).

If a ship violates environmental laws and regulations while exercising its right of transit passage, causing or threatening major damage to the marine environment of the straits, the states bordering the straits may take appropriate enforcement measures. LOS Convention, Article 233. See Mary George, Transit Passage and Pollution Control in Straits under the 1982 Law of the Sea Convention, 33 Ocean Dev. & Intl. L. 189 (2002).

F. ARCHIPELAGIC SEA LANES PASSAGE

The LOS Convention establishes a new regime governing archipelagic waters, under which all ships enjoy the right of archipelagic sea lanes passage. Article 53. There are parallel rights for aircraft overflight along designated air routes. Id. Archipelagic sea lanes passage means navigation in the normal mode solely for the purpose of continuous and expeditious transit between one area of the high seas or exclusive economic zone and another area of the high seas or exclusive economic zone. Id. at Article 53(3). An archipelagic state may designate sea lanes or traffic schemes that conform to generally accepted international regulations, id. at Article 53(1), but any proposals for such sea lanes or traffic separation schemes must be submitted to the International Maritime Organization (IMO) for adoption. Id. at Article 53(8)–(9). See, for example, the adoption of certain archipelagic sea lanes for Indonesian archipelagic waters at IMO Res. MSC.72(69) (1998). If an archipelagic state does not designate sea lanes, the right of archipelagic sea lanes passage may be exercised through the routes normally used for international navigation. LOS Convention, Article 53(12). For discussion of what constitutes an archipelagic state and archipelagic waters, see Chapter 5, Section I.

In archipelagic waters other than designated sea lanes (or, in the absence of designated sea lanes, the routes normally used for international navigation), ships of all states enjoy the right of innocent passage, except in internal waters delimited by straight lines drawn across mouths of rivers, bays, and entrances to ports. Id. at Articles 50, 52, 54. Whereas innocent passage may be suspended in archipelagic waters other than archipelagic sea lanes if "essential for the protection of the archipelagic state's security," id. at Article 53(2), an archipelagic state may not suspend passage through archipelagic sea lanes. Id. at Article 54 (with cross-reference to Article 44). See generally J. Peter A. Bernhardt, The Right of Archipelagic Sea Lanes Passage: A Primer, 35 Va. J. Intl. L. 719 (1995).

Attempts by archipelagic states to limit or suspend the rights of archipelagic passage have drawn objections from maritime states. For example, when Indonesia temporarily closed Sunda and Lombok Straits in 1988 to permit the Indonesian navy to engage in maneuvers, several states objected, including Australia, the United States, the United Kingdom, and West Germany. See Donald R. Rothwell, The Indonesian Straits Incident: Transit or Archipelagic Sea Lanes Passage?, 14 Marine Policy 491, 492–494 (1990). See also the U.S. protest of the Philippines' declaration that its archipelagic waters constituted internal waters through which no right of archipelagic passage exists, U.S. Dept. of State, Pub. No. 112, Limits in the Seas: United States Responses to Excessive Maritime Claims 77–78 (1992), and the U.S. protest of a proposal requiring compulsory pilotage through the Torres Strait that

Australia had submitted to the IMO. 2005 Digest of U.S. Practice in International Law 686.

G.   CONTIGUOUS ZONE

In a zone contiguous to its territorial sea, the coastal state may exercise the control necessary to prevent infringement of its customs, fiscal, immigration, or sanitary laws and regulations within its territory or territorial sea, or to punish such infringements committed within its territory or territorial sea. LOS Convention, Article 33(1); 1958 Territorial Sea Convention, Article 24(1). The contiguous zone may not extend beyond twenty-four nautical miles from the baseline from which the breadth of the territorial sea is measured. LOS Convention, Article 33(2). The coastal state does not possess "sovereignty" over the contiguous zone, as it does in the territorial sea, but instead enjoys jurisdiction in the contiguous zone for the limited purposes specified above.

The United States has historically exercised jurisdiction in waters adjacent to its territorial seas for the purpose of enforcing its customs laws. In 1790 the first U.S. Congress enacted a statute that allowed U.S. authorities to board and inspect vessels within four leagues (approximately twelve miles) of its coasts for purposes of enforcing its customs laws. Act of Aug. 4, 1790, 1 Stat. 145. In Church v. Hubbart, 6 U.S. 187 (1804), the U.S. Supreme Court recognized the right of a coastal state to exercise jurisdiction beyond the limits of its territorial sea to prevent violation of its customs laws. In The Grace and Ruby, 283 F. 475 (D. Mass. 1922), a U.S. court upheld the seizure of a British vessel located outside U.S. territorial waters but within four leagues of the U.S. coast for smuggling liquor in violation of U.S. prohibition laws. For further discussion of the development of the contiguous zone, see generally A.V. Lowe, The Development of the Contiguous Zone, 52 Brit. Y.B. Intl. L. 109 (1981).

Under the 1930 Tariff Act, which remains in effect today, a U.S. customs officer is authorized to board any vessel within U.S. "customs waters" to examine its manifest and inspect and search the vessel, whether or not such vessel is bound for the United States. 19 U.S.C. § 1581. If a violation of U.S. law has occurred, the vessel is subject to arrest and seizure. Id. The U.S. Supreme Court has upheld the reasonableness of boarding and inspecting a vessel in customs waters under the Fourth Amendment of the U.S. Constitution, even where there is no suspicion of wrong-doing. United States v. Villamonte–Marquez, 462 U.S. 579 (1983). "Customs waters" are defined as "the waters within four leagues of the coast of the United States," unless a foreign vessel is subject to a treaty or other arrangement between a foreign government and the United States enabling or permitting U.S. authorities to board the foreign vessel, in which event customs waters are as designated by such treaty. 19 U.S.C. § 1401(j). For example, under Article 2 of the 1924 United States–United Kingdom Anti–

Smuggling Convention, the right to board a foreign vessel may be exercised up to a distance from the coast that can be traversed by that vessel in one hour.

The Anti–Smuggling Act of 1935, 19 U.S.C. § 1701, authorized the President to declare a "customs-enforcement area" that could extend sixty-two miles outward from the coast and laterally up to 100 miles in each direction around a particular vessel "hovering" off the coast of the United States and suspected of smuggling. The United Kingdom objected, even though the Act exempted its vessels because of the existence of the 1924 United States–United Kingdom Anti–Smuggling Convention. Marjorie M. Whiteman, 4 Digest of International Law 490–492 (1965). Only five such zones were established, primarily to enforce U.S. prohibition laws. They were discontinued in 1946. 1948–1949 U.S. Naval War College, International Legal Documents 176–180. For discussion of the use of special U.S. customs enforcement areas under the 1980 Marijuana on the High Seas Act, see United States v. Gonzalez, 776 F.2d 931 (11th Cir. 1985).

In 1999, President Clinton extended the U.S. contiguous zone to twenty-four nautical miles from its baseline, but in no case within the territorial sea of another country. Exec. Procl. No. 7219, 64 Fed. Reg. 48701 (1999). The proclamation provides that it does not amend existing U.S. laws. Although Congress has acted to amend some statutes, such as the Maritime Drug Law Enforcement Act, 46 U.S.C. § 70502, to incorporate the twenty-four-mile contiguous zone, many statutes, such as the four-league definition of "custom waters," 19 U.S.C. § 1401(j), remain unaffected by the proclamation. See generally John E. Noyes, Establishment of a 24–Mile US Contiguous Zone, 15 Intl. J. Marine & Coastal L. 269 (2000).

H. THE U.S. TERRITORIAL SEA AND THE RIGHTS OF THE STATES OF THE UNITED STATES

In 1947, the U.S. Supreme Court held that the United States was "possessed of paramount rights in, and full dominion and power over, the lands, minerals and other things" underlying the sea to the extent of three nautical miles measured from the low-water mark on the coast or from the outer limit of internal waters, and that the coastal states had "no title thereto or property interest therein." United States v. California, 332 U.S. 19 (1947), and Decree, 332 U.S. 804, 805 (1947). The Submerged Lands Act of 1953, 43 U.S.C. §§ 1301–1315, ceded to the coastal states all the property rights of the United States in submerged lands within three miles of the baseline (and up to nine miles in the Gulf of Mexico if a state established a historic title to such broader area). Id. at §§ 1311–1312. It vested in the states "the right and power to manage, administer, lease, develop and use" the submerged land and natural resources of the ceded area. Id. at § 1311(a). The United States retained, however, "powers of regulation and control of said lands and navigable waters for the constitutional purposes of commerce, navigation, national defense, and international affairs." Id. at § 1314(a).

When the United States extended its territorial sea from three to twelve miles in 1988, see Section C, the President indicated that his proclamation would not affect the offshore limits of state jurisdiction, which remained at three miles for purposes of several statutes. See Bruce E. Alexander, The Territorial Sea of the United States: Is It Twelve Miles or Not?, 20 J. Mar. L. & Com. 449 (1989). For additional discussion of the Submerged Lands Act and its companion legislation, the Outer Continental Shelf Lands Act, see Chapter 10, Section H.

In the absence of conflicting federal legislation, the conservation and management of fisheries in a state's three-mile territorial sea is within the police power of the individual states. Corsa v. Tawes, 149 F.Supp. 771 (D. Md.), aff'd, 355 U.S. 37 (1957). With the adoption of the Fishery Conservation and Management Act in 1976 (now known as the Magnuson–Stevens Fishery Conservation and Management Act, 16 U.S.C. §§ 1801 et seq.), the federal government asserted sovereign rights and exclusive fishery management authority over fisheries within the U.S. exclusive economic zone and continental shelf, id. at § 1811(a), reserving to states the right to continue to exercise jurisdiction over fisheries within the state's three-mile territorial sea, with some exceptions. Id. at § 1856. See also Chapter 9, Section G. The federal government offers assistance to the states in the development of fishery conservation and management plans within their three-mile territorial seas under the Coastal Zone Management Act of 1972, 16 U.S.C. §§ 1451 et seq.

Numerous courts have addressed the extent of federal preemption of state jurisdiction in the areas of fishing, conservation, and regulation of vessels and vessel traffic within and outside of the states' territorial seas. See, for example, Douglas v. Seacoast Products, Inc., 431 U.S. 265 (1977) (federal laws governing the licensing of vessels preempt state laws that prohibit federally licensed vessels from fishing within a state's territorial waters); Livings v. Davis, 465 So.2d 507 (Fla. 1985) (Florida may exercise fishery jurisdiction beyond its three-mile territorial sea where there is no conflict with a federal law or fishery management plan concerning that fishery); Beveridge v. Lewis, 939 F.2d 859 (9th Cir. 1991) (city mooring and anchoring requirements not preempted by the federal Ports and Waterways Safety Act). See also Mike Mastry, Extraterritorial Application of State Fishery Management Regulations under the Magnuson–Stevens Fishery Conservation and Management Act: Have the Courts Missed the Boat?, 25 UCLA J. Envtl. L. & Policy 225 (2006).

I. SHIPWRECKS AND UNDERWATER CULTURAL HERITAGE

Article 303(1) of the LOS Convention imposes a duty on all states to protect objects of an archaeological and historical nature found at sea. Within its territorial sea, the coastal state has the exclusive right to regulate activities concerning the salvage and excavation of shipwrecks, relics, and other items of underwater cultural heritage. Id. at Article 2; 1958 Territorial Sea Convention, Articles 1–2. Article 303(2) of the LOS Convention further authorizes coastal states to exercise jurisdiction to prevent or punish the unauthorized removal of such objects from the seabed within its contiguous zone. The coastal state is not granted authority under the LOS Convention to regulate activities pertaining to underwater cultural heritage in its exclusive economic zone or on the continental shelf beyond the contiguous zone.

Although the coastal state has the right to regulate activities concerning the salvage and excavation of shipwrecks, relics, and other items of underwater cultural heritage in its territorial sea and contiguous zone as described above, the coastal state does not necessarily own the shipwrecks or other underwater items salvaged. The law of salvage and the law of finds, which exist as a part of the general maritime law of nations, determine the ownership of such items, unless such laws are modified by applicable national laws of the coastal state or by international conventions to which the coastal state is bound. Article 303(3) of the LOS Convention specifically preserves "the rights of identifiable owners, the law of salvage or other rules of admiralty."

The law of salvage, which is favored over the law of finds, recognizes that title to shipwrecks or other items of underwater cultural heritage is vested in the owner thereof, but grants an award, either monetary or in kind, to the successful salvor for the reasonable value of the salvor's services, secured by a lien against the salvaged property. If the ship or other items have been abandoned by the owner, the law of finds applies rather than the law of salvage, and title to the abandoned items is granted to the person who first finds and possesses them.

Under U.S. law, an exception to the law of finds exists with regard to abandoned shipwrecks or other abandoned items that are embedded in the internal waters, archipelagic waters, or territorial sea of a coastal state. With regard to embedded items, title belongs to the coastal state. The 1987 Abandoned Shipwreck Act vests title to an abandoned shipwreck embedded in the submerged lands of a U.S. state to that state. 43 U.S.C. § 2105. For discussion of the application by U.S. courts of the laws of salvage and finds to shipwrecks, including a discussion of the 1987 Abandoned Shipwreck Act, see Donna R. Christie & Richard G. Hildreth, Coastal and Ocean Management Law in a Nutshell 162–179 (3d ed. 2007).

The 2001 UNESCO Underwater Cultural Heritage Convention entered into force on January 2, 2009. As of June 1, 2009, twenty-five states were parties. Article 1(a) of the Convention broadly defines "underwater cultural heritage" as "all traces of human existence having a cultural, historical or archaeological character which have been partially or totally under water, periodically or continuously, for at least 100 years." Proposals to include a "significance" test were rejected.

Article 2(4) of the UNESCO Convention obligates parties to take appropriate measures, either individually or jointly, as are necessary to protect underwater cultural heritage, using the best practicable means at their disposal and in accordance with their capabilities. In implementing protective measures, the protection of underwater cultural heritage through in situ preservation shall be considered as the first option. Id. at Annex, Rule 1. The UNESCO Convention is to be applied consistently with other international law, including the LOS Convention. Id. at Article 3. Unlike Article 303(3) of the LOS Convention, which specifically acknowledges rights established under the laws of salvage and finds, the UNESCO Convention specifically displaces the laws of salvage and finds, unless authorized by the competent authorities, and then only if the application of such laws is consistent with the UNESCO Convention and ensures that any recovery of the underwater cultural heritage achieves its maximum protection. UNESCO Convention, Article 4. See generally Guido Carducci, New Developments in the Law of the Sea: The UNESCO Convention on the Protection of Underwater Cultural Heritage, 96 Am. J. Intl. L. 419 (2002).

The United States and several other countries maintain that sunken vessels or aircraft owned by the government belong exclusively to the flag state and are not subject to the laws of salvage or finds, unless expressly and affirmatively abandoned by the flag state. 2004 Digest of U.S. Practice in International Law 716–719. In Sea Hunt v. The Unidentified Shipwrecked Vessel, 221 F.3d 634 (4th Cir. 2000), the court upheld Spain's ownership of two Spanish Navy frigates against the claims of Virginia, in whose territorial waters the ships had sunk. Subsequent to the Sea Hunt case, Congress enacted the Sunken Military Craft Act, which prohibits the granting of salvage rights or awards with respect to any U.S. sunken military craft without the express permission of the United States, or, with respect to any foreign sunken military craft located in U.S. waters, without the express permission of the relevant foreign state. Pub. L. No. 108–375, 118 Stat. 1811 (2004). See David J. Bederman, Congress Enacts Increased Protections for Sunken Military Craft, 100 Am. J. Intl. L. 649 (2006).

The status of warships was a matter of debate in the negotiations leading up to the 2001 UNESCO Underwater Cultural Heritage Convention. According to that Convention, as finally adopted, a coastal state has jurisdiction to regulate activities relating to a sunken warship or government aircraft within its territorial sea and contiguous zone, but "should" inform the flag state "with a view to cooperating on the best methods of protecting" the site. Articles 7(3), 8. For sunken warships or government aircraft located on the continental shelf or in the exclusive economic zone beyond the contiguous zone, the flag state must agree to any activities involving the vessel or plane. Id. at Article 10(7). For sunken warships or government aircraft located beyond the exclusive economic zone or continental shelf, no activities may be undertaken without the consent of the flag state. Id. at Article 12(7).

CHAPTER 9

EXCLUSIVE ECONOMIC ZONE

A. INTRODUCTION

The establishment of the exclusive economic zone (EEZ) is closely related to negotiations at the Third United Nations Conference on the Law of the Sea. The EEZ is one of the two novel maritime zones—the other being the Area, which is discussed in Chapter 11—that were created by the LOS Convention. The EEZ extends beyond the territorial sea up to 200 nautical miles from a coastal state's baseline. LOS Convention, Articles 55, 57; see Illustration 1 at p. 12. The EEZ encompasses the seabed and the subsoil as well as the superjacent waters. However, the regime of the continental shelf, addressed in Chapter 10, also regulates the seabed and subsoil, id. at Article 56(3). The LOS Convention also contains numerous provisions relating to the protection and preservation of the marine environment of the EEZ, examined in Chapter 12.

This Chapter focuses on living resources and economic activities in the water column of the EEZ. As indicated in the table below, the developed states have been the main beneficiaries of the EEZ, not only with respect to area, but also with respect to fish catches and volume of water possessed. Since living resources are not equally spread out over the oceans, columns one (area) and two (fish catches) do not necessarily follow the same ranking. The volume of water, noted in column three, can be an important factor if states want to exploit thermal

Table 1: Exclusive Economic Zone Statistics			
	Area (in M^2/km^2)	2007 fish catches (in metric tons)	Volume (in km^3)
United States	3.0/10.3	4.8	33.8
France	2.0/6.8	0.5	not available
Australia	1.8/6.1	0.1	18.2
New Zealand	1.7/5.8	0.4	11.4
Indonesia	1.5/5.1	4.9	12.7
Russia	1.3/4.4	3.4	/
Japan	1.1/3.7	4.3	15.8
Brazil	0.9/3.0	0.7	10.5
Canada	0.8/2.7	1	/

Note: These figures are only indicative, as they vary widely according to the parameters used for calculating them. The area figures are based on Robert W. Smith, Exclusive Economic Zone Claims: An Analysis and Primary Documents 13–16 (1986). A list of all fish catches in the EEZs of coastal states is not readily available on a comparative basis. Instead, the 2007 fish catch figures were derived from the total annual volume of aquatic species caught by country or area, species, and Food and Agriculture Organization (FAO) major fishing areas for all commercial, industrial, recreational, and subsistence purposes, as provided by FAO in its Fishery and Aquaculture Country Profiles. See www.fao.org/fishery/countryprofiles/search/en. In most cases where specific information on catches within EEZs is available, these figures indicate that states catch most of their marine living resources in their own EEZs. The volume figures are based on Takatoshi Matsuzawa, What is the Volume of Japan's 200–nm Exclusive Economic Zone?, Maritime Studies, Issue 157, at 23 (Nov.-Dec. 2007). The entry "/" means that the country is not one of the ten countries with the largest EEZ volume. "M" refers to nautical miles.

energy conversion, as discussed in Section I. The United States, which ranked first in all three domains in 2007, is one of the main beneficiaries of the EEZ.

Section B of this Chapter briefly outlines the genesis of the EEZ concept. Section C addresses the fisheries management and conservation rules in that zone. Special topics related to living resources include: the rights of geographically disadvantaged and land-locked states (Section D); special regimes for certain species of fish (Section E); enforcement (Section F); the practice of the United States (Section G); and the role of the European Community with respect to fisheries (Section H). In addition to living resources, the coastal state has other rights in its EEZ with respect to the production of energy from the water, currents, and wind (Section I), the conduct of marine scientific research (Section J), and the construction of artificial islands and installations, including deepwater ports (Section K).

B. FROM FISHERY ZONES TO AN EXCLUSIVE ECONOMIC ZONE

Until the middle of the twentieth century, all waters beyond the territorial sea and the contiguous zone were viewed as high seas over which no state had jurisdiction. G.H. Hackworth, 2 Digest of International Law 651 (1941); 1958 High Seas Convention, Article 1.

The impetus for extending the jurisdiction of coastal states over waters adjacent to the territorial sea related closely to the growing demand for better conservation and management of coastal fisheries. Increased exploitation of fisheries in waters contiguous to the coast led several coastal states, beginning in the nineteenth century, to enter bilateral and multilateral agreements to conserve and manage fisheries in adjacent zones. Examples include the 1818 United States–Great Britain Fisheries Convention, the 1839 France–Great Britain Fisheries Convention, the 1882 North Sea Fisheries Convention, and the 1911 Fur Seal Convention. See Stefan A. Riesenfeld, Protection of Coastal Fisheries under International Law (1942).

In 1945 President Truman simultaneously issued proclamations concerning the continental shelf and coastal fisheries in certain areas of the high seas. The Continental Shelf Proclamation asserted the right of the United States to claim jurisdiction over the natural resources of the subsoil and seabed of the continental shelf adjacent to the United States. See Chapter 10, Section B. The Fisheries Proclamation asserted U.S. authority to establish fishery conservation zones in the high seas adjacent to its coasts on the basis that existing agreements did not adequately protect such fisheries. The United States claimed sole fishery conservation and management authority in those areas where its nationals had historically fished exclusively. The Fisheries Proclamation also provided for joint fishery conservation and management arrangements in those areas where the nationals of other states had fished along with U.S. nationals, with these arrangements to be

agreed upon by the concerned states. Exec. Procl.
2668, 10 Fed. Reg. 12,304 (1945). In fact, the United States never established conservation zones under the authority of the Fisheries Proclamation.
Other states did not appear eager to enter into
agreements limiting their catches off the U.S. coast.

A combined reading of both Truman proclamations nevertheless prompted a number of South
American states to establish zones of up to 200
miles in which they claimed complete sovereignty
over the seabed, its subsoil, and superjacent waters
"in order to reserve, protect, preserve and exploit
the natural resources of whatever nature found on,
within and below the said seas." 1947 Presidential
Declaration of Chile, Marjorie M. Whiteman, 4 Digest of International Law 794, 795 (1965). See also
1947 Presidential Decree No. 781 of Peru, id. at
797; 1951 Ecuadorean Congressional Decree, id. at
799. The United States objected to these and similar decrees on the bases that the decrees asserted
complete national sovereignty over the zones and
failed to accord recognition to the rights and interests of other states. Id. at 796–801. In 1952, Chile,
Peru, and Ecuador signed the Declaration of Santia-
go on the Maritime Zone, which proclaimed that
each country possessed "sole sovereignty and jurisdiction over the area of sea adjacent to the coast of
its own country and extending not less than 200
nautical miles." Id. at 1089, 1090. See generally
Ann L. Hollick, Origins of the 200–Mile Offshore
Zones, 71 Am. J. Intl. L. 404 (1977).

The 1958 Fishing on the High Seas Convention (to which thirty-eight states, including the United States, were parties as of June 1, 2009) embodies the principle of special rights of coastal states in the conservation, management, and exploitation of fisheries in areas contiguous to its coast. The Convention does not, however, grant coastal states exclusive rights in the conservation, management, and exploitation of these fisheries, nor does it apply to other resources in those areas. Article 6 provides that a coastal state is entitled to take part in any fishery conservation measures in the high seas adjacent to its territorial waters, even if its nationals do not fish there. Other states whose nationals fish in that area must, at the request of the coastal state, enter into negotiations with that state. If such negotiations fail, the coastal state may unilaterally enact and enforce conservation measures that are urgently needed. Such measures must be based on scientific findings and may not be discriminatory. Id. at Article 7. In addition, any conservation measures must be designed to render possible "the optimum sustainable yield from those resources so as to secure a maximum supply of food and other marine products." Id. at Article 2.

After the Second United Nations Conference on the Law of the Sea failed, by one vote, in 1960 to adopt a compromise solution that would have extended coastal states' exclusive fishing jurisdiction to twelve miles, see Marjorie M. Whiteman, 4 Digest of International Law 122–137 (1965), many countries extended their exclusive fishery jurisdiction to twelve miles by national legislation. See, for example, the Exclusive Fisheries Zone Act of 1966, Pub. L. No. 89–658, 80 Stat. 908 (1966) (establishing a U.S. twelve-mile exclusive fishery zone, which was repealed by the Fishery Conservation and Management Act of 1976). During the 1960s the United States and other "distant fishing" states continued to resist assertions of exclusive fishery jurisdiction beyond twelve miles.

In 1972 Iceland established a fifty-mile exclusive fishery zone, which was strongly contested by the United Kingdom and the Federal Republic of Germany, countries that historically had fished in that area. The International Court of Justice recognized that a coastal state has preferential rights in the exploitation of fisheries in the seas around its coast, but found that such preferential rights could not be exercised without taking into account the fishing rights of other states whose vessels traditionally have fished in the same waters and whose coastal communities depend on such fishing for their livelihood and economic well-being. According to the Court, the governments must negotiate in good faith for an equitable solution of their differences, taking into account both Iceland's preferential rights and the other states' established fishing rights in the areas concerned. Fisheries Jurisdiction Cases (United Kingdom v. Iceland; Federal Republic of Germany v. Iceland), 1974 I.C.J. 3, 34; 1974 I.C.J. 175, 205–206.

The concept of a 200–mile zone in which a coastal state would have exclusive rights not only in relation to fisheries, but also for the purpose of exploring, exploiting, and managing all of the living and nonliving natural resources in that zone, was developed at the Third United Nations Conference on the Law of the Sea. See UN Doc. A/CONF./62/L.8/ Rev.1 Annex II, 3–4 (1971). During these negotiations, several coastal states unilaterally enacted laws and regulations reserving exclusive rights for the purpose of conservation, management, and exploitation of the natural resources in waters adjacent to their territorial seas. See, for instance, the 1976 Fishery Conservation and Management Act, 16 U.S.C. §§ 1801 et seq. (establishing a 200–mile fishery conservation zone); National Legislation and Treaties Relating to the Law of the Sea, UN Doc. ST/LEG/SER.B/18, 271–377 (1976) and UN Doc. ST/LEG/SER.B/19, 349–394 (1980) (compiling the legislation of other states around that time period).

According to Articles 55 and 57 of the LOS Convention, the EEZ lies beyond and adjacent to the territorial sea, extending up to 200 nautical miles from the baselines from which the breadth of the territorial sea is measured. Thus, a state claiming a twelve-mile territorial sea may have a 188–mile EEZ beyond the territorial sea. The coastal state has sovereign rights for the purpose of exploring, exploiting, conserving, and managing all the living resources in the EEZ. The coastal state also has such rights with respect to nonliving resources of the seabed, its subsoil, and superjacent waters, and with respect to other activities undertaken for the economic exploration and exploitation of the zone, such as the production of energy from the water, currents, and wind. Id. at Article 56. Within the EEZ, a coastal state has limited jurisdiction with regard to: the establishment and use of artificial islands, installations, and structures; the protection and preservation of the marine environment; and marine scientific research. Id. at Articles 56(1)(b), 60, Parts XII–XIII.

Although Article 77(3) of the LOS Convention provides that the rights of coastal states over the continental shelf do not depend on occupation or any express proclamation (see Chapter 10, Section E), Part V of the Convention, which concerns the EEZ, contains no such provision. State practice indicates that unless states claim such a zone, these waters remain governed by the regime of the high seas. As of May 28, 2008, 126 states had proclaimed an EEZ. See UN Division for Ocean Affairs and the Law of the Sea, Summary of National Claims to Maritime Zones, available at http://www.un.org/Depts/los/LEGISLATIONANDTREATIES/claims. htm. Taking into consideration the number of land-locked countries (see Section D), this represents a high percentage of all coastal states. A small number of coastal states have not claimed an EEZ, but continue to rely on the notion of a fishery zone to expand their competence in that field to a 200–mile zone, the United Kingdom being a prime example. See Shalva Kvinikhidze, Contemporary Exclusive Fishery Zones or Why Some States Still Claim an EFZ, 23 Intl. J. Marine & Coastal L. 271 (2008). Finally, the Mediterranean Sea has long been devoid of EEZs, although this situation is gradually changing. In sum, the 200–mile limit, which has at times been under pressure from coastal states wanting to extend their powers beyond that limit, seems so far to have stood the test of time. See Erik Franckx, The 200–mile Limit: Between Creeping Jurisdiction and Creeping Common Heritage?, 48 Ger. Y.B. Intl. L. 117 (2005).

Within the EEZ, all states may exercise the high seas freedoms of navigation and overflight and of the laying of submarine cables and pipelines. They may also engage in other internationally lawful uses of the sea that are related to these freedoms, such as the operation of ships and aircraft. LOS Convention, Article 58(1)–(2), with cross-references to Articles 87–115. In exercising these freedoms, however, all states must give due regard to the rights and duties of the coastal state and shall comply with the laws and regulations of the coastal state that are consistent with the LOS Convention and international law. Id. at Article 58(3). Reciprocally, the coastal state must give due regard to the rights and duties of other states while the coastal state exercises its rights and performs its duties in the EEZ. Id. at Article 56(2).

The creation of the EEZ concept in international law serves as a good example of a process whereby a clause in an international convention, which is in itself not a source of law because the convention has not yet entered into force, may serve as a starting point for an international customary rule to emerge. The International Court of Justice had already acknowledged the possibility of such a transformation in the North Sea Continental Shelf Cases (Federal Republic of Germany/Denmark; Federal Republic of Germany/Netherlands), 1969 I.C.J. 3, ¶¶ 70–81. That case involved the question of whether Article 6 of the 1958 Continental Shelf Convention relating to delimitation between adjacent and opposite states, even though not codifying customary international law at its inception, could subsequently have become a customary rule binding on Germany, which was not a party to that 1958 Convention. The Court ruled that the requirements for such a transformation, namely sufficient state practice by non-parties as well as the belief that the practice is obligatory (opinio juris), were not fulfilled with regard to the equidistance-special circumstance rule embodied in Article 6. Id. at ¶ 81.

The International Court of Justice touched on the matter of the customary international law status of the EEZ for the first time in February 1982, before states had even signed the LOS Convention. In a classic example of an obiter dictum, in a section on historic rights and in a case that only concerned the continental shelf, the Court stated that the concept of the EEZ "may be regarded as part of modern international law." Continental Shelf Case (Tunisia/Libya), 1982 I.C.J. 18, ¶ 100. In 1984 a Chamber of the International Court of Justice noted that certain provisions concerning the EEZ "may ... be regarded as consonant at present with general international law." Gulf of Maine Case (Canada/United States), 1984 I.C.J. 246, ¶ 94. Then in 1985 the

International Court of Justice stated in much more affirmative language: "It is in the Court's view incontestable that ... the institution of the exclusive economic zone ... is shown by the practice of states to have become a part of customary law." Continental Shelf Case (Libya/Malta), 1985 I.C.J. 13, ¶ 34. About a decade before the entry into force of the LOS Convention, one of the novel concepts created by it had crystallized as customary international law.

On March 10, 1983, President Reagan issued Proclamation 5030, claiming a 200–mile EEZ in which the United States had rights and jurisdiction substantially similar to those of coastal states set forth in the LOS Convention. Exec. Procl. No. 5030, 48 Fed. Reg. 10,605 (1983). According to the statement of the President accompanying the Proclamation, the Proclamation was "consistent with those fair and balanced results in the Convention" that "generally confirm existing maritime law and practice." 22 Intl. Leg. Materials 461, 464 (1983). As noted in Section A, the United States had much to gain from this new concept.

The United States and other major maritime states take the position that the EEZ continues to be a part of the high seas, although subject to special rights of coastal states. Other states insist that the zone is a special zone of the coastal state subject to the freedoms of navigation and overflight. Today the EEZ is normally characterized as sui generis. The allocation of certain rights and responsibilities in the zone remains a matter of debate, however, and states have some leeway to try to strengthen their respective claims. For example, a number of coastal states have enacted legislation restricting specific forms of navigation in the EEZ, leading some scholars to question whether certain high seas freedoms continue to have vitality in the zone. See Jon M. Van Dyke, The Disappearing Right to Navigational Freedom in the Exclusive Economic Zone, 29 Marine Policy 107 (2005). The negotiators of the LOS Convention recognized that not every activity in the EEZ is specifically addressed. The LOS Convention thus provides that in cases where the Convention does not attribute rights or jurisdiction, conflicts between states "should be resolved on the basis of equity and in the light of all the relevant circumstances, taking into account" not only the respective importance of the interests of the states directly involved, but also the interests of "the international community as a whole." LOS Convention, Article 59. See Syméon Karagiannis, L'article 59 de la Convention des Nations Unies sur le droit de la mer (ou les mystères de la nature juridique de la zone économique exclusive), 37 Belgian Rev. Intl. L. 325 (2004).

Some "gray areas" have already created tensions between states. One example involves bunkering vessels that supply fuel to fishing vessels. The question whether bunkering vessels make an internationally lawful use of the sea related to the freedom of navigation, or instead are involved in a commercial operation directly related to fishing activities that a coastal state has the right to regulate, has engendered debate. See David Anderson, The Regulation of Fishing and Related Activities in Exclusive Economic Zones, in The Exclusive Economic Zone and the United Nations Convention on the Law of the Sea, 1982–2000: A Preliminary Assessment of State Practice 43 (Erik Franckx & Philippe Gautier eds., 2003). The International Tribunal for the Law of the Sea did not squarely address this controversy in the M/V Saiga (No. 2) Case (Saint Vincent and the Grenadines v. Guinea), ITLOS Case No. 2, ¶¶ 103–109 (1999), in which Guinea arrested a Vincentian bunkering vessel that had been supplying fuel to fishing vessels in Guinea's EEZ outside its contiguous zone. Guinea pressed only the claim that the arrested vessel was violating Guinea's customs laws, avoiding paying tax on the bunker oil; Guinea did not assert that its fishing or environmental laws had been violated. The Tribunal ruled for the flag state, Saint Vincent and the Grenadines, finding that except "in respect of artificial islands, installations and structures" in the EEZ, Guinea's customs authority extended only to its territorial sea and contiguous zone. Id. at ¶ 127. See Section K and Chapter 8, Sections B and G. The Tribunal did not rely on Article 59 of the LOS Convention, discussed in the preceding paragraph, and rejected Guinea's arguments that "public interest," a "state of necessity," or "self-protection" justified arresting the vessel. The Saiga decision emphasizes that, under international law, a coastal state lacks jurisdiction with respect to some matters in its EEZ—in this case, jurisdiction with respect to violations of the coastal state's customs laws.

For further reading on the EEZ, see generally David Joseph Attard, The Exclusive Economic Zone in International Law (1987); Barbara Kwiatkowska, The 200 Mile Exclusive Economic Zone in the New Law of the Sea (1989); Francisco Orrego Vicuña, The Exclusive Economic Zone: Regime and Legal Nature under International Law (1989). For later developments, see The Exclusive Economic Zone and the United Nations Convention on the Law of the Sea, 1982–2000: A First Assessment of State Practice (Erik Franckx & Philippe Gautier eds., 2003).

C. MANAGEMENT AND CONSERVATION OF THE LIVING RESOURCES WITHIN THE EEZ

The coastal state has two primary responsibilities in the management and conservation of living resources within its EEZ. First, the coastal state is under a duty, taking into account the best scientific evidence available to it, to ensure through proper conservation and management measures that the living resources of the EEZ are not endangered by over-exploitation. LOS Convention, Article 61(2). The coastal state must maintain or restore populations of harvested fisheries at levels that produce a "maximum sustainable yield." Id. at Article 61(2)–(3). Maximum sustainable yield is the level of fishing of a stock of fish at which the maximum tonnage of fish can be harvested without depleting the stock. Although maximum sustainable yield is based primarily on scientific and biological data, the coastal state must also take into account the effects on interrelated fishery stocks, fishing patterns, and any generally recommended international minimum standards. The notion of maximum sustainable yield is further qualified by the economic needs of the fishing communities of the coastal state and the special requirements of developing countries in the region. Id. at Article 61(3)–(4).

The second primary responsibility of the coastal state is to promote the objective of "optimum utilization" of the living resources within its EEZ, a more flexible concept than "full utilization." Id. at Article 62(1). To this end, the coastal state shall determine the allowable catch of the living resources within its EEZ and its own capacity to harvest the allowable catch. Id. at Articles 61(1), 62(2). The coastal state's discretion to determine the allowable catch in its EEZ is not prejudiced by its responsibility to promote optimum utilization. Id. at Article 62(1). Therefore, a coastal state may set the entire allowable catch at a level equal to its capacity to harvest, even if such level is below the level that would ensure optimum utilization of fishery resources, thus cutting off access by foreign countries to any surplus that the coastal state cannot harvest. A coastal state may not, however, determine an allowable catch that would lead to over-exploitation of harvested species. Id. at Article 61(2).

If a coastal state sets an allowable catch at levels above which the coastal state has the capacity to harvest, it must grant access to other states to harvest the available surplus. Id. at Article 62(2). In granting access to other states, the coastal state must, among other considerations, give due regard to the rights and needs of land-locked states and geographically disadvantaged states in the region. Id. Land-locked states and geographically disadvantaged states obtained this concession after protracted negotiations at the Third United Nations Conference on the Law of the Sea Conference. However, these states obtained no rights with respect to the exploitation of nonliving resources in the EEZ. For a more detailed presentation of the rights of land-locked and geographically disadvantaged states in the EEZ, see Section D.

In addition to considering the rights and needs of land-locked and geographically disadvantaged states in the region, a coastal state must take other factors into account when it gives other states access to its EEZ. These factors include the coastal state's own economic and other national interests, the requirements of developing states in the region, and "the need to minimize economic dislocation in states whose nationals have habitually fished in the [EEZ] or which have made substantial efforts in research and identification of stocks" in the EEZ. Id. at Article 62(3).

Article 62(4) of the LOS Convention sets forth a nonexhaustive list of matters that a coastal state may regulate in its EEZ, including:

(a) the licensing of fishermen, fishing vessels, and equipment and the payment of fees (see, e.g., 16 U.S.C. § 1824);

(b) establishing quotas and species that may be caught (see, e.g., the Atlantic Herring Fishery Management Plan, 50 C.F.R. § 648.200);

(c) regulating the seasons and areas of fishing, and the types, sizes, and amount of gear and fishing vessels that may be used (see, e.g., the Gulf of Mexico and South Atlantic Spiny Lobster Fishery Management Plan, id. at §§ 640.20–.24);

(d) the age and size of fish that may be caught (see, e.g., the Monkfish Management Plan, id. at § 648.93);

(e) reporting requirements relating to fish caught (see, e.g., reporting requirements for Caribbean, Gulf, and South Atlantic fisheries, id. at § 622.5);

(f) fishery research programs (see, e.g., 15 U.S.C. § 713c–3(c));

(g) placing observers or trainees on foreign vessels (see, e.g., 16 U.S.C. § 1827);

(h) the landing of catch by foreign vessels in the ports or waters of the coastal state (see, e.g., 46 U.S.C. § 55114);

(i) the terms of joint ventures;

(j) the training of personnel and transfer of fisheries technology; and

(k) enforcement procedures (see, e.g., 16 U.S.C. § 1861).

Where nationals of other states are granted access to a coastal state's EEZ, they must comply with the conservation measures and other lawful regulations and laws of the coastal state. LOS Convention, Articles 58(3), 62(4).

The LOS Convention provides that if a coastal state has neglected its duties under Articles 61 and 62 in some important respects, other states concerned may submit the matter to a compulsory conciliation procedure. This procedure can be invoked in particular when:

[(a)] a coastal State has manifestly failed to comply with its obligations to ensure through proper conservation and management measures that the maintenance of living resources in the exclusive economic zone is not seriously endangered;

[(b)] a coastal State has arbitrarily refused to determine, at the request of another State, the allowable catch and its capacity to harvest living resources with respect to stocks which that other State is interested in fishing; or

[(c)] a coastal State has arbitrarily refused to allocate to any State ... the whole or part of the surplus it has declared to exist.

Id. at Article 297(3)(b). This procedure applies only in disputes between parties to the LOS Convention, so it cannot be invoked by the United States if it does not become a party to the Convention. For more on dispute settlement, see Chapter 15.

For further discussion of the conservation and management of living resources in the EEZ, see generally William T. Burke, The New International Law of Fisheries: UNCLOS 1982 and Beyond (1994); Harry N. Scheiber, Ocean Governance and the Marine Fisheries Crisis: Two Decades of Innovation—and Frustration, 20 Va. Envtl. L.J. 119 (2001).

D. RIGHTS OF GEOGRAPHICALLY DISADVANTAGED AND LAND-LOCKED STATES IN THE EEZ

Geographically disadvantaged states are coastal states that can claim no EEZ of their own and coastal states, including states bordering closed or semi-enclosed seas, whose geographical situations make them dependent on the exploitation of the living resources of the EEZs of other coastal states in the region. LOS Convention, Article 70(2). These states include, for example, coastal states with a short coastline, such as Singapore or the Democratic Republic of the Congo. For discussion of the criteria used in determining which states are geographically disadvantaged in the framework of the LOS Convention and their listing, see Lewis M. Alexander & Robert D. Hodgson, The Role of the Geographically–Disadvantaged States in the Law of the Sea, 13 San Diego L. Rev. 558 (1976). Land-locked states are states that do not border open, enclosed, or semi-enclosed seas. As of June 1, 2009, there were forty-two land-locked states if one restricts the count to member states of the United Nations, thus excluding other potential candidates such as Kosovo, South Ossetia, or the Vatican City.

The LOS Convention affirmed several previously recognized rights with respect to land-locked states and geographically disadvantaged states, such as their rights to use the high seas and to have vessels fly their flag. LOS Convention, Articles 87, 90. However, the LOS Convention introduced their right to participate, on an equitable basis, in the exploitation of any fishery surplus in the EEZs of coastal states in the region, taking into account the relevant economic and geographic circumstances of all the states concerned. Id. at Articles 69(1), 70(1). Developed land-locked and developed geographically disadvantaged states may participate in the exploitation of surplus fisheries of the EEZs of other developed coastal states in the region only after the developed coastal state has given due regard to the need to minimize detrimental effects on states whose nationals have habitually fished in the zone. Id. at Articles 69(4), 70(5).

The terms of participation of geographically disadvantaged and land-locked states in a given EEZ shall be established by bilateral, subregional, or regional agreement. In establishing such terms, the states concerned must take into account the following factors:

(a) the need to avoid effects detrimental to the coastal state's fishing communities or fishing industry;

(b) the extent to which the land-locked or geographically disadvantaged state is participating or entitled to participate in the exploitation of other states' EEZs;

(c) the need to avoid a particular burden for any single coastal state; and

(d) the nutritional needs of the populations of the states concerned.

Id. at Articles 69(2), 70(2).

When the harvesting capacity of a coastal state approaches a point that would enable it to harvest the entire allowable catch, the coastal state must cooperate in establishing equitable arrangements to allow the participation of developing land-locked and developing geographically disadvantaged states of the region in the exploitation of the living resources of the EEZ. These arrangements are to be "appropriate in the circumstances and on terms satisfactory to all parties" concerned, taking into account the factors noted in the preceding paragraph. Id. at Articles 69(3), 70(4). For more details concerning these rights, see Antonio Martínez Puñal, The Rights of Land–Locked and Geographically Disadvantaged States in Exclusive Economic Zones, 23 J. Mar. L. & Com. 429 (1992). These articles of the LOS Convention have not been widely implemented in practice. See Stephen Vasciannie, Land–Locked and Geographically Disadvantaged States,

31 Commonwealth L. Bull. 59 (2005), who at the same time emphasizes that the Third United Nations Conference on the Law of the Sea achieved success in affirming for land-locked states the right of access to and from the sea and the freedom of transit. See LOS Convention, Articles 125–126.

E.   SPECIES SUBJECT TO SPECIAL RULES

1.   *Straddling and Highly Migratory Fish Stocks*

Where the same fish stock occurs within the EEZs of two or more coastal states, or in an EEZ and an adjacent area of the high seas frequented by foreign fishermen, the states concerned must cooperate directly or through an international organization in enacting appropriate conservation and management measures. LOS Convention, Article 63. A similar duty is imposed regarding highly migratory species, such as tuna, which are listed in Annex I of the LOS Convention. Id. at Article 64. As discussed in Chapter 13, Section C, application of these articles has given rise to controversy.

2.   *Marine Mammals*

A coastal state or an international organization may regulate the exploitation of marine mammals more strictly than Part V of the LOS Convention, concerning the EEZ, otherwise provides. LOS Convention, Article 65. The international organization primarily concerned with cetaceans is the International Whaling Commission (IWC), established by the 1946 Whaling Convention. Although the IWC was originally established to protect the whaling interests of states, the Commission's totally open membership provision (1946 Whaling Convention, Article 10(2)), has allowed the IWC gradually to move towards the other side of the spectrum, i.e., towards protection of cetaceans. In 1982 the IWC adopted a temporary moratorium on commercial whaling. The moratorium remains in place today, with exceptions for aboriginal subsistence hunting (1946 Whaling Convention, Schedule ¶ 13) and scientific research (id. at Article 8 and Schedule ¶ 30). Pursuant to the opt-out provisions of Article 5(3) of the Convention, several member states, including Japan, Norway and the Soviet Union, exempted themselves from the application of the moratorium by registering timely objections. Japan subsequently withdrew its objection, but continues to issue permits for the taking of whales under its controversial scientific research program. Iceland, which withdrew from the 1946 Convention in 1992, exempted itself from the commercial whaling moratorium by means of filing a much-contested reservation at the time of its re-adherence to the Convention in early 2000. For discussion of the history of the moratorium and its current application, see Gerry J. Nagtzaam, The International Whaling Commission and the Elusive Great White Whale of Preservationism, 33 Wm. & Mary Envtl. L. & Policy Rev. 375 (2009). For discussion of the exemption for aboriginal subsistence hunting, see A.W. Harris, Making the Case for Collective Rights: Indigenous Claims to Stocks of Marine Living Resources, 15 Geo. Intl. Envtl. L. Rev. 379 (2003).

The United States enacted a comprehensive protection plan for marine mammals in the Marine Mammal Protection Act of 1972, 16 U.S.C. §§ 1361 et seq. The U.S. Fish & Wildlife Service has listed several species of marine mammals, including whales, as endangered under the Endangered Species Act, 16 U.S.C. §§ 1531 et seq., which prohibits the harming and killing of endangered species and the importation or trading of products derived from endangered species. The 1971 Pelly Amendment to the Fisherman's Protective Act grants the President discretion to ban imports from countries that the U.S. Secretary of Commerce has certified as "engaging in trade or taking which diminishes the effectiveness of any international program for endangered or threatened species," so long as such sanctions are consistent with U.S. obligations under the General Agreement on Tariffs and Trade and other trade agreements. 22 U.S.C. § 1978. Under the 1979 Packwood Amendment to the Magnuson–Stevens Fishery Conservation and Management Act, if the U.S. Secretary of Commerce certifies to the President that the nationals of a foreign state are engaged in action that "diminishes the effectiveness" of the 1946 Whaling Convention, the U.S. Secretary of State must reduce the foreign state's fishing quota in the U.S. EEZ by not less than fifty percent. 16 U.S.C. § 1821(e)(2). For discussion of Japan's certification under both the Pelly and Packwood Amendments as a result of the expansion of its scientific whaling program in the North Pacific, see Sean D. Murphy, Contemporary Practice of the United States Relating to International Law, 95 Am. J. Intl. L. 132, 149–152 (2001).

Legislative measures adopted by the European Community also provide a high standard of protection for whales. Directive 92/43 (EEC) on the conservation of natural habitats and of wild fauna and flora, 1992 O.J.L. 206, 7, lists all cetacean species in its Annex IV and prohibits their capture and killing within Community waters. Regulation 338/97 (EC), 1997 O.J.L. 61, 1, bans the introduction of cetaceans or parts or products derived therefrom into the Community for primarily commercial purposes.

For further discussion of international and U.S. efforts to protect marine mammals, see Donna R. Christie & Richard G. Hildreth, Coastal and Ocean Management Law in a Nutshell 219–265 (3d ed. 2007); Donald C. Baur, Michael L. Gosliner & Nina M. Yong, The Law of Marine Mammal Conservation, in Ocean and Coastal Law and Policy 477 (Donald C. Baur, Tim Eichenberg & Michael Sutton eds., 2008).

3. Anadromous and Catadromous Stocks

Anadromous stocks (such as salmon) and catadromous stocks (such as eels) are subject to special rules. States in whose rivers anadromous stocks originate have the primary interest in and responsibility for them, and states in which catadromous stocks spend the greater part of their life cycle similarly have such primary interest and responsibility. The coastal state must cooperate with other states whose nationals fish for anadromous or catadromous stock outside the coastal state's EEZ, or with other states through whose waters these stocks migrate, and appropriate conservation and management measures should be entered into by agreement. In particular, arrangements are to minimize economic dislocation to other states fishing for these anadromous and catadromous stocks. LOS Convention, Articles 66–67. For an example of such an agreement, see the 1985 Canada–United States Treaty Concerning Pacific Salmon, as amended.

4.   Sedentary Species

Sedentary species are organisms that, at the harvestable stage, either are immobile on or under the seabed or are unable to move except in constant physical contact with the seabed or the subsoil and are a part of the natural resources of the continental shelf. LOS Convention, Article 77. The provisions of the LOS Convention governing fisheries in the EEZ do not establish the rules for coastal state management and exploitation of sedentary species. Id. at Article 68. Instead, a coastal state's rights over sedentary species are governed by rules applicable to the continental shelf. See Chapter 10, Section F.

F. ENFORCEMENT OF CONSERVATION AND MANAGEMENT MEASURES

Within the EEZ, a coastal state has the right to enforce all laws and regulations enacted to conserve and manage living resources. LOS Convention, Article 73. The authorities of the coastal state, in enforcing such laws and regulations, may board and inspect a ship, arrest a ship and its crew, and institute judicial proceedings against them. Arrested ships and crews must be promptly released on the posting of a reasonable bond or other security. If such release is delayed, and if the states concerned are parties to the Convention, the flag state may make an application for prompt release to the International Tribunal for the Law of the Sea. Id. at Articles 73(1)–(2), 292. See Chapter 15, Section D. Of the fifteen cases this Tribunal has dealt with as of June 1, 2009, nine have concerned prompt release issues. This prompt release procedure can also be used with respect to certain cases where vessels have been arrested or detained for serious pollution offenses. See LOS Convention, Articles 220, 226; Chapter 12, Section K.2. As of June 1, 2009, Article 73 has been the only legal basis relied on by parties in these prompt release proceedings.

A coastal state's penalties for violations of its conservation and management measures may not include imprisonment, in the absence of agreements to the contrary by the states concerned, or any other form of corporal punishment. Id. at Article

73(3). Several countries, including some parties to the LOS Convention, nevertheless still provide for imprisonment. The United States, which, as of July 15, 2009, was not a party to the LOS Convention, belongs to this group. See Section G. The coastal state must inform the flag state of any vessel arrests or enforcement actions taken. Id. at Article 73(4). The coastal state may engage in hot pursuit to arrest any ship that violates conservation or management measures within the coastal state's EEZ, provided such pursuit does not continue into the territorial waters of another state. Id. at Article 111(2)–(3); see also United States v. F/V Taiyo Maru, 395 F.Supp. 413 (D. Me. 1975). For discussion of hot pursuit, see Chapter 4, Section D.6.

G. U.S. LEGISLATION RELATING TO CONSERVATION AND EXPLOITATION OF THE LIVING RESOURCES IN THE EEZ

The United States has always claimed exclusive sovereignty over the living (and nonliving) resources in its territorial sea. Traditionally, states of the United States regulated fisheries in the territorial sea; the Submerged Lands Act of 1953, 43 U.S.C. § 1311(a), confirmed the jurisdiction of states extending to, in most cases, three miles from U.S. baselines. According to Skiriotes v. Florida, 313 U.S. 69, 77 (1941), a state could also regulate fishing by its citizens beyond the territorial sea where there is no conflict with acts of Congress. See Chapter 8, Section H.

In 1966, Congress established a nine-mile fishery zone contiguous to the territorial sea in which the United States claimed exclusive fishing rights, subject to the continuation of fishing by countries that had traditionally fished in those waters. Pub. L. No. 89–658, 80 Stat. 908 (1966). This act did not establish a comprehensive program for the conservation or management of fisheries within the zone.

In 1976, Congress enacted the Fishery Conservation and Management Act, which extended U.S. fishery conservation and management jurisdiction over a newly established 200–mile fishery conservation zone. Pub. L. No. 94–265, 90 Stat. 331 (1976). This enactment, known as the Magnuson Act, specified standards for establishing comprehensive conservation and management plans for each species of fishery stock within the 200–mile zone, to be developed by regional fishery management councils. 16 U.S.C. §§ 1801 et. seq. For a listing of the eight regional fishery management councils established under the Act and the geographical areas over which each has authority, see id. at § 1852. The councils' fishery management plans must prevent over-exploitation of the fisheries within the zone and must promote on a continuing basis the harvest of an "optimum yield" from each fishery. Id. at § 1851(a)(1). "Optimum yield" is defined as a yield that "will provide the greatest overall benefit to the Nation, particularly with respect to food production and recreational opportunities, and taking into account the protection of marine ecosystems," that is determined "on the basis of the maximum sustainable yield from the fishery, as reduced by any relevant social, economic, or ecological factor," and that "in the case of an overfished fishery, provides for rebuilding to a level consistent with producing the maximum sustainable yield in such fishery." Id. at § 1802(33).

Fishery management plans must comply not only with the scientific and other standards set forth in Section 1851, but must also take into account "any Indian treaty fishing rights." Id. at § 1853(a)(2). In Hoh Indian Tribe v. Baldrige, 522 F.Supp. 683, 685 (W.D. Wash. 1981), the court determined that the 1981 salmon fisheries plan established by the Pacific Fishery Management Council failed to adequately consider and protect fishing rights granted to the Hoh and other Indian tribes under the 1856 Treaty of Olympia. Many other countries have also confirmed the fishery rights of indigenous peoples. For discussion of indigenous fishing rights recognized by Canada and Norway, see Anthony Davis & Svein Jentoft, The Challenge and the Promise of Indigenous Peoples' Fishing Rights—From Dependency to Agency, 25 Marine Policy 223 (2001).

In addition to establishing conservation and management authority in the 200–mile zone, the Magnuson Act established a system for controlling foreign access to the zone. The Act authorized foreign fishing within the zone only if (1) a treaty or international agreement in force at the time of enactment required access, or (2) the flag state entered "a governing international fishery agreement" with the United States after enactment of the Act acknowledging U.S. fishery conservation and management jurisdiction in the zone. 16 U.S.C. § 1821(b)–(c). Foreign vessels meeting either of these requirements may be issued a fishing permit only to harvest that portion of the "optimum yield" not harvested by U.S. fishermen. Id. at § 1821(d). Determining optimum yield, U.S. harvest capacity, and the allocation of any surplus among foreign fishermen is the responsibility of the regional councils. Id. at § 1853(a).

A 1980 amendment to the Magnuson Act provided complicated optional methods for determining the total allowable level of foreign fishing within the zone. Access to available surplus shall be allocated in part on a "market access" basis, giving preference to nationals of states that grant preferential access to their available surpluses to U.S. nationals. The rights of fishing vessels that have historically fished in the zone must also be taken into account. Id. at § 1821(e). Moreover, foreign states must extend substantially the same fishing privileges to fishing vessels of the United States if their fishermen want to fish in the U.S. EEZ. Id. at § 1821(f). Another amendment to the Fishery and Conservation Management Act minimized joint ventures by which U.S. fishermen transferred their catches to foreign fish processing vessels, by limiting such transfers to the portion of catches that exceeded the capacity of U.S. onshore processing facilities. Id. at § 1824(b)(6)(B). Today, foreign fishing and joint ventures in the U.S. EEZ are minimal.

The Fishery Conservation and Management Act provides for both civil and criminal penalties for violations of the Act. Id. at §§ 1858–1859. The Act permits seizure of any fishing vessel violating the Act, but provides for a stay of execution on payment of a bond. Id. at § 1860(d)(1).

By 1996, a widespread sense existed that regulation of fisheries in the U.S. EEZ had long been lax and that "many fisheries were severely overfished and that probably even more were overcapitalized." Josh Eagle, Domestic Fishery Management, in Ocean and Coastal Law and Policy 275, 286 (Donald C. Baur, Tim Eichenberg & Michael Sutton eds., 2008). In that year, Congress passed the Sustainable Fisheries Act, which significantly revised the Magnuson Act (now known as the Magnuson–Stevens Fishery Conservation and Management Act). The Sustainable Fisheries Act, codified primarily, as amended, at 16 U.S.C. §§ 1801–1883, inter alia, requires that fishery management plans specify essential fish habitats, provides for bycatch reduction, provides for fishery monitoring and research, and obligates the Secretary of Commerce to develop plans to rebuild depleted fish stocks if the regional fishery management councils do not do so. See Natural Resources Defense Council v. Daley, 209 F.3d 747 (D.C. Cir. 2000) (allowable level of take under a rebuilding plan must have at least a fifty percent chance of rebuilding an overfished stock). The 1996 Act also creates a program to reduce the size of a fishing fleet if the Secretary of Commerce certifies a fishery resource disaster, 16 U.S.C. §§ 1861a, 1864, and the Act suspended temporarily new government loan guarantees for the construction of fishing vessels that would increase harvesting capacity in the U.S. EEZ. Pub. L. No. 104–297, § 302(b), 110 Stat. 3559, 3615. For a recent analysis of this Act from a New England perspective, see Roger Fleming, Peter Shelley & Priscilla M. Brooks, Twenty-eight Years and Counting: Can the Magnuson–Stevens Act Deliver on Its Conservation Promise?, 28 Vt. L. Rev. 579 (2004).

Many observers of the U.S. regulatory process have maintained, and continue to maintain, that the regional councils have been dominated by the fishing industry and have been insufficiently responsive to conservation and other public interest concerns. The Magnuson–Stevens Reauthorization Act of 2006, Pub. L. No. 109–479, 120 Stat. 3575 (2007), addressed some of these concerns by requiring members of regional fishery councils to undertake training related to a range of factors involved in the fishery management process and by clarifying conflict-of-interest and recusal provisions. 16 U.S.C. § 1852(j)–(k). The 2006 Reauthorization Act also requires that, beginning in 2009, regional councils must take steps "immediately" to end overfishing. Id. at § 1854(e)(3)(A). Furthermore, regional councils now must "develop annual catch limits for each of its managed fisheries that may not exceed the fishing level recommendations of its scientific and statistical committee" or a peer review process. Id. at § 1852(h).

In its current form, the Magnuson–Stevens Act sets broad "national standards" for fishery conservation and management. Some of these standards, such as preventing overfishing while achieving optimum yield, id. at § 1851(a)(1), and basing conservation and management measures on "the best scientific information available," id. at § 1851(a)(2), set strong conservation policies. Other standards, however, reflect a concern not to cause short-term economic disruption in the fishing industry. For example, regional councils must minimize bycatch, but need do so only "to the extent practicable." Id. at § 1851(a)(9). Another standard requires the councils to "minimize adverse economic impacts on" fishing communities, and although "the conservation requirements of th[e] Act" cannot be sacrificed to achieve short-term economic gains, id. at § 1851(a)(8), conservation objectives may in practice be qualified. See, e.g., Natural Resources Defense Council v. Daley, 209 F.3d 747 (D.C. Cir. 2000).

The Magnuson–Stevens Act preserves the jurisdiction of the coastal states of the United States over a three-mile territorial sea, including fishery management jurisdiction, so long as state jurisdiction relates to fishery stocks not predominantly fished beyond the territorial sea, and so long as any state actions do not adversely affect the fishery management plans adopted by the regional councils under the Act. 16 U.S.C. § 1856(b). U.S. states are given an important role in the development of fishery conservation and management plans within the zone beyond the territorial sea by their representation on the eight regional fishery management councils set up under the Act. Id. at § 1852. States may also regulate fishing vessels outside the boundaries of the states under certain conditions, such as if no fishery management plan has been established, the state's regulations are consistent with such plan, or the plan delegates management authority to the state. Id. at § 1856(a)(3). In People v. Weeren, 26 Cal.3d 654, 163 Cal.Rptr. 255, 607 P.2d 1279 (1980), the California Supreme Court held, for instance, that California had jurisdiction to regulate fishing in the fishery conservation zone adjacent to California's territorial waters, since no federal rules had yet been promulgated under the 1976 Magnuson Act. The Court also found that its authority under the Act to regulate a vessel "registered" in the state applied to a federally documented vessel (see Chapter 3, Section C.4) that had a California commercial fishing license, since section 1856(a) would become "virtually meaningless" if state jurisdiction extended only to pleasure boats and small commercial fishing vessels that did not qualify for federal documentation. Id. at 668, 607 P.2d at 1286. The federal government has also enacted legislation to assist states in conserving and managing fisheries within their territorial seas, if they request such assistance. Coastal Zone Management Act of 1972, as amended, 16 U.S.C. §§ 1451 et seq.

In 1990 the U.S. National Marine Fisheries Service established its first individual fishing quota (IFQ) program, 55 Fed. Reg. 24,184 (1990), a conservation and management tool pioneered by New Zealand in the 1980s. Under an IFQ program, the total allowable catch of a designated fishery is allocated among licensees, based on specific eligibility criteria established in the program's implementing regulations. 16 U.S.C. §§ 1802(23), 1853(b)(6), 1853a. For an analysis of the effectiveness of the Alaskan halibut and sablefish fisheries IFQ program, see Alison Rieser, Prescriptions for the Commons: Environmental Scholarship and the Fishing Quotas Debate, 23 Harv. Envtl. L. Rev. 393, 412–414 (1999). Due to concerns about the fairness of the quota allocations, the 1996 Sustainable Fisheries Act placed a moratorium on the implementation of any new IFQ programs. Pub. L. No. 104–297, § 108(e), 110 Stat. 3559, 3576 (1996). The 2006 Magnuson–Stevens Reauthorization Act provides for the establishment of "limited access privilege programs," including IFQs. Among other requirements, the 2006 Reauthorization Act obligates regional fishery management councils to establish procedures to "ensure fair and equitable initial allocations." 16 U.S.C. § 1853a(c)(5). See Peter Schikler, Student Author, Has Congress Made It Harder to Save the Fish? An Analysis of the Limited Access Privilege Program (LAPP) Provisions of the Magnuson–Stevens Fishery Conservation and Management Reauthorization Act of 2006, 17 N.Y.U. Envtl. L.J. 908 (2008). For discussion of state practice regarding the implementation and allocation of IFQs, see FAO Fisheries Technical Paper No. 411, Case Studies on the Allocation of Transferable Quota Rights in Fisheries (R. Shotton ed., 2001), available at ftp://ftp.fao.org/docrep/fao/004/y2684e/y2684e00.pdf.

For additional discussion of U.S. management of fishery resources, see Donna R. Christie & Richard G. Hildreth, Coastal and Ocean Management Law in a Nutshell 188–218 (3d ed. 2007); Josh Eagle, Domestic Fishery Management, in Ocean and Coastal Law and Policy 275 (Donald C. Baur, Tim Eichenberg & Michael Sutton eds., 2008).

H. THE EUROPEAN COMMUNITY AND FISHERIES

As a party to the LOS Convention, the European Community (EC) deserves attention, since its twenty-seven member states have transferred competence with respect to the conservation and management of fisheries to this organization. The EC's exclusive competence with respect to fisheries conservation and management means that the EC adopts the relevant rules and regulations for fisheries in the EEZs of its member states, and that the EC deals directly with third states and international organizations with respect, inter alia, to waters under national jurisdiction. Declaration made at the time of formal confirmation by the EC pursuant to Article 5(1) of Annex IX to the LOS Convention, available at www.un.org/Depts/los/convention_

agreements/convention_declarations.htm.   Third
states seeking access to EC waters, therefore, must
conclude agreements with the EC, and not with the
individual member states in whose waters they
would like to fish. Enforcement of these conservation and management rules, however, remains a
competence of the individual EC member states.

This division of competence between the EC and
its member states is not static. Even though the EC
was established in 1957 by the Treaty of Rome, a
common policy in the area of fisheries was only
adopted in 1970. See Regulation (EEC) No. 2141/70,
1970 O.J.L. 236, 1 (laying down a common structur-
al policy for the fishing industry). Moreover, the
first basic regulation concerning the conservation
and management of fisheries was not adopted until
1983. See Regulation (EEC) No. 170/83, 1983 O.J.L.
24, 1 (establishing a Community system for the
conservation and management of fishery resources).
This regulation was revised in 1992 and most recently in 2002. Regulation (EC) No. 2371/2002,
2002 O.J.L. 358, 59 (on the conservation and sustainable exploitation of fisheries resources under
the Common Fisheries Policy). The European Court
of Justice has also played an important role in the
development of this common fisheries policy and in
clarifying the gray zone between legislative and
enforcement competence in this domain. See Erik
Franckx, Sea Fisheries Cases before the European
Court of Justice, in Max Planck Encyclopedia of
Public International Law (2008), available at http://
www.mpepil.com. In addition, in the area of en-

forcement certain subtle changes can be noted, such as the establishment of a Community Fisheries Control Agency, which became operational in 2007, as well as slightly enhanced enforcement powers for the European Commission and the EC member states. Constance Johnson, Fisheries Enforcement in European Community Waters Since 2002: Developments in Non–Flag Enforcement, 23 Intl. J. Marine & Coastal L. 249 (2008).

Two fundamental concepts form the basis of the EC's common fisheries policy, namely the principle of equal access and the principle of relative stability. The former, based on the principle of nondiscrimination, ensures that EC fishermen have a right of equal access to the fishing grounds of all member states. The latter, making inroads on the principle of equal access, governs the yearly distribution of quotas among the EC member states based on the adoption of total allowable catches. It aims to assure member states a share of the EC's total allowable catch on the basis of their respective catches as they existed before the quota system was put into operation in 1983 or, for member states that acceded to the EC after 1983, as of the time of their accession.

For further reading on the EC fisheries competence, see Daniel Vignes, La communauté européenne dans le domaine du droit général de la mer, in The Law of the Sea: The European Union and its Member States 7 (Tullio Treves & Laura Pineschi eds., 1997); Claire Bury & Jörn Sack, The European Union, in The Exclusive Economic Zone and the

United Nations Convention on the Law of the Sea, 1982–2000: A First Assessment of State Practice 67 (Erik Franckx & Philippe Gautier eds., 2003); Europe and the Sea: Fisheries, Navigation and Marine Environment 13–118 (Rafael Casado Raigón ed., 2005).

I. ENERGY PRODUCTION AND THE EEZ

In addition to exploiting the living resources of the EEZ, the coastal state may undertake other exploitation activities in the zone, such as the production of energy from the water, currents, and wind. LOS Convention, Article 56. More and more windmill farms are today installed beyond the limits of the territorial sea in order to minimize their visibility from land. With respect to the United States, the 2005 Energy Policy Act authorizes the Secretary of the Interior to grant offshore leases, easements, and rights of way for a range of energy-related activities, including the "production, transportation, or transmission of energy from sources other than oil and gas," such as wind. 43 U.S.C. § 1337(p). See Symposium, Coastal Wind Energy Generation: Capacities and Conflicts, 31 B.C. Envtl. Aff. L. Rev. 177 (2004).

Several countries have also regulated the production of energy from the differentials in temperatures between the warm surface and the cooler subsurface waters of the ocean (ocean thermal energy conversion (OTEC)). The thermal energy produces electricity, which can be transferred to shore by submarine cables or used at the site of production to manufacture energy-intensive chemicals such as ammonia. In 1980 the U.S. Congress enacted the Ocean Thermal Energy Conversion Research, Development, and Demonstration Act, 42 U.S.C. §§ 9001 et seq., to promote the development of OTEC in the waters adjacent to the United States, and the Ocean Thermal Energy Conversion Act, 42 U.S.C. §§ 9101 et seq., to authorize and regulate the construction and operation of OTEC facilities in the territorial and adjacent waters of the United States. Only U.S. citizens, U.S. government entities, and entities organized under the laws of any state of the United States whose executive officers and a controlling number of governing board members meet U.S. citizenship requirements may apply for a license under the Act. Id. at §§ 9102(18), 9111(f). A foreign vessel may not call at an OTEC facility unless its flag state has recognized U.S. jurisdiction over the vessel while within any safety zone that has been established around the facility. Id. at § 9118(d)(3). Licensees must not interfere with lawful uses of the high seas by other countries. Id. at § 9119(a).

J. MARINE SCIENTIFIC RESEARCH

During the Third United Nations Conference on the Law of the Sea, coastal states, especially developing states, raised the concern that developed states might use marine scientific research as a pretext to gain sensitive intelligence. See Chapter 2, Section C.6. Coastal states also recognized that scientific research of fish necessarily involved the taking of fish and were concerned that such research might interfere with coastal state fisheries management. These concerns resulted in limits on marine scientific research in the EEZ. The coastal state has the right to regulate, authorize, and conduct marine scientific research within its EEZ in accordance with the relevant provisions of the LOS Convention. Other states or international organizations may not conduct marine scientific research without the consent of the coastal state. Where the proposed research is to be conducted for peaceful purposes for the benefit of the scientific knowledge of all humankind, a coastal state may not normally withhold such consent, unless the proposed research: is of direct significance for the exploration and exploitation of natural resources; involves drilling or the use of explosives or other harmful substances; involves the construction or use of artificial islands; contains inaccurate information relating to the nature and objectives of the project; or if the applicant has outstanding obligations to the coastal state from a prior research project. LOS Convention, Article 246.

Other states or international organizations authorized to conduct marine scientific research may not unjustifiably interfere with a coastal state's lawful activities. Id. at Article 246(8). The other state or international organization must provide certain information regarding the nature and objective of the research project to the coastal state at least six months in advance, and provide the coastal state with project reports and resulting data. Id. at Articles 248, 249(1). The other state or international organization must ensure the right of the coastal state, if it so desires, to participate or to be represented in the marine scientific research projects conducted in its EEZ, without payment of any remuneration to the scientists of the coastal state and without any obligation of the coastal state to contribute towards the costs of the project. Id. at Article 249(1)(a). If the other state or international organization does not comply with these provisions, a coastal state may suspend the project. Id. at Article 253.

Between parties to the LOS Convention, disputes arising from the interpretation or application of these provisions shall be submitted to special conciliation procedures. However, disputes involving the discretion of the coastal state to withhold its consent in accordance with Article 246 or to suspend a research project in accordance with Article 253 shall not be subject to dispute resolution. LOS Convention, Article 297(2). For discussion of the LOS Convention's dispute settlement provisions, see Chapter 15.

In a statement accompanying Proclamation 5030, establishing a 200–mile EEZ for the United States (see Section B), President Reagan specifically excluded any claim of U.S. jurisdiction over marine scientific research within the zone. 22 Intl. Leg. Materials 461, 464 (1983). Most other countries, however, claim jurisdiction over marine scientific research in the EEZ, which usually means that scientific researchers must obtain consent from a coastal state before engaging in such research. See generally Judith Fenwick, International Profiles on Marine Scientific Research (1992). The U.S. State Department coordinates international scientific activities for the United States, processing a few hundred requests from U.S. oceanographers to engage in research in other states' EEZs each year, and assisting in the transmission of post-research cruise data reports to other countries. See Comments of Ambassador Mary Beth West, in Perspectives on International Oceanographic Research 28, 30 (Carnegie Endowment for International Peace, 2002), available at http://www.state.gov/documents/organization/19900.pdf.

The most prominent international organization in the field of marine scientific research is the Intergovernmental Oceanographic Commission (IOC), a body with functional autonomy within the United Nations Educational, Scientific and Cultural Organization. If a coastal state is a member of an international organization, such as the IOC, the coastal state is deemed to consent to marine scientific projects proposed by the organization in the coastal state's EEZ if the coastal state had approved the project when the organization decided to undertake it, unless the coastal state objects within four months of notification of the project. LOS Convention, Article 247. In 2005 the IOC Assembly approved a procedure to apply Article 247 of the LOS

Convention to facilitate marine scientific research undertaken under the auspices of international organizations in the EEZs of their member states. See IOC Resolution XXIII–8 available at http://www.gc. noaa.gov/documents/procedure_article247.pdf.

Whether military survey activities are subject to the rules governing marine scientific research is a matter of debate. The United States, for example, takes the position that military surveillance does not constitute marine scientific research, and does not require the consent of coastal states when conducted within their EEZs. During 2000–2002, the collection of military survey data by the *USNS Bowditch* within the EEZs of certain coastal states triggered diplomatic protests by the countries involved. See Sam Bateman, Hydrographic Surveying in the EEZ: Differences and Overlaps with Marine Scientific Research, 29 Marine Policy 163 (2005).

K. ARTIFICIAL ISLANDS AND INSTALLATIONS, INCLUDING DEEPWATER PORTS

In the EEZ, the coastal state has the exclusive right to construct and regulate the construction, operation, and use of any artificial islands. This right extends to other types of installations and structures for economic purposes and as necessary to allow the coastal state to exercise its rights within the EEZ as provided under Article 56. LOS Convention, Article 60(1). Artificial islands, installations, and structures may not be established so as to interfere with the use of recognized sea lanes essential to international navigation. Id. at Article 60(7).

The coastal state has exclusive jurisdiction over such artificial islands, installations, and structures, including jurisdiction with regard to customs, fiscal, health, safety, and immigration laws and regulations. Id. at Article 60(2). Where necessary, the coastal state may establish safety zones not in excess of 500 meters around such artificial islands, installations, and structures, and may take appropriate measures therein to ensure the safety of navigation and the structures themselves. Id. at Article 60(4)–(5).

Abandoned or disused installations or structures must be removed by the coastal state to ensure safety of navigation. Such removal must be undertaken in accordance with applicable international standards or regulations and with due regard to fishing, the protection of the marine environment, and the rights and duties of other states. Id. at Article 60(3). The International Maritime Organization has promulgated guidelines for the removal of such installations and structures. See Guidelines and Standards for the Removal of Offshore Installations and Structures on the Continental Shelf and in the Exclusive Economic Zone, IMO Res. A.672(16) (1989). This issue will become increasingly significant as structures age: "[i]n the North Sea area alone there are approximately 440 steel and concrete installations with a total mass of nearly 8 [million tons] and 18,370 kilometres of pipeline."

John Woodliffe, Decommissioning of Offshore Oil and Gas Installations in European Waters: The End of a Decade of Indecision?, 14 Intl. J. Marine & Coastal L. 101, 103 (1999). See generally Morakinyo Adedayo Ayoade, Disused Offshore Installations and Pipelines: Towards "Sustainable Decommissioning" (2002).

In addition to their frequent use as deepwater ports and oil drilling rigs, artificial islands and similar structures have been proposed over time for numerous other purposes including airports, nuclear power plants, broadcasting facilities, fish processing, gambling resorts, and even waste disposal.

The U.S. Outer Continental Shelf Lands Act (OCSLA) of 1953, as amended, provides:

> The Constitution and laws and civil and political jurisdiction of the United States are extended ... to all artificial islands, and all installations and other devices permanently or temporarily attached to the seabed, which may be erected thereon for the purpose of exploring for, developing, or producing resources therefrom, or any such installation or other device (other than a ship or vessel) for the purpose of transporting such resources.

43 U.S.C. § 1333(a)(1). Some courts have construed this statutory language as extending not only to structures related to natural resources such as oil and gas, but also to installations used for wind energy exploration, development, or production. Alliance to Protect Nantucket Sound, Inc. v. United

States Army Corps of Engineers, 288 F. Supp. 2d 64 (D. Mass. 2003).

When the OCSLA was proposed, conflict-of-laws questions arose concerning the law that would apply to individuals and activities on structures on the U.S. continental shelf. See Warren M. Christopher, The Outer Continental Shelf Lands Act: Key to a New Frontier, 6 Stan. L. Rev. 23, 37–43 (1953). Although the answers to such questions have not been completely resolved, U.S. federal courts are directed to apply as federal law "the civil and criminal laws of each adjacent State" on "artificial islands and fixed structures erected" on the continental shelf beyond the boundaries of state jurisdiction (see Chapter 5, Section A), to the extent that such state laws are not inconsistent with federal laws. 43 U.S.C. § 1333(a)(2)(A). Admiralty and maritime law apply to vessels, and it is thus essential to determine whether various types of drilling rigs are "vessels" or "structures." See Chapter 3, Section E. See David W. Robertson, The Outer Continental Shelf Lands Act's Provisions on Jurisdiction, Remedies, and Choice of Law: Correcting the Fifth Circuit's Mistakes, 38 J. Mar. L. & Com. 487 (2007).

Federal law directly regulates many issues related to artificial islands, structures, and installations in the U.S. EEZ. The OCSLA adopts the federal Longshore and Harbor Workers' Compensation Act, 33 U.S.C. §§ 901 et seq., as the applicable law with respect to death or disability resulting from injuries incurred in operations on the outer continental shelf related to natural resources. 43 U.S.C.

§ 1333(b). The U.S. Coast Guard also has the authority under the OCSLA to make and enforce regulations with respect to lights, warning devices, safety equipment, and other safety matters on artificial islands and installations. Id. at § 1333(d)(1). The Coast Guard must require, on all drilling and production operations begun after 1978, and wherever practicable regarding installations constructed earlier, the use of the best available and safest technologies that are economically feasible. Id. at § 1347(b). For the safety regulations promulgated by the Coast Guard, see 33 C.F.R. Parts 140–147. The OCSLA acknowledges the Department of Labor's authority to regulate labor conditions. 43 U.S.C. § 1347(d). However, where safety and health regulations overlap, and the Coast Guard first exercises its authority, the authority of the Department of Labor is displaced. Marshall v. Nichols, 486 F.Supp. 615 (D. Tex. 1980).

The Secretary of the Army has authority to prevent artificial islands, installations, or structures from obstructing navigation. 43 U.S.C. § 1333(e). For regulations establishing a 500–meter safety zone around artificial islands, installations, and structures, see 33 C.F.R. Part 147. For the regulation of navigation around artificial islands and similar installations, see id. at Part 67.

The Deepwater Port Act of 1974, 33 U.S.C. §§ 1501 et seq., establishes the legal framework for licensing the construction and operation of port facilities in waters beyond the boundaries of U.S. state jurisdiction (see Chapter 5, Section A) for facilitation of tanker and supertanker traffic. For regulations governing the issuance of construction licenses, pollution prevention, safety, navigation, operations, and enforcement, see 33 C.F.R. Parts 148–150. Subject to recognized principles of international law, safety zones may be established on a port-by-port basis. 33 U.S.C. § 1509(d). See, e.g., 33 C.F.R. 150.940, establishing safety zones for specific deepwater ports. The Deepwater Port Act does not apply to ports constructed in connection with offshore drilling platforms and used exclusively for storage and shipment of oil or gas produced there. Get Oil Out! Inc. v. Exxon Corp., 586 F.2d 726 (9th Cir. 1978). For discussion of U.S. offshore oil and gas regulation, see Chapter 10, Section H.

Except in a situation involving force majeure, a foreign flag vessel may not utilize a deepwater port unless its flag state has recognized the jurisdiction of the United States over the vessel and its personnel while at the deepwater port and while in any authorized safety zones. 33 U.S.C. § 1518(c). See, e.g., 1979 United States–United Kingdom Offshore Oil Ports Agreement.

CHAPTER 10

CONTINENTAL SHELF

A. INTRODUCTION

The continental shelf is the submerged offshore seabed and subsoil that constitutes the natural prolongation of a coastal state. The continental shelf has become a significant source of oil and gas production. Development projects are now located in water more than 8000 feet (2438.4 meters) deep, exploration wells have been drilled in over 10,000 feet (3048 meters) of water, and searches for oil and gas resources are being conducted beyond 200 miles offshore. See Sen. For. Rel. Comm., Hearings on the United Nations Convention on the Law of the Sea, 110th Cong., 1st Sess., Sen. Hrg. 110–592, at 135–136 (2007) (prepared statement of Paul L. Kelly, Consultant, Rowan Companies, Inc.; President, Gulf of Mexico Foundation). The continental shelf is also exploited for other mineral resources and sedentary fisheries.

This Chapter explains early developments respecting the continental shelf (Section B), the definition and outer limits of the continental shelf (Section C), and the roles of the Commission on the Limits of the Continental Shelf (Section D). Subsequent Sections concern the rights and duties of the coastal state over the continental shelf (Section E) and rules respecting sedentary fisheries (Section F) and marine scientific research (Section G). The Chapter concludes with a brief examination of U.S. practice and legislation concerning the continental shelf (Section H).

B. EARLY DEVELOPMENTS

Early concerns about the rights of states in the seabed and its subsoil related primarily to the exploitation of sedentary fisheries. In his pioneering article, Whose is the Bed of the Sea?, 4 Brit. Y.B. Intl. L. 34 (1923), Cecil Hurst, after surveying the practices of several states, concluded that a state could acquire rights of sovereignty in the seabed adjacent to it where the state effectively and continuously occupied the seabed for a long period. This occupation could be demonstrated through exclusive exploitation of sedentary species such as pearls, oysters, sponges, or coral. Rights of sovereignty in the seabed adjacent to a state could not conflict with the freedom of navigation of the superjacent waters nor with the common right of the public to fish nonsedentary species in the area.

In 1945 President Truman issued two proclamations, one pertaining to fisheries in the high seas contiguous to the territorial sea of the United States (see Chapter 9, Section B) and the second pertaining to the natural resources of the subsoil and seabed of the continental shelf adjacent to the United States. In his Continental Shelf Proclamation, President Truman stated that in view of the "long range worldwide need for new sources of petroleum and other minerals,"

> the Government of the United States regards the natural resources of the subsoil and sea bed of the continental shelf beneath the high seas but contiguous to the coasts of the United States as appertaining to the United States, subject to its jurisdiction and control.... The character as high seas of the waters above the continental shelf and the right to their free and unimpeded navigation are in no way thus affected.

Exec. Procl. 2667, 10 Fed. Reg. 12,303 (1945).

The International Court of Justice has acknowledged the Truman Proclamation as "the starting point of the positive law on the subject [of the continental shelf]." North Sea Continental Shelf Cases (Federal Republic of Germany/Denmark; Federal Republic of Germany/Netherlands), 1969 I.C.J. 3, 32–33. The Truman Proclamation did not actually claim sovereignty over the continental shelf, but only stated the U.S. policy regarding the natural resources of the subsoil and seabed of the continental shelf. Nevertheless, the Proclamation (and the companion U.S. fisheries proclamation) prompted numerous claims of sovereignty over the continental shelf, its seabed and subsoil, its superjacent waters, and, in some instances, the overlying air space. Many of these claims were made by Latin American states that border on the Pacific Ocean and that lack extensive physical continental shelves.

For discussion of these claims and the U.S. reaction to them, see Chapter 9, Section B.

In 1953, the United States enacted the Outer Continental Shelf Lands Act to regulate the exploration and exploitation of the continental shelf. 43 U.S.C. §§ 1331 et seq. See Section H. Other countries also enacted laws regulating activities on the continental shelf. See, e.g., Australia, Pearl Fisheries Act and Regulations of 1952–54, Supplement to Laws and Regulations on the Regime of the High Seas, UN Doc. ST/LEG./SER.B/8, 4, 8 (1959).

In 1958 the First United Nations Conference on the Law of the Sea, building on the preparatory work of the International Law Commission, concluded a Continental Shelf Convention. The Convention embodies the principle of sovereign rights of the coastal state over the continental shelf for the purpose of exploring its seabed and subsoil and exploiting its natural resources. 1958 Continental Shelf Convention, Article 2. These rights do not affect the legal status of the superjacent waters as high seas, and the exercise of these rights may not unjustifiably interfere with the exercise of the high seas freedoms by other states. Id. at Articles 3, 5(1). The LOS Convention incorporated these principles, which in some instances have been refined and expanded. In addition, the LOS Convention imposes some duties on the coastal state in favor of other states and the international community. LOS Convention, Articles 76–85. The rights and duties of coastal states relating to the continental shelf are discussed in Section E.

C. DEFINITION AND OUTER LIMITS

The term "continental shelf" apparently was first used in a physical sense in the late nineteenth century. The continental shelf is known, geologically and geomorphologically, as those submarine areas that extend from the shore to the point at which there is a marked fall-off (the continental slope) to the ocean floor of the deep seabed. Illustration 9 shows one typical formation of the continental margin, which comprises the continental shelf, the continental slope, and the continental rise (a build-up of sediment at the base of the slope). Nevertheless, there is considerable variation in the continental margin, with some margins exhibiting terraces, troughs, plateaux, and multiple slopes. See Philip A. Symonds et al., Characteristics of Continental Margins, in Continental Shelf Limits: The Scientific and Legal Interface 25 (Peter J. Cook & Chris M. Carleton eds., 2000).

Illustration 9:
Continental Shelf
and Margin

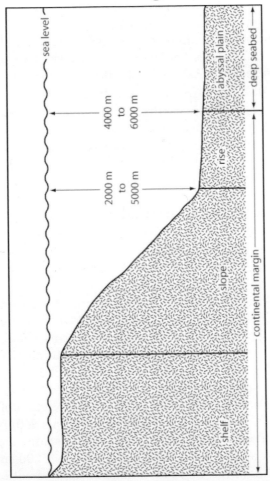

The average breadth of the physical continental shelf is about forty miles, but the breadth varies greatly in different parts of the world. Several Latin American states bordering the Pacific, for example, have narrow continental shelves that fall off very close to shore, while other states, such as the Latin American states bordering the Atlantic, have much wider continental shelves, extending for hundreds of miles.

The term "continental shelf" acquired legal significance after its use in the Truman Proclamation and in other similar decrees that various states issued shortly thereafter. The Proclamation did not define "continental shelf," but an accompanying press release stated that it was generally considered to be the subsoil and seabed of the submarine areas contiguous to the coasts of the United States and covered by no more than 100 fathoms (600 feet or 182.9 meters) of water. 13 Dept. St. Bull. 484 (1945).

Article 1 of the 1958 Continental Shelf Convention defines the continental shelf as "the seabed and subsoil of the submarine areas adjacent to the coast [including the coast of islands] but outside the area of the territorial sea, to a depth of 200 meters or, beyond that limit, to where the depth of the superjacent waters admits of the exploitation of the natural resources of the said areas." This definition, formulated after much study and debate, adopts two criteria. The first criterion, the 200–meter depth limit, is based on a general approximation of the point at which the continental shelf normally ends. In fact, the increase in slope marking the edge of the continental shelf is known to occur at less than 150 meters and more than 400 meters. The drafters of the 1958 Convention regarded the 200–meter depth limit as necessary to provide uniformity and certainty to the concept of the continental shelf. The second criterion, exploitability, assured the right of coastal states to exploit natural resources of the seabed beyond the 200–meter mark in the event that technology improved to permit such exploitation in the future. See Report of the International Law Commission, UN Doc. A/3159, 1956 2 Y.B. Intl. L. Commn. 253, 296–297; J.A.C. Gutteridge, The 1958 Geneva Continental Shelf Convention, 35 Brit. Y.B. Intl. L. 102 (1959).

The delegates to the Third United Nations Conference on the Law of the Sea (UNCLOS III) found the definition of continental shelf embodied in the 1958 Continental Shelf Convention to be unsatisfactory. Coastal states desired to extend their sovereignty over a wider belt of the continental shelf in view of technological advances making such areas exploitable. Yet the exploitability criterion of the 1958 definition was too imprecise and unclear. The 200–meter criterion was also unsatisfactory, since it was an overbroad generalization that did not relate to the concept of the continental shelf as an extension of the land mass of the coastal state. The delegates endorsed the International Court of Justice's holding in the North Sea Continental Shelf Cases (Federal Republic of Germany/Denmark; Federal Republic of Germany/Netherlands), 1969 I.C.J.

3, 31, that the continental shelf is a "natural prolongation" of the land mass of the adjacent coastal state and based the new definition of the continental shelf on that concept. The delegates also recognized that a new definition of the continental shelf would have to be compatible with the concept of a 200–mile exclusive economic zone. See generally the discussion in the Second Committee, 2 UNCLOS III, Off. Rec. 142–169, 171 (1974).

The LOS Convention expands the definition of the continental shelf to include "the seabed and subsoil of the submarine areas that extend beyond its territorial sea throughout the natural prolongation of its land territory to the outer edge of the continental margin, or to a distance of 200 nautical miles from the baselines from which the breadth of the territorial sea is measured where the outer edge of the continental margin does not extend up to that distance." Article 76(1). Where the outer edge of the continental margin (which term includes not only the shelf, but the slope and rise) extends beyond 200 miles, the coastal state may determine the outer limit of its continental shelf by using either (1) a line drawn by reference to points no more than sixty nautical miles from the foot of the slope, or (2) a line drawn by reference to points at which the thickness of sediments is at least one percent of the shortest distance to the foot of the continental slope. Id. at Article 76(4). This set of alternative limits is known as the "Irish formula." The continental margin "does not include the deep ocean floor with its oceanic ridges or the subsoil thereof." Id. at Article 76(3). In addition, in no event may the outer limits of the shelf exceed 350 nautical miles from the baseline of the territorial sea or 100 nautical miles from the 2500–meter isobath (a line every point of which is on the seabed at a depth of 2500 meters below the water surface). Id. at Article 76(5). Illustration 10 refers to these two alternative limits as "cutoff." The Soviet Union originally proposed a 300-mile cutoff to the continental shelf, but its proposal was modified by UNCLOS III negotiators to extend to 350 nautical miles (referred to as the "Russian formula" in Illustration 10). Bernard H. Oxman, The Third United Nations Conference on the Law of the Sea: The Eighth Session (1979), 24 Am. J. Intl. L. 1, 19–22 (1980). On "submarine ridges," other than "submarine elevations that are natural components of the continental margin, such as its plateaux, rises, caps, banks and spurs," only the 350–mile limit applies. Id. at Article 76(6). See Second Report of the Committee on Legal Issues of the Outer Continental Shelf, in Intl. L. Assn., Report of the Seventy–Second Conference, Toronto 215 (2006). According to one study, twenty-nine different areas, involving fifty-six different coastal states, have legal continental shelves extending beyond 200 nautical miles from baselines. Victor Prescott, National Rights to Hydrocarbon Resources of the Continental Margin Beyond 200 Nautical Miles, in Boundaries and Energy: Problems and Prospects 51, 55–61 (Gerald Blake et al. eds., 1998). Illustration 10 shows the complex outer limits of the legal continental shelf.

Illustration 10:
Diagram of Article 76*

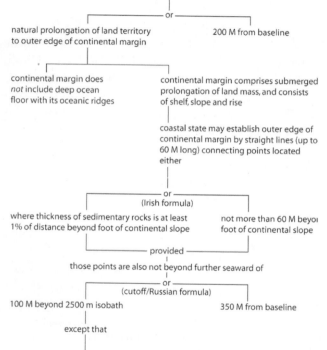

Limit of continental shelf may not
extend beyond further seaward of either

— or —

natural prolongation of land territory
to outer edge of continental margin

200 M from baseline

continental margin does
not include deep ocean
floor with its oceanic ridges

continental margin comprises submerged
prolongation of land mass, and consists
of shelf, slope and rise

coastal state may establish outer edge of
continental margin by straight lines (up to
60 M long) connecting points located
either

— or —
(Irish formula)

where thickness of sedimentary rocks is at least
1% of distance beyond foot of continental slope

not more than 60 M beyor
foot of continental slope

— provided —

those points are also not beyond further seaward of

— or —
(cutoff/Russian formula)

100 M beyond 2500 m isobath

350 M from baseline

except that

only the 350 M cutoff may be applied on submarine ridges if those ridges are not
submarine elevations that are natural components of continental margin such as
its plateaux, rises, caps, banks and spurs

* Modified from Bernard H. Oxman, The Third United Nations
Conference on the Law of the Sea: The Ninth Session (1980), 75
Am. J. Intl. L. 211, 229 (1981). Used with permission of the
American Society of International Law.

As defined by the LOS Convention, and as now accepted in customary international law, there are in effect two legal conceptions of the continental shelf. The first corresponds generally to the geological and geomorphological concept of the continental margin and extends to the outer edge of the continental margin, albeit with cut-offs that in some circumstances may leave the legal continental shelf short of its full geological or geomorphological extent. The second corresponds with the coastal state's 200–mile exclusive economic zone (EEZ) where the coastal state's geological and geomorphological continental shelf does not extend that far. In both cases, the legal continental shelf begins where the territorial sea ends.

Since the coastal state's jurisdiction in its EEZ includes rights to the resources of the underlying seabed and subsoil, the doctrine of the continental shelf grants important additional rights in those areas of the legal continental shelf that extend beyond 200 nautical miles. However, even within the EEZ, the doctrine of the continental shelf grants some additional rights to the coastal state. For example, in contrast to its rights relating to EEZ fisheries (see Chapter 9, Section C), the coastal state is not required to share with other states any surplus of the natural resources of the continental shelf, including sedentary fisheries. See Sections E and F.

Where the coastal state does have a continental shelf extending beyond 200 nautical miles, its rights and duties in that area vary in some important respects from its rights and duties on the continental shelf within the 200–mile zone. For example, see Section E, relating to exploitation of nonliving resources beyond 200 miles by parties to the LOS Convention, and Section G, relating to marine scientific research.

Before examining in more detail the coastal state's rights and duties in its continental shelf, however, we consider the work of the Commission on the Limits of the Continental Shelf, a body established by the LOS Convention. The Commission exercises an important procedural role with respect to a state's establishment of final and binding outer limits of its continental shelf.

D. THE COMMISSION ON THE LIMITS OF THE CONTINENTAL SHELF

The Commission on the Limits of the Continental Shelf (CLCS) is established pursuant to Article 76(8) and Annex II of the LOS Convention. Its twenty-one members are experts in geology, geophysics, or hydrography. Parties to the LOS Convention elect the Commission members for five-year terms "from among their nationals, having due regard to the need to ensure equitable geographical representation," but the members serve in their personal capacities. LOS Convention, Annex II, Article 2(1). The first election took place in March 1997.

One function of the CLCS is to consider information that coastal states are required to submit concerning the outer limits of the continental shelf beyond 200 nautical miles from baselines, and to make recommendations related to those limits. LOS Convention, Article 76(8); Annex II, Article 3(1)(a). Although each coastal state establishes its own continental shelf limits, only limits set "on the basis of" CLCS recommendations are "final and binding." Id. at Article 76(8); Annex II, Article 7. The CLCS is to make recommendations "in accordance with article 76" and a 1980 Statement of Understanding intended to apply to the Bay of Bengal. Id. at Annex II, Article 3(1)(a). The CLCS in essence is intended to act "as a watchdog," P.R.R. Gardiner, Reasons and Methods for Fixing the Outer Limit of the Legal Continental Shelf Beyond 200 Nautical Miles, 11–12 Rev. iranienne des relations internationales 145, 161 (1978), or as a " 'canary in the mineshaft' respecting exaggerated continental shelf outer limit claims." Ted L. McDorman, The Role of the Commission on the Limits of the Continental Shelf: A Technical Body in a Political World, 17 Intl. J. Marine & Coastal L. 301, 324 (2002).

A second CLCS function is to provide technical and scientific advice, should a coastal state request it, to help the state prepare for its submission. LOS Convention, Annex II, Article 3(1)(b). The CLCS has organized training courses and seminars to advise states about their submissions. A voluntary trust fund also provides some resources to assist developing states in preparing their submissions. See GA Res. 55/7, Annex II, UN Doc. A/RES/55/7 (2000); GA Res. 58/240, Annex, UN Doc. A/RES/58/240 (2003).

According to Annex II, Article 4 of the LOS Convention, each state intending to establish limits of the continental shelf beyond 200 nautical miles from baselines must submit proposed limits and supporting data to the CLCS no later than ten years after the date of entry into force of the LOS Convention for that state. For states that had accepted the Convention before it entered into force in 1994, this ten-year period expired on November 16, 2004. However, in light of the difficulties developing states were experiencing in preparing their submissions, the parties to the LOS Convention decided, at their 2001 annual meeting, that "it is understood that the ten-year period ... shall have been taken to have commenced on 13 May 1999," which was the date on which the CLCS adopted its Scientific and Technical Guidelines. SPLOS/72 (2001). In June 2008 the parties to the LOS Convention, noting the Commission's heavy workload and the financial and technical challenges faced by developing states, decided that any state could satisfy the new deadline if it filed preliminary information indicating the outer limits of the continental shelf and described when it intended to make its formal submission to the CLCS. SPLOS/183 (2008).

The CLCS received its first submission from Russia in 2001, followed by Brazil (2004), Australia (2004), Ireland (2005), New Zealand (2006), and Norway (2006), as well as a joint submission from France, Ireland, Spain, and the United Kingdom concerning the Celtic Sea and the Bay of Biscay (2006). As of June 1, 2009—shortly after the extended ten-year period expired—the CLCS had received fifty-one submissions and partial submissions and an additional forty-two preliminary information filings. See http://www.un.org/Depts/los/clcs_new/ commission_submissions.htm; http://www.un.org/ Depts/los/clcs_new/commission_preliminary.htm. The CLCS had adopted eight recommendations as of June 1, 2009. See http://www.un.org/Depts/clcs_ new/commission_recommendations.htm.

Whether a non-party to the LOS Convention may make a submission to the CLCS, seeking to obtain a recommendation that the non-party could then rely on to set a generally recognized, final, and binding continental shelf outer limit, has been a disputed question, but as of June 1, 2009 only states parties to the Convention had made submissions.

Should a coastal state disagree with the recommendations of the CLCS, that state "shall, within a reasonable time, make a revised or new submission to the Commission." LOS Convention, Annex II, Article 8. In the case of Russia's 2001 submission concerning the continental shelf under the Arctic Ocean, for example, the CLCS recommended that Russia make certain revisions. See UN Doc. A/57/57/Add.1, ¶¶ 38–41 (2002). The LOS Convention does not provide a formal dispute settlement mechanism for resolving a disagreement between a state and the CLCS over the content of CLCS recommendations. In the event of an interstate dispute concerning the outer limit of a coastal state's continental shelf, however, the dispute settlement provisions of the Convention would apply. See Chapter 15.

In reviewing a coastal state's continental shelf outer limits, another state may find it difficult or impossible to learn all the underlying data that the CLCS used to make its recommendations and that the coastal state relied on to establish its outer limits. The Commission, sensitive to the need to maintain the confidentiality of information submitted to it, conducts much of its work behind closed doors. The CLCS's evaluation of a coastal state's data is undertaken by a seven-person subcommission whose deliberations are closed except to representatives of the submitting state. Coastal states are required to publish an executive summary of their submissions, however, and the CLCS subcommission also publishes an executive summary of its recommendations. Rules of Procedure of the Commission on the Limits of the Continental Shelf, CLCS/40/Rev.1, Annex III, ¶ 11(3) (2008). Some coastal states also may, in the interest of transparency, disclose the data justifying their outer limits. See Ron McNab, The Case for Transparency in the Delimitation of the Outer Continental Shelf, 35 Ocean Dev. & Intl. L. 1 (2004); Alex G. Oude Elferink, "Openness" and Article 76 of the Law of the Sea Convention: The Process Does Not Need to Be Adjusted, 40 Ocean Dev. & Intl. L. 36 (2009).

After a coastal state receives the CLCS's recommendations and sets the outer limits of its continental shelf, the state must "deposit with the Secretary–General of the United Nations charts and relevant information, including geodetic data, permanently describing the outer limits of its continental shelf." The Secretary–General must in turn publicize this information. LOS Convention, Article 76(9).

Approximately three-fourths of the situations in which the legal continental shelf extends beyond 200 nautical miles from baselines involve situations requiring maritime boundary delimitations among adjacent or opposite states. See Chapter 6. The actions of the CLCS cannot "prejudice matters relating to delimitation of boundaries between states with opposite or adjacent coasts." LOS Convention, Annex II, Article 9; see LOS Convention, Article 76(10). The CLCS has determined that it will not consider state submissions if they implicate a land or maritime dispute, although the Commission may do so if all states that are parties to such a dispute consent. Rules of Procedure of the Commission on the Limits of the Continental Shelf, CLCS/40/Rev.1, Annex I, ¶ 5(a) (2008). The CLCS could make its recommendations in situations involving disputed boundaries if all states concerned with an area of the continental shelf jointly made a submission. Five of the fifty-one submissions the CLCS had received as of June 1, 2009 were joint submissions. The states making a joint submission could then settle any disputed boundaries later, while the CLCS is considering the submitted data or even after the CLCS has made its recommendations concerning an outer limit. Alternatively, a state may make a partial submission, saving for a later date the submission of data concerning an area in which maritime boundaries are disputed. See Donald R. Rothwell, Issues and Strategies for Outer Continental Shelf Claims, 23 Intl. J. Marine & Coastal L. 185, 202–209 (2008).

One controversial question has been whether states may set outer limits to the continental shelf off the continent of Antarctica. Article IV(2) of the 1959 Antarctic Treaty, which prohibits any "new claim, or enlargement of an existing claim, to territorial sovereignty in Antarctica," raises concerns about any effort to set continental shelf limits off Antarctica. The CLCS has "decided not to consider the part of [Australia's] submission" that concerns Antarctica. CLCS/44, ¶ 23 (2005). See Alex G. Oude Elferink, The Continental Shelf of Antarctica: Implications of the Requirement to Make a Submission to the CLCS under Article 76 of the LOS Convention, 17 Intl. J. Marine & Coastal L. 485 (2002).

The CLCS must independently consider a large volume of complex technical data submitted by coastal states. Yet, in addition to the challenges associated with considering this data expertly and expeditiously, the CLCS must inevitably construe Article 76 of the LOS Convention. Some interpretations are sensitive. For example, the terms "oceanic ridge" and "submarine ridge" are not defined in the LOS Convention, but, as noted in Section C, the terms carry legal significance. An "oceanic ridge" is not part of the continental margin at all, and on a "submarine ridge" the maximum outer limit of the continental shelf is 350 miles. The CLCS has indicated that it will examine the issue of ridges, which arise from a variety of geological processes, "on a case-by-case basis," taking into account such factors as "natural prolongation of land territory and land mass, morphology of ridges and their relation to the continental margin ..., and continuity of ridges." Scientific and Technical Guidelines of the Commission on the Limits of the Continental Shelf, CLCS/ 11, ¶¶ 7.2.10–7.2.11 (1999). For discussion of the ridges issue, see Robert W. Smith & George Taft, Legal Aspects of the Continental Shelf, in Continental Shelf Limits 17 (Peter J. Cook & Chris M. Carleton eds., 2000); Second Report of the Committee on Legal Issues of the Outer Continental Shelf, in Intl. L. Assn., Report of the Seventy–Second Conference, Toronto 215, 219–222 (2006).

E. RIGHTS AND DUTIES OF THE COASTAL STATE OVER THE CONTINENTAL SHELF

The coastal state has sovereign rights over the continental shelf for the purpose of exploring it and exploiting its natural resources. The rights of the coastal state do not depend on actual exploration, exploitation, or other assertion of the rights. In the event the coastal state does not exercise its rights, no one else may explore or exploit its continental shelf without the express consent of the coastal state. LOS Convention, Articles 77, 81; 1958 Continental Shelf Convention, Article 2. See United States v. Ray, 423 F.2d 16 (5th Cir. 1970) (consent of the United States required to construct man-made island on coral reefs located on the U.S. continental shelf).

The coastal state does not have sovereign rights over the continental shelf for purposes other than the exploration or exploitation of its natural resources. Treasure Salvors, Inc. v. Unidentified Wrecked and Abandoned Sailing Vessel, 569 F.2d 330 (5th Cir. 1978) (U.S. jurisdiction under the Outer Continental Shelf Lands Act as modified by the 1958 Continental Shelf Convention does not extend to nonresource-related material in the shelf area and does not cover objects such as wrecked ships and their cargoes lying on or under the seabed). For consideration of the law of salvage and finds and other law applicable to wrecked ships and underwater cultural heritage, see Chapter 8, Section I.

Natural resources include the mineral and other nonliving resources of the seabed and subsoil, along with sedentary fisheries (organisms that are, at the harvestable stage, either immobile on or under the seabed or unable to move except in constant physical contact with the seabed or the subsoil). LOS Convention, Article 77(4); 1958 Continental Shelf Convention, Article 2(4). See Section F regarding sedentary fisheries. The U.S. Submerged Lands Act of 1953 defines "natural resources" to include, "without limiting the generality thereof, oil, gas, and all other minerals, and fish, shrimp, oysters, clams, crabs, lobsters, sponges, kelp, and other marine animal and plant life;" the term "does not include water power, or the use of water for the production of power." 43 U.S.C. § 1301(e). In United States v. Ray, 423 F.2d 16, 21–22 (5th Cir. 1970), the court held that coral reefs and their coral and pescatorial inhabitants are "natural resources" as defined by the Act and the 1958 Continental Shelf Convention.

The rights of the coastal state over the continental shelf do not affect the legal status of the superjacent waters and airspace. In exercising its rights, the coastal state may not infringe on or unjustifiably interfere with navigation and the other high seas freedoms of overflight, fishing, laying submarine cables and pipelines, and conducting scientific research. LOS Convention, Articles 78, 87; 1958 Continental Shelf Convention, Articles 3, 5(1). The coastal state may, however, take reasonable measures to prevent and control pollution from pipelines, and the delineation of the course of a pipeline (but not a submarine cable) is subject to the coastal state's consent. Cables or pipelines constructed for exploitation or exploration of the natural resources of the continental shelf or for use in artificial islands, installations, and structures on the continental shelf or in the EEZ are subject to the coastal state's jurisdiction, as are cables or pipelines that enter the coastal state's territorial sea. LOS Convention, Article 79.

Without the coastal state's consent, other states may not drill on the continental shelf for any purpose, including the exercise of high seas freedoms such as scientific research. Id. at Article 81.

Article 60 of the LOS Convention governing artificial islands, installations, and structures in the EEZ applies mutatis mutandis to artificial islands, installations, and structures on the continental shelf. See Chapter 9, Section K.

The LOS Convention imposes certain obligations on parties to the Convention with regard to the exploitation of the nonliving resources of the continental shelf beyond 200 miles from the baseline from which the territorial sea is measured. The coastal state (except for certain developing states) must make payments or contributions in kind annually after the first five years of production occurring at a site beyond the 200–mile zone. In the sixth year, the coastal state shall pay one percent of the value or volume of production at the site, which rate increases each year until it reaches seven percent. The graduated rate structure is intended to permit the coastal state to recoup start-up costs before having to make the payments or contributions. The term "production" does not include resources used in connection with the exploitation. LOS Convention, Article 82. The Article 82 payments or contributions in kind shall be made "through" the International Seabed Authority (ISA) established to regulate and govern deep seabed mining. For discussion of the ISA and the regime governing nonliving resources beyond the limits of national jurisdiction, see Chapter 11. The ISA will distribute the Article 82 payments or contributions to states that are parties to the LOS Convention on an equitable sharing basis, taking into account the interests and needs of developing states, particularly the least developed states and land-locked states.

The obligation to make payments or contributions in kind was the result of a negotiating compromise during the Third United Nations Conference on the Law of the Sea. The expansion of continental shelves to include the seabed and subsoil beyond 200 miles from baselines meant fewer seabed mineral resources would be subject to the deep seabed mining regime of the LOS Convention, and, as discussed in Chapter 11, that regime provided for some equitable sharing of benefits with developing states. See Michael W. Lodge, The International Seabed Authority and Article 82 of the UN Convention on the Law of the Sea, 21 Intl. J. Marine & Coastal L. 323 (2006). The United States has taken the position that the Article 82 regime is not binding on states not parties to the LOS Convention. See 1976 Digest of U.S. Practice in International Law 345.

F. SEDENTARY FISHERIES

The coastal state has sovereign rights over the sedentary fisheries of its continental shelf. LOS Convention, Article 77; 1958 Continental Shelf Convention, Article 2(4). In contrast to its obligations within the EEZ (see Chapter 9, Section C), the coastal state is not required to manage and conserve its sedentary fisheries to provide for an "optimum yield," nor must the coastal state grant access to any portion of its sedentary fisheries to other states. LOS Convention, Article 68.

At the First United Nations Conference on the Law of the Sea, the drafting of a definition of "continental shelf resources" was highly controversial. Marjorie M. Whiteman, 4 Digest of International Law 856–864 (1965). As finally drafted, it was not clear whether certain species of crustacea and other organisms fell within the definition. See S.V. Scott, The Inclusion of Sedentary Fisheries Within the Continental Shelf Doctrine, 41 Intl. & Comp. L.Q. 788 (1992). In 1960 the U.S. Department of State stated that "clams, oysters, abalone, etc. are included in the definition, whereas shrimp, lobsters, and finny fish are not." Sen. For. Rel. Comm., Hearings on the Law of the Sea Conventions, 86th Cong., 2d Sess., 82, 88 (1960). But see the 1953 Submerged Lands Act definition of "natural resources" noted in Section E, which includes shrimp and lobster. In 1964 Congress enacted the Bartlett Act, Pub. L. No. 88–308, 78 Stat. 194 (1964) (superseded in 1976 by the Fishery Conservation and Management Act), which prohibited foreign vessels from taking "any Continental Shelf fishery resource." Japan protested the inclusion of Alaskan king crabs within the definition, asserting that they are a high seas fishery resource. Marjorie M. Whiteman, 4 Digest of International Law 864–865 (1965). Similarly, France objected to Brazil's assertion of jurisdiction over lobsters, id. at 864, and various states have made other protests regarding a coastal state's exercise of jurisdiction over allegedly sedentary species. Generally, the coastal state has prevailed.

The Fishery Conservation and Management Act of 1976, as amended, 16 U.S.C. §§ 1801 et seq., governs the conservation and management of sedentary fisheries located on the U.S. continental shelf. The term "continental shelf" has not yet been amended to reflect the definition in the LOS Convention, but reiterates the 1958 Continental Shelf Convention definition. Id. at § 1802(6). The term "Continental Shelf fishery resources" is defined to include several species of coral, crustacea (including crabs and lobster), abalone, conch, clams, quahog, and sponges. Id. at § 1802(7). The Secretary of Commerce is authorized to include other species within the term by regulation. Id.

G. MARINE SCIENTIFIC RESEARCH ON THE CONTINENTAL SHELF

The provisions of the LOS Convention governing marine scientific research in the EEZ apply to such research on the continental shelf. LOS Convention, Articles 246–255. See Chapter 9, Section J. However, beyond 200 nautical miles, the coastal state may not exercise its discretion to withhold consent on the basis that a proposed research project has direct significance for the exploration or exploitation of natural resources, if research is to be conducted in areas other than those in which the coastal state has begun exploitation or detailed exploratory operations or in which it will begin such operations within a reasonable period of time. Id. at Article 246(6).

H. U.S. PRACTICE AND LEGISLATION RELATING TO THE CONTINENTAL SHELF

After issuance of the Truman Proclamation, disputes arose among states of the United States and the federal government over the rights of each in the natural resources of the continental shelf. Many U.S. states enacted legislation establishing a regulatory system for the leasing, exploration, and exploitation of the natural resources of the continental shelf in the territorial sea adjacent to their coasts. The United States instituted several actions to enjoin the states from implementing these regulatory schemes, and to claim ownership of the natural resources of the continental shelf in these areas. In 1947, the U.S. Supreme Court held that the United States was "possessed of paramount rights in, and full dominion and power over, the lands, minerals and other things" underlying the waters seaward of the low-water mark and outside of the inland waters of the coastal states, and that the coastal states had "no title thereto or property interest therein." United States v. California, 332 U.S. 19 (1947), and Decree, 332 U.S. 804, 805 (1947). The principle of federal sovereignty over the natural resources of the continental shelf was applied again in United States v. Louisiana, 339 U.S. 699 (1950), and Decree, 340 U.S. 899 (1950), and in United States v. Texas, 339 U.S. 707 (1950), and Decree, 340 U.S. 900 (1950).

In 1953, Congress enacted the Outer Continental Shelf Lands Act (OCSLA), which established a regulatory system for the leasing, exploration, and exploitation of the nonliving resources of the continental shelf beyond three miles (or nine miles in certain historic cases) from the baseline from which the territorial sea is measured. 43 U.S.C. §§ 1331 et seq. The Act is to be construed so that "the character of the waters above the outer Continental Shelf as high seas and the right to navigation and fishing therein shall not be affected." Id. at § 1332(2). The simultaneously enacted Submerged Lands Act relinquished all rights, title, and interest of the United States in the continental shelf and its resources within three miles of the baseline (or within nine miles in certain historic cases) to the adjacent states. Id. at §§ 1301 et seq. The United States reserved its powers of regulation and control in those areas for purposes of commerce, navigation, national defense, and international affairs, and specifically reserved its rights in and title to the continental shelf seaward of the conceded areas. Id. at § 1314(a). The OCSLA defines the "outer Continental Shelf" as the subsoil and seabed seaward of the conceded areas that "appertain" to the United States and are "subject to its jurisdiction and control." Id. at § 1311(a). The OCSLA has not been amended to incorporate the definition of "continental shelf" as set forth in either Article 1 of the 1958 Continental Shelf Convention or Article 76 of the LOS Convention.

In United States v. Louisiana, 363 U.S. 1 (1960), and United States v. Florida, 363 U.S. 121 (1960), the Supreme Court found that, based on historic circumstances, the relevant boundary for Texas and the Gulf side of Florida for purposes of the Submerged Lands Act extended to nine miles beyond the baseline. The other states were entitled only to those lands, minerals, and other natural resources underlying the Gulf to a distance from the baseline of three "geographical miles" (which the Court, see 363 U.S. at 9 n.6, equated to nautical miles). See also Chapter 5, Section A.

In its originally enacted form, the OCSLA established very general guidelines and directives for the Secretary of the Interior in managing the resources of the "outer Continental Shelf" (the continental shelf beyond the areas conceded to the states) and in leasing tracts for oil, gas, and other mineral exploration and development. The increased need for exploration and exploitation of continental shelf resources resulting from the oil shortage of the 1970s produced dissatisfaction, primarily from the states and environmental groups, with the over-general directives of the OCSLA. The OCSLA was amended in 1978 to establish a comprehensive national policy for continental shelf exploration and exploitation, to revise the federal leasing system, to provide coastal states with an increased role in federal exploration and exploitation decisions on the continental shelf beyond state boundaries, to provide for safety standards on off-shore installations and other exploration and exploitation operations, to enhance environmental protection, and to establish an oil spill liability fund. Congress subsequently repealed the oil spill liability provision in 1990 when it enacted the Oil Pollution Act. See Chapter 12, Section J. For a detailed discussion of the 1978 amendments, see G. Kevin Jones, The Legal Framework for Energy Development on the Outer Continental Shelf, 10 UCLA–Alaska L. Rev. 143 (1981).

The Secretary of the Interior may grant oil and gas leases on the outer continental shelf, and the OCSLA, as amended, sets out several alternative methods for awarding leases. 43 U.S.C. § 1337(a)(1). The most typical method involves payments of bonus bids (up-front cash payments to secure a lease), annual rents on the leases that are granted (payable until production begins), and royalties on production. The 1995 Deep Water Royalty Relief Act authorized reduced royalty payments for certain deep water areas in the Gulf of Mexico, in an effort to promote development and increase production. Id. at § 1337(a)(3)(B)–(C). Additional drilling incentives and other efforts to encourage production were enacted in the Energy Policy Act of 2005, Pub. L. No. 109–58, Title III, 119 Stat. 594, 683 (2005); see 43 U.S.C. § 1337(p)(3), and the Gulf of Mexico Energy Security Act of 2006, Pub. L. No. 109–432, Div. C, Title 1, 120 Stat. 2922, 3000 (2006). Federal revenues from offshore leases have been significant, ranging during the period 1997–2006 from a low of US$3.2 billion in 1999 to a high of US$7.6 billion in 2006. See Marc Humphries,

Outer Continental Shelf: Debate Over Oil and Gas Leasing and Revenue Sharing, CRS Report for Congress 6 (RL33493, updated Oct. 27, 2008). A portion of oil and gas revenues is distributed to U.S. coastal states. See id. at 6–9; 43 U.S.C. §§ 1337(g), 1356a.

The OCSLA oil and gas leasing and development program, which is administered by the Minerals Management Service (MMS) of the Department of the Interior (see http://www.mms.gov), proceeds through five stages: development of a leasing plan; lease sales; exploration; development; and decommissioning of structures. In the first stage, the MMS prepares and periodically revises an oil and gas leasing plan, comprising five-year schedules of proposed lease sales. 43 U.S.C. § 1344(a). The goal for the timing and location of leasing is to obtain, "to the maximum extent practicable, . . . a proper balance between the potential for environmental damage, the potential for the discovery of oil and gas, and the potential for adverse impact on the coastal zone." Id. at § 1344(a)(3). Environmental studies must be prepared for each area included in any oil and gas lease sale and must be submitted for public review. Id. at § 1346. To ensure that the MMS takes into account all relevant policy considerations, the 1978 amendments provided for participation by affected state and local governments, relevant federal agencies, and the public. Id. at § 1344. When Alaska and California challenged the 1980–1985 oil and gas lease plan prepared by the Secretary of the Interior, the court found much of the Secretary's program free from fault, but held that he erred in several regards, including a failure "to strike a proper balance incorporating environmental and coastal zone factors and not simply administrative need and economic factors such as potential oil and gas recovery." California v. Watt, 668 F.2d 1290, 1325 (D.C. Cir. 1981). A revised plan for 1982–1987 was upheld; it set forth a leasing program that would offer, in forty-one oil and gas lease sales, almost all of the one billion acres comprising the U.S. outer continental shelf. California v. Watt, 712 F.2d 584 (D.C. Cir. 1983).

The second stage in the OCSLA leasing and development program typically consists of a competitive bidding process leading to lease sales. This stage also follows environmental studies conducted in cooperation with affected states. Beginning in the 1980s environmental and tourist industry concerns prompted leasing moratoria for most of the U.S. outer continental shelf. During this period, leasing has been allowed only off parts of Alaska and in the Gulf of Mexico (except near Florida). The 2000 United States–Mexico Continental Shelf Delimitation Treaty set the U.S.-Mexican boundary of the continental shelf in the Western Gap of the Gulf of Mexico, allowing the United States to offer additional deep-water lease sales. Both the Consolidated Security, Disaster Assistance, and Continuing Appropriations Act for 2009, Pub. L. No. 109–432, enacted September 30, 2008, and the Omnibus Appropriations Act of Pub. L. No. 111–8, enacted March 11, 2009, omitted language, contained in previous appropriations acts, providing for outer continental shelf moratoria off the Atlantic and Pacific coasts. The 2008 and 2009 enactments opened the possibility of leases and eventual oil and gas development in those offshore areas.

Following a lease sale, in the third stage of the OCSLA program, lessees may submit a proposed exploration plan, along with an environmental report and an oil spill response plan. 43 U.S.C. § 1340(c); 30 C.F.R. §§ 250.219, 250.227. Should the MMS approve the exploration plan (which it may do with or without modifications), it will issue an exploration permit. Fourth, if the lessee discovers oil or gas, it may submit a detailed development and production plan, again accompanied by an environmental report and oil spill response plan. 43 U.S.C. § 1351(a), (c); 30 C.F.R. §§ 250.250, 250.261. In order for the production and development plan to be approved, it must comply with applicable laws, including the coastal management program of an affected state, and it must not threaten national security or pose serious harm to life (including fish and other aquatic life), property, or the environment. 43 U.S.C. § 1351(d), (h). Fifth, following production and termination of a lease, decommissioning obligations, including the removal of structures, must be met. 30 C.F.R. Part 250, Subpart Q. Throughout operations on the continental shelf, the MMS exercises comprehensive regulatory authority concerning "air emissions, effluent discharges, archaeological resources, Endangered Species Act fauna and flora, Marine Mammal Protection Act mammals, shut down and emergen-

cy evacuation procedures, drilling fluid requirements, pollution control, blow-out preventers, production safety, production rates, safety training for
personnel, and a myriad of other specific requirements." Milo C. Mason, Offshore Energy Development, in Ocean and Coastal Law and Policy 409,
419 (Donald C. Baur, Tim Eichenberg & Michael
Sutton eds., 2008) (footnotes omitted).

In addition to the OCSLA, other federal statutes
may apply to U.S. outer continental shelf oil and
gas leasing and development. An environmental impact statement may be required at various stages of
the process, pursuant to the National Environmental Policy Act. 42 U.S.C. § 4332. See, e.g., Natural
Resources Def. Council, Inc. v. Morton, 458 F.2d
827 (D.C. Cir. 1972) (environmental impact statement relating to oil and gas lease sale off the coast
of Louisiana was inadequate due to failure to discuss the environmental risks incident to alternative
energy sources). Some challenges to lease sales have
invoked the Endangered Species Act, which is designed to protect the continued existence and habitat of endangered species and to preclude federal
agency actions that make "any irreversible or irre-
trievable commitment of resources" that would
foreclose reasonable alternative measures. 16 U.S.C.
§ 1536(a)(2), (d). See, e.g., Tribal Village of Akutan
v. Hodel, 869 F.2d 1185 (9th Cir. 1988) (upholding
lease sales despite Department of Interior's failure
to adopt alternatives proposed by National Marine
Fisheries Service intended to protect endangered
gray whales from oil spill risks). When California

invoked the Coastal Zone Management Act (CZMA), 16 U.S.C. §§ 1451 et seq., seeking a showing that lease sales had to be consistent with the state's coastal zone management program, the U.S. Supreme Court held that lease sales on the outer continental shelf were not activities "directly affecting" the coastal zone and therefore need not be shown to be consistent with a state's management plan. Secretary of Interior v. California, 464 U.S. 312 (1984). Pursuant to 1990 amendments, the CZMA now indicates that lease sales must, "to the maximum extent practicable," be consistent with state coastal management programs. 16 U.S.C. § 1456(c)(1)(A); see California v. Norton, 311 F.3d 1162 (9th Cir. 2002). See also Amoco Prod. Co. v. Village of Gambell, 480 U.S. 531 (1987) (Alaska National Interest Lands Conservation Act, 16 U.S.C. § 3120, which requires federal agencies to consider the effects of using public lands on the subsistence uses and needs of indigenous peoples, does not apply to activities on the outer continental shelf).

The OCSLA also provides for U.S. jurisdiction over other hard mineral resources. The Act contains provisions governing sulphur rights, e.g., 43 U.S.C. §§ 1335(b), 1337(h)–(i), and refers to the extraction of sand, gravel, and shell resources (which may be arranged by a negotiated contract rather than competitive bidding, if the resources are used for shore protection, beach or wetlands restoration projects, or federally funded construction projects). Id. at § 1337(k)(2). With respect to other minerals, the

OCSLA, in general language, gives the Secretary of the Interior the right to grant "on a basis of competitive bidding leases of any mineral other than oil, gas, and sulphur." Id. at § 1337(k)(1). The MMS has issued regulations to govern prospecting, leasing, and exploitation of other minerals. 30 C.F.R. Parts 280–282.

For discussion of the use of structures on the U.S. continental shelf to produce wind, see Chapter 9, Section I. For discussion of the laws applicable to activities on offshore U.S. structures, see Chapter 9, Section K.

CHAPTER 11

THE DEEP SEABED AND ITS MINERAL RESOURCES

A. INTRODUCTION

The main focus of international law concerning the "Area" (defined in Article 1(1) of the LOS Convention as "the seabed and ocean floor and subsoil thereof, beyond the limits of national jurisdiction") has been nonliving resources. Section B surveys early legal developments respecting the deep seabed and its mineral resources. Section C describes the 1982 LOS Convention's seabed mining regime, along with U.S. objections to it. Section D discusses efforts to modify or replace the LOS Convention provisions, and Section E then sets out the current international seabed mining regime. As of June 1, 2009, no commercial exploitation of deep seabed minerals had yet occurred.

Uses of the Area for purposes other than the exploration and exploitation of its mineral resources include marine scientific research (Section F) and the recovery of genetic materials from organisms at hydrothermal vents (Section G). Section H briefly reviews the legal status of other human activity on the deep seabed, including the laying of pipelines and cables, bottom trawling, and the recovery of objects of historical and archaeological significance.

B. EARLY DEVELOPMENTS

While the doctrine of the continental shelf emerged in the mid-twentieth century and was recognized at the First United Nations Conference of the Law of the Sea (see Chapter 10), the general belief that the exploration and exploitation of the seabed and subsoil beyond national jurisdiction would not be technologically possible in the near future precluded serious consideration of the issue at that time. See The Régime of the High Seas and Régime of the Territorial Sea, UN Doc. A/CONF.4/97 (1956), 1956–2 Y.B. Intl. L. Commn. 1, 9 (comments of the Special Rapporteur of the International Law Commission), and 6 UNCLOS I Off. Rec. 40 (1958) (comments of U.S. delegate).

The *HMS Challenger* oceanographic expedition in 1872–1876 first discovered "manganese nodules" on the deep ocean floor. It was not until the 1960s, however, that the presence of these nodules, which in shape and size resemble potatoes, became widely known and the technology developed to permit their recovery. These nodules contain nickel, copper, and cobalt, as well as manganese, and today are commonly referred to as "polymetallic nodules."

New interest in polymetallic nodules brought the issue of the legal status of the deep seabed to the international forefront. Three divergent views developed regarding the deep seabed's legal status.

One view asserted that the mineral resources of the deep seabed were the common heritage of humankind and could be exploited only by or under the auspices of an international authority acting on behalf of all countries. Until the establishment of such an authority, no state or person could claim, explore, or exploit these resources. A second view defined the exploration and exploitation of mineral resources of the deep seabed as a freedom of the high seas. Under this view, no state could claim or acquire sovereign or exclusive rights over any part of the deep seabed or its mineral resources. However, unless or until a state agreed to be bound otherwise, it could authorize or engage in the exploration and exploitation of deep seabed mineral resources, provided that such activities were conducted with reasonable regard for the rights of other states or persons to engage in similar activities and to exercise the freedoms of the high seas. A third view, which came to have little influence, argued that the deep seabed, like unclaimed land, belonged to no one (res nullius) and could be appropriated to the exclusion of all others by the first state that claimed and exploited a particular portion of the seabed beyond national jurisdiction. See, e.g., L.F.E. Goldie, Customary International Law and Deep Seabed Mining, 6 Syracuse J. Intl. L. & Com. 173 (1978–1979). For discussion of these divergent views and their legal premises, see Jon Van Dyke & Christopher Yuen, "Common Heritage" v. "Freedom of the High Seas": Which Governs the Seabed?, 19 San Diego L. Rev. 493 (1982).

Malta's Ambassador Arvid Pardo gave an important address at the General Assembly of the United Nations in 1967, in which he emphasized the potential for deriving great wealth from deep seabed minerals and the dangers of militarization of the seabed. He proposed treating the seabed beyond national jurisdiction under a common heritage principle, calling for "an effective international regime" under which a widely representative special agency separate from the United Nations would exercise regulatory powers. UNGAOR, 22d Sess., First Comm., 1515th and 1516th meetings, UN Doc. A/C.1/PV 1515 and UN Doc. A/C.1/PV 1516 (1967). The U.N. General Assembly established an ad hoc committee to study the issue in 1967, followed in December 1968 by the Committee on the Peaceful Uses of the Seabed and the Ocean Floor beyond the Limits of National Jurisdiction. GA Res. 2467–A, UNGAOR, 23d Sess., Supp. No. 18, UN Doc. A/2718 (1968). The Moratorium Resolution, passed by the General Assembly in 1969, favored a prohibition on deep seabed exploitation activities (but not exploration). The vote was sixty-two in favor, twenty-eight against (including the United States and most other developed states), with twenty-eight abstentions. GA Res. 2574–D, UNGAOR, 25th Sess., Supp. No. 30, UN Doc. A/7630, 11 (1969).

In 1970, the General Assembly adopted, by a unanimous vote (including the United States and most developed countries) with fourteen abstentions, the Declaration of Principles Governing the Sea–Bed and the Ocean Floor, and the Subsoil

Thereof, Beyond the Limits of National Jurisdiction. GA Res. 2749 (XXV), 25 UNGAOR Supp. No. 28, UN Doc. A/8028, 24 (1970). According to the Declaration of Principles, the deep seabed and its natural resources "are the common heritage of mankind" and the exploitation of these resources shall be carried out for the benefit of humankind as a whole, taking into particular consideration the interests and needs of the developing countries. The Declaration provides that all activities regarding the exploration and exploitation of the resources of the deep seabed shall be governed by an international regime to be established under a generally accepted international treaty of a universal character based on the principles of the Declaration.

The Declaration of Principles did not expressly forbid or authorize the exploration and exploitation of the mineral resources of the deep seabed pending the establishment of a generally accepted international treaty of a universal character. The United States and several other countries made statements, at the time of its adoption, that the Declaration was not binding and did not constitute an interim deep seabed mining regime. UN Doc. A/C.1/PV.1799, 1, 3–4 (1970). In particular, the United States rejected the earlier Moratorium Resolution and reserved its right to begin exploration and exploitation of the deep seabed on a nonexclusive basis with regard to the rights of other states until it became a party to an international agreement establishing a new international regime. Id.

The Declaration of Principles served as a basis for negotiating an international regime for the exploration and exploitation of deep seabed minerals at the Third United Nations Conference on the Law of the Sea (UNCLOS III). Arriving at the precise contours of this regime, however, proved to be one of the most challenging issues during UNCLOS III. Industrialized states saw polymetallic nodules as a future source of strategic minerals, and many of these states sought an arrangement whereby national companies could securely invest in their own mining operations; the role of an international institution would be minimal, limited essentially to issuing licenses to avoid overlapping claims. Many developing states (known as the Group of 77) favored an international regime that would include a strong regulatory international institution, a mining arm of this institution to conduct all mining operations, and the distribution of mining proceeds to developing states. Both industrialized and developing states that were net exporters of the minerals contained in polymetallic nodules sought protections for their land-based producers. States with broad and narrow continental shelves also debated the limits of national jurisdiction (and hence of the Area). See Chapter 10, Section C.

C. THE DEEP SEABED MINING PROVISIONS OF THE 1982 LOS CONVENTION

After difficult negotiations in which the United States participated fully, a seabed mining regime emerged at the Third United Nations Conference on the Law of the Sea (UNCLOS III). Industrialized states agreed to include in the LOS Convention some seabed mining provisions that they regarded as less than ideal because they achieved negotiating concessions on other issues, such as navigation rights and coastal zones. Nevertheless, the U.S. administration of President Ronald Reagan, which took office in January 1981, announced near the end of UNCLOS III that the United States would not accept the LOS Convention because of difficulties the administration had with the Convention's deep seabed mining provisions. This Section briefly describes those provisions and the U.S. objections to them. Section E reviews the current deep seabed mining regime, which is comprised in part by portions of the 1982 LOS Convention and in part by 1994 revisions that significantly modify the original 1982 arrangement.

The LOS Convention establishes a regulatory mechanism to govern "activities in the Area." "Activities in the Area" are "all activities of exploration for, and exploitation of, the resources of the Area." LOS Convention, Article 1(2). "Resources" are in turn defined, for purposes of Part XI (which governs deep seabed mining), as "all solid, liquid or gaseous mineral resources *in situ* in the Area at or beneath the seabed." Id. at Article 133(a).

Part XI sets out general principles, tracking those established in the Declaration of Principles. These include the principle that "[t]he Area and its resources are the common heritage of mankind." Id.

at Article 136. The common heritage principle is not defined, but in this context encompasses other norms set out in Part XI. These include: the prohibition against states claiming or exercising sovereignty or sovereign rights over the Area or its resources (Article 137(1)); the vesting of resources in humankind as a whole (Article 137(2)); the carrying out of activities in the Area for the benefit of humankind as a whole, taking into particular consideration the interests and needs of developing states, especially those that are land-locked and geographically disadvantaged (Articles 140(1), 143(3)(b), 144, 148); the sharing, on an equitable and nondiscriminatory basis, of economic benefits derived from activities in the Area (Article 140(2)); the reservation of the Area for peaceful purposes (Article 141); and the protection of the marine environment from harmful effects arising from activities in the Area (Article 145). See also Christopher C. Joyner, Legal Implications of the Concept of the Common Heritage of Mankind, 35 Intl. & Comp. L.Q. 190 (1986).

The LOS Convention establishes an International Seabed Authority (ISA) with enumerated responsibilities concerning the Area and its resources. LOS Convention, Articles 137(2), 153, 156–157. All parties to the LOS Convention are members of the ISA. Id. at Article 156(2). The ISA's principal organs are an Assembly, a Council, and a Secretariat. Id. at Article 158(1). The LOS Convention designates the Assembly, with one representative from each member of the ISA, as the ISA's "supreme organ," responsible for establishing general policies. Id. at Articles 159–160. The LOS Convention identifies the thirty-six-member Council as the "executive organ" of the ISA, charged with establishing "specific policies" and approving "plans of work" for each mining project. Id. at Article 162. The Secretariat and the ISA's Secretary–General are authorized to perform administrative duties under the 1982 regime. Id. at Article 166.

The "Enterprise" is an autonomous organ of the ISA that was designed to carry out mining activities in the Area, either directly or through joint ventures with national or private companies. Id. at Article 170. When applicants, who must be controlled by parties to the LOS Convention or by their citizens, applied for a license to explore and exploit the deep seabed, they were to submit a "plan of work" that, inter alia, presented two sites of estimated equal commercial value. If the plan was approved, the ISA would reserve one of the sites for the Enterprise (which the Authority could in turn transfer to a developing state), and the applicant would acquire, in the form of a contract with the ISA, exploration and exploitation rights in the other. Id. at Annex III, Articles 3, 8–9. This was known as the "parallel system."

The 1982 seabed mining provisions subjected applicants and contractors to other significant obligations. In order to apply for a plan of work and to explore and exploit the resources of the Area, an applicant had to pay the ISA. Payments included a one-time US$500,000 administrative fee, id. at Annex III, Article 13(2), and, if a proposed plan of work was approved and a contract was issued, an annual fixed fee of US$1 million until commercial production began and thereafter the greater of US$1 million or a "production charge" determined through a complex formula. Id. at Annex III, Article 13(3). In order to protect the economies of developing states that were mining the minerals contained in deep seabed resources, the ISA could establish, pursuant to detailed parameters, production limits for seabed mining. Id. at Article 151(2). In addition, an applicant was required to disclose to the ISA information relating to the equipment and methods to be used under the plan of work, along with other nonproprietary technology. Id. at Annex III, Article 5(1). On approval of a plan, the contractor was to make available to the Enterprise (or to a developing country exploiting the reserved site), on "fair and reasonable commercial terms and conditions," the technology to be used in the project if the technology was not reasonably available on the open market. Id. at Annex III, Article 5(3).

Since the Enterprise might not have sufficient funds to begin exploitation of a reserved site, parties to the LOS Convention were to make available to the Enterprise funds and loan guarantees necessary for commercial exploitation of an initial site, in accordance with the scale of assessments for the U.N. general budget. Id. at Annex IV, Article 11(3). Economic benefits derived from activities in the Area were to be shared equitably, "taking into particular consideration the interests and needs of developing States and peoples who have not attained full independence or other self-governing status." Id. at Articles 140(1), 162(2)(f)(i).

Provisions of Part XI of the LOS Convention could be changed, fifteen years after the start of commercial production, pursuant to a Review Conference. Id. at Article 155. This Review Conference could adopt amendments to the Convention that would bind all parties if the amendments were ratified by three-fourths of the parties. Id. at Article 155(4).

The LOS Convention also established a seabed mining dispute settlement system that remains unchanged after the 1994 modifications. See Section E and Chapter 15, Section D. For a detailed presentation of the 1982 LOS Convention's deep seabed mining regime, see Wolfgang Hauser, The Legal Regime for Deep Seabed Mining Under the Law of the Sea Convention (Frances Bunce Dielmann trans., 1983).

In 1982, UNCLOS III approved the LOS Convention by 130 votes to 4 (Israel, Turkey, the United States, and Venezuela), with 17 abstentions. The United States refused to sign the LOS Convention on the basis that the deep seabed mining regime provisions of the LOS Convention were "hopelessly flawed." White House Office of Policy Information, The Law of the Sea Convention, Issue Update No. 10 (Apr. 15, 1983), 8. The United States considered this text unacceptable because it would: deter future development of deep seabed mineral resources (because of lack of certainty with regard to the granting of mining contracts, the artificial limitations on seabed mineral production, and the imposition of burdensome financial requirements); not give the United States an adequate role in the decision-making process; allow amendments to the Convention to enter into force for the United States without its approval; provide for mandatory transfer of private technology related to seabed mining; and potentially allow the ISA to transfer to national liberation movements a portion of funds received from the miners. U.S. Policy and the Law of the Sea, Presidential Statement and White House Fact Sheet, Jan. 29, 1982, Dept. St. Bull., Mar. 1982, at 54. The Reagan administration emphasized that the United States supported other parts of the LOS Convention and that if the objectionable provisions of Part XI could be corrected, the "Administration will support ratification." Id.

D.   THE SEARCH FOR A GENERALLY ACCEPTED DEEP SEABED MINING REGIME: DEVELOPMENTS TO 1994

The United States was not the only industrialized state with concerns about the Part XI seabed mining regime of the LOS Convention. Like the United States, the Federal Republic of Germany and the United Kingdom did not sign the Convention, and other developed states held off ratifying it. Before the LOS Convention entered into force in 1994, efforts to shape the legal regime for deep seabed mining proceeded along three tracks outside the Third United Nations Conference on the Law of the Sea (UNCLOS III). First, the United States and several other industrialized states adopted unilateral legislation, authorizing their citizens to explore and exploit seabed minerals. Second, the Preparatory Commission, a body created at UNCLOS III to plan for the entry into force of the LOS Convention, worked on seabed mining matters. Third, an initiative of the U.N. Secretary–General, which began in 1990, eventually resulted in the 1994 Implementation Agreement. This Agreement significantly modified the 1982 Part XI regime and paved the way for widespread acceptance of the modified LOS Convention by industrialized and additional developing states.

The first track involved unilateral legislation. In 1980 the United States adopted the Deep Seabed Hard Mineral Resources Act to regulate the exploration for and commercial recovery of hard mineral resources of the deep seabed by U.S. citizens. 30 U.S.C. §§ 1401 et seq. The Act was intended to be transitional until the entry into force with respect to the United States of the LOS Convention or another treaty concerning the deep seabed. Id. at § 1441(3). The Act acknowledges U.S. support of the Declaration of Principles, but states the U.S. legal opinion that the exploration and exploitation of the deep seabed is a freedom of the high seas, subject to a duty of reasonable regard to the rights and interests of other states. Id. at § 1401. Under the Act, U.S. "citizens," including U.S. corporations and foreign corporations controlled by U.S. nationals, are prohibited from engaging in the exploration or commercial recovery of deep seabed mineral resources except pursuant to the Act. Id. at §§ 1403(14), 1411(a). The Act authorizes applications for a ten-year license for exploration (renewable for five-year periods) and a permit for commercial recovery (extending at least twenty years) of deep seabed mineral resources. Id. at § 1417. Applicants must meet requirements for financial responsibility and technological capabilities, id. at § 1413(c), and comply with several provisions to safeguard the environment. See id. at §§ 1401(b)(4), 1413(a)(2)(C), 1415(a)(4), (b)(2), (c)(1)(B), 1419–1420.

Several other industrialized countries (the Federal Republic of Germany, the United Kingdom, France, the Soviet Union, Japan, and Italy) also enacted interim national legislation regulating the exploration and exploitation of deep seabed mineral resources. See respectively 20 Intl. Leg. Materials 393 (1981), as amended, 21 id. 832 (1982); 20 id. 1217 (1981); 21 id. 808 (1982); 21 id. 551 (1982); 22 id. 102 (1983); 24 id. 983 (1985). Developing states opposed this legislation as illegal under international law. See the legal position of the Group of 77, UN Doc. A/CONF.62/106 (1980), 14 UNCLOS III Off. Rec. 111 (1982). For a comparison of national acts, see Richard Todd Luoma, A Comparative Study of National Legislation Concerning the Deep Sea Mining of Manganese Nodules, 14 J. Mar. L. & Com. 243 (1983).

If different states were to authorize exploration for or exploitation of deep seabed minerals under unilateral legislation, conflicting claims to mine sites might arise. National legislation addressed this difficulty by providing that the holder of a license or permit issued under the legislation gained certain exclusive rights. The holder could explore or engage in exploration or commercial recovery to the exclusion of both any other citizen of the country granting the license or permit, and any citizen of a "reciprocating state" with similar interim legislation. See, e.g., 30 U.S.C. §§ 1412(b)(2), 1428. Treaties were concluded to avoid overlapping claims authorized under national acts. See, e.g., the 1984 Provisional Understanding Regarding Deep Seabed Matters, concluded by Belgium, the Federal Republic of Germany, France, Italy, Japan, the Netherlands, the United Kingdom, and the United States.

A second deep seabed mining track involved the Preparatory Commission for the International Seabed Authority and for the International Tribunal for the Law of the Sea (Prepcom), established by Resolution I of the UNCLOS III Final Act. Prepcom was charged with planning for the operation of the International Seabed Authority (ISA) once the LOS Convention entered into force. Some hoped that Prepcom, during this planning process, might take steps to persuade industrialized states to accept the Convention. Prepcom made a few minor adjustments to the 1982 regime. For example, Prepcom indicated that certain states and multinational consortia that had made early investments in seabed mining (so-called "pioneer investors"), could, under the parallel system, designate which of two parts of a site was to be licensed to them and which was to be reserved for the Enterprise—rather than, as indicated in the LOS Convention, allowing the ISA to choose first. Cf. LOS Convention, Annex III, Article 8. Yet Prepcom was not authorized to make fundamental changes to the text of the Convention itself.

Prepcom took some important steps. First, it co-operated in agreements to avoid overlapping mine sites, taking the practical position that it was important to avoid conflicts not just among states that were participating in Prepcom (i.e., states that had signed or acceded to the LOS Convention), but also among states, such as the United States, that were not participating in Prepcom. See, e.g., the 1987 Agreement on the Resolution of Practical Problems with Respect to Deep Seabed Mining Areas and related bilateral notes. Second, Prepcom registered several pioneer investors, which gained an exclusive right, in areas allocated to them, to undertake activities related to the discovery and evaluation of polymetallic nodules and to determine whether exploitation would be technologically and economically feasible. UNCLOS III Final Act, Resolution II, ¶¶ 1(a)–(b), 6. These registered pioneer investors include: the government of India (registered in 1987); IFEMER/AFERNOD of France (1987); the Deep Ocean Resources Development Co. of Japan

(1987); Yuzhmorgeologiya, a Russian state enterprise (1987); COMRA, an association of the People's Republic of China (1991); Interoceanmetal Joint Organization, a consortium formed by Bulgaria, Cuba, the Czech Republic, Poland, the Russian Federation, and Slovakia (1991); and the government of the Republic of Korea (1994). See E. Riddell–Dixon, The Preparatory Commission on the International Sea–bed Authority: "New Realism"?, 7 Intl. J. Estuarine & Coastal L. 195 (1992).

Fundamental changes in the deep seabed mining regime finally resulted from a third track, which began with informal consultations initiated by the U.N. Secretary–General in 1990. This track, in which the United States actively participated, resulted in the July 1994 Implementation Agreement. In November 1993, the LOS Convention gained its sixtieth ratification, which meant that the Convention would enter into force one year later. LOS Convention, Article 308(1). The pending entry into force of the LOS Convention lent impetus to the negotiations concerning seabed mining, since no major Western power had yet accepted the Convention. The world faced the prospect of the Convention entering into force and the ISA beginning its operations under the 1982 regime without the participation of industrialized states. The 1994 changes, explained in the next Section, attracted the support of industrialized states as well as developing states.

E.   THE 1994 IMPLEMENTATION AGREEMENT AND THE CURRENT DEEP SEABED MINING REGIME

It was important to create a unified seabed mining regime that incorporated the changes agreed on in the 1994 Implementation Agreement along with the seabed mining provisions of the LOS Convention that remained unaffected. Before considering the substantive changes made in the 1994 Agreement, this Section notes how a unified regime was achieved.

The 1994 Agreement is to be read together with Part XI of the LOS Convention as a single instrument, and if an inconsistency arises between the Agreement and Part XI, the provisions of the Agreement prevail. 1994 Implementation Agreement, Article 2(1). Although the U.N. General Assembly adopted the Agreement, UN Doc. A/RES/48/263 (1994), states had to accept it in order to be legally bound by it. States cannot accept the 1994 Implementation Agreement without also accepting the LOS Convention; by contrast, states may become parties to the 1995 Fish Stocks Convention, which is also designated as an agreement that "implements" the LOS Convention, without also joining the LOS Convention. 1994 Implementation Agreement, Article 4(2); see Chapter 13. States accepting the LOS Convention after July 28, 1994, the date on which the Agreement was concluded, are deemed to consent also to the Agreement. Id. at Article 4(1). States that had previously accepted the Convention were given a range of procedural options, some of them easily satisfied, by which they could accept the Agreement. Id. at Articles 4(3), 5. See Annick de Marffy–Mantuano, The Procedural Framework of the Agreement Implementing the 1982 United Nations Convention on the Law of the Sea, 89 Am. J. Intl. L. 814 (1995).

The 1994 Agreement also authorized its provisional application beginning in November 1994, when the LOS Convention entered into force. 1994 Implementation Agreement, Article 7. The International Seabed Authority (ISA) thus has operated consistently under the merged LOS Convention/1994 Agreement arrangements both before and after the 1994 Agreement itself entered into force in 1996. As of July 15, 2009, there were 159 parties to the LOS Convention and 137 parties to the 1994 Implementation Agreement. Despite this disparity, only the merged LOS Convention/1994 Agreement provides the international mechanism for seabed mining; no other treaty-based mechanism competes with it.

The 1994 Implementation Agreement's Preface notes "the political and economic changes, including market-oriented approaches, affecting the implementation of Part XI" and recognizes that "the objective of universal participation in the [LOS] Convention may best be achieved by the adoption of an agreement relating to the implementation of Part XI." Although in name the Agreement only relates to Part XI's "implementation," in reality the Agreement significantly modifies the seabed mining provisions of the LOS Convention. In general, the Agreement streamlined operations of the ISA, increased the decision-making authority of the United States and other industrialized states, and provided that numerous provisions of Part XI to which the United States and other industrialized states had objected would not apply. The general principles governing the Area and its resources that had been set out in the LOS Convention (see Section C) remain in effect, but how those principles are to be implemented has changed considerably.

The ISA's principal organs—the Assembly, the Council, and the Secretariat—continue to exist, but their functions have changed. The broadly representative Assembly must now collaborate with the limited membership Council, 1994 Implementation Agreement, Annex § 3(1), and any Assembly decisions on administrative, budgetary, or financial matters "shall be based on the recommendations of the Council." Id. at Annex § 3(4). The 1994 Implementation Agreement augments the role of industrialized states in the Council, on which the United States, should it accept the LOS Convention, is now guaranteed a seat. Id. at Annex § 3(15)(a). The Council must take some steps by consensus (i.e., without any formal objection), including the recommendation of rules, regulations, and procedures about distributing economic benefits. For other substantive matters, the Council requires a super-majority vote of two-thirds of members present and voting if consensus cannot be achieved. Id. at Annex § 3(2)–(3), (5); LOS Convention, Articles 159(8),

161(8)(d), 162(2)(*o*)(i). In addition, the Council may not approve a matter over the objection of a majority of members of any of four chambers into which the Council is organized. 1994 Implementation Agreement, Annex § 3(9)(a), (15)–(16). Two of the chambers will be controlled by the industrialized states; the other two chambers are composed of developing states and major net exporters of the minerals to be derived from the Area. Furthermore, any Assembly or Council decision "having financial or budgetary implications shall be based on the recommendations" of a new Finance Committee, id. at Annex § 3(7), which operates by consensus and on which the major contributors to the Authority's budget (including the United States, should it join the Convention) have seats. Id. at Annex § 9(3), (8).

Several provisions of the LOS Convention that opponents of the original Part XI regime regarded as insufficiently protective of market mechanisms no longer apply. Seabed mining production ceilings "shall not apply," id. at Annex § 6(7), and have been replaced by market-oriented restrictions on subsidies and other principles contained in the General Agreement on Tariffs and Trade. Id. at Annex § 6. The 1982 provisions that might have resulted in a mandatory transfer of technology to the Enterprise, the mining arm of the ISA, "shall not apply." Id. at Annex § 5(2). Instead, "consistent with the effective protection of intellectual property rights," the ISA may only "request" that contractors and their sponsoring states "cooperate . . . in facilitating the acquisition of deep seabed mining technology

... on fair and reasonable commercial terms and conditions;" parties "undertake to cooperate" with the ISA "for this purpose." Id. at Annex § 5(1)(b). Onerous provisions concerning the financial terms of contracts have been modified. The US$1 million annual fee for mining companies or other production charges required by the LOS Convention "shall not apply," and the initial fee to apply for a plan of work has been reduced from US$500,000 to US$250,000 (or less, if the costs of processing the application are less). Id. at Annex § 8(2)–(3).

The 1994 Implementation Agreement also helps to insure that discretionary actions of the ISA cannot block qualified mining companies from gaining contracts. Applications are approved on a first-come, first-served basis, based on standards set out in rules, regulations, and procedures that the Council adopts by consensus and that relate to an applicant's financial and technical capabilities. Miners' applications approved by a majority vote in a Legal and Technical Commission "shall be deemed to have been approved" unless the Council decides not to approve by a super-majority vote (which vote could be blocked by any chamber of the Council). Id. at Annex §§ 1(6), 3(11), (13). Should the United States accept the LOS Convention, U.S. consortia that the United States certifies have made investments under the U.S. Deep Seabed Hard Mineral Resources Act are deemed to have met the necessary financial and technical requirements, and will receive arrangements "no less favorable than" those accorded pioneer investors that registered with Prepcom. Id. at Annex § 1(6). See Section D.

Once approved, applicants gain exclusive rights to a mine site, security of tenure, and title to the minerals they extract. Should any party to the LOS Convention consider that minerals other than polymetallic nodules are worth developing, the ISA must adopt the necessary rules, regulations, and procedures. Id. at Annex § 1(15)(b); LOS Convention, Article 162(2)(*o*)(ii).

The Enterprise will operate initially through joint ventures "that accord with sound commercial principles." 1994 Implementation Agreement, Annex § 2(2). A private mining contractor must still contribute a reserved area for the use of the Enterprise, but the contractor has a right of first refusal to enter a joint venture with the Enterprise. Id. at Annex § 2(5). The LOS Convention requirement that parties fund a mine site for the Enterprise "shall not apply." Id. at Annex § 2(3).

Article 145 of the LOS Convention stresses the importance of protecting the marine environment against harmful effects arising from activities in the Area and requires the ISA to adopt rules, regulations, and procedures to this end. See also LOS Convention, Articles 147, 162(2)(w)-(x), 165(2)(d)-(e), (k), and Annex III, Articles 2(1)(b), 17(1)(b)(xii), 17(2)(f). The 1994 Implementation Agreement further emphasizes this issue, requiring the ISA, inter alia, to monitor the development of marine technology relating to the protection of the marine environment and to review environmental impact assessments that are contained in applications for plans of work. 1994 Implementation Agreement, Annex § 1(5)(g)–(i), (k), (7).

Provisions of Article 155 of the LOS Convention concerning the Review Conference that might have resulted in amendments to Part XI binding on a party without its consent "shall not apply." Id. at Annex § 4. Instead, parties may amend Part XI of the LOS Convention through other standard avenues provided for in the Convention. LOS Convention, Articles 312–314.

Continuing unchanged from the LOS Convention are provisions for the settlement of seabed mining disputes. The Seabed Disputes Chamber, a part of the International Tribunal for the Law of the Sea (see Chapter 15), has jurisdiction "with respect to activities in the Area" in several categories of contentious cases. LOS Convention, Article 187. These categories include, inter alia: disputes between parties concerning the interpretation or application of the LOS Convention's deep seabed regime; disputes between a party and the ISA; disputes between parties to a contract and the ISA or the Enterprise concerning the interpretation or application of a contract or plan of work; and disputes between the ISA and an applicant concerning the denial of a contract. The 1994 Implementation Agreement emphasizes that disputes concerning disapproval of a plan of work, or disputes concerning rules and regulations based on the modified principles concerning financial terms of contract, are subject to the LOS Convention's dispute settlement procedures. 1994 Implementation Agreement, Annex §§ 3(12), 8(1)(f). Some technical disputes relating to contracts may be submitted to binding commercial arbitration. LOS Convention, Article 188(2). Finally, the Seabed Disputes Chamber may render an advisory opinion at the request of the Assembly or Council concerning "legal questions arising within the scope of their activities," id. at Article 191, and the Assembly may request the Chamber to give an advisory opinion "on the conformity with th[e] [LOS] Convention of a proposal before the Assembly on any matter." Id. at Article 159(10).

For discussion of the deep seabed mining regime after the 1994 changes, see David H. Anderson, Resolution and Agreement Relating to the Implementation of Part XI of the UN Convention on the Law of the Sea: A General Assessment, 55 Zeitschrift für ausländisches Recht und Völkerrecht 275 (1995); Bernard H. Oxman, The 1994 Agreement and the Convention, 88 Am. J. Intl. L. 687 (1994). For the consolidated text of Part XI of the LOS Convention and the 1994 Implementation Agreement, see 6 United Nations Convention on the Law of the Sea 1982: A Commentary 875 (Satya N. Nandan ed.-in-chief, 2002).

The ISA is now fully operational, headquartered in Kingston, Jamaica. See http://www.isa.org.jm. It operates on a small annual budget of approximately US$4 million, contributed by parties to the LOS Convention. The ISA is preparing a comprehensive mining code. As of June 1, 2009, regulations governing prospecting (an activity that gives no exclusive rights) and exploring for polymetallic nodules (which does entail exclusive rights) had been adopted. ISBA/6/A/18 (2000). Regulations for polymetallic sulfides and cobalt-rich ferromanganese crusts are also being developed. Recent increases in the prices of metals have led to increased interest in deep seabed mining. The ISA has approved plans of work and concluded contracts for exploration for the seven pioneer investors that Prepcom registered. In 2006 the ISA also approved an exploration contract with Germany's Federal Institute for Geosciences and Natural Resources. Most of the contracts apply to the Clarion–Clipperton zone in the Pacific Ocean. The ISA also has received recent applications for approval of plans of work for exploration from two other companies, one sponsored by Nauru and one by Tonga. In addition, the ISA collects and disseminates public information about deep seabed minerals, metal markets, nonproprietary seabed mining technology, and the deep seabed environment. See Report of the Secretary–General of the International Seabed Authority, ISBA/14/A/2 (2008).

A preponderant majority of states—both industrialized and developing, and from all regional groups—has accepted the regime established by the LOS Convention as modified by the 1994 Implementation Agreement. These states have conformed their practice to this regime. Shortly after the 1994 Implementation Agreement was concluded, and even before it entered into force in 1996, one highly respected commentator concluded that the position that "deep seabed mining is a freedom of the high seas" is "no longer tenable, in light of the fact that almost all the major technologically advanced countries have adopted and signed" the 1994 Agreement. L.D.M. Nelson, The New Deep Sea–Bed Mining Regime, 10 Intl. J. Marine & Coastal L. 189, 202 (1995).

As of July 15, 2009, the United States had neither ratified the LOS Convention nor repealed the Deep Seabed Hard Mineral Resources Act. However, all U.S. exploration licenses had lapsed or been relinquished as of that date. See Sen. For. Rel. Comm., Hearings on the United Nations Convention on the Law of the Sea, 110th Cong., 1st Sess., Sen. Hrg. 110–592, at 254, 260 (2007) (written testimony of Caitlyn L. Antrim). No exploitation permits have been granted under the U.S. Act. Mining consortia, seeking the stability associated with a widely recognized international system, have been pursuing their options under the LOS Convention/1994 Implementation Agreement regime, through companies incorporated in countries that are parties to the LOS Convention. Any company pursuing exploitation under the U.S. Act would have not only the administrative burdens and fees associated with obtaining a U.S. permit, but might face international challenges to its security of tenure to a mine site or trade restrictions.

F. MARINE SCIENTIFIC RESEARCH IN THE AREA

All states and "competent international organizations" (e.g., the Intergovernmental Oceanographic Commission, a body with functional autonomy within the United Nations Educational, Scientific and Cultural Organization) have the right to conduct marine scientific research in the Area, but this activity must be "in conformity with the provisions of Part XI." LOS Convention, Article 256. Parties shall also promote cooperation in marine scientific research in the Area. Id. at Article 143(3).

The International Seabed Authority (ISA) itself may carry out marine scientific research and is charged with encouraging such research and coordinating and disseminating the results of such research. Id. at Article 143(2); 1994 Implementation Agreement, Annex § 1(5)(h). Article 143(1) of the LOS Convention emphasizes that marine scientific research in the Area is to be carried out exclusively for the benefit of humankind. In 2006 the ISA established an endowment fund to promote and encourage marine scientific research in the Area. See http://www.isa.org.jm/en/efund.

G. HYDROTHERMAL VENTS AND GENETIC RESOURCES

Sales of marine biotechnology-related products amount to over US$100 billion annually. Biotechnology companies have patented and used genetic materials from living organisms found at deep-sea hydrothermal vents, which are home to abundant and diverse ecosystems. Salvatore Arico & Charlotte Salpin, UNU–IAS Report: Bioprospecting the Genetic Resources in the Deep Seabed §§ 3.2.2.2, 4.2 (2005), available at http://www.ias.unu.edu/binaries 2/DeepSeabed.pdf.

The legal status of "bioprospecting" for organisms found at geothermal vents is a matter of debate. Under one view, activities related to marine genetic materials in the Area are an exercise of high seas freedoms. In particular, the freedoms of navigation, fishing, and marine scientific research may apply. According to this view, living resources are not "resources" as defined in Article 133(a) of the LOS Convention. That definition restricts the meaning of the term to mineral resources for the purposes of Part XI of the Convention; Part XI and the International Seabed Authority (ISA) do not govern living resources. See Craig H. Allen, Protecting the Oceanic Gardens of Eden: International Law Issues in Deep–Sea Vent Resource Conservation and Management, 13 Geo. Intl. Envtl. L. Rev. 563 (2001). However, high seas freedoms must be exercised "with due regard for the rights under this Convention with respect to activities in the Area," LOS Convention, Article 87(2), which suggests that bioprospecting could not unduly interfere with ISA regulations applicable to deep seabed mining.

A contrasting view maintains that living material found at hydrothermal vents is part of the common heritage of humankind, and any legal regime for such material must take account of the common heritage principle. This view builds on the premise that the Area itself, comprising the deep seabed and its subsoil beyond the limits of national jurisdiction, is best understood as distinct from the water column above it. See id. at Article 1(1). In particular, the "seabed" may include hydrothermal vents, which emit heated water from beneath the seabed, and certain other features that differ from the superjacent water column, such as hypersaline brine pools, mud volcanoes, and cold seeps. See generally Arico & Salpin, supra, § 2.1. Proponents of this view accept that the detailed regulatory regime of Part XI and the 1994 Implementation Agreement applies only to mineral resources. Nevertheless, they argue that the Area itself and living resources on the seabed—not just mineral resources—are part of the common heritage of humankind. As a result, the general principles of Part XI apply to living organisms and genetic material at deep-sea hydrothermal vents. These principles include the norm of non-appropriation and the precept that marine scientific research in the Area must benefit humankind as a whole. See Sections C and F; Alex G. Oude Elferink, The Regime of the Area: Delineating the Scope of Application of the Common Heritage Principle and Freedom of the High Seas, 22 Intl. J. Marine & Coastal L. 143 (2007).

Genetic material found at hydrothermal vents is important to biological diversity, and states acknowledge the importance of the 1992 Convention on Biological Diversity with respect to future efforts to regulate and clarify the legal status of bioprospecting. For discussion of that Convention, see Chapter 13, Section C.3. See generally Letter dated 15 May 2008 from the Co–Chairpersons of the Ad Hoc Open-ended Informal Working Group to study issues relating to the conservation and sustainable use of marine biological diversity beyond areas of national jurisdiction addressed to the President of the General Assembly ¶¶ 32–39, UN Doc. A/63/79 (2008); Report of the Ad Hoc Open-ended Informal Working Group to study issues relating to the conservation and sustainable use of marine biological diversity beyond areas of national jurisdiction, UN Doc. A/61/65 (2006).

H. OTHER ACTIVITIES IN THE AREA

Nonextractive uses of the Area, notably the laying of submarine cables and pipelines, are unambiguously treated as high seas freedoms. LOS Convention, Article 87. See Chapter 2, Section C.

Bottom trawling for fish may cause great damage to coral, hydrothermal vents, and other geological features of the Area, disrupting ecosystems associated with these features. One debated issue is what entity and process could best regulate this practice or establish marine protected areas where the practice is prohibited. Some have suggested that the International Seabed Authority (ISA) could create marine protected areas. According to Article 145 of the LOS Convention, the ISA shall adopt appropriate environmental rules, regulations, and procedures to, inter alia, prevent "damage to the flora and fauna of the marine environment." However, the focus of the ISA is on environmental damage that may arise from mining activities. The U.N. General Assembly, which took the lead in addressing the use of driftnets on the high seas, and regional fisheries organizations could also play important roles in addressing bottom trawling. For discussion of restrictions on high seas fishing, regional fisheries organizations, and the General Assembly's role in regulating the use of driftnets, see Chapter 13.

Wrecks of historical and archaeological interest have been found in the Area. Recovery of objects from these wrecks has traditionally been governed under the general maritime law of salvage. See R.M.S. Titanic v. Wrecked & Abandoned Vessel, 435 F.3d 521 (4th Cir. 2006); R.M.S. Titanic, Inc. v. Haver, 171 F.3d 943 (4th Cir.), cert. denied, 528 U.S. 825 (1999). In addition, Article 49 of the LOS Convention generally provides that "objects of an archaeological and historical nature found in the Area shall be preserved or disposed of for the benefit of mankind as a whole." The ISA requires that contractors prospecting or exploring for polymetallic nodules notify the ISA when they find any object of an historical or archaeological character, and that they take reasonable efforts not to disturb the object. The ISA in turn will notify the Director–General of the United Nations Educational, Scientific and Cultural Organization about the discovery.

Regulations on Prospecting and Exploration for Polymetallic Nodules in the Area, ISBA/6/A/18 (2000),
Regs. 8, 34. See also 2001 UNESCO Underwater
Cultural Heritage Convention, Article 11. For discussion of the law of salvage and underwater cultural heritage, see Chapter 8, Section I.

CHAPTER 12

PROTECTION AND PRESERVATION OF THE MARINE ENVIRONMENT

A. INTRODUCTION

The LOS Convention broke new ground on the protection and preservation of the marine environment. In sharp contrast to the prior piecemeal approach in this domain, the LOS Convention represents "the first comprehensive statement of international law on the issue," to use the words of the Secretary–General of the United Nations in his special report on the subject. UN Doc. A/44/461, 5 (1989). Because of the advanced nature of these provisions, codified primarily in Part XII, the LOS Convention has been described as "the strongest comprehensive environmental treaty now in existence or likely to emerge for quite some time." John R. Stevenson & Bernard H. Oxman, The Future of the United Nations Convention on the Law of the Sea, 88 Am. J. Intl. L. 488, 496 (1994).

Section B of this Chapter begins with a general comparison of the old and new marine environmental protection regimes, followed by discussions of the different general sources of pollution distinguished by the LOS Convention: vessel-source pol-

367

lution (Section C); pollution from land-based sources (Section D); ocean dumping (Section E); pollution from seabed activities subject to national jurisdiction (Section F); pollution from deep seabed mining (Section G); and pollution from or through the atmosphere (Section H). Section I addresses more specific LOS Convention measures applicable to marine areas that require special protection. Section J analyzes different environmental liability regimes established by the Convention, followed by a discussion of enforcement issues (Section K). The Chapter concludes by discussing the notification and cooperation requirements imposed on states in case of pollution disasters (Section L) and the application of international rules concerning protection of the marine environment to government noncommercial vessels (Section M).

B.   GENERAL PRINCIPLES

Prior to several marine environmental disasters in the 1960s, few international conventions addressed the preservation of the marine environment and its protection against pollution. Several states had enacted unilateral legislation prohibiting the pollution of their internal waters and their territorial seas, but these acts were inadequate to prevent pollution of waters beyond zones of national jurisdiction, and they dealt primarily with pollution caused by the deliberate or grossly negligent discharge of oil from vessels. See, for instance, the U.S. Oil Pollution Act of 1924, 43 Stat. 604 (amended by

80 Stat. 1246 (1966), repealed by 86 Stat. 816 (1972)).

The First United Nations Conference on the Law of the Sea did not develop a comprehensive regime relating to the prevention of pollution and the preservation of the marine environment, but some general provisions relating to the obligations of states in this regard were adopted. Article 24 of the 1958 High Seas Convention imposes a general obligation on states to regulate the discharge of oil from ships or pipelines or resulting from the exploration or exploitation of the seabed and its subsoil. Article 25 requires states to take measures to prevent pollution of the seas from the dumping of radioactive waste, and it requires states to cooperate with the appropriate international organizations in taking measures for the prevention of pollution of the seas resulting from any activities with radioactive materials or other harmful agents. Article 5(7) of the 1958 Continental Shelf Convention requires coastal states to undertake, in safety zones around artificial installations, all appropriate measures for the protection of the living resources of the sea from harmful agents.

The marine disasters of the 1960s fostered the growing recognition that cooperative international action was necessary to protect adequately the marine environment. On March 18, 1967, the grounding of the *Torrey Canyon*, a Liberian oil tanker carrying 119,000 tons of crude oil, on Pollard Rock, about seven miles off the Scilly Isles, United Kingdom, caused the worst oil pollution recorded at that time. The oil spill affected over 120 miles (190 kilometers) of British and 50 miles (80 kilometers) of French coastlines. Since the grounding occurred on a Saturday and contact with the Liberian authorities proved impossible at the time, the British government ordered the Royal Air Force to bomb the ship, located outside its then three-nautical-mile territorial sea, in an attempt to burn up some of the oil. This incident triggered the adoption of the 1969 Convention on High Seas Intervention in Oil Pollution Casualties, followed by a Protocol in 1973 extending its application to substances other than oil. These instruments authorized each coastal state to take necessary measures to prevent, mitigate, or eliminate danger to its coastline or related interests from pollution resulting from a maritime casualty, after due consultation with other states affected by the casualty, including the flag state of the vessel involved.

In 1972 in Stockholm, the United Nations Conference on the Human Environment adopted a Declaration establishing principles and guidelines for government action. For an analysis of the Declaration in relation to the marine environment, see The Stockholm Declaration and Law of the Marine Environment (Myron H. Nordquist, John Norton Moore & Said Mahmoudi eds., 2003). Principle 7 of the Declaration adopted by the Conference provides that "[s]tates shall take all possible steps to prevent pollution of the seas." Principle 21 provides that states must ensure, in exercising their sovereign rights to exploit their resources, "that activities within their jurisdiction or control do not cause damage to the environment of other States or of areas beyond the limits of national jurisdiction." UN Doc. A/CONF.48/14/Rev.1, 3, 4–5 (1972). The latter principle is derived from the seminal Trail Smelter Case, in which the United States and Canada submitted to an international arbitral tribunal a dispute involving injuries caused in the state of Washington by large amounts of sulphur dioxide emitted by a smelter plant in Trail, British Columbia. The Tribunal declared as a principle of international law that "no state has the right to use or permit the use of its territory in such a manner as to cause injury by fumes in or to the territory of another or the properties or persons therein, when the case is of serious consequence and the injury is established by clear and convincing evidence." 3 Rep. Intl. Arb. Awards 1938, 1965 (1941). See Transboundary Harm in International Law: Lessons from the Trail Smelter Arbitration (Rebecca M. Bratspies ed., 2006).

In the 1960s and 1970s, several regional and multilateral conventions emerged, governing various aspects of the marine environment. The principles and standards incorporated in the Stockholm Declaration and in these conventions served as a basis for the negotiation of a comprehensive regime for the protection and preservation of the marine environment at the Third United Nations Conference on the Law of the Sea (UNCLOS III). Article 192 of the LOS Convention sets forth the general obligation of states to protect and preserve the marine environment. To fulfill this obligation, states are required to take, individually or jointly, all measures necessary to prevent pollution of the marine environment from any source, using the best practicable means at their disposal and in accordance with their capabilities. LOS Convention, Article 194(1). These measures must take into account internationally agreed rules and standards, and, in some circumstances, must be not less effective than generally accepted international rules and standards. See id. at Articles 207(1), 208(3), 209(2), 210(6), and 211(2). The measures taken must encompass all sources of pollution of the marine environment, including:

(1) The release of toxic, harmful or noxious substances from land-based sources, from or through the atmosphere, or by dumping;

(2) Pollution from vessels;

(3) Pollution from installations and devices used in the exploration or exploitation of the natural resources of the seabed and subsoil and from other installations operating in the marine environment.

Id. at Article 194(3). In taking measures to prevent marine pollution, states may not transfer, directly or indirectly, damage or hazards from one area to another or transform one type of pollution into another. Id. at Article 195. The LOS Convention defines "pollution of the marine environment" broadly as "the introduction by man, directly or indirectly, of substances or energy into the marine environment ... which results or is likely to result in such deleterious effects as harm to living resources and marine life, hazards to human health, hindrance to marine activities, including fishing and other legitimate uses of the sea, impairment of quality for use of sea water and reduction of amenities." Id. at Article 1(4).

Article 197 of the LOS Convention requires states to cooperate on a regional and global basis, directly or through competent international organizations, in formulating international rules and standards for the protection of the marine environment. A source of controversy throughout UNCLOS III was whether standards should be established on a global or regional basis. See Competing Norms in the Law of Marine Environmental Protection (Henrik Ringbom ed., 1997); J.W. Kindt, The Effect of Claims by Developing Countries on LOS International Marine Pollution Negotiations, 20 Va. J. Intl. L. 313, 328–332 (1980). To achieve consensus, several parallel provisions were adopted. With regard to pollution from land-based sources and from seabed activities within zones of national jurisdiction, states shall endeavor to harmonize their policies at a regional level. LOS Convention, Articles 207(3), 208(4). With regard to pollution from land-based sources, seabed activities subject to national jurisdiction, pollution by dumping, and pollution of the marine environment through or from the atmosphere, states shall endeavor to establish global and regional rules and standards, acting especially through competent international organizations or diplomatic conferences. Id. at Articles 207(4), 208(5), 210(4), 212(3). With regard to control of pollution from land-based sources, the economic capacity of developing states and their need for economic development must be considered in establishing such standards. Id. at Article 207(4).

The International Seabed Authority is to adopt rules, regulations, and procedures relating to the protection of the marine environment in connection with deep seabed mining activities. Id. at Articles 145, 209. See also id. at Articles 147, 162(2)(w)-(x), 165(2)(d)–(e), (k); Chapter 11, Section E.

C. VESSEL SOURCE POLLUTION

Article 211 of the LOS Convention requires states, acting through the competent international organization (primarily the International Maritime Organization (IMO)) or general diplomatic conference (such as the Brussels Conferences), to establish international rules and standards governing vessel-source pollution, including the adoption of routing systems designed to avoid collisions at sea. Under the LOS Convention, differing types of regulatory jurisdiction are accorded to coastal states with respect to vessels within their ports, within their territorial sea, and within their exclusive economic zone, and to flag states. LOS Convention, Article 211(3)–(6).

1. Flag State Jurisdiction

Flag states are obligated to adopt laws and regulations for the prevention of pollution of the marine environment from their vessels. These measures must be at least as effective as generally accepted international standards. In particular, flag states must regulate the design, construction, equipment, operation, and manning of their vessels; and they must take measures for preventing accidents (including the designation of routing systems), dealing with emergencies, ensuring the safety of operations at sea, and preventing both intentional and unintentional discharges. Id. at Articles 194(3)(b), 211. The flag state has the primary responsibility for ensuring that its ships comply with international rules and standards and those of the flag state. Id. at Article 217. See Section K.

In exercising its flag state authority, the United States imposes on U.S. vessels stringent standards for the design, construction, operation, and manning of vessels that are intended to protect the marine environment. See, e.g., 46 U.S.C. § 3701 et seq. (relating to U.S. vessels carrying cargoes of hazardous materials in bulk as well as to foreign vessels operating in the U.S. exclusive economic zone). See also the 1980 Act to Prevent Pollution from Ships, 33 U.S.C. §§ 1901 et seq., implementing the 1973 Convention for the Prevention of Pollution from Ships, as modified by the 1978 Protocol (MARPOL), and accompanying regulations at 33

C.F.R. Part 151. The United States is a party to the 1972 Convention on the Prevention of Collisions at Sea, and it has enacted regulations with which all U.S. vessels (and foreign vessels passing through waters subject to U.S. jurisdiction) must comply. 33 U.S.C. §§ 1601 et seq.

2. Coastal State Jurisdiction in Ports and in the Territorial Sea

Coastal states may adopt laws and regulations for the prevention, reduction, and control of marine pollution from foreign vessels within their territorial sea, including vessels exercising the right of innocent passage. However, such measures may not impede innocent passage. LOS Convention, Article 211(4). States may establish standards for pollution prevention as a condition for entrance into their ports or internal waters or for a call at their offshore terminals (see Chapter 7, Section C.3), but must publicize such requirements, both directly and through the competent international organization, i.e., the IMO. When a port state has harmonized its port entrance policies with other states in the region, a flag state shall require its vessels destined to a port in that region to furnish certain information relating to their compliance with port entry requirements when requested by any cooperating state through whose territorial sea the vessels are passing. Id. at Article 211(3).

The United States prohibits the discharge by vessels, including foreign vessels, of oil or hazardous substances within its navigable waters or contiguous zone, 33 U.S.C. § 1321(b)(3), defined for purposes of this statute as waters within twelve nautical miles of its baselines. Id. at § 1362(7)–(9). For a list of hazardous substances subject to this provision, see 40 C.F.R. § 116.4. The 1972 Clean Water Act regulates the discharge of sewage by vessels operating in U.S. navigable waters, defined for purposes of this Act as waters within three nautical miles of U.S. baselines. 33 U.S.C. § 1362(7)–(8). The Act requires the installation on most vessels of "marine sanitation devices" that meet specified standards (depending upon the size and age of the ship) for the treatment of sewage. Id. at § 1322; 33 C.F.R. Part 159; 40 C.F.R. Part 140. Sewage may be discharged within U.S. navigable waters only if specified effluent standards are met, and may be prohibited entirely in certain marine areas, including "no-discharge zones" established by U.S. states under 33 U.S.C. § 1322(f). The discharge of sewage by vessels beyond three miles of U.S. baselines is subject to the 1973 Convention for the Prevention of Pollution from Ships, as modified by the 1978 Protocol (MARPOL), Annex IV. See 33 C.F.R. Part 151. For discussion of U.S. laws regulating sewage and other discharges from vessels, see U.S. Environmental Protection Agency, Cruise Ship Discharge Assessment Report (Dec. 29, 2008), available at http://www.epa.gov/owow/oceans/cruise_ships/pdf/0812cruiseshipdischargeassess.pdf.

The Clean Water Act generally prohibits the discharge of pollutants into U.S. waters unless a permit is issued. However, in 1973 the U.S. Environmental Protection Agency (EPA) issued regulations exempting discharges incidental to the normal operation of vessels from the requirement of a discharge permit, including the discharge of "gray water" and marine engine discharges. 38 Fed. Reg. 13,528 (1973). This long-standing exclusion of normal vessel discharges from the permitting process was successfully challenged in Northwest Environmental Advocates v. United States EPA, 537 F.3d 1006 (9th Cir. 2008). Effective December 18, 2008, all vessels operating in U.S. waters, including waters within three miles of U.S. baselines, must obtain a "general vessel permit" for discharges incidental to normal operation, unless a specific exemption applies. 73 Fed. Reg. 79,473 (2008). The 2008 Clean Boating Act exempts recreational vessels from the general vessel permit process, 33 U.S.C. § 1342(r), and creates a new regulatory regime requiring the EPA, in consultation with the Coast Guard and interested U.S. states, to establish "management practices" for recreational vessels. Id. at § 1322(o). Congress also established a two-year moratorium during which time general vessel permits are not required for discharges (other than ballast water discharges) from commercial fishing vessels and nonrecreational vessels less than seventy-nine feet in length. Pub. L. 110–299, 122 Stat. 2995. See generally U.S. EPA, National Pollutant Discharge Elimination System (NPDES) Vessel General Permit (VGP) for Discharges Incidental to the Normal Operation of Ves-

sels Fact Sheet, available at http://www.epa.gov/
npdes/pubs/vessel_vgp_factsheet.pdf.

The 1978 Port and Tanker Safety Act conditions
entrance of tankers and other vessels carrying bulk
cargoes to U.S. ports on the fulfillment of specified
requirements aimed at minimizing risks to the marine environment. 33 U.S.C. § 1228; 33 C.F.R. Part
157; 46 C.F.R. Subchapter D. The Act also authorizes the establishment of port access routes designed to prevent collisions. 33 U.S.C. § 1223(c).
These requirements do not apply to foreign vessels
exercising their right of innocent passage or transit
passage through an international strait. Id. at
§ 1223(d).

3. Coastal State Jurisdiction in the EEZ

Where a coastal state believes that international
rules and standards are inadequate to protect an
area of its exclusive economic zone (EEZ), the coastal state may submit a request to the competent
international organization for a determination that
special conditions exist that merit additional coastal
state regulation of vessel-source pollution in that
area. Upon a finding that special conditions exist,
the coastal state may adopt laws and regulations for
the area, relating to discharges or navigational practices. These laws may not, however, relate to design, construction, manning, or equipment standards, other than generally accepted international
standards. LOS Convention, Article 211(6). See also
Section I.

The United States prohibits the discharge of oil or hazardous substances within its EEZ, except where permitted under the the 1973 Convention for the Prevention of Pollution from Ships, as modified by the 1978 Protocol (MARPOL). 33 U.S.C. § 1321(b)(3). In addition, regulations enacted to implement the 1978 MARPOL Protocol, 33 U.S.C. §§ 1901 et seq., and the 1972 Convention on the Prevention of Collisions at Sea, 33 U.S.C. §§ 1601 et seq., apply to foreign vessels within the U.S. EEZ. As a result of the 1989 *Exxon Valdez* oil spill disaster in Prince William Sound, Alaska, the United States enacted the 1990 Oil Pollution Act, which introduced a double-hull requirement for new tankers and a phase-in of double hulls for existing oil tankers operating in the U.S. EEZ. 46 U.S.C. § 3703a(a). At the time, this requirement was nonexistent on the international plane. With regard to tank vessels, the U.S. government may establish, inter alia, design, construction, manning, and equipment standards "that exceed standards set internationally." Id. at § 3703(a).

Europe also has had its share of maritime disasters near its coasts. For example, the *Erika* broke apart in heavy weather in the Gulf of Biscay at the end of 1999, spilling 10,000 tons of heavy fuel oil, while taking the remaining 20,000 tons down with it to a depth of approximately 400 feet (120 meters). The *Prestige* underwent the same fate about three years later off the Spanish Atlantic coast, with more than double the amount of oil on board; it now lies at a depth of two and a half miles (4,000 meters). As in the field of fisheries (see Chapter 9, Section H), the European Community (EC) has a certain competence with respect to the marine environment. Unlike the situation with respect to the conservation and management of fishery resources, this competence is not exclusive, but shared. The EC thus has exclusive competence only to the extent that provisions of the LOS Convention, or legal instruments adopted to implement it, affect common rules established by the EC. When EC rules exist but are not affected, such as EC provisions that establish only minimum standards, the member states normally retain competence, albeit without prejudice to the competence of the EC to act in this field. In all other cases competence rests with the EC member states. Declaration made at the time of formal confirmation by the EC pursuant to Article 5(1) of Annex IX to the LOS Convention, available at http://www.un.org/Depts/los/convention_agreements/convention_declarations. htm.

This competence, just as in the case of fisheries, is not static, for the 1957 Treaty of Rome did not contain any provision on environmental policy or law. It was only in 1973 that the EC first adopted a general action plan in this domain. As a result of the above-mentioned disasters, the EC adopted a number of so-called *Erika* packages. These measures did not always strictly follow existing international regulations. For example, the EC required a quicker timetable for a double-hull requirement for oil tankers than international regulations mandated. Rather than steering the EC into sailing a separate course, these EC initiatives have pushed the IMO to move forward. See Alan Boyle, EU Unilateralism and the Law of the Sea, 21 Intl. J. Marine & Coastal L. 15 (2006).

4. Topics of Special Concern

In order to keep organisms from sticking to the hulls of ships, so-called "anti-fouling" paints are normally applied. These paints, however, can significantly damage biological systems through the active substance they disperse while the ship is sailing. In order to mitigate these unwanted side effects, a convention has been adopted under the auspices of the IMO, namely the 2001 Convention on the Control of Harmful Anti-fouling Systems, which entered into force in September 2008.

Ships need to take ballast water on board when sailing without cargo for stability reasons. This practice may have adverse environmental consequences, since about three to ten billion tons of ballast water are transferred from one area to another each year, discharging species into a non-native environment. See http://www.imo.org; see generally Maria Helena Fonseca de Souza Rolim, The International Law on Ballast Water: Preventing Biopollution (2008). To address this issue, the IMO convened a diplomatic conference, resulting in the adoption of the 2004 Convention for the Control and Management of Ships' Ballast Water and Sediments, which had not entered into force as of June

1, 2009. The 2004 Convention mandates certain reception facilities for the repair and cleaning of ballast tanks, requires the monitoring of ballast water management efforts, creates a mechanism for ship surveys, certificates, and inspections, and sets specified distances from shore for ballast water discharges. Pending its entry into force, some states have agreed, on a regional level, to apply this global convention on a voluntary interim basis in the Baltic Sea and northeast Atlantic. See General Guidance on the Voluntary Interim Application of the D1 Ballast Water Exchange Standard in the North–East Atlantic and the Baltic Sea, available at http://www.helcom.fi.

D. POLLUTION FROM LAND–BASED SOURCES

All states, whether coastal or land-locked, must take measures, including the adoption of laws and regulations, to prevent pollution of the marine environment from land-based sources. Land-based sources include rivers, estuaries, pipelines, and outfall structures. The measures addressing such sources must "tak[e] into account" global or regional rules and standards. States, moreover, "shall endeavor" not only to harmonize their policies at the regional level, but also to establish global and regional rules. LOS Convention, Article 207(1)–(4). The use of the term "endeavor" in Article 207 with respect to regional and global cooperation is more cautious than that found in articles relating to other sources of marine pollution, and indeed is the weakest directive to be found in the LOS Convention, indicating an effort to accommodate the territorial sovereignty of states. Erik Franckx, Regional Marine Environment Protection Regimes in the Context of UNCLOS, 13 Intl. J. Marine & Coastal L. 307, 312–314 (1998). Standards that are even lower may be established for developing country regions. See Section B.

Although land-based pollution is by far the largest source of marine pollution, no global agreement dealing specifically with its prevention and control has yet seen the light of day. As of June 1, 2009, the only achievement on the global level has been the adoption in 1995 of a nonbinding Global Program of Action for the Protection of the Marine Environment from Land–Based Activities. UN Doc. UNEP(OCA)/LBA/IG.2/7 (1995). Although states are the main implementors of the Global Program of Action (GPA), this task was facilitated by the establishment of a secretariat—the United Nations Environment Programme (UNEP) GPA Coordination Office—a few years later. Intergovernmental review meetings have been taking place every five years. See http://www.gpa.unep.org.

On the regional level, however, several binding multilateral agreements address land-based pollution. These regional agreements are all related today, in one way or another, to the Regional Seas Program of UNEP, which was established in 1974 on the premise that states sharing a common body of water might be more inclined to protect this

shared marine environment. See http://www.unep.
org/regionalseas/default.asp. As of June 1, 2009, the
following regional programs had been established:

Baltic Sea: 1974 Convention on the Protection of
the Marine Environment of the Baltic Sea, as
replaced by the 1992 Convention on the Protection of the Marine Environment of the Baltic Sea
Area (HELCOM). This regional program was not
established under the auspices of UNEP, but participates in global meetings, shares experiences,
and exchanges policy advice and support. This
type of program is referred to as an "independent
partner program."

Northeast Atlantic: 1974 Convention for the Prevention of Marine Pollution from Land-based
Sources, as replaced by the 1992 Convention for
the Protection of the Marine Environment of the
North–East Atlantic (OSPAR). This is an independent partner program.

Mediterranean: 1980 Protocol on the Protection
of the Mediterranean Sea against Pollution from
Land–Based Sources. The 1980 Protocol was replaced by a 1996 Protocol, which entered into
force in May 2008. This program is established
under the auspices of UNEP and is directly administered by it.

Southeast Pacific: 1983 Protocol for the Protection of the South East Pacific against Pollution
from Land–Based Sources. This program is established under the auspices of UNEP but is not
directly administered by it.

Persian Gulf: 1990 Protocol for the Protection of the Marine Environment against Pollution from Land–Based Sources. This program is established under the auspices of UNEP but is not directly administered by it.

Black Sea: 1992 Protocol on Protection of the Black Sea Marine Environment against Pollution from Land–Based Sources. This program is established under the auspices of UNEP but is not directly administered by it.

Wider Caribbean Region: 1999 Protocol Concerning Pollution from Land–Based Sources and Activities (not in force as of June 1, 2009). This program is established under the auspices of UNEP and is directly administered by it.

Caspian Sea: 2003 Framework Convention for the Protection of the Marine Environment of the Caspian Sea, Article 7. This is an independent partner program. Although this Convention is not as elaborate as the previous treaties, it does obligate the parties, individually or jointly, to take appropriate measures to prevent, reduce, combat, and control land-based sources of pollution.

Of the ten remaining regions that currently form part of the UNEP Regional Seas Program, the South Asian Seas Program also addresses land-based pollution in some detail, albeit by means of a nonlegally binding document. See 1995 Action Plan for the Protection and Management of the Marine and Coastal Environment of the South Asian Region, Annex IV: Protection of the Marine Environment from Land–Based Activities.

Overall, these regional seas programs have been a useful tool to promote closer cooperation among states that share a marine environment, but their effectiveness very much depends on the political will of the particular countries involved and therefore differs widely from one region to another.

Land-based pollution gave rise to the protracted MOX Plant dispute, in which Ireland contested the planned release of radioactive contaminants by a mixed oxide plant located in the United Kingdom near the Irish Sea. See Chapter 15, Section C. After the involvement of not less than four different international dispute settlement forums, the merits of the environmental aspects of the dispute remained undecided as of June 1, 2009.

The discharge of pollutants from land-based sources into U.S. navigable waters is strictly regulated under the 1972 Clean Water Act, as amended, 33 U.S.C. §§ 1251 et seq. The "discharge of any pollutant," defined as "any addition of any pollutant to navigable waters from any point source" and "any addition of any pollutant to the waters of the contiguous zone or the ocean from any point source other than a vessel or other floating craft," id. at § 1362(12), is prohibited unless a permit is issued in compliance with the Act. Id. at § 1311. The term "navigable waters" is defined for purposes of the Act to include waters within three nautical miles of U.S. baselines; "contiguous zone" is defined by reference to Article 24 of the 1958 Territorial Sea Convention, i.e., an additional nine nautical miles beyond the limits of the three-nautical-mile territorial sea. Id. at § 1362(7)–(9).

Permits may not be issued for the discharge of high-level radioactive wastes and other designated toxic pollutants. Id. at § 1311(f). Permits for the discharge of other pollutants shall be issued only if such discharge meets effluent limitations at the source of the discharge and does not violate ambient water quality standards. Id. at §§ 1311, 1313. Additionally, permits for the discharge of land-source pollutants into coastal waters must comply with guidelines separately promulgated to avoid degradation of the "waters of the territorial seas, the contiguous zone, and the oceans." Id. at § 1343; 40 C.F.R. §§ 125.120–125.124. See generally Robin Kundis Craig, Urban Runoff and Ocean Water Quality in Southern California: What Tools Does the Clean Water Act Provide?, 9 Chap. L. Rev. 313 (2006). See Section C.2 for discussion of the regulation of the discharge of pollutants from vessels under the Clean Water Act.

E. OCEAN DUMPING

States are required to adopt laws and regulations to prevent pollution of the marine environment by the deliberate dumping of sewage, sludge, and other waste materials into the ocean. These laws and regulations must be no less effective than global rules and standards. States must ensure that dumping is not carried out without the permission of the proper authorities of the state involved. The coastal state has the right to permit, regulate, and control dumping within the territorial sea and the exclusive economic zone or onto the continental shelf, and no such dumping may occur without the express prior approval of the coastal state. LOS Convention, Article 210. For a definition of dumping, see id. at Article 1(5).

Several conventions have been concluded on this subject, some of which predate the LOS Convention. The first was a regional instrument: the 1972 Convention for the Prevention of Marine Pollution by Dumping from Ships and Aircraft, as later amended and finally replaced by the 1992 Convention for the Protection of the Marine Environment of the North–East Atlantic (OSPAR). This first regional step was followed later the same year by the adoption of a global convention, the 1972 Convention on the Prevention of Marine Pollution by Dumping of Wastes and Other Matter, to which the United States is a party. This Convention, listing substances that cannot be dumped at all (Annex I) or only with a permit (Annex II), will eventually be replaced by a 1996 Protocol. The Protocol will supersede the 1972 Convention as between parties to the 1972 Convention that are also parties to the 1996 Protocol. 1996 Protocol, Article 23. As of June 1, 2009, the United States was not a party to this Protocol. The Protocol applies the so-called negative listing approach, i.e., it lists only substances that may be dumped, thus implying that all other substances can no longer be dumped.

A 2006 amendment to this 1996 Protocol allows for the sequestration of carbon dioxide under the seabed, as complemented by the 2007 Specific Guidelines for Assessment of Carbon Dioxide Streams for Disposal into Sub-seabed Geological Formations. In the northeast Atlantic, OSPAR implementing measures, effective as of early 2008, allow for the storage of carbon dioxide streams in sub-soil geological formations, while at the same time prohibiting the placement of such streams in the water column or on the seabed. See OSPAR Decisions 2007/1 and 2007/2, available at http://www.ospar.org. Ocean fertilization—using iron to sequester carbon dioxide directly from the atmosphere—is an issue that, according to scientists, still requires further study. See http://www.gesamp.org. These twenty-first-century developments indicate the role oceans can play in trying to alleviate the negative consequences of climate change, as mentioned in Section H.

In the framework of the UNEP Regional Seas Program (see Section D), special protocols on dumping have also been adopted. These include: for the Mediterranean, the 1976 Protocol for the Prevention of Pollution in the Mediterranean Sea by Dumping from Ships and Aircraft, as amended by the 1995 Protocol for the Prevention and Elimination of Pollution in the Mediterranean Sea by Dumping from Ships and Aircraft or Incineration at Sea (1995 Protocol not in force as of June 1, 2009);

for the Pacific, the 1986 Protocol for the Prevention of Pollution of the South Pacific Region by Dumping; for the Black Sea, the 1992 Protocol on the Protection of the Black Sea Marine Environment Against Pollution by Dumping; and for the Persian Gulf, the 1998 Protocol on the Control of Marine Transboundary Movements and Disposal of Hazardous Wastes and Other Wastes.

The treatment of ocean dumping has evolved over time, as evidenced by these international agreements. While in the past banned substances were listed in an annex, modern treaties instead make use of negative listing, i.e., enumerating only those substances that may be dumped. This negative listing approach reverses the previous presumption that nonlisted substances could legally be dumped.

The 1972 Marine Protection, Research and Sanctuaries Act, 33 U.S.C. §§ 1401 et seq., makes unlawful the dumping of material by U.S. vessels into any ocean waters seaward of the U.S. baseline, and by foreign vessels within twelve miles of U.S. baselines, unless in compliance with the Act. Id. at § 1411. This Act does not regulate the routine discharge of sewage or effluent incidental to the operation of vessels. Id. at § 1402(c), (f). See Section C.2. The Secretary of the Army is authorized to issue permits for the dumping of dredged materials, id. at § 1413, and the Administrator of the Environmental Protection Agency (EPA) has permit authority for the dumping of all other materials. Id. at § 1412. After notice and opportunity for public hearing, the EPA Administrator may issue permits for ocean dumping after determining that such dumping will not "unreasonably degrade or endanger human health, welfare, or amenities, or the marine environment, ecological systems, or economic potentialities." Id. at § 1412(a). In making a determination, the EPA Administrator must take into consideration designated factors, including: the need for the proposed dumping; the effect of the dumping on human health and welfare, fisheries resources, shorelines, and marine ecosystems; and the use of land-based alternatives. Id. The EPA Administrator must designate sites where permitted disposals may occur. Id. at § 1412(c). Sites are "selected to minimize the interference of disposal activities with other activities in the marine environment, particularly avoiding areas of existing fisheries . . . and regions of heavy commercial or recreational navigation." 40 C.F.R. § 228.5. For a list of designated dumping sites, see id. at § 228.15. See generally Charles B. Anderson, Ocean Dumping and the Marine Protection, Research and Sanctuaries Act, 1 Loy. Mar. L.J. 79 (2002).

U.S. EPA permits may not be issued for radiological, chemical, and biological warfare agents, high-level radioactive waste, and medical waste. 33 U.S.C. § 1412(a). The dumping of low-level radioactive waste materials requires a "radioactive material disposal impact assessment" as well as the explicit approval of Congress. Id. at § 1414(i). For a discussion of ocean dumping of radioactive wastes, see Marianne Mackintosh, The Development of International Law in Relation to the Dumping and

Disposal of Radioactive Waste at Sea, 9 J. Intl. Mar. L. 354 (2003).

Since 1992 U.S. law has prohibited the dumping of sewage sludge (a common practice among coastal cities) or industrial waste. 33 U.S.C. § 1414b(a)(1)(B). Only emergency dumping of industrial waste is still possible if it has been demonstrated that the waste would otherwise pose an unacceptable risk to human health and that no other feasible solution exists. Id. at § 1412a(a). The EPA's interpretation of the ban on the dumping of industrial waste to include the prohibition of ocean incineration of wastes was upheld in Seaburn, Inc. v. United States EPA, 712 F.Supp. 218 (D.D.C. 1989).

F. POLLUTION FROM SEABED ACTIVITIES SUBJECT TO NATIONAL JURISDICTION

States are obligated to adopt laws, regulations, and other measures to prevent pollution of the marine environment arising from or in connection with their exploration and exploitation of the seabed and subsoil, or from artificial islands, installations, and structures under their jurisdiction. Such laws, regulations, and measures must be no less effective than international rules, standards, and recommended practices and procedures. LOS Convention, Articles 194(3)(c), 208(1). Moreover, states, "acting especially through competent international organizations or diplomatic conference, shall establish global and regional" rules, standards, and practices to address seabed pollution. Id. at Article 208(5).

No such global convention has yet been adopted, but at the regional level a number of specific protocols have been adopted under the umbrella of the United Nations Environment Programme (UNEP) Regional Seas Program (see Section D). These include the 1989 Persian Gulf Protocol concerning Marine Pollution Resulting from Exploration and Exploitation of the Continental Shelf and the 1994 Protocol for the Protection of the Mediterranean Sea against Pollution Resulting from Exploration and Exploitation of the Continental Shelf (not in force as of June 1, 2009). See also the 1992 Convention on the Protection of the Marine Environment of the Baltic Sea Area (HELCOM), Annex VI, and the 1992 Convention for the Protection of the Marine Environment of the North–East Atlantic (OSPAR), Annex III. Furthermore, several nonbinding documents have been adopted to address this topic, including: UNEP, Guidelines for Offshore Mining and Drilling (1982), available at http://www.unep. org/law/PDF/UNEPEnv–LawGuide & PrincN04.pdf; International Maritime Organization, Code for the Construction and Equipment of Mobile Offshore Drilling Units, IMO Doc. A.649(16) (1989); Arctic Council Working Group on Protection of the Arctic Marine Environment, Arctic Offshore Oil and Gas Guidelines (2002), available at http://old.pame.is/ sidur/uploads/ArcticGuidelines.pdf; International Council for the Exploration of the Sea, Guidelines for the Management of Marine Sediment Extraction (2003), available at http://www.ices.dk/reports/ MHC/2003/WGEXT03.pdf; and International Finance Corporation of the World Bank Group, Environmental, Health, and Safety Guidelines for Offshore Oil and Gas Development (2007), available at http://www.ifc.org/ifcext/enviro.nsf/AttachmentsBy Title/gui_EHSGuidelines2007_OffshoreOiland Gas/$FILE/Final + - + Offshore + Oil + and + Gas + Development.pdf.

Under the U.S. Outer Continental Shelf Lands Act, environmental studies must be conducted by the Secretary of the Interior in all regions in which oil and gas leases will be sold. 43 U.S.C. § 1346. Environmental impact statements must be prepared by the Secretary of the Interior for a production plan submitted by a lessee, which must provide environmental safeguards. The Secretary shall disapprove any plan that may cause serious harm or damage to the marine environment. Id. at § 1351(h). See also Chapter 10, Section H.

According to U.S. law, licenses for the construction and operation of deepwater ports may not be issued until an environmental impact statement has been prepared and reviewed. 33 U.S.C. §§ 1504–1505. Regulations have been issued to prevent pollution of the marine environment, to clean up any pollutants that may be discharged, and to minimize any adverse environmental impact from the construction and operation of deepwater ports. 33 C.F.R. Parts 149–150.

G. POLLUTION FROM DEEP SEABED MINING

For parties to the LOS Convention, international rules, regulations, and procedures to prevent pollution of the marine environment from specified deep seabed activities are to be issued in accordance with Part XI of the Convention governing the Area. See Chapter 11. Article 145 of Part XI authorizes the International Seabed Authority to adopt appropriate rules and regulations to protect the marine environment with respect to mineral exploration and exploitation in the Area. In 2000 the Authority issued Regulations on Prospecting and Exploration for Polymetallic Nodules in the Area, of which Part V deals specifically with the protection and preservation of the marine environment. ISBA/6/A/18 (2000), Regs. 31–34. A year later, its Legal and Technical Commission adopted Recommendations for the Guidance of the Contractor for the Assessment of the Possible Environmental Impacts arising from Exploration for Polymetallic Nodules in the Area. ISBA/7/LTC//Rev.1. Both documents can be found at http://www.isa.org.jm.

The 1980 U.S. Deep Seabed Hard Mineral Resources Act incorporates extensive rules relating to the protection of the marine environment against pollution that might result from deep seabed activities carried on by persons subject to U.S. jurisdiction. 30 U.S.C. §§ 1401(b)(4), 1413(a)(2)(c), 1415(a)(4), (b)(2), (c)(1)(B), 1419–1420. Each licensee or permittee is required to monitor the environmental effects of any deep seabed exploration and mining activities and to submit relevant information to the government. Id. at § 1424. For discussion of liability for pollution arising from deep seabed activities, see Section J. For further discussion of this Act, see Chapter 11, Section D.

H. POLLUTION FROM OR THROUGH THE ATMOSPHERE

Each state is required to adopt laws, regulations, and measures to prevent pollution of the marine environment from or through the atmosphere. These rules and regulations shall govern activities within the state's sovereign air space and shall apply to its vessels and aircraft. In adopting such rules and regulations states must take into account international rules and standards. LOS Convention, Article 212.

No multilateral convention deals specifically with marine pollution from or through the atmosphere. The 1963 Limited Test Ban Treaty and the 1996 Comprehensive Test Ban Treaty (1996 Treaty not in force as of June 1, 2009) address the possible pollution of the sea by radioactive fallout from nuclear weapons testing. The regional 1979 Convention on Long-range Transboundary Air Pollution, which responded to the acid rain phenomenon in Europe, tries, by means of protocols, to achieve emission targets for specific substances. Moreover, the International Maritime Organization has adopted regulations for the prevention of air pollution from ships by means of a 1997 Protocol that adds a new Annex VI to the 1973 Convention for the Prevention of Pollution from Ships, as modified by 1978 Protocol (MARPOL), setting limits on emissions from ship exhausts and allowing for the establishment of sulphur oxide emission control areas. This Annex was further revised in 2008, and the revisions will become operational in 2010.

Global climate change and the oceans are interrelated. Oceans are not only a factor influencing the change in the earth's climate through their movement of heat and sediments by means of their surface and sub-surface currents, but they also bear the consequences of climate change, with sea-level rise as a prime example. See Chapter 5, Section K. Additionally, oceans are seen as part of the solution to this problem through the enhancement of their use as sinks and reservoirs of greenhouse gases. 1992 United Nations Framework Convention on Climate Change, Article 4(1)(d). See Christopher A.G. Tulou et al., Climate Change and the Marine Environment, in Ocean and Coastal Law and Policy 571 (Donald C. Baur, Tim Eichenberg & Michael Sutton eds., 2008).

I. AREA–BASED MANAGEMENT TOOLS

States are obligated to take measures necessary to protect and preserve rare or fragile ecosystems as well as the habitat of depleted, threatened, or endangered species and other forms of marine life. Where the area to be protected forms part of a state's exclusive economic zone (EEZ), special international arrangements must be made to prevent the pollution of such an area. LOS Convention, Articles 194(5), 211(6). To establish these "particular, clearly defined areas" of the EEZ, the coastal state must submit a proposal to the competent international organization, i.e., the International Maritime Organization (IMO). Id. at Article 211(6)(a), (c). The coastal state can only establish such areas if the IMO agrees.

A coastal state also has the right to adopt and enforce nondiscriminatory laws and regulations for the prevention, reduction, and control of marine pollution from vessels in ice-covered areas within the limits of its EEZ, where particularly severe climatic conditions and the presence of ice for most of the year create obstructions or exceptional hazards to navigation. Such laws and regulations are needed especially where pollution of the marine environment could cause major harm to, or irreversible disturbance of, the ecological balance. Id. at Article 234. This Article provides the only instance in the LOS Convention where national rules concerning vessel-source pollution do not have to conform to generally accepted international rules and standards. The potential commercial usage of the Northeast Passage (or Northern Sea Route, as it is called by Russia) and the Northwest Passage in the Arctic as a result of climate change will increase international attention on Article 234, which is the only LOS Convention article relating specifically to ice-covered areas. See Erik Franckx, Should the Law Governing Maritime Areas in the Arctic Adapt to Changing Climatic Circumstances?, in Climate Governance in the Arctic 119, 133–135 (Timo Koivurova, E. Carina H. Keskitalo & Nigel Bankes eds., 2009) (stressing the adaptive capacity of Article 234).

The Article 234 principles reflect the consensus developed at the Third United Nations Law of the Sea Conference. Previously, a controversy was caused by Canada's 1970 enactment of the Canadian Arctic Waters Pollution Prevention Act, the purpose of which was to preserve "the peculiar ecological balance that now exists in the water, ice and land areas" of the Canadian Arctic. 18–19 Eliz. II, c. 47 (1969–70), Can.Rev.Stat. ch. C–2 (1970), 9 Intl. Leg. Materials 543 (1970). That legislation established and applied safety control zones to foreign ships. These zones extended 100 miles from the nearest Canadian land, north of the sixtieth parallel of latitude, and included both liquid and frozen waters within that area. All ships not complying with far-reaching Canadian regulations were banned from these zones. For the U.S. objections to the Canadian measures and the Canadian response, see id. at 605.

In addition to the LOS Convention framework, various other types of area-based management tools currently exist. For an overview of these tools, see Report of the Secretary–General to the U.N. General Assembly, Oceans and the Law of the Sea, UN Doc. A/62/66/Add.2, ¶¶ 122–186 (2007). In the fisheries context these tools include such notions as "marine protected areas" (as contemplated under Article 8 of the 1992 Convention on Biological Diversity), "specially protected areas" (see the 1995 Protocol Concerning Specially Protected Areas and Biological Diversity in the Mediterranean), and "spatial and temporal closures" (as regularly used by regional fisheries management organizations). In the shipping context, area-based management involves "special areas" (such as the Sulphur Oxide Emissions Control Areas created through Annex VI of MARPOL, mentioned in Section H), and "particularly sensitive sea areas" (as regulated by IMO Revised Guidelines for the Identification and Designation of Particularly Sensitive Sea Areas, IMO Doc. A/24/RES/982 (2006)). In addition, area-based management tools include "sanctuaries" (e.g., the Southern Ocean Whale Sanctuary established by the International Whaling Commission, http://www.iwcoffice.org/index.htm) and "reserves" (such as the network of biosphere reserves established to protect biodiversity under the UNESCO Man and the Biosphere Program, http://portal.unesco.org/science/en/ev.php-URL_ID=6393 & URL_DO=DO_TOPIC & URL_SECTION=201.html). The exact relationship between all these different area-based management tools is not always crystal clear. For discussion, for instance, of the relationship between Article 211(6) of the LOS Convention, "special areas," and "particularly sensitive areas," see Louise Angélique de la Fayette, The Marine Environment Committee: The Conjunction of the Law of the Sea and International Environmental Law, 16 Intl. J. Marine & Coastal L. 155, 190–194 (2001).

Under the 1972 Marine Sanctuaries Act, 16 U.S.C. §§ 1431 et seq., the United States established a National Marine Sanctuary System. Id. at § 1431(c). Sanctuaries created pursuant to this System may extend into the EEZ, consistent with international law. Id. at § 1432(3). As of June 1, 2009, the National Marine Sanctuary System consists of thirteen marine sanctuaries, 15 C.F.R. Part 922, and the Papahanaumokuakea Marine National Monument (formerly known as the Northwestern Hawaiian Islands Marine National Monument), 50 C.F.R. Part 404. Several of these areas extend beyond the U.S. twelve-mile territorial sea. They range in size from less than one square mile (Fagatele Bay off the southwest coast of American Samoa) to approximately 140,000 square miles (362,580 square kilometers) (the Papahanaumokuakea Marine Monument—the world's largest protected marine area). The regulations governing these protected areas must conform to generally recognized principles of international law as well as to treaties to which the United States is a party. 16 U.S.C. § 1435(a); 15 C.F.R. § 922.4; 50 C.F.R. § 404.12. In April 2008 the IMO designated the Papahanaumokuakea Marine National Monument as a particularly sensitive sea area. Res. MEPC. 171(57), IMO Doc. MEPC 57/21, Annex 12 (2008). Entering the Monument waters without permission is generally prohibited. However, vessels may exercise their right of innocent passage so long as the vessel participates in a compulsory vessel monitoring system. 50 C.F.R. § 404.4. For discussion of U.S. law relevant to marine sanctuaries, see Kim Diana Connolly, Jennifer L. Schorr & Darren Misenko, Marine Protected Areas, in Oceans and Coastal Law and Policy 535 (Donald C. Baur, Tim Eichenberg & Michael Sutton eds., 2008).

J.   RESPONSIBILITY AND LIABILITY

A state that fails to fulfill its obligations to protect and preserve the marine environment is liable in accordance with international law. LOS Convention, Article 235(1). Under international law, a state may be required to prevent, reduce, or terminate the activity threatening or causing pollution, or to pay reparation for injury caused. See, e.g., the Trail Smelter Case (United States v. Canada), 3 Rep. Intl. Arb. Awards 1911 (1938), 1938 (1941). Where a state's violation of anti-pollution rules or standards results in injury to private interests, the state must ensure that recourse is available in accordance with its legal system for prompt and adequate compensation or other relief. LOS Convention, Article 235(2).

States are obligated to cooperate in developing and implementing international law in order to assure prompt and adequate compensation for damage caused by pollution of the marine environment. These measures may include criteria and procedures for payment of adequate compensation, such as compulsory insurance or compensation funds. Id. at Article 235(3).

Several international conventions deal with the liability of persons responsible for the violation of international anti-pollution rules or standards. Although nuclear ships pose a special concern, comprehensive international regulation of nuclear-powered civilian vessels and warships has been difficult to achieve. A specific convention was concluded on the topic of nuclear ships in 1962. But this Convention on Liability for Operators of Nuclear Ships, which included warships in its scope of application, met with strong opposition from the United States as well as the Soviet Union and never entered into force. The 1963 Convention on Civil Liability for Nuclear Damage, as amended, explicitly excludes nuclear-powered ships from its coverage. Article I(1)(j). Under the auspices of the International Maritime Organization (IMO), the Convention Relating to Civil Liability in the Field of Maritime Carriage of Nuclear Material was adopted in 1971. However, this Convention, which entered into force in 1975, has attracted only a limited number of ratifications, and as of June 1, 2009 did not include the United States among its member states.

Questions of liability for nuclear vessels may arise in conjunction with questions about port access and required notice to coastal states. Civilian nuclear-powered ships have so far not been a commercial success; only in the Northern Sea Route do such ships currently operate under the Russian flag, mostly as oceanic or river ice-breakers and exceptionally as cargo vessels. Whether a coastal state can require previous notification of ships carrying nuclear material or waste in innocent passage through its territorial sea has stirred controversy; similar controversy has arisen with regard to prior coastal state notification with respect to nuclear-powered warships. See Chapter 8, Section D.3, and Marco Roscini, The Navigational Rights of Nuclear Ships, 15 Leiden J. Intl. L. 251 (2002). The access of military nuclear-powered ships to foreign ports is often regulated on a bilateral basis. How such access relates to existing security and collective defense treaties has at times given rise to tension. See, e.g., J.C. Woodliffe, Port Visits by Nuclear Armed Naval Vessels: Recent State Practice, 35 Intl. & Comp. L.Q. 730 (1986); see also Chapter 7, Section C.4. The United States has a policy to compensate for damage resulting from a nuclear incident involving a nuclear reactor of a U.S. warship in times of peace. 42 U.S.C. § 2211; see also Chapter 7, Section C.5.

The 1969 Convention on Civil Liability for Oil Pollution Damage established a system of strict liability for the shipowner for oil pollution damage caused in the territory and territorial sea of a contracting state as a result of an incident. Articles 2–3. The registered owner is obligated to maintain compulsory insurance. Id. at Article 7. A second tier of compensation was established in the 1971 Convention concerning an International Fund for Compensation for Oil Pollution Damage. Contributions to the Fund are to be made by persons receiving shipments of oil by sea, in proportion to the tonnage received. Article 10. These conventions were amended by means of two 1992 protocols that entirely supersede the parent conventions. 1992 Protocol to Amend the International Convention on Civil Liability for Oil Pollution Damage, Article 12; 1992 Protocol to Amend the International Convention on the Establishment of an International Fund for Compensation for Oil Pollution Damage, Article 31. The applicable treaties are now known as the 1992 Civil Liability Convention and the 1992 Fund Convention. In addition to an increase in the compensation limits, major changes include the extension of each Convention's application to the exclusive economic zone (Articles 2(a)(ii) and 3(a)(ii), respectively) as well as, indirectly, the expiration of private industry arrangements such as the 1969 Tanker Owners Voluntary Agreement Concerning Liability for Oil Pollution (TOVALOP) and the 1971 Oil Companies' Contract Regarding an Interim Supplement to Tanker Liability for Oil Pollution (CRISTAL). See Susan Bloodworth, Student Author, Death on the High Seas: The Demise of TOVALOP and CRISTAL, 13 J. Land Use & Envtl. L. 443 (1998). A new third tier of compensation has been added by means of a 2003 Protocol to the 1992 Fund Convention. This supplementary scheme, available only to parties to the 1992 Fund Convention, also calls for contributions by persons receiving shipments of oil by sea. 2003 Protocol, Article 10. The total amount of compensation payable for any one incident under this scheme is limited to a combined total of 750 million Special Drawing Rights (just over US$1 billion), including the amount of compensation paid under the 1992 Civil Liability and Fund Conventions. Finally, the 2001 Convention on Civil Liability for Bunker Oil Pollution Damage, which entered into force in November 2008, obligates a vessel's registered owner to maintain compulsory insurance for damage caused in the territory, territorial sea, or exclusive economic zone of a contracting party. Articles 2, 7.

Besides the above-mentioned conventions, which focus on pollution by oil, the IMO has also addressed other hazardous and noxious substances. These substances have been subjected to a two-tier system like that of the 1992 Civil Liability Convention and the 1992 Fund Convention, by means of the 1996 International Convention on Liability for Damage in Connection with the Carriage of Hazardous and Noxious Substances by Sea (not in force as of June 1, 2009), which incorporates provisions for setting up a fund. The 1996 Convention will apply to inland waters and territory, the territorial sea, and the exclusive economic zone. Article 3. As of June 1, 2009, a Protocol is being negotiated to address the practical problems that have caused states to withhold their ratification of this 1996 Convention.

A private 1974 Offshore Pollution Liability Agreement (OPOL), as amended, concerns liability for pollution connected with offshore drilling. The parties to OPOL are operators of offshore oil and gas exploration and production facilities who agree to accept strict liability for possible pollution damage up to a certain maximum limit. Clause IV(A). See http://www.opol.org.uk.

As of June 1, 2009, the United States is not a party to any of the agreements established within the framework of the IMO mentioned above. After a number of major oil incidents, including the *Exxon Valdez* disaster (see Section C.3), which spilled an estimated 10.8 million gallons (40.9 million liters) of crude oil in Alaskan waters, the United States adopted the 1990 Oil Pollution Act (OPA), Pub. L. No. 101–380, 104 Stat. 484 (1990) (codified as amended primarily at 33 U.S.C. §§ 2701 et seq. and 46 U.S.C. §§ 3701 et seq.). The OPA imposes strict liability for removal costs and other damages on persons responsible for the discharge of oil (or a substantial threat of an oil discharge) from a vessel or facility in or on U.S. navigable waters, shore-lines, or its exclusive economic zone. 33 U.S.C. § 2702(a). However, liability may not exceed the limits set forth in the OPA, which as of July 31, 2009, range from US$854,400 to US$373,800,000, depending on the type and/or size of the vessel or facility involved. Id. at § 2704(a), (d); 74 Fed. Reg. 31,357 (2009).

These limits do not apply in cases of gross negli-gence or willful misconduct of the responsible party. 33 U.S.C. § 2704(c)(1). Liability is not imposed on a potentially responsible party where a discharge is caused solely by an act of God, an act of war, or an act or omission of a third party, id. at § 2703(a), unless the responsible party fails or refuses to re-port an incident, to provide all reasonable cooperation with respect to removal activities, or to comply with an applicable order. Id. at § 2703(c). An Oil Spill Liability Trust Fund is available to pay for state and federal government removal, assessment, and restoration costs, as well as other uncompensated claims and damages allowed under the OPA (including allowable damages that have been incurred by individuals). 26 U.S.C. § 9509; 33 U.S.C. §§ 2712–2713. However, all claims for removal costs or damages must first be presented to the responsible party. Id. at § 2713(a). For discussion of the OPA and its application, see Lawrence I. Kiern, Liability, Compensation, and Financial Responsibility Under the Oil Pollution Act of 1990: A Review of the First Decade, 24 Tul. Mar. L. J. 481 (2000).

The OPA specifically reserves the right of U.S. states to impose "additional liability or requirements with respect to ... the discharge of oil or other pollution by oil" within the state. 33 U.S.C. § 2718(a), (c). Many states have imposed their own liability regimes. See, for example, Conn. Gen. Stat. § 22a–452, which imposes unlimited liability for oil spill removal costs arising from "the negligence or other actions" of responsible parties. Some state enactments, however, have been successfully challenged. See United States v. Locke (Intertanko), 529 U.S. 89 (2000), in which the U.S. Supreme Court found that Congress had pre-empted the state of Washington's personnel and training requirements for oil tankers. For a discussion of state pre-emption issues, see Steven R. Swanson, OPA 90 + 10:

The Oil Pollution Act of 1990 After Ten Years, 32 J. Mar. L. & Com. 135, 142–152 (2001).

The Federal Water Pollution Control Act (FWPCA) imposes civil penalties on any owner, operator, or person in charge of a vessel or facility from which oil or a hazardous substance is discharged in harmful quantities into the navigable waters of the United States, its territorial sea, or exclusive economic zone, or in connection with continental shelf exploitation activities or deepwater ports. These penalties range up to a maximum amount (as of June 1, 2009) of US$32,500 per day of violation or an amount up to US$1,100 per barrel of oil or unit of reportable quantity of hazardous substances discharged. 33 U.S.C. § 1321(b)(7)(A); 33 C.F.R. § 27.3. These amounts increase in cases of gross negligence or willful misconduct. 33 U.S.C. § 1321(b)(7)(D); 33 C.F.R. § 27.3. In determining the exact amount of the civil penalty, the court considers a number of factors, including the gravity of the offense and the efforts of the person to mitigate the effects of such discharge. 33 U.S.C. § 1321(b)(8). Although civil penalties may only be imposed by a federal district court, id. at § 1321(b)(7)(E), the Administrator of the Environmental Protection Agency or the secretary of the department in which the Coast Guard is operating (the Department of Homeland Security as of June 1, 2009) has authority to assess lesser administrative penalties. Id. at § 1321(b)(6). Criminal penalties may also be imposed for failure to notify the government of a discharge. Id. For criminal penalties relating to other violations of the Clean Water Act, see id. at § 1319(c).

The FWPCA also provides for the recovery of the costs of removal of the discharge of oil or hazardous substances from the owner or operator of a vessel or onshore or offshore facility, unless caused solely by an act of God or war, negligence on the part of the government, or the act or omission of a third party. 33 U.S.C. § 1321(f). Under the FWPCA, unlike under the OPA, private persons and state governments have no recourse; only the U.S. government may recover such costs, id., and the limits of liability are lower than under the OPA. As of June 1, 2009, removal cost liability was limited to the greater of US$125 per gross ton or US$125,000 for oil barges, and in the case of any other vessel, US$150 per gross ton (or US$250,000 for vessels carrying oil or a hazardous substance as a cargo), whichever is greater. Id. These limitations do not apply if the discharge is the result of willful negligence or misconduct, in which case costs are recoverable in full. Id. For discharges of oil or a hazardous substance from onshore or offshore facilities, the government may recover up to US$50,000,000 from the responsible person, or all of such costs if the discharge is the result of willful negligence or misconduct. Id. The FWPCA also preserves the authority of states of the United States to enact more stringent rules than those on the federal level, unless expressly provided otherwise. Id. at §§ 1370, 1321(*o*)(2).

U.S. courts have held that the oil spill liability limitations established under the FWCPA may not be circumvented by allowing the government to pursue other forms of action, such as maritime tort, against the discharger. United States v. Dixie Carriers, Inc., 627 F.2d 736 (5th Cir. 1980). Similarly, in South Port Marine, LLC v. Gulf Oil Ltd. Pshp., 234 F.3d 58, 65 (1st Cir. 2000), the court ruled that Congress intended enactment of the OPA to supplant existing federal admiralty and maritime law claims applicable to oil spills, and thus denied a claim for punitive damages.

In addition to the liability schemes established for oil spills under the OPA and for oil and hazardous substances under the FWCPA, the Comprehensive Environmental Response, Compensation, and Liability Act (CERCLA), 42 U.S.C. §§ 9601 et seq., imposes strict liability on responsible parties for removal costs and other damages caused by the discharge of hazardous substances. The CERCLA does not apply to discharges of petroleum (including crude oil) or natural gas (including liquified natural gas). Id. at § 9601(14). The owner or operator of any vessel or facility subject to U.S. jurisdiction from which there is a release or threatened release of a hazardous substance is strictly liable for all costs of removal or remedial action and damages for injury to, destruction of, or loss of natural resources (defined to include land, fish, wildlife, biota, air, water, and other resources, including the resources of the exclusive economic zone). Id. at §§ 9607(a), 9601(16). Unlike other categories of responsible parties under the CERCLA (who face unlimited liability), owners and operators of vessels face liability that varies according to the size and type of vessel. For example, vessels carrying hazardous cargoes may be liable up to the greater of US$5,000,-000 or US$300 per gross ton. Id. at § 9607(c)(1). However, the limitations of liability are not available where the discharge is a result of willful misconduct or negligence, where the primary cause of such discharge is a violation of applicable safety, construction, or operation regulations, or where the person responsible fails to provide all reasonable cooperation and assistance to remedial activities. Id. at § 9607(c)(2). Liability is not imposed if the discharge is caused solely by an act of God, an act of war, or certain acts or omissions of third parties. Id. at § 9607(b). Penalties may be imposed for failure to notify the proper government authority immediately of a discharge. Id. at § 9603(b). In addition, punitive damages may be assessed where the liable person fails without cause to provide removal or remedial action on the order of the President. Id. at § 9607(c)(3).

For discussion of U.S. legislation in this area in general, see John E. Noyes, Case Study of the United States of America, in Vessel-source Pollution and Coastal State Jurisdiction: The Work of the ILA Committee on Coastal State Jurisdiction Relating to Marine Pollution (1991–2000) 357 (Erik Franckx ed., 2001).

K. ENFORCEMENT

Jurisdiction to enforce rules and regulations relating to the marine environment can be exercised by flag states, coastal states, and port states in varying degrees, depending on the source of pollution and the location of the violation or the resulting environmental damage.

1. Flag State Enforcement

The flag state has the primary obligation to ensure that its ships comply with applicable international rules and standards established through the competent international organization or general diplomatic conference, and with the flag state's laws and regulations implementing such standards. LOS Convention, Article 217(1). Flag states may not permit their ships to sail unless they meet such requirements, including standards relating to design, construction, equipment, and manning, as evidenced by certificates of compliance. Id. at Article 217(2). Furthermore, flag states must periodically inspect their ships to verify that such certificates are in conformity with the ship's actual condition. Other states must accept these certificates as evidence of the condition of the ship, unless there are clear grounds for believing otherwise. Id. at Article 217(3).

If a ship does not meet international rules and standards, the flag state must provide for immediate investigation and, where appropriate, institute proceedings irrespective of where the violation or injury has occurred. Id. at Article 217(4). The state that is the victim of a violation by a ship (or, in the case of pollution of the common environment, any state) may complain to the flag state and request it to take appropriate actions, id. at Article 217(6), and, if dissatisfied with the action taken by the flag state, may invoke against the flag state the remedies available under international law. Id. at Article 235(1). Flag states must provide penalties sufficient in severity to discourage violations by their ships whenever they occur. Id. at Article 217(8).

2. *Coastal State Enforcement*

The authority of the coastal state to bring proceedings against an offending foreign vessel varies in some respects, depending on where the vessel is located and where the violation occurred. The coastal state has jurisdiction to prescribe, adjudicate, and enforce with respect to any matter relating to acts of pollution committed in its ports. In addition, the coastal state can institute proceedings against a ship voluntarily in port or against its crew for a violation of its laws that occurred within its territorial sea or exclusive economic zone, provided that its laws were adopted in accordance with generally accepted rules and standards. An offshore terminal is assimilated for these purposes to a port. Id. at Article 220(1).

Where there are clear grounds for believing that a foreign ship, passing through the territorial sea of the coastal state, has, during that passage, violated laws and regulations of that state adopted in accordance with applicable international rules and standards, the coastal state may, subject to certain procedural safeguards, see id. at Article 226, undertake physical inspection of the vessel in the territorial sea in order to ascertain the facts relating to the violation. It may, where evidence so warrants, institute proceedings, including detention of the ship, in accordance with its laws. If the act of pollution in the territorial sea was willful and serious, the coastal state may impose any penalties authorized by its law. Id. at Articles 220(2), 230(2).

When a ship has violated international anti-pollution rules or standards in the exclusive economic zone of the coastal state, and the ship is still in the exclusive economic zone or the territorial sea of the coastal state, that state can take various steps, depending on the gravity of the violation. Where clear grounds exist for believing that a violation has occurred, the coastal state may require the ship to provide information regarding its identity and port of registry, its last and its next port of call, and other relevant information needed to establish whether a violation has occurred. Id. at Article 220(3). If there are clear grounds for believing that the violation resulted in "a substantial discharge causing or threatening significant pollution of the marine environment," and the ship either refuses to give information or the information supplied is manifestly in variance with the evident facts, the coastal state is entitled to proceed with a physical inspection. Id. at Article 220(5). Only when there is "clear objective evidence" that the ship committed the violation and that the discharge is causing or threatens to cause "major damage to the coastline or related interests of the coastal state, or to any resources of its territorial sea or exclusive economic zone," is that state entitled to institute proceedings in accordance with its laws and to detain the ship. Id. at Article 220(6).

To ensure that in no case is a ship unduly detained, appropriate procedures must be established, either through the competent international organization or by special agreement, for bonding or other appropriate financial security. If the ship makes the necessary arrangements, the coastal state is obligated to allow the vessel to proceed. Id. at Article 220(7). See also Chapter 15, Section D for discussion of prompt release applications before the International Tribunal of the Law of the Sea. The coastal state may only apply monetary penalties, unless the violation was committed in the territorial sea and the act of pollution was willful and serious. In that case, the vessel may be confiscated and the person responsible may be tried and punished. LOS Convention, Article 230.

3. Port State Enforcement

For a discussion of the LOS Convention provisions that authorize a port state to undertake investigations and institute proceedings relating to a discharge by a foreign vessel that has occurred within or outside its coastal waters, see Chapter 7, Section E.

Under the 1973 Convention for the Prevention of Pollution from Ships, as modified by the 1978 Protocol (MARPOL), a contracting party is authorized to verify the existence of valid certificates while a ship is in one of its ports. Article 5(2). A contracting party may also verify whether a ship has discharged any harmful substances in violation of the provisions of MARPOL regulations, and if such inspection indicates a violation, the report of such violation is forwarded to the flag state for further action. Id. at Article 6(2).

Prosecution for violation of separate national record-keeping laws may also be possible in cases involving oil or other discharges from vessels. See United States v. Royal Caribbean Cruises Ltd., 11 F. Supp. 2d 1358 (S.D. Fla. 1998), which is discussed in Chapter 7, Section E.

4. Overlapping Jurisdiction

The flag state is entitled to have penal proceedings against its ship in a foreign state suspended as soon as the flag state has itself instituted proceedings against the ship. There are three exceptions. The state that has instituted the proceedings need not suspend them if: (1) the violation was committed in its territorial sea or internal waters; (2) the coastal state suffered major damage; or (3) the flag state "has repeatedly disregarded its obligations to enforce effectively the applicable international rules and standards in respect of violations committed by its vessels." When the proceedings are suspended, they have to be terminated on completion of proceedings in the flag state. LOS Convention, Article 228. If the coastal state is dissatisfied with the action taken by the flag state after the case has been transferred, it may, in accordance with general international law, complain both to the flag state and to the competent international organization; and, if the lack of enforcement recurs, the coastal state may next time refuse to suspend proceedings. Id. at Article 228(1).

5. Liability for Wrongful Enforcement

If a state took measures against a foreign ship that were unlawful or exceeded those reasonably required in the light of available information, it must pay the flag state appropriate compensation for any injury or loss attributable to such measures. It must also provide for recourse in its legal system for private actions in respect of such injury or loss. Id. at Article 232.

The 1958 High Seas Convention contains various measures for wrongful enforcement, but none relate to environmental enforcement actions. See Articles 20 (piracy), 22(3) (stopping certain suspected ships on the high seas), and 23(7) (hot pursuit). Article 6 of the 1969 Convention on High Seas Intervention in Oil Pollution Casualties provides that any party that has taken measures in contravention of the provisions of that Convention "shall be obliged to pay compensation to the extent of the damage caused by measures which exceed those reasonably necessary" to prevent, mitigate, or eliminate grave and imminent danger. Under the 1973 Convention for the Prevention of Pollution from Ships, as modified by the 1978 Protocol (MARPOL), a ship that is unduly detained or delayed by measures taken under that Convention "shall be entitled to compensation for any loss or damage suffered." Article 7(2).

L.   NOTIFICATION AND COOPERATIVE ACTION

When a state becomes aware that the marine environment has been injured or is in imminent danger of being injured, it has the duty to notify immediately other states likely to be affected by such injuries as well as the competent global or regional international organization. LOS Convention, Article 198.

States in an area affected by a maritime pollution disaster have the duty to cooperate in eliminating the effects of pollution and in preventing or minimizing the injury. To be better able to deal with such emergencies, neighboring states must develop and be ready to put into operation contingency plans for responding to pollution incidents affecting the marine environment in their vicinity. Id. at Article 199. On the global level, the International Maritime Organization adopted the 1990 Convention on Oil Pollution Preparedness, Response and Co-operation, followed in 2000 by a protocol extending its field of application to hazardous and noxious substances. The United States, which is a party to the 1990 Convention, has also concluded a number of bilateral agreements on the subject. See, for example, the 1980 United States–Mexico Marine Pollution Agreement. Regional initiatives include specific protocols adopted under the framework of the Regional Seas Program of the United Nations Environment Programme. See the 1978 Protocol concerning Regional Co-operation in Combating Pollution by Oil and other Harmful Substances in Cases of Emergency (Persian Gulf); the 1981 Protocol Concerning Co-operation in Combating Pollution in Cases of Emergency (Western Africa region); the 1981 Agreement on Regional Cooperation in Combating Pollution in the South East Pacific by Hydrocarbons and Other Harmful Substances in Cases of Emergency and its complementary 1983 Protocol; the 1982 Protocol Concerning Regional Co-operation in Combating Pollution by Oil and Other Harmful Substances in Cases of Emergency (Red Sea and Gulf of Aden); the 1983 Protocol Concerning Co-operation in Combating Oil Spills in the Wider Caribbean Region; the 1985 Protocol Concerning Co-operation in Combating Marine Pollution in Cases of Emergency in the Eastern African Region; the 1986 Protocol Concerning Co-operation in Combating Pollution Emergencies (South Pacific region); the 1992 Protocol on Cooperation in Combating Pollution of the Black Sea Marine Environment by Oil and Other Harmful Substances in Emergency Situations; and the 2002 Protocol Concerning Cooperation in Preventing Pollution from

Ships and, in Cases of Emergency, Combating Pollution of the Mediterranean Sea.

M. GOVERNMENT NONCOMMERCIAL SHIPS

Government noncommercial ships are not subject to the international rules, standards, and enforcement procedures discussed above. However, each state must ensure, through the adoption of appropriate measures, that such ships act so far as practicable in a manner consistent with international rules and standards. LOS Convention, Article 236.

CHAPTER 13

CONSERVATION AND MANAGEMENT OF HIGH SEAS LIVING RESOURCES

A. INTRODUCTION

The topic of "conservation and management of the living resources of the high seas" has sometimes been considered the missing chapter of the LOS Convention. This assertion is not totally correct, for the LOS Convention has a section in Part VII (High Seas) bearing exactly the same title. As will be seen, however, that section is neither elaborate nor does it reflect much progressive development from the 1958 Fishing on the High Seas Convention. The LOS Convention provisions quickly proved ill-adapted to new pressures on high seas living resources created by technological developments and the establishment of the concept of the exclusive economic zone (Chapter 9).

This Chapter begins by explaining the marked similarities between the regimes governing the conservation and management of high seas living resources established at the First (UNCLOS I) and Third (UNCLOS III) United Nations Conferences on the Law of the Sea (Section B). The insufficiency of these provisions has resulted in the creation of a

number of new instruments (Section C). Section C
first discusses several legally binding and nonbinding instruments adopted specifically to address the
conservation and management of the high seas living resources, and then turns to other conventions
that have been applied to protect these resources,
even though their original focus was not the law of
the sea.

B. FROM UNCLOS I TO UNCLOS III

All states have the right to fish on the high seas
subject to their treaty obligations and the rights
and duties of coastal states. See Chapter 2, Section
C.3. In addition, all states have the duty to take, or
to cooperate with other states in taking, such measures as may be necessary for the conservation of the
living resources of the high seas, and to ensure that
their nationals comply with these measures. States
whose nationals exploit identical fisheries or fisheries in the same area must enter negotiations to
conserve these resources. LOS Convention, Articles
117, 118; 1958 Fishing on the High Seas Convention, Articles 1(2), 2, 4. Additionally, under the LOS
Convention states must cooperate with each other
in managing—and thus not only conserving—the
living resources in the high seas and shall, when
appropriate, cooperate to establish subregional or
regional organizations to this end. LOS Convention,
Article 118. Moreover, in determining the allowable
catch and establishing other conservation measures
for high seas fisheries, states must take nondiscrim-

inatory measures designed to maintain or restore species at levels that "can produce the maximum sustainable yield, as qualified by relevant environmental and economic factors," taking into account the requirements of developing states, fishing patterns, the interdependence of stocks, and generally recommended international standards. Id. at Article 119(1)(a). States must also consider the effects on associated species. Id. at Article 119(1)(b). Article 119 is patterned after Article 61 concerning the responsibilities of the coastal state with respect to living resources in its exclusive economic zone (EEZ). See Chapter 9, Section C.

Overall, the provisions of the LOS Convention on the conservation and management of the living resources of the high seas are not conceptually new, but rather reflect the system established under the 1958 Fishing on the High Seas Convention, adapted to the creation of the EEZ. This approach reflects the general lack of attention that the UNCLOS III negotiators accorded the part of the LOS Convention that concerns high seas fisheries. During UNCLOS III almost all efforts directed towards the issue of conservation and management of living resources concentrated on the newly established EEZ. This focus was due in part to the fact that the overwhelming majority of the commercial exploitation of fisheries was occurring inside the 200–mile limit. High seas fisheries were believed at that time to constitute approximately ten percent of the world's capture fisheries production, and consequently the UNCLOS III negotiators did not consider high seas fisheries to be a major issue. Gordon Munro, Annick Van Houtte & Rolf Willmann, The Conservation and Management of Shared Fish Stocks: Legal and Economic Aspects, Food and Agriculture Organization (FAO) Fisheries Technical Paper No. 465, 34–35 (2004), available at http://www.fao.org/docrep/007/y5438e/y5438e00.htm.

Although coastal states were granted extensive, if not comprehensive, rights with respect to the living resources inside their EEZs, coastal states' rights were strictly limited beyond the 200–mile limit. The articles of Part V of the LOS Convention (Exclusive Economic Zone) dealing with species to be found inside as well as outside this 200–mile zone deserve special attention in this regard. Article 63(2) of the LOS Convention, concerning stocks to be found inside the EEZ as well as in the area beyond and adjacent to that zone—so-called straddling stocks—remained on the agenda of UNCLOS III until the very end of the negotiations. The basic compromise in Article 63(2) requires that coastal states and distant water fishing states "shall seek ... to agree upon the measures necessary for the conservation of" straddling stocks in the area adjacent to the EEZ. Some countries wanted to tilt authority in favor of the coastal state if no such agreement could be reached, but the wording remained unchanged during UNCLOS III. The LOS Convention thus does not grant any preference with respect to who should be responsible for conserving these straddling stocks in the area of the high seas adjacent to the EEZ. These stocks normally occur where extended continental shelves reach beyond 200 miles. The coastal states most likely affected are Argentina, Australia, Canada, New Zealand, Norway, Russia, and the United States.

A similar approach applies to highly migratory fish stocks. Annex I of the LOS Convention lists these stocks, which include tuna, tuna-like species (such as swordfish), sharks, and cetaceans. Article 64(1) obligates coastal and other states whose nationals fish for such species in the region to cooperate either directly or through appropriate international organizations to ensure conservation and promote optimum utilization of such highly migratory species both within and beyond the EEZ. This "shall cooperate" provision, like the language of Article 63(2) concerning straddling stocks, also survived many proposals for substantial change during UNCLOS III. Article 64(1) therefore does not seem to indicate any preference for either the coastal state or other states whose nationals fish such highly migratory species.

The United States for a number of years held a unique position with respect to highly migratory fish species, since the Fishery Management and Conservation Act specifically excluded such species from U.S. fishery management authority. The United States claimed jurisdiction over highly migratory species out to twelve miles in its own waters, and only recognized claims of other countries to the same distance, reflecting the U.S. view that tuna management ought to be conducted by international agreement. The United States recognized the right of other countries to claim jurisdiction over tuna inside their own EEZs only on November 28, 1990, with the new policy becoming effective as of January 1, 1992. See United States, Aide-mémoire Concerning Amendments to the Magnuson Fishery Conservation and Management Act: Amendment to Include Highly Migratory Tuna as Species of Fish under United States Jurisdiction, 22 May 1991, 19 L. Sea Bull. 21 (1991); 16 U.S.C. §§ 1812, 1822(e). See also Christopher Kelly, The Law of the Sea: The Jurisdictional Dispute over Highly Migratory Species of Tuna, 26 Colum. J. Transnatl. L. 476, 500–504, 513 (1988) (expressing clear doubts about the compatibility of pre–1990 U.S. legislation with the LOS Convention); 1987 Treaty on Fisheries Between the Governments of Certain Pacific Island States and the Government of the United States (indicating a change in U.S. policy, even before 1990, with respect to recognition of coastal state management of tuna within the EEZ). For an account of the evolution in U.S. policy, see Christopher J. Carr, Transformations in the Law Governing Highly Migratory Species: 1970 to the Present, in Bringing New Law to Ocean Waters 55 (David D. Caron & Harry N. Scheiber eds., 2004).

In contrast to how it treats straddling stocks and highly migratory species, the LOS Convention gives primary authority with respect to the capture of anadromous stocks (such as salmon) to the state of origin and not the coastal state in whose waters these species may be found. The state of origin's authority extends even beyond the 200–mile limit.

"Due regard" is to be given to the conservation requirements and the needs of the state of origin. LOS Convention, Article 66(3)(a). The state of origin must cooperate in minimizing economic dislocation for states that fish salmon on the high seas, while taking into account the past practice of such states concerning the volume, mode, and areas of fishing for such stocks. Id. at Article 66(3)(b). However, the general rule is that anadromous stocks can normally only be fished inside the 200–mile limit; fishing outside the EEZ is allowed only if application of the general rule would result in economic dislocation for a state that has fished such resource on the high seas in the past. The two multilateral agreements that cover the two main salmon regions of the world—the north Atlantic and the north Pacific—both now prohibit direct fishing for salmon on the high seas. See 1982 North Atlantic Salmon Treaty, Article 2(1); 1992 North Pacific Salmon Treaty, Article 3(1)(a). Japan has also stopped direct fishing for salmon on the high seas. The U.S. Fishery Management and Conservation Act expressly extends U.S. management and enforcement authority over anadromous species through and beyond the 200–mile zone, except that such management authority shall not extend to such species when they are found in any waters of a foreign country. 16 U.S.C. §§ 1801(b)(1), 1811(b)(1). See William T. Burke, Implications for Fisheries Management of U.S. Acceptance to the 1982 Convention on the Law of the Sea, 89 Am. J. Intl. L. 792, 800–801 (1995) (arguing that this legislation would not be inconsistent with the

LOS Convention if the United States were to accede to the Convention).

Some special rules apply to cetaceans and other marine mammals. Coastal states may regulate the exploitation of marine mammals more strictly in their EEZs than the rules normally applicable there would otherwise permit. See LOS Convention, Article 65; Chapter 9, Section E.2. Through Article 120 of the LOS Convention, this regime has been extended to the high seas, making it possible for states or international organizations to set up a stricter regime than the one provided for in Articles 118–119. LOS Convention, Articles 65, 120. Since seven families of cetaceans are listed as highly migratory, id. at Annex I, the objective of optimum utilization otherwise applicable to highly migratory species must be brought into harmony with management and study requirements concerning marine mammals. Compare id. at Articles 64–65.

The International Whaling Commission (IWC), established under the 1946 Whaling Convention, exercises global competence concerning whales. The IWC has established uniform regulations applicable inside and outside the EEZ. For a discussion of the IWC and current whaling regulations, see Chapter 9, Section E.2.

The LOS Convention does not fully and adequately address the relationship between fishing inside and outside the 200–mile limit, especially for highly migratory species and straddling stocks. As stated in a document prepared by the U.N. Office of Legal

Affairs in 1992, the LOS Convention lacks clarity with respect to high seas living resources, giving rise to a need for an "enhanced understanding" of the rights of coastal and distant water fishing states. The Law of the Sea: The Regime for High-seas Fisheries: Status and Prospects, UN Pub. Sales No. E.92.V.12, 98 (1992). The commercial importance of straddling and highly migratory species has led to developments concerning the conservation and management of high seas living resources outside of the LOS Convention, as discussed in Section C.

C. BEYOND UNCLOS III

One effect of the LOS Convention's extension of coastal state jurisdiction over living resources beyond the territorial sea was to increase pressure on high seas resources. As a result of the creation of an exclusive economic zone (EEZ) in which the coastal state was attributed sovereign rights for the exploration and exploitation of the living resources, most of the commercially exploited fish resources lost their high seas status. The high seas freedom of fishing no longer applied to them. Many distant water fishing fleets, confronted with the choice between having to buy their way into the EEZ of coastal states or relocating their fishery efforts for stocks beyond that zone, opted for the latter course of action. This tactic resulted in increased catch efforts for straddling and highly migratory fish stocks beyond the 200–mile limit, as well as for so-called discrete high seas stocks, i.e., those stocks that are found entirely in the high seas. A recent Food and Agriculture Organization (FAO) study indicates that these stocks do not have much room for increased exploitation. See Table 2, which is based on Jean–Jacques Maguire et al., The State of World Highly Migratory, Straddling and Other High Seas Fishery Resources and Associated Species, FAO Fisheries Technical Paper No. 495 (2006), available at http://www.fao.org/docrep/009/a0653e/a0653e00.htm.

Table 2: Highly Migratory, Straddling, and Discrete High Seas Fish Stocks Statistics (in Percentages)			
	Moderately exploited	Fully exploited	Over-exploited	Depleted
Highly migratory species (HMS): Tuna and tuna-like	21	50	21	8
HMS: Sharks	10	35	40	15
HMS: Others, excluding cetaceans	Limited information, but generally ranging between moderately and fully exploited			
Selected straddling stocks	12	19	58	6
Discrete high seas stocks	Limited information, but generally ranging between fully exploited and depleted			

Note: Of the remaining 5% of the "selected straddling stocks" category, 4% are under-exploited and 1% is recovering.

This same study indicates that fishing for oceanic deep-water resources has increased sharply since the middle of the 1970s, confirming the impact of the LOS Convention on the fishing patterns of distant water fishing fleets, which have gained the technological capacity to fish in ever deeper waters. Id. at 64. Since FAO statistics do not distinguish between fish caught in the EEZ and resources harvested beyond that limit, the percentages provided in Table 2 do not necessarily imply that the overexploitation or depletion of certain highly migratory species and straddling stocks is solely due to fishing on the high seas. Id. at 68. Nevertheless, in a recent State of World Fisheries and Aquaculture report, the FAO, after concluding that there are clear indications that the maximum wild capture fishery potential from the world's oceans has been reached in general, emphasizes that the situation seems more critical with respect to some highly migratory, straddling, and discrete high seas fish stocks. In particular, over half of the stocks of highly migratory sharks and almost two-thirds of straddling and discrete high seas stocks are listed as over-exploited or depleted. FAO, The State of World Fisheries and Aquaculture 2006, 33 (2007), available at http:// www.fao.org/docrep/009/A0699e/A0699e00.htm.

Existing regional fisheries management organizations proved ill-adapted to face these new challenges. See generally Are K. Syndes, Regional Fishery Organizations: How and Why Diversity Matters,

32 Ocean Dev. & Intl. L. 349 (2001). Consider, for example, the Northwest Atlantic Fisheries Organization (NAFO), which became operational in 1979, superseding an arrangement that dated from 1949. 1978 Convention on Future Multilateral Cooperation in the Northwest Atlantic Fisheries, Articles 22(3), 23. NAFO's so-called opting-out procedure deserves particular notice. The NAFO Commission, which is the Organization's decision-making body, can adopt conservation, management, and enforcement measures applicable outside the EEZ by simple majority vote (id. at Article 14), and these measures then become binding on all contracting parties. Id. at Article 11(7). But any party may object to a measure, which then becomes nonbinding for that party. Id. at Article 12(1).

In the 1990s this opting-out procedure created difficulties for Canada, one of the countries confronted with straddling fish stocks because of the extended continental shelf in front of its Atlantic coast. Even though the Grand Banks off the coast of Newfoundland are for the most part located inside the 200–mile Canadian EEZ, the "Nose" and "Tail" of this rich fishing ground reach beyond that limit, and therefore fall under the competence of NAFO. After the European Community opted out from a NAFO Commission measure reducing its catch quota for turbot by fifty percent, and after other attempts to arrive at mutually accepted quotas failed, Canada implemented unilateral measures. In 1995 the Canadian coast guard arrested the *Estai*, a Spanish fishing vessel, on the high seas for violation of these measures, illustrating the inability of the regional fisheries management organization to resolve the discord. See generally Rebecca Bratspies, Finessing King Neptune: Fisheries Management and the Limits of International Law, 25 Harv. Envtl. L. Rev. 213 (2001). The issue was finally solved by direct negotiations between the parties. Agreed Minute on the Conservation and Management of Fish Stocks, 20 April 1995, 34 Intl. Leg. Materials 1260 (1995). Spain also introduced a case before the International Court of Justice, challenging Canada's use of force in arresting the *Estai*. The Court found it lacked jurisdiction, however, since Canada had explicitly narrowed the scope of its acceptance of the Court's jurisdiction before it enacted its legislation allowing for the seizure of vessels beyond the 200–mile limit. Fisheries Jurisdiction Case (Spain v. Canada), 1998 I.C.J. 432.

Efforts to achieve a viable regime for high seas fisheries have led to the adoption of a number of new documents, both legally binding as well as nonlegally binding ones.

1. *Legally Binding Documents*

The FAO, in collaboration with the Government of Mexico, organized a conference in 1992, which resulted in a call for states to cooperate to "establish, reinforce and implement effective means and mechanisms to ensure responsible fishing on the high seas, in accordance with relevant provisions of [the LOS Convention]." Declaration of Cancun, 8

May 1992, Point 11, available at http://www.fao.org/docrep/003/V5321E/V5321E11.htm#ch9.5.   The United Nations Conference on Environment and Development (UNCED), held in Rio de Janeiro about a month later, took up this challenge. States at UNCED stressed that cooperation is essential, especially for highly migratory species and straddling stocks, and decided to convene a United Nations Conference on Straddling Fish Stocks and Highly Migratory Fish Stocks. Agenda 21, ¶¶ 17.45, 17.50 (1992), available at http://www.un.org/esa/dsd/agenda21/res_agenda21_17.shtml.

Awaiting the outcome of this conference, which started its work in April 1993 and lasted until August 1995, the FAO took the initiative, based on the Declaration of Cancun and Agenda 21 of UNCED, to regulate high seas fisheries. These efforts resulted in the 1993 FAO Flag State Compliance Agreement, which focused on the obligations of flag states. A second legally binding document emerged from the above-mentioned U.N. Conference on Straddling Fish Stocks and Highly Migratory Fish Stocks—the 1995 Fish Stocks Convention.

Despite their common background, the 1993 FAO Flag State Compliance Agreement and the 1995 Fish Stocks Convention follow substantially different approaches. The 1993 Agreement applies to the high seas, without any restriction as to species. This Agreement basically tries to tackle the problem of over-fishing on the high seas by introducing new rights, and especially new obligations, for one single actor, the flag state. Each flag state is obligated to exercise control by licensing, at a minimum, all vessels measuring twenty-four meters (78.74 feet) or more in length that fly its flag and fish on the high seas. No such license should be granted if the flag state is unable to exercise sufficient control over the vessel to allow the flag state to fulfill its obligations under the 1993 Agreement, or if a vessel, previously registered in the territory of another state, has undermined the effectiveness of international conservation and management measures. The flag state must maintain a record of fishing vessels, must ensure that all its vessels fishing on the high seas are properly marked, and must ensure that its vessels provide detailed information about the volume and areas of catches and landings. 1993 FAO Flag State Compliance Agreement, Articles 3–4. Another basic pillar of the 1993 Agreement involves the transfer of information to the FAO, allowing the Organization to run a global ship register covering the whole world in order to try to limit the practice of shopping around for a flag most convenient for particular fishing activities. Id. at Article 6. Not all flag states have implemented these basic obligations, a state of affairs that has triggered an international initiative to subject flag states to a performance assessment. See Report of the Secretary–General to the U.N. General Assembly, Oceans and the Law of the Sea, UN Doc. A/63/63, ¶¶ 250–251 (2008). The 1993 FAO Flag State Compliance Agreement required twenty-five instruments of acceptance to enter into force (Article 11(1)), a condition that was not satisfied until April 24, 2003. As of June 1, 2009, thirty-seven states (including the United States) and the European Community were parties to this Agreement.

The 1995 Fish Stocks Convention is the result of multilateral negotiations "implementing" the LOS Convention outside the framework of FAO. Nevertheless, despite the "implementing" nature of this agreement, membership in the LOS Convention is not required. Compare the 1994 Implementation Agreement, discussed in Chapter 11, Section E. The 1995 Convention entered into force on December 11, 2001, thirty days after receiving the necessary thirty instruments of ratification or accession. 1995 Fish Stocks Convention, Article 40. As of June 1, 2009, seventy-four states (including the United States) and the European Community were parties to this Convention. As indicated by its full title (see Table of Treaties), the 1995 Convention applies only to highly migratory species and straddling stocks. Moreover, these stocks are only covered when sojourning in the high seas. Id. at Article 3(1). With regard to flag states, the 1995 Fish Stocks Convention covers similar ground as the 1993 FAO Flag State Compliance Agreement. For example, flag states have to introduce a system of obligatory licenses, exercise effective control over their vessels, keep a record of fishing vessels, properly mark their fishing vessels, and report catches and landings. Id. at Article 18. However, unlike the 1993 Agreement, which applies to vessels that are twenty-four meters or longer, these obligations apply to all vessels, regardless of length. In addition, the 1995 Fish

Stocks Convention provides for a limited exchange of information between directly interested states, but this information need not be sent to the FAO or other global organizations. Id. at Article 18(3)(c).

The primary difference between the 1995 Fish Stocks Convention and the 1993 FAO Flag State Compliance Agreement is that the Fish Stocks Convention addresses roles for actors other than the flag state, in case the flag state proves either unwilling or unable to discharge its obligations. Negotiating the choice of these actors and their roles was a very delicate exercise, given the fundamental divisions between coastal states and distant water fishing states. The 1995 Fish Stocks Convention negotiators were careful not to prefer one group over the other. See William T. Burke, Compatibility and Precaution in the 1995 Straddling Stock Agreement, in Law of the Sea: The Common Heritage and Emerging Challenges 105, 115 (Harry N. Scheiber ed., 2000). Instead, strengthening and creating shared obligations to ensure effective conservation and management proved to be the key to success. In order to achieve the much-needed international cooperation, the 1995 Convention attributes a central role to regional fisheries management organizations, either already in existence or still to be created, on which both coastal states and distant water fishing states should be represented, based on their "real interest" in the fisheries concerned. 1995 Fish Stocks Convention, Article 8(3). States fishing in the area covered by a particular regional fisheries management organization are supposed to join that organization or at least give effect to its measures. If a state fishing in the area does not do so, that state may no longer license its vessels to fish in the convention or regulatory area of that regional fisheries management organization. Id. at Article 8(4).

The 1995 Fish Stocks Convention also spells out a number of principles, which were not widely adopted at the time, governing the conservation and management of the relevant fish stocks. Foremost among these principles is the precautionary approach, namely that "[t]he absence of adequate scientific information shall not be used as a reason for postponing or failing to take conservation and management measures." Id. at Article 6(2). The conservation and management objectives of the 1995 Convention are to be met by establishing so-called precautionary limit (conservation) reference points or target (management) reference points. Id. at Annex II. The 1995 Convention also contains other new principles not found in the LOS Convention. These principles include long-term sustainability (id. at Article 5(a)), biodiversity protection (id. at Article 5(g)), taking "measures to prevent or eliminate over-fishing" (id. at Article 5(h)), and taking "into account the interests of high seas artisanal and subsistence fishers." Id. at Article 5(i). Other principles, such as ecosystem management (id. at Article 5(e)–(d)), further develop provisions of the LOS Convention. See André Tahindro, Conservation and Management of Transboundary Fish Stocks: Comments in Light of the Adoption of the

1995 Agreement for the Conservation and Management of Straddling Fish Stocks and Highly Migratory Fish Stocks, 28 Ocean Dev. & Intl. L. 1 (1997).

The differences between the 1993 FAO Flag State Compliance Agreement and the 1995 Fish Stocks Convention become even more apparent when their compliance and enforcement provisions are compared. The 1993 Agreement contains no specific part concerning compliance and enforcement. Since the whole Agreement is centered around the flag state, the only compliance and enforcement provisions are to be found in Article 3 governing the responsibilities of the flag state. The flag state is obligated to make a violation of the Agreement's requirements an offense under national legislation, with sanctions severe enough to secure compliance. 1993 FAO Flag State Compliance Agreement, Article 3(8). Under the 1995 Fish Stocks Convention, however, national measures imposed by flag states concerning monitoring, control, and surveillance have to yield to those established by regional fisheries management organizations. 1995 Fish Stocks Convention, Article 18(4). Moreover, the 1995 Convention contains a specific chapter on compliance and enforcement, namely Part VI, which contains the crux of the substantially novel provisions introduced by this Convention. Not only must the flag state enforce conservation and management measures adopted by regional fisheries management organizations against its own vessels, but it also must accept that the vessels flying its flag will be subjected to a system of regional surveillance and enforcement. Under this system, all members of a regional fisheries management organization may board and inspect vessels flying the flag of any state party to the 1995 Fish Stocks Convention. Id. at Article 21(1). The flag state retains a preemptive right to further investigate and take enforcement measures, but it may forego this right, leaving the task to the inspecting state. Id. at Article 21(6)–(7). For certain severe violations, defined in the Convention, vessels may even be taken to port if the flag state remains inactive. Id. at Article 21(8). Finally, port states are also granted a general right, and have a corresponding obligation, to inspect documents, fishing gear, and catches when foreign vessels voluntarily enter their ports. Id. at Article 23. The 1995 Convention thus expands the system of port-state jurisdiction introduced in the LOS Convention with respect to certain pollution offenses (see Chapter 7, Section E and Chapter 12, Section K.3) to the area of fisheries.

Finally, the provisions concerning the settlement of disputes are totally different in the 1993 FAO Flag State Compliance Agreement and the 1995 Fish Stocks Convention. The 1993 Agreement, even though providing for third-party settlement if the parties themselves are unable to resolve their disputes, nevertheless requires the consent of all parties to each and every individual case. 1993 FAO Flag State Compliance Agreement, Article 9. The 1995 Fish Stocks Convention, however, incorporates by reference Part XV of the LOS Convention for obligatory dispute settlement. 1995 Fish Stocks Convention, Article 30. As a result, consent to jurisdiction is, as a rule, implied by becoming a party to the 1995 Convention. On the dispute settlement system of the LOS Convention, see Chapter 15, Section C.

The 1995 Fish Stocks Convention undoubtedly contains several innovations, such as the precautionary approach mentioned above, that sometimes appear to do more than merely implement the LOS Convention. But some of these innovations have been questioned as to their conformity with the basic rule of international law that treaties cannot create obligations for non-parties without their consent. Consider the following two examples. First, the Fish Stocks Convention introduces the new principle that the access to fishery resources in a particular region of the high seas is restricted to states that are either members of the competent regional fisheries management organization, or agree to apply the conservation and management measures established by such organization. 1995 Fish Stocks Convention, Article 8(4). Second, the Convention's compliance and enforcement provisions, which authorize the boarding and inspection of ships on the high seas that do not fly the same flag as the ship undertaking the inspection, are also new. Id. at Article 21(1). Yet a close reading of the 1995 Convention reveals that only parties to the Convention are bound by these novel provisions. The rights of non-parties remain unaffected, at least as far as the principles of international treaty law are concerned. Erik Franckx, *Pacta Tertiis* and the Agreement for the Implementation of the Straddling and Highly Migratory Fish Stocks Provisions of the United Nations Convention on the Law of the Sea, 8 Tulane J. Intl. & Comp. L. 49 (2000).

The 1995 Fish Stocks Convention, which attributes an enhanced role for regional fisheries management organizations, has noticeably impacted existing organizations. Many of them are seeking to adapt their structures to the new international legal framework. For example, NAFO, discussed above, successfully completed such a process in September 2007. According to the new NAFO provisions, which had not entered into force as of June 1, 2009, the opting-out procedure still exists, but an elaborate dispute settlement procedure has been added, which ultimately results in an obligatory third-party settlement of disputes related to the opting-out procedure. 2007 Amendment to the 1978 Convention on Future Multilateral Cooperation in the Northwest Atlantic Fisheries, Article 3, available at http://www.nafo.int (deleting and replacing inter alia the old Articles 14–15). Also, the regional fisheries management organizations established after the adoption of the 1995 Fish Stocks Convention often use the 1995 Convention as a blueprint when drafting their organizational documents. The 2001 Convention on the Conservation and Management of Fishery Resources in the South East Atlantic Ocean is a particularly good example, evidencing the influence of the 1995 Convention on the structure of a regional fisheries management organization whose competence falls outside the scope of the 1995 Convention, namely, the management of discrete high seas stocks (rather than straddling or highly migratory stocks).

Unfortunately, despite all these efforts, regional fisheries management organizations have so far not lived up to expectations. They have not been able to stem the tide of illegal, unreported, and unregulated fishing on the high seas, and serious concerns remain about their ability to deliver an effective management regime. See High Seas Task Force, Closing the Net: Stopping Illegal Fishing on the High Seas 43 (2006), available at http://www.high-seas.org/docs/HSTFfinal/HSTF–Final–Report–09–03–06.pdf. The work of these organizations is being closely scrutinized, and best practices have been proposed in order to try to alleviate the situation. Michael W. Lodge et al., Recommended Best Practices for Regional Fisheries Management Organizations: Report of an Independent Panel to Develop a Model for Improved Governance by Regional Fisheries Management Organizations (2007), available at http://www.chathamhouse.org.uk/files/10301_rfmo0807.pdf. Since increased competence should go hand in hand with enhanced responsibility, it has been suggested that regional fisheries organizations should subject themselves to performance assessments that are internal, external, or conducted by a combined panel of reviewers. Id. at 118. The North East Atlantic Fisheries Commission was the first to complete such an assessment by means of a combined panel in March 2007. See http://www.neafc.org. These and other novel trends, such as requiring increased transparency and cooperation between regional fisheries organizations, receive the support of the international community, as witnessed by the recent U.N. General Assembly resolution on sustainable fisheries. UN Doc. A/RES/62/177, ¶¶ 85–92 (2008).

In addition to the 1993 FAO Flag State Compliance Agreement and the 1995 Fish Stocks Convention discussed above, which focus on the flag state and regional fisheries management organizations respectively to regulate high seas fisheries, on November 25, 2009 the FAO governing Conference approved the Agreement on Port State Measures to Prevent, Deter and Eliminate Illegal, Unreported and Unregulated Fishing. This new Agreement, which will enter into force upon ratification by twenty-five states, relies on port state control to curb illegal, unreported, and unregulated fishing.

2. Nonlegally Binding Documents

Modern treaty law is based on state consent. Sometimes, however, nonlegally binding documents may become the basis for the emergence of a new legally binding norm if sufficient converging state practice presents itself. Nonbinding documents, often termed "soft law," are normally easier to adopt than binding treaties. States and nongovernmental organizations nevertheless may, through soft law, ultimately influence the creation of new legally binding norms. Soft law may help set the scene for future treaty negotiations or may influence national legislation and policy. In addition, soft law may well develop into rules of customary international law if the conviction of legal obligation (opinio juris) can be demonstrated for those states implementing the rules in question.

A number of nonlegally binding documents relating to the conservation and management of high seas fisheries have been drafted, foremost by the FAO. This Organization has prepared a nonbinding Code of Conduct for Responsible Fisheries, adopted by consensus in 1995, of which the 1993 FAO Flag State Compliance Agreement forms an integral part. Code of Conduct for Responsible Fisheries, Article 1(1), available at http://www.fao.org/docrep/005/v9878e/v9878e00.htm. Since 1999, the FAO has also adopted four voluntary International Plans of Action relating to: the conservation and management of sharks (1999); the reduction of incidental catch of seabirds in longline fisheries (1999); the management of fishing capacity (1999); and the prevention, deterrence, and elimination of illegal, unreported, and unregulated fishing (2001). See http://www.fao.org/fishery/ccrf/2,3/en. For a discussion of these and other nonbinding documents in the area of fisheries, including the gray zone between binding and nonbinding instruments, see William Edeson, Soft and Hard Law Aspects of Fisheries Issues: Some Recent Global and Regional Approaches, in The Stockholm Declaration and Law of the Marine Environment 165 (Myron H. Nordquist, John Norton Moore & Said Mahmoudi eds., 2003).

The nonbinding U.N. General Assembly resolutions adopted since 1989 concerning large-scale pelagic high seas driftnet fishing have also been influential. These resolutions culminated in a call for a general moratorium as of December 31, 1992. See UN Doc. A/RES/46/215 (1991). Even though not legally binding, this moratorium seems to have been a relative success in practice. The moratorium has been implemented by a number of bilateral and regional conventions, such as the 1989 Convention for the Prohibition of Fishing with Long Driftnets in the South Pacific, as well as by national legislation. Grant J. Hewison, The Legally Binding Nature of the Moratorium on Large-scale High Seas Driftnet Fishing, 25 J. Mar. L. & Com. 557 (1994). The United States has adopted legislation denying port access to offending vessels and prohibiting fish imports from states whose vessels violate the moratorium. 16 U.S.C. §§ 1826, 1826a–1826g, 1857(1)(M). The European Community has prohibited the use of drift nets of over 2.5 kilometers in length by means of a number of regulations. See Council Regulation (EC) No. 894/97, laying down certain technical measures for the conservation of fishery resources, 1997 O.J. L. 132, 1; Council Regulation (EC) No. 812/2004, laying down measures concerning incidental catches of cetaceans in fisheries, 2004 O.J. L. 150, 12; Council Regulation (EC) No. 2187/2005 for the conservation of fishery resources through technical measures in the Baltic Sea, the Belts and the Øresund, 2005 O.J. L. 349, 1; and Council Regulation (EC) No. 809/2007 amending Regulations (EC) No. 894/97, (EC) No. 812/2004 and (EC) No. 2187/2005 as concerns drift nets, 2007 O.J. L. 182, 1. But problems do remain. See Richard Caddell, The Prohibition of Driftnet Fishing in European Community Waters: Problems, Progress and Prospects, 13 J. Intl. Mar. L. 265 (2007) (discussing problems on the regional level). A recent U.N. General Assembly resolution on sustainable fisheries stated that driftnet fishing still remains a threat. UN Doc. A/RES/62/177, 4 (2008).

At times the U.N. General Assembly and the FAO have worked in tandem in this domain. The yearly resolutions of the former body on sustainable fisheries, which have been issued since 2003, became much more concrete in 2006 with respect to the protection of the deep sea from destructive fishing practices by requesting states to take "action immediately." UN Doc. A/RES/61/105, ¶ 80 (2007). The FAO, which had been tasked with establishing standards for the management of deep sea fisheries (id. at ¶ 89), responded by adopting the International Guidelines for the Management of Deep-sea Fisheries in the High Seas, 47 Intl. Leg. Materials 998 (2008). The Guidelines were developed for fisheries occurring in areas beyond national jurisdiction that can only be sustained at low exploitation rates and that are taken with fishing gear likely to make contact with the seafloor. Id. at ¶ 8. The exact impact of these nonbinding Guidelines on the future regulation of deep-sea fisheries remains to be seen.

3. *Conventions Not Focusing on the Law of the Sea*

Effective compliance and enforcement mechanisms remain one of the weak links in the regulatory chain established to conserve the living resources of the high seas. In the quest for more effective compliance and enforcement, regimes established under conventions whose main focus is not the law of the sea may look attractive if they have a wide membership and an effective enforcement mechanism. The 1973 Convention on Trade in Endangered Species of Wild Fauna and Flora (CITES) fulfills these requirements. Its convenient system of import and export permits and certificates could provide a useful alternative to cost-intensive enforcement at sea. Even though commercially exploited aquatic species had not initially been considered as within the CITES field of application, the situation started to change at the end of the 1990s. Since then an increasing number of proposals under CITES have been aimed specifically at the protection of certain economically important species of fish. In lieu of arguing which system has precedence over the other, the preferred outcome is closer cooperation with a view of enhancing the effectiveness of the global protection of certain species. See Erik Franckx, The Protection of Biodiversity and Fisheries Management: Issues Raised by the Relationship Between CITES and LOSC, in The Law of the Sea: Progress and Prospects 210 (David Freestone, Richard Barnes & David Ong eds., 2006).

Another system with wide membership and a developed dispute settlement procedure is the World Trade Organization (WTO), established under the 1994 World Trade Organization Agreement. Environmental protection is not a primary concern of this Organization. Instead, the WTO system has been invoked to try to counter trade-related measures by regional fisheries management organizations aimed at preventing fish from reaching the market, if the fish have been captured in an illegal, unreported, or unregulated manner. Such trade-related measures may consist of landing restrictions, catch documentation schemes, or even import bans. States have also invoked the WTO system to try to set aside unilateral measures that states have taken to implement certain environmental goals, including the protection of high seas living resources. When the United States, for instance, started to ban imports from countries that harvested shrimp in ways that damaged sea turtles, directly affected countries turned to the WTO for relief. United States–Import Prohibition of Certain Shrimp and Shrimp Products, WTO, Report of the Appellate Body, AB–1998–4 (1998), 38 Intl. Leg. Materials 121 (1999). Even though the WTO Appellate Body found that the U.S. measures were inconsistent with WTO rules in this case, the Appellate Body at least indicated that states could implement some evolving environmental norms under certain conditions. Provisions of the 2006 U.S. Magnuson Stevens Reauthorization Act that mandate unilateral trade-related environmental measures against illegal, unreported, and unregulated fishing had not been tested in a WTO procedure as of June 1, 2009. See 16 U.S.C. §§ 1826h–1826j. In 1994 the WTO also created a Committee on Trade and Environment. See http://www.wto.org/english/tratop_e/envir_e/wrk_committee_e.htm.

WTO dispute settlement has been invoked in situations involving high seas fisheries disputes, in situations in which other dispute settlement forums are also available. A state will typically prefer to introduce a case in a forum that is inclined to support the position of the complaining state. The dispute relating to the conservation of swordfish in the South Pacific between Chile and the European

Community, discussed also in Chapter 7, Section C.1, illustrates this proposition. When Community vessels were not allowed to unload swordfish in Chilean ports, either for landing or transshipment, in order to put pressure on the European Community to accept Chilean fisheries conservation measures beyond the 200–mile limit, the European Community introduced proceedings in the WTO in 2000 focusing on the trade-related aspects of the dispute. See http://www.wto.org/english/tratop_e/dispu_e/cases_e/ds193_e.htm. Chile, on the other hand, started proceedings under the dispute settlement mechanisms of the LOS Convention (see Chapter 15, Sections C and D), concentrating on the aspects of the dispute related to the conservation of highly migratory species on the high seas. After Chile and the European Community reached a provisional agreement in 2001, both proceedings were suspended by the parties; as of June 1, 2009, these two cases were still pending. For discussion of the relationship between the WTO and the marine environment, see Alan Boyle, The World Trade Organization and the Marine Environment, in The Stockholm Declaration and Law of the Marine Environment 109 (Myron H. Nordquist, John Norton Moore & Said Mahmoudi eds., 2003).

A third convention, which originally did not focus on the high seas, treats an issue that the LOS Convention does not address—biological diversity. The 1992 Convention on Biological Diversity was the direct result of UNCED. This Convention's relationships with the LOS Convention and the 1995

Fish Stocks Convention are rather complex, especially if one tries to determine an hierarchical order among these documents. See Rüdiger Wolfrum & Nele Matz, The Interplay of the United Nations Convention on the Law of the Sea and the Convention on Biological Diversity, 4 Max Planck Y.B. U.N. L. 445 (2000); Nele Matz, The Interaction Between the Convention on Biological Diversity and the UN Convention on the Law of the Sea, in Marine Issues: From a Scientific, Political and Legal Perspective 203 (Peter Ehlers, Elisabeth Mann Borgese & Rüdiger Wolfrum eds., 2002); Alan Boyle, Relationship between International Environmental Law and Other Branches of International Law, in The Oxford Handbook of International Law 125, 138–140 (Daniel Bodansky, Jutta Brunnée & Ellen Hey eds., 2007). In 2004, the Conference of the Parties of the 1992 Convention on Biological Diversity decided to establish an ad hoc open-ended working group on protected areas. The mandate of this working group is to establish marine protected areas beyond the limits of national jurisdiction. See http://www.cbd.int/convention/wgpa.shtml; Chapter 12, Section I.

Complex challenges remain with respect to devising an effective system for the conservation and management of high seas living resources. One challenge is the lack of cooperation among the different regional fisheries management organizations, a deficiency that has only just recently been squarely placed on the international agenda. Other issues that loom large include the impact of deep-sea fishing activities on vulnerable marine ecosystems, including sea mounts, hydrothermal vents, and cold water corals, and the exact legal regime applicable to marine genetic resources found in the deep oceans. See Chapter 11, Section G. The subject of conservation and management of high seas living resources is far from settled. This subject may well be one particular area of the law of the sea where another "implementing" agreement could seriously be considered in the not-too-distant future.

CHAPTER 14

MARITIME TERRORISM AND SECURITY

A. INTRODUCTION

Acts of terrorism have occurred throughout history. Some incidents, such as the murder of Israeli athletes at the 1972 Olympic Games in Munich, occurred near or during the Third United Nations Conference on the Law of the Sea (UNCLOS III). Nonetheless, terrorism was not a topic of pressing concern at UNCLOS III; the term does not appear in the text of the LOS Convention. Security issues were viewed primarily as a national concern. The LOS Convention recognizes, for example, the right of a coastal state to suspend temporarily innocent passage if essential for the protection of its security. LOS Convention, Article 25(3). Although the LOS Convention obligates states to cooperate in several domains, including, for example, the repression of piracy and the protection of the marine environment, id. at Articles 100, 197, it does not contemplate international cooperation in combating terrorism or other threats to maritime security.

The modern era of maritime terrorism dawned in October 1985, when members of the Palestine Liberation Front (PLF) boarded the Italian cruise ship, the *Achille Lauro,* as passengers and seized control of the vessel after it left port. When Israel refused to accede to the PLF's demands for the release of Palestinian prisoners, the PLF members killed an invalid Jewish–American passenger and threw his body and wheelchair overboard. See also Chapter 4, Section D.2. The *Achille Lauro* incident resulted in an awareness of the necessity of international cooperation to address acts of maritime terrorism and recognition of the lack of an adequate system under either the LOS Convention or other existing agreements. The September 11, 2001 al-Qaida attacks against the World Trade Center and the Pentagon gave further impetus to the development of international mechanisms for preventing and responding to terrorism.

Section B discusses provisions of the LOS Convention and other international agreements that established a framework for the implementation of subsequent regional and global efforts to suppress maritime terrorism. Section C examines the post-UNCLOS III activities of states and international organizations in adopting both legally and nonlegally binding instruments to prevent maritime terrorism. Section D focuses on national laws and policies designed to enhance maritime security, particularly those of the United States, some of which have influenced international anti-terrorism efforts.

B. HISTORICAL DEVELOPMENT OF INTERNATIONAL COOPERATION IN THE SUPPRESSION OF TERRORISM

Historically, each state was responsible for the protection of its maritime security interests, including the safety of its ports and vessels and the security of its shipping routes. Several law of the sea rules facilitate a state's ability to protect its national interests, including a coastal state's sovereignty over its ports and territorial sea. See Chapters 7 and 8. Concern for coastal state security was one impetus behind the origins of the territorial sea and its expansion to twelve miles. Although some states have argued for even broader territorial seas, it can be difficult for a coastal state to police effectively its territorial sea. Coastal state authority does not, in and of itself, ensure maritime security.

Other traditional law of the sea rules that can promote a state's maritime security include the principle of freedom of navigation for warships as well as merchant fleets and the jurisdiction of a flag state over its vessels. See Chapters 2 and 4. Many countries, including the United States, have relied heavily on naval power as an integral component in protecting maritime and other national security interests. In the nineteenth and early twentieth centuries, maritime security was achieved primarily through the development of the law of naval warfare, naval arms limitation agreements, and collective defense agreements. See generally James Kraska, Grasping "The Influence of Law on Sea Power," 62 Naval War College Rev. 113, 116–120 (2009).

Although traditionally maritime security was not promoted through global collaboration, the repression of piracy emerged as an exception to this rule. For centuries, states have recognized the importance and necessity of international cooperation in safeguarding the right of all vessels to exercise the freedom of navigation without disruption by pirates. Accordingly, all states have an obligation to cooperate in repressing piracy. LOS Convention, Article 100; 1958 High Seas Convention, Article 14. See Chapter 4, Section D.2. The law of the sea developed a framework to implement this duty, granting warships of all countries the right to board a vessel on the high seas (other than a warship or noncommercial government vessel) when there are reasonable grounds to believe that the vessel is engaged in piracy. LOS Convention, Article 110(1)(a); 1958 High Seas Convention, Article 22(1)(a). In addition to this right to visit, a ship engaged in piracy on the high seas may be seized by a warship or government vessel of any state. LOS Convention, Articles 105, 107; 1958 High Seas Convention, Articles 19, 21.

The LOS Convention provides frameworks for regional and global cooperation in other areas of criminal law, including the suppression of illegal trafficking in drugs, LOS Convention Article 108, and the suppression of unauthorized broadcasting from the high seas. Id. at Article 109. The LOS Convention also grants warships the right to visit a vessel flying another state's flag (other than a warship or noncommercial government vessel) when reasonable grounds exist to believe that the vessel is engaged in the slave trade. LOS Convention, Article 110; 1958 High Seas Convention, Article 22. Several other international agreements complement the LOS Convention in these matters. See, for example, the 1961 Single Convention on Narcotic Drugs, the 1971 Convention on Psychotropic Substances, and the 1988 Convention against Illicit Traffic in Narcotic Drugs, which implement the duty of states to cooperate in the suppression of illegal drug trafficking.

The International Maritime Organization (IMO) was established to "provide machinery for co-operation among Governments" in matters relating to international shipping. 1948 Convention on the Intergovernmental Maritime Consultative Organization, Article 1. The IMO, with 169 member states as of June 1, 2009, has successfully promoted international cooperation and standardization in a wide array of matters affecting shipping. As discussed in Section C, its widely accepted conventions, particularly the 1974 Safety of Life at Sea Convention (SOLAS), have proven to be an important platform for the implementation of several recent maritime security measures.

During the same general time frame as the UNCLOS III negotiations, several international agreements were concluded to prevent acts of terrorism in nonmaritime settings. See, for example, the 1970 Convention for the Suppression of the Unlawful Seizure of Aircraft and the 1971 Convention for the Suppression of Unlawful Acts against the Safety of

Civil Aviation, which were developed in response to aircraft hijackings in the 1960s and 1970s. Several incidents involving the taking of civilian and government hostages resulted in the 1973 Internationally Protected Persons Convention and the 1979 Hostages Convention. Regional agreements, such as the 1977 European Convention on the Suppression of Terrorism, were also implemented. These and other treaties reflected the increasing importance of collaboration among states in combating terrorism. See M. Cherif Bassiouni, International Terrorism: Multilateral Conventions (1937–2001) (2001).

C. COOPERATIVE INTERNATIONAL EFFORTS TO PREVENT MARITIME TERRORISM AND ENHANCE MARITIME SECURITY

Although national efforts continue to play an important role in maritime security, the international nature of shipping demands the involvement and cooperation of numerous parties in security matters. Important actors include the flag state, port states in which vessels are loaded and off-loaded, states bordering international straits through which large volumes of ships pass, and coastal states through whose territorial seas vessels travel. Vessel owners and operators, cargo owners, vessel crews, and port workers are also stakeholders. The international community has responded by implementing both binding and nonbinding collaborative international regimes designed to promote maritime security, including the safety and security of vessels, cargoes, crews, passengers, port facilities, and international shipping routes. For a detailed analysis of the risk factors facing the maritime transport system and the potential economic impact of maritime terrorist attacks, see Organization for Economic Co-operation and Development Maritime Transport Committee Report, Security in Maritime Transport: Risk Factors and Economic Impact (2003), available at http://www.oecd.org/dataoecd/19/61/18521672.pdf.

1. *1988 Convention for the Suppression of Unlawful Acts against the Safety of Maritime Navigation*

Following the *Achille Lauro* incident, the U.N. General Assembly adopted Resolution 40/61, condemning "all acts, methods and practices of terrorism wherever and by whomever committed" and requesting the International Maritime Organization (IMO) "to study the problem of terrorism aboard or against ships with a view to making recommendations on appropriate measures." UN Doc. A/RES/40/61, ¶¶ 1, 13 (1985). Subsequently, the IMO promulgated the 1988 Convention for the Suppression of Unlawful Acts against the Safety of Maritime Navigation, the first treaty to establish a legal regime specifically addressing maritime security and terrorism. This Convention entered into force in March 1992; as of June 1, 2009, there were 153 parties.

The 1988 Convention does not define terrorism; it refers instead to "offences." 1988 Convention for the Suppression of Unlawful Acts against the Safety of Maritime Navigation, Article 3. Although there is no universally accepted definition of terrorism, most definitions include conduct by a nonstate party that involves violence resulting in physical injury or death (or fear thereof) to achieve a particular purpose. See Reuven Young, Defining Terrorism: The Evolution of Terrorism as a Legal Concept in International Law and Its Influence on Definitions in Domestic Legislation, 29 B.C. Intl. & Comp. L. Rev. 23 (2006). See also Chapter 4, Section D.2 regarding the definition of piracy.

Under the 1988 Convention, it is an offense for a person to "unlawfully and intentionally" commit, attempt to commit, or assist in committing any of the following acts (regardless of the person's purpose in undertaking such acts):

(a) the seizure or exercise of control over a ship by force or any other form of intimidation;

(b) performing an act of violence against a person on board a ship if that act is likely to endanger the safe navigation of the ship;

(c) destroying or causing damage to a ship or its cargo that is likely to endanger the safe navigation of the ship;

(d) placing a device or substance on a ship that is likely to destroy or cause damage to the ship or its cargo and endanger the safe navigation of the ship;

(e) destroying, seriously damaging, or interfering with maritime navigational facilities if such act is likely to endanger the safe navigation of the ship;

(f) communicating false information that endangers the safe navigation of the ship; and

(g) injuring or killing any person in connection with the commission or the attempted commission of any of the above offenses.

1988 Convention for the Suppression of Unlawful Acts against the Safety of Maritime Navigation, Article 3. Each party must make the foregoing offenses punishable by appropriate penalties. Id. at Article 5. A party must cooperate in the prevention of the proscribed offenses. Cooperative acts include the exchange of information and the adoption of measures to prevent preparation within its territory for the commission of the offenses. Id. at Article 13(1).

A state has jurisdiction to prosecute if an offense is committed against or on board a ship if: the ship is flying the flag of the state at the time the offense is committed; the ship is located in the territory of that state, including its territorial sea; or a national of that state commits the offense. Id. at Article 6(1). Discretionary jurisdiction may also be exercised in other situations, including an incident of terrorism in which a national of the state is seized, threatened, injured, or killed. Id. at Article 6(2). A state in whose territory an alleged offender is present must either prosecute the alleged offender or extradite the person to a state that has jurisdiction. Id. at Articles 6(4), 10(1).

The Convention applies to a ship (other than a warship or ship used as a naval auxiliary or for customs or police purposes) that "is navigating or is scheduled to navigate into, through or from waters beyond the outer limit of the territorial sea." Id. at Articles 2, 4. The Convention does not apply to ships that do not intend to travel outside of the territorial sea of one or more states.

The 1988 Protocol for the Suppression of Unlawful Acts against the Safety of Fixed Platforms applies similar provisions to artificial islands, installations, and structures located on the continental shelf beyond a state's territorial sea. As of June 1, 2009, 141 parties had adopted this Protocol. See Stuart Kaye, International Measures to Protect Oil Platforms, Pipelines, and Submarine Cables from Attack, 31 Tul. Mar. L.J. 377 (2007).

Following terrorist attacks against the *USS Cole* in October 2000, the World Trade Center in September 2001, and the French tanker *M/V Limburg* in October 2002, efforts began to expand the categories of unlawful offenses to include the transportation of weapons of mass destruction, the transportation of known terrorists, and other matters. On October 14, 2005, an IMO Diplomatic Conference in London adopted a Protocol to the 1988 Convention for the Suppression of Unlawful Acts against the Safety of Maritime Navigation. The 2005 Protocol, which had not entered into force as of June 1, 2009, adds several offenses. Some activities are offenses only if carried out with the intent "to intimidate a population, or to compel a government or an international organization to do or to abstain from doing any act," including:

(a) using against or on a ship, or discharging from a ship, any explosive, radioactive material, or biological, chemical or nuclear weapon in a manner likely to cause death, serious injury, or damage;

(b) discharging oil, liquefied natural gas, or other hazardous or noxious substance from a ship in such quantity or concentration likely to cause death, serious injury, or damage;

(c) using a ship in a manner that causes death, serious injury, or damage.

Id. at Article 4(5) (adding new Article 3 bis to the 1988 Convention).

The Protocol also adds as offenses the transport on board a ship of:

(a) any biological, chemical, or nuclear weapon;

(b) any explosive or radioactive material, knowing that it is intended to be used to cause or threaten death or serious injury for the purpose of intimidating a population or compelling a government or an international organization to do or to abstain from doing any act;

(c) any source material or equipment, knowing that it is to be used in connection with nuclear explosions or the construction of biological, chemical, or nuclear weapons, unless authorized pursuant to an International Atomic Energy Agency safeguard agreement;

(d) a person whom the transporter knows has committed an offense under the 1988 Convention, its Protocols, or other treaties intended to suppress terrorism, but only if the transporter's intent is to assist the offender in evading criminal prosecution.

Id. at Article 4(5)–(7) (adding new Articles 3 bis, 3 ter, and 3 quater to the 1988 Convention).

Another important addition establishes "right to visit" procedures. Id. at Article 8(2) (adding new Article 8 bis to the 1988 Convention). With the consent of the flag state, a party may board and investigate a ship flying the flag of another party if the ship is outside of any state's territorial sea and there are reasonable grounds to suspect that the ship or a person on board the ship is, has been, or is about to be involved in the commission of an offense under the Convention. Id. On receipt of a request to board by another party, the flag state may authorize or deny the request. If authorized to board, the requesting party may take any appropriate measures, such as a search of the vessel, subject to any conditions imposed by the flag state. Id. The Protocol also allows parties to file one of two forms of notification with the IMO Secretary–General.

The first of these forms consents automatically to all requests to board submitted by other parties, while the second provides for deemed consent to a request to board if the flag state fails to respond within four hours of its receipt of the request. Either form of pre-authorized consent may be withdrawn at any time. Id. The requesting party must inform the flag state of the results of any authorized boarding. Id. The use of force is to be avoided except when necessary to ensure the safety of officials and persons on board or where the officials are obstructed in performing authorized actions. Id. See Natalie Klein, The Right of Visit and the 2005 Protocol on the Suppression of Unlawful Acts against the Safety of Maritime Navigation, 35 Denv. J. Intl. L & Policy 287, 317–329 (2007).

2. ISPS Code and Related 1974 Safety of Life at Sea Convention Amendments

Following the September 11, 2001 al-Qaida attacks, the IMO Maritime Safety Committee began work on a series of measures to strengthen maritime security. The Committee approached maritime security as a risk management activity that requires the assessment of vulnerabilities, the development of appropriate responses, and the acquisition and exchange of knowledge concerning potential maritime security threats. The Committee developed an International Ship and Port Facility Security (ISPS) Code that requires, among other measures, the regular assessment of ships and ports to identify security threats and the development and implementation of security plans based on those assessments. The Committee also proposed amendments to existing provisions of the 1974 Safety of Life at Sea Convention (SOLAS) to improve vessel identification, monitoring, and security systems. The ISPS Code and related SOLAS amendments include important provisions regarding the generation and exchange of security-related information among governments. The IMO adopted the ISPS Code and related SOLAS amendments in December 2002, and they became effective in July 2004. By using the widely-accepted SOLAS Convention as a platform for incorporating these changes, the enhanced security measures affect ninety-nine percent of the world's international merchant and passenger fleet.

Under the ISPS Code, incorporated as Chapter XI–2 of the 1974 SOLAS Convention, all international passenger ships and cargo ships of 500 tons or more must conduct a ship security assessment and prepare a ship security plan based thereon for submission to and approval by the flag state or its agent. IMO Doc. SOLAS/CONF.5/34, Annex 1, Part A ¶¶ 8–9 (2002). Shipping companies must designate a company security officer and a ship security officer for each of its ships. Ships must also provide security training for crews. Id. at Part A ¶¶ 11–13.

The 2002 amendments to SOLAS require all ships to be equipped with an Automatic Identification System that communicates information regarding the ship's identification, position, heading, and speed. 1974 SOLAS Convention, Ch. V. More re-

cently, the IMO established an arrangement for
sharing long-range identification and tracking information between SOLAS parties for security and
search and rescue purposes. IMO Maritime Safety
Committee Resolution 211 (81), MSC 81/25/Add.1,
Annex 14 (2006). Ships must also be equipped with
a ship-to-shore security alert system, 1974 SOLAS
Convention, Ch. XI–2/6, and carry a Continuous
Synopsis Record, which includes current and historical data relating to the ship's registration, identification number, and owner. Id. at Ch. XI–1/5.

As evidence of compliance with the ISPS Code
and the other maritime security provisions of the
1974 SOLAS Convention, ships must obtain an International Ship Security Certificate issued by the
flag state or its designated agent. IMO Doc. SO-
LAS/CONF.5/34, Annex 1, Part A ¶ 19 (2002). Ships
that fail to comply with these requirements and
thus do not obtain a Certificate may be denied
entrance to parties' ports or expelled from port.
1974 SOLAS Convention, Ch. XI–2/9. A port state
that is a party to SOLAS may board a foreign vessel
flying the flag of another party while it is in port to
verify its International Ship Security Certificate. If
there are clear grounds to believe that the ship does
not comply with the ISPS Code or other SOLAS
maritime security provisions, additional inspections
and other appropriate control measures may be
taken by the port state, including expulsion of a
ship from port. Id. A port state may also take
control measures applicable to ships that intend to
enter port, including requests for information re-

garding the ship and its prior port calls. Failure to comply with the port state's control measures may result in the denial of port entrance. Id. at Ch. XI–2/9.2; see also IMO Guidance Relating to the Implementation of SOLAS Chapter XI–2 and the ISPS Code, MSC/Circ.1111 (2004); Chapter 7, Section C.3.

Under the ISPS Code, each party must assess all port facilities within its territory that are used by ships engaging in international voyages and must prepare port facility security plans. Each port's security assessment and plan must be periodically reviewed and updated. IMO Doc. SOLAS/CONF.5/34, Annex 1, Part A ¶¶ 15–16 (2002). A port security officer must be designated for each port facility, and port facilities must provide security training, drills, and exercises for its personnel. Id. at Part A ¶¶ 17–18.

Consistent with its risk management approach to maritime security, the ISPS Code requires each party, on an on-going basis, to determine the level of risk of a security threat to its port facilities and vessels. There are three levels of threat. Level 1 represents a normal risk level, level 2 a heightened risk level, and level 3 a probable or imminent threat. Id. at Part A ¶¶ 2.1.9–.11, 4. Port facility security plans must provide measures for each level of security threat; ship security plans must provide measures to be implemented in response to a level 3 security threat. Id. at Part A ¶¶ 14, 9.4.5

The IMO has reported high compliance by governments, ships, and port facilities with the ISPS

Code and related maritime security amendments to the 1974 SOLAS Convention. See http://www.imo. org/.

3. *Seafarer Identification*

Recognizing the security risks posed by falsification of seafarer identification, the International Labour Organization (ILO) developed an improved system for issuing identification documents to seafarers. The ILO's 2003 Convention Revising the Seafarers' Identity Documents Convention (No. 185) entered into force in February 2005. This Convention creates a new biometric identification system for the world's estimated 1.2 million maritime workers. Biometric identification relies on physical characteristics unique to each person, such as fingerprints, retina, iris, or voice. See also Section D.1 regarding U.S. biometric identification cards.

4. *U.N. Security Council Decisions*

The U.N. Security Council has the authority, under Chapter VII of the U.N. Charter, to adopt legally binding decisions to prevent threats to international peace and security. The Security Council has exercised this authority on several occasions in response to specific incidents involving the unlawful use of force. See, for example, the discussion in Chapter 2, Section D.2 of Security Council Resolutions 661 and 665 adopted after Iraq's invasion of

Kuwait. Following the September 11, 2001 al-Qaida attacks, the Security Council invoked its Chapter VII powers in a much broader context. Security Council Resolution 1373 requires all U.N. member states to adopt counter-terrorism measures, including measures that suppress financing of terrorism activities, criminalize the provision of resources to terrorists, and deny safe haven to terrorists, and to take "other necessary steps to prevent terrorism." UN Doc. S/RES/1373, ¶¶ 1–2 (2001). The Security Council established a Counter–Terrorism Committee to monitor implementation of Resolution 1373 by states, which were called on to report within ninety days of the adoption of the Resolution on the actions taken by each state. Id. at ¶ 6.

In 2004, the U.N. Security Council adopted Resolution 1540 requiring member states to establish "domestic controls to prevent the proliferation of nuclear, chemical, or biological weapons and their means of delivery." According to Resolution 1540, member states must implement measures to account for, secure, and physically protect sensitive materials and must develop effective border and export controls. UN Doc. S/RES/1540, ¶ 2 (2004). The Security Council established the 1540 Committee to monitor state activities taken to prevent the proliferation of weapons of mass destruction. Id. at ¶ 9. For a database of legislation adopted by states to implement Resolution 1540, see http://www.un.org/sc/1540/legisdocuments.shtml.

The adoption of Resolution 1540 caused several states to express their "basic concerns over the increasing tendency of the Council in recent years to assume new and wider powers of legislation on behalf of the international community, with its resolutions binding on all States." UN Doc. S/PV.4950, 5 (Mexico), 14 (Nepal), 17 (Namibia), 23 (India), 30 (Cuba) (2004). See also the 2008 decision of the European Court of Justice, which annulled regulations enacted by the Council of the European Union in implementing certain anti-terrorism measures, including the freezing of assets, mandated by Security Council resolutions issued under Chapter VII. The Court determined that "the obligations imposed by an international agreement cannot have the effect of prejudicing the constitutional principles of the EC Treaty," including the right to be heard, the right to effective judicial review, and the right to property. Kadi & Al Barakaat International Foundation v. Council & Commission, Joined Cases C–402/05 P & C–415/05 P, 2008 E.C.R. I–06351, ¶ 285. See Takis Tridimas & Jose A. Gutierrez– Fons, EU Law, International Law, and Economic Sanctions against Terrorism: The Judiciary in Distress?, 32 Fordham Intl. L.J. 660 (2009).

In Resolution 1718 the U.N. Security Council reasserted its concern regarding the threat to international peace and security posed by weapons of mass destruction (WMD). It called on all states to prevent the Democratic People's Republic of Korea (North Korea) from obtaining materials that could be used in its nuclear, WMD, or missile programs. UN Doc. S/RES/1718 (2006). After North Korea conducted nuclear tests in May 2009, the U.N.

Security Council issued Resolution 1874, calling on all states to inspect, consistent with international law, all cargo to and from North Korea located in its territory, including seaports, if the inspecting state has reason to believe that the cargo contains prohibited items. UN Doc. S/RES/1874 (2009).

5.   *Proliferation Security Initiative*

In May 2003 President George W. Bush announced the Proliferation Security Initiative (PSI) as an international partnership to stop the shipment of WMD. Ten countries originally joined with the United States to shape and promote the PSI, including Australia, France, Germany, Italy, Japan, the Netherlands, Poland, Portugal, Spain, and the United Kingdom. As of June 1, 2009, ninety-five countries participated in the PSI. U.S. Department of State, Proliferation Security Initiative Participants, available at http://www.state.gov/t/isn/c 27732.htm. The purpose of the PSI is "to establish a more coordinated and effective basis through which to impede and stop shipments of WMD ... consistent with national legal authorities and relevant international law and frameworks, including the U.N. Security Council." Interdiction Principles for the Proliferation Security Initiative, available at http://www.state.gov/t/isn/c27726.htm. Participating states commit to adopt various types of measures to accomplish the PSI's purpose, including measures to interdict the transfer or transport of WMD or related materials and streamlined procedures for rapid exchange of relevant information among participating states concerning suspected proliferation. Id.

The United States has entered several bilateral agreements with open-registry states that provide procedures for the boarding and investigation of vessels of the other party if there are reasonable grounds to suspect that the vessel is transporting WMDs or related materials. For a list of agreements, see http://www.state.gov/t/isn/c27733.htm. Several of the agreements provide for implied consent to board if the flag state fails to respond to a request within a few hours. See, for example, 2004 United States–Liberia Agreement concerning Cooperation to Suppress the Proliferation of Weapons of Mass Destruction, Article 4(3)(d). See Section D for a discussion of other measures adopted by the United States in furtherance of the PSI.

The U.N. Security Council welcomed multilateral arrangements such as the PSI in Resolution 1540. UN Doc. S/RES/1540 (2004). However, several maritime countries, including China and North Korea, have criticized the PSI, citing concerns regarding the legality of interdictions. For further discussion of the PSI, see Daniel H. Joyner, The Proliferation Security Initiative: Nonproliferation, Counterproliferation, and International Law, 30 Yale J. Intl. L. 507 (2005).

D. NATIONAL LEGISLATION

Many countries have adopted legislation to enhance maritime security and prevent maritime terrorism. Some of these laws fulfill a state's obligations under treaties, such as the 1974 Safety of Life at Sea Convention (SOLAS); others are unilateral· measures taken to protect the safety of a state's ports and vessels and to reduce the threat of terrorist attacks.

After the *Achille Lauro* incident, the United States enacted the 1986 International Maritime and Port Security Act, Pub. L. No. 99–399, title IX, 100 Stat. 889 (1986), which required the Secretary of Transportation to prepare annual reports to Congress analyzing the threat to U.S. ports and vessels from acts of terrorism. In 1997 the U.S. Department of Transportation published Port Security: A National Planning Guide to provide an overview of the essential aspects of port security, identifying many of the challenges facing ports and presenting a common basis on which to establish port security standards. In September 1999 a congressionally approved task force prepared "An Assessment of the U.S. Marine Transportation System," available at http://ntl.bts.gov/DOCS/report/, that identified seven strategic areas for action, including the security of the nation's marine transportation system. As a result of this report, in 2000 eighteen federal agencies formed a new Interagency Committee for the Marine Transportation System to ensure the development and implementation of national maritime transportation system policies. Additionally, in 2000 the U.S. Secretary of Transportation established the Marine Transportation System National Advisory Council. Thus, the United States was positioned to move forward with increased maritime security measures when the World Trade Center and Pentagon were attacked by terrorists on September 11, 2001.

Following the September 11, 2001 al-Qaida attacks, the United States made maritime security a top national priority and adopted many laws affecting the security of the "maritime domain." The maritime domain is described as "all areas and things of, on, under, relating to, adjacent to, or bordering on a sea, ocean, or other navigable waterway, including all maritime-related activities, infrastructure, people, cargo, and vessels and other conveyances." White House, National Maritime Strategy 1 n.1 (2005). As discussed below, several U.S. laws have been influential in shaping international maritime security strategies.

1. U.S. 2002 Maritime Safety and Transportation Act

In November 2002 the U.S. Congress enacted the Maritime Transportation Security Act, 46 U.S.C. §§ 70101 et seq., to protect U.S. ports and waterways from terrorist attacks. The Act incorporates several elements of the ISPS Code and other amendments to the 1974 Safety of Life at Sea

Convention (SOLAS) that were under consideration by the IMO at the same time Congress was deliberating this legislation. The Act establishes the following cornerstones for the security of the U.S. maritime transportation system:

(a) the assessment of the vulnerability of port facilities and vessels to terrorist attacks and other transportation security incidents, 46 U.S.C. §§ 70101–70102;

(b) the development and implementation of national and regional maritime security plans, as well as individual security plans for port facilities and vessels, id. at §§ 70103–70104;

(c) the prohibition of entrance of individuals to secure areas of port facilities unless the individual has been issued a biometric transportation security card, id. at § 70105;

(d) the assessment of the effectiveness of the anti-terrorism measures maintained at foreign ports, id. at § 70108, and implementation of conditions restricting entrance of vessels into the United States if departing from any foreign ports that do not maintain effective anti-terrorism measures, id. at § 70110;

(e) the implementation of systems to collect and assess information regarding vessels operating in U.S. waters and bound for U.S. ports, including automatic identification and long-range tracking systems for vessels, id. at §§ 70114–70115; and

(f) the establishment of standards for screening cargo prior to loading in a foreign port for shipment to the United States and for securing cargo while in transit, id. at § 70116.

The U.S. Coast Guard, under the direction of the Secretary of Homeland Security, has significant responsibility for implementing the maritime security program established under the Act. Substantially all U.S. port facilities had conducted assessments and implemented security plans by the July 1, 2004 deadline. See 33 C.F.R. Part 105, Subpart D, for required security plan contents for port facilities. Subject to funding availability, the Coast Guard must verify the effectiveness of each port facility security plan by conducting at least two on-site inspections each year, one of which must be unannounced. 46 U.S.C. § 70103(c)(4)(D).

By August 2007 the Coast Guard had organized forty-six Area Maritime Security Committees for various geographic areas around the country, each of which has prepared an Area Maritime Transportation Security Plan that coordinates with the national and other area plans. The Committees share information with each other, the Coast Guard, and other agencies involved in maritime security operations. See U.S. General Accounting Office, Maritime Security: The SAFE Port Act: Status and Implementation One Year Later, Rpt. No. GAO–08–126T, 12–14 (2007). In 2005 the Coast Guard established the Port Security Training Exercise Program (Port-STEP) and Area Maritime Security Training and Exercise Program (AMStep), to conduct exercises to test the effectiveness of area plans. All ports have undergone a security exercise at least annually since the implementation of these two programs.

The Transportation Security Administration (TSA), a division of the Department of Homeland Security, is responsible for the development and issuance of biometric transportation worker identification cards, or TWICs, to control access to secure port facilities. Before issuing a TWIC, the TSA conducts background checks on transportation workers to ensure they do not impose a security risk. To obtain a TWIC, an individual must provide biographic data and biometric information (such as fingerprints), sit for a digital photograph, and successfully pass a security threat assessment. 49 C.F.R. §§ 1572.17–.21. Enrollment and issuance of TWICs began at the Port of Wilmington, Delaware on October 16, 2007. See generally U.S. General Accounting Office, Transportation Security: Transportation Worker Identification Credential: A Status Update, Rpt. No. GAO–08–1151T (2008).

In April 2004 the Coast Guard developed its International Port Security Program to assess security measures at foreign ports. Under this program, the Coast Guard negotiates with the port state to establish conditions of an on-site visit for the purpose of reviewing the port's implementation of international security measures, including the ISPS Code. The port state also has the right to make reciprocal visits to U.S. ports to assess U.S. implementation of international standards. If the Coast Guard determines that a foreign port does not maintain effective anti-terrorism measures, it may prescribe conditions of entry into the United States for any vessel arriving from that port. 46 U.S.C. § 70110(a). See, for example, Notification of the Imposition of Conditions of Entry for Certain Vessels Arriving to the United States from Venezuela, 74 Fed. Reg. 3092 (2009). In 2008 the Coast Guard completed its assessment of foreign ports in 140 countries and began a cycle of reassessments. The Coast Guard has faced resistance from several countries that believe that the frequency of the reassessments (once every two to three years) interferes with the host country's sovereignty. See U.S. General Accounting Office, Maritime Security: The SAFE Port Act: Status and Implementation One Year Later, Rpt. No. GAO–08–126T, 15–19 (2007).

In October 2003 the Coast Guard issued final regulations specifying the categories of ships that must be equipped with automatic identification systems (AIS) while operating in U.S. waters designated as Vessel Traffic Service areas. 33 C.F.R. § 164.46. As of June 1, 2009, proposed regulations expanding the AIS requirement to cover more vessels and to apply in all U.S. navigable waters had not yet been finalized. 73 Fed. Reg. 76,295 (2008). In addition to AIS requirements, foreign passenger vessels, cargo vessels of 300 tons or more, and mobile drilling units while underway must be equipped with long-range vessel identification and tracking systems. Such vessels must also transmit periodic position reports to the United States if they intend to enter a U.S. port or if they are engaged in an international voyage within 1,000 miles of U.S. baselines. 46 U.S.C. § 70115; 33 C.F.R. Part 169, Subpart C. These regulations are consistent with long-range vessel identification and tracking system regulations adopted by the IMO Maritime Safety Committee. MSC Res. 202(81), MSC Doc. 81/25/ Add.1, Annex 2 (2006). See generally U.S. General Accounting Office, Maritime Security: Vessel Tracking Systems Provide Key Information, but the Need for Duplicate Data Should Be Reviewed, Rpt. No. GAO–09–337 (2009).

2. *U.S. 2005 National Strategy for Maritime Security*

In December 2004 President Bush established the Maritime Security Policy Coordinating Committee, comprised of several U.S. agency representatives, and directed it to coordinate U.S. maritime security programs "to achieve a comprehensive and cohesive national effort involving appropriate Federal, State, local, and private sector entities." National Security Presidential Directive–41, 1 (2004). This effort resulted in the National Strategy for Maritime Security, announced on September 20, 2005. The document emphasizes the importance of international cooperation to protect the "common interest in global maritime security," and identifies as overarching principles the preservation of the freedom of navigation, facilitation of the free flow of commerce, and screening of dangerous people and goods. White House, The National Strategy for Maritime Security 7–8 (2005), available at http://www. dhs.gov/xlibrary/assets/HSPD13_MaritimeSecurity Strategy.pdf. In accordance with these principles, the Strategy enunciates the following U.S. maritime security objectives: preventing terrorist attacks; protecting maritime-related population centers and critical infrastructures; minimizing damage and expediting recovery in the event of a terrorist attack; and safeguarding the ocean and its resources. Id. at 8.

To achieve these objectives, the document identifies five strategic actions: enhance international cooperation; maximize awareness of the "maritime domain;" embed security into commercial practices; deploy layered security that "integrates the capabilities of governments and commercial interests throughout the world;" and assure continuity of the marine transportation system. Id. at 13, 20. Annex I of the Strategy, id. at 27, identifies eight supplementary plans to implement the national maritime strategy, including the National Plan to Achieve Maritime Domain Awareness, the Global Maritime Intelligence Integration Plan, the Maritime Operational Threat Response Plan, the International Outreach and Coordination Strategy, the Maritime Infrastructure Recovery Plan, the Maritime Transportation System Security Plan, the Maritime Commerce Security Plan, and the Domestic Outreach Plan, all of which are available at http://www.dhs.gov/files/programs/editorial_0608. shtm. For a discussion of the National Strategy for Maritime Security and supporting plans, see U.S.

General Accounting Office, Maritime Security: National Strategy and Supporting Plans Were Generally Well–Developed and Are Being Implemented, Rpt. No. GAO–08–672 (2008).

3. U.S. 2006 SAFE Port Act

The U.S. Customs and Border Protection (formerly the U.S. Customs Service) is the agency primarily responsible for inspecting cargo entering the United States. It was one of the first U.S. agencies to take steps after the September 11, 2001 al-Qaida attacks to improve maritime security. In November 2001 it announced its voluntary Customs–Trade Partnership Against Terrorism (C–TPAT) program, and in January 2002 it introduced its Container Security Initiative (CSI). Both of these administrative measures became part of U.S. statutory law with the enactment of the 2006 Security and Accountability for Every Port Act (SAFE Port Act), Pub. L. No. 109–347, §§ 211–223, 120 Stat. 1884 (2006).

Under the C–TPAT program, U.S. Customs officials review the compliance history, security profile, and practices of private companies that elect to participate in the program. As of June 1, 2009, more than 8,000 companies were enrolled, including importers, customs brokers, forwarders, terminal operators, carriers, foreign manufacturers, and other entities in the international supply chain and transportation system. 6 U.S.C. § 963. If a company is certified, it receives certain benefits, such as reduced examinations of cargo or reduced delays if its cargos are examined. Id. at §§ 964–966.

Most of the world's nonbulk cargo is transported in marine shipping containers. After the September 11, 2001 al-Qaida attacks, attention quickly shifted to the possibility that containers could be used to conceal weapons of mass destruction or terrorists. OECD Maritime Transport Committee Report, Security in Maritime Transport: Risk Factors and Economic Impact ¶¶ 20–22 (2003). In January 2002 U.S. Customs announced the CSI, consisting of four core elements:

(a) development of security criteria to identify high-risk containers,

(b) screening high-risk containers before they arrive in U.S. ports in cooperation with foreign governments,

(c) use of scanning technology to efficiently screen high-risk containers, and

(d) development of smart and secure containers.

U.S. Customs identified twenty ports as potential CSI partners, based on the highest volume of ocean container shipments to the United States. Within its first year, the United States had entered agreements with fifteen foreign governments for the placement of U.S. Customs personnel at twenty-four foreign ports (including eighteen of the twenty target ports). U.S. General Accounting Office, Container Security: Expansion of Key Customs Programs Will Require Greater Attention to Critical

Success Factors, GAO Rpt. No. 03–770, 20 (2003). In 2008 fifty-eight foreign ports participated in the CSI. U.S. Customs and Border Protection, CSI in Brief (2008).

In February 2003 U.S. Customs announced its "24–hour rule" requiring all sea carriers (with the exception of bulk carriers) to provide proper cargo descriptions and valid consignee addresses twenty-four hours before cargo is loaded at a foreign port for shipment to the United States. 19 C.F.R. § 4.7. The purpose of the rule is to permit U.S. Customs officers to analyze the contents of the container and identify potential terrorist threats before loading the U.S.-bound container at the foreign seaport. The Organization for Economic Co-operation and Development (OECD) reported that this rule, which exceeded existing international requirements as established under the ISPS Code, was "probably the most contentious of all of the security measures announced to date." OECD Maritime Transport Committee Report, Security in Maritime Transport: Risk Factors and Economic Impact ¶ 138 (2003).

U.S. Customs developed the "Automated Targeting System" to assess the risks of individual cargo containers by using a complex mathematical model to assign a risk score to each in-bound shipment based on cargo manifests and other shipping information. 6 U.S.C. § 943. If a shipment is determined to be high-risk, U.S. Customs personnel refer the shipment to the foreign port officials, who then decide whether to inspect the shipment. See U.S. General Accounting Office, Maritime Security: The

SAFE Port Act: Status and Implementation One Year Later, GAO Report 08–126T, 27 (2007).

The SAFE Port Act of 2006, which incorporated the CSI into a statute, required all containers entering the United States through the twenty-two highest volume U.S. ports to be scanned for radiation by December 2007. Pub. L. No. 109–347, § 121(a), 120 Stat. 1884, 1898. The Act authorized the Department of Homeland Security to establish a pilot program at several overseas ports to determine if 100% scanning of containers bound for all U.S. ports would be possible in the future. Id. at § 121(h), 120 Stat. at 1899. The Act also required pilot testing of new integrated scanning systems that combine nonintrusive imaging equipment and radiation detection equipment for more efficient scanning. Id. at § 231, 120 Stat. at 1915. In 2007 Congress amended the SAFE Port Act by requiring all containers bound for the United States to be screened for radioactive materials by July 1, 2012, with exceptions to be given on a case-by-case basis under strict parameters. Pub. L. No. 110–53, § 1701(a), 121 Stat. 266, 489–490. The requirement of 100% scanning of U.S.-bound containers has raised objections throughout the international community. See World Shipping Council, Statement Regarding Legislation to Require 100% Container Scanning (2007), available at http://www.worldshipping.org/wsc_legislation_statement.pdf.

In 2007 the Department of Homeland Security initiated the Secure Freight Initiative at six foreign ports, using a combination of existing technology and nuclear detection methods to test whether 100% scanning can be accomplished. See http:// www.dhs.gov/files/programs/gc_1166037389664. shtm. Under the Megaports Initiative established by the Department of Energy's National Nuclear Security Administration, as of June 1, 2009, the United States had installed radiation detection equipment at nineteen foreign ports, enabling foreign government personnel to screen shipping containers for nuclear and other radioactive material. See http:// nnsa.energy.gov/nuclear_nonproliferation/1641.htm.

Both the C–TPAT and CSI have served as worldwide models to improve the security of the global supply chain. In June 2005 member countries of the World Customs Organization (WCO) adopted the WCO Framework of Standards to Secure and Facilitate Global Trade (SAFE Framework). As of June 1, 2009, 157 WCO member countries had signed letters of intent to implement the SAFE Framework. World Customs Organization, WCO SAFE Framework of Standards (2007). The SAFE Framework consists of four core elements: harmonizing advance electronic cargo information requirements on inbound, outbound, and transit shipments; adoption by all participating countries of a consistent risk management approach to address security threats; providing for inspection of high-risk containers on the reasonable request of a receiving country by nonintrusive detection equipment such as large-scale X-ray machines and radiation detectors; and establishing benefits to be provided to businesses that meet specified supply chain security standards and best practices.

To facilitate trade, the U.S. Customs and Border Protection has also implemented an "in-bond shipment" system that allows imported goods to move in transit from one U.S. port to another without being assessed U.S. duties and without officially entering the U.S. commerce system. See U.S. General Accounting Office, International Trade: Persistent Weaknesses in the In-bond Cargo System Impede Customs and Border Protection's Ability to Address Revenue, Trade, and Security Concerns, GAO Rpt. No. 07–561 (2007).

4.   U.S. Criminal Laws

The USA PATRIOT Improvement and Reauthorization Act of 2005, Pub. L. 109–177, 120 Stat. 233 (2005), included several criminal measures to penalize terrorist activities committed on U.S. vessels or vessels subject to U.S. jurisdiction. Among other measures, the Act established several new crimes, including: the failure of a vessel to heave to on request by an authorized official, 18 U.S.C. § 2237; providing false information concerning a vessel's cargo, origin, destination, registration, ownership, nationality, or crew, id.; placing a dangerous substance or device in U.S. navigable waters with the intent to damage a vessel or its cargo or to interfere with maritime commerce, id. at § 2282A; tampering with any navigational aid maintained by the Coast Guard, id. at § 2282B; and knowingly transporting a terrorist or a weapon of mass destruction or related materials aboard any U.S. vessel or a foreign vessel in waters subject to U.S. jurisdiction or on the high seas. Id. at §§ 2283–2284. As noted in Section C.5, the United States has entered agreements with other states allowing either party to board and investigate vessels of the other party on the high seas if there are grounds to suspect that the vessel is transporting weapons of mass destruction.

5. Legislation of Other Countries

Although the international community recognizes the importance of regional and global collaboration to combat maritime terrorism, national implementation and enforcement of anti-terrorism measures remain critical to their success. In its Report on the Work of the United Nations Open-ended Informal Consultative Process on Oceans and the Law of the Sea at its Ninth Meeting, UN Doc. A/63/174, ¶ 5 (2008), the co-chairs of the Consultative Process asked the U.N. General Assembly to "[r]eaffirm that flag, port and coastal States all bear responsibility for ensuring the effective implementation and enforcement of international instruments relating to maritime security and safety, in accordance with international law."

A discussion of the legislation adopted by various countries to enhance maritime security is beyond the scope of this text. Not surprisingly, different countries have adopted varying approaches. For discussion of European and U.S. perspectives on maritime security and other matters relating to jurisdiction over vessels, see The Exercise of Jurisdiction over Vessels: Transatlantic Perspectives (New Developments in the Fields of Pollution, Fisheries, Crimes at Sea and Trafficking of Weapons of Mass Destruction) (Erik Franckx & Philippe Gautier eds., 2009). In spite of some differences as to the most effective and appropriate anti-terrorism mechanisms, countries are united in their determination to promote maritime security and have achieved significant progress in developing comprehensive and widely accepted measures to achieve this goal.

CHAPTER 15

SETTLEMENT OF DISPUTES

A. INTRODUCTION

As cases cited throughout this book have shown, a variety of forums may hear and help to resolve law of the sea disputes. National courts decide many such disputes involving private parties, as do some international courts, such as the European Court of Justice. Interstate disputes may be resolved informally, through negotiation or responses to diplomatic protests, or with the assistance of a third-party mediator or conciliator. States sometimes bring cases to third-party tribunals that are authorized to render binding decisions. Arbitral tribunals, the International Court of Justice (ICJ), and the International Tribunal for the Law of the Sea (ITLOS), which is a court created by the LOS Convention, have heard many law of the sea cases. This Chapter focuses primarily on binding third-party dispute settlement mechanisms in interstate cases. Section B provides an overview of third-party dispute settlement. Section C then introduces the dispute settlement provisions of the LOS Convention, and Section D addresses the ITLOS.

B. OVERVIEW OF THIRD–PARTY INTERNATIONAL DISPUTE SETTLEMENT

A state is not bound to go to an international tribunal unless it has accepted previously that tribunal's jurisdiction or agrees by a special agreement (a so-called "compromis") to submit a particular dispute to the tribunal. States have, for example, used special agreements to ask arbitral tribunals or the International Court of Justice (ICJ) to help resolve maritime boundary disputes. See the cases noted in Chapter 6. Prior to the entry into force of the LOS Convention, when a state had a dispute with another state about an alleged violation of a law of the sea rule, usually no international tribunal would have jurisdiction to decide the issue. If negotiations between two governments did not lead to a settlement of the dispute, and if the states did not agree to submit the dispute to a tribunal by special agreement, then the dispute might linger, disturbing relations between the two states for a long time.

To avoid this situation, many treaties relating to law of the sea issues contain a so-called compromissory clause by which the parties to the treaty agree to submit to the ICJ or an international arbitral tribunal any dispute relating to the interpretation or application of that treaty. See, e.g., 1969 Convention on High Seas Intervention in Oil Pollution Casualties, Article 8 and Annex, Articles 13–19; 1988 Convention for the Suppression of Unlawful

Acts Against the Safety of Maritime Navigation,
Article 16; 1996 Protocol to the 1972 Convention on
the Prevention of Marine Pollution by Dumping of
Wastes from Ships and Aircraft, Article 16. At the
1958 United Nations Conference on the Law of the
Sea, no agreement could be reached on obligatory
submission of disputes to adjudication; instead, an
optional protocol was prepared allowing states to
accept the jurisdiction of the ICJ for the purpose of
deciding any dispute relating to the interpretation
or application of the four conventions adopted by
the Conference. 1958 Optional Protocol concerning
the Compulsory Settlement of Disputes. Fewer than
forty states accepted this Protocol. In the United
States, the Senate vote for it was only 49 to 30, thus
falling short of the necessary two-thirds. Marjorie
M. Whiteman, 12 Digest of International Law 1333
(1971).

The ICJ may, as an alternative to basing its
jurisdiction on a special agreement or a compromissory clause in a treaty, rest its jurisdiction in contentious interstate cases on declarations by both
parties, filed with the ICJ in advance of a case.
States have sometimes made these so-called "optional clause declarations" (named for the optional
clause in Article 36 of the ICJ's Statute) conditional
by attaching reservations to them. The 1946 U.S.
acceptance of the ICJ's optional clause jurisdiction
was limited by two broad reservations. One (the
Connally Amendment) excluded from the ICJ's jurisdiction all "disputes with regard to matters
which are essentially within the domestic jurisdic-

tion of the United States of America as determined by the United States of America." Another U.S. reservation (the Vandenberg Amendment) excluded from the ICJ's jurisdiction all "disputes arising under a multilateral treaty, unless (1) all parties to the treaty affected by the decision are also parties to the case before the Court, or (2) the United States of America specially agrees to jurisdiction." Decl. of Aug. 14, 1946, 61 Stat. 1218 (1946). Since declarations under the optional clause are based on reciprocity, any other state could invoke these reservations against the United States at that state's discretion. In a case between the United States and Bulgaria, Bulgaria invoked the domestic jurisdiction clause, thus avoiding ICJ jurisdiction with respect to an issue—shooting down an Israeli airplane with U.S. passengers on board—that was an international law matter. See Leo Gross, Bulgaria Invokes the Connally Amendment, 56 Am. J. Intl. L. 357 (1962). The United States has now withdrawn altogether its optional clause declaration. In Armed Activities in and against Nicaragua (Nicaragua v. United States), 1984 I.C.J. 392, 1986 I.C.J. 14, the Court found that the optional clause provided one basis for its jurisdiction and ruled that the United States had violated the principle of non-intervention and had illegally used force against Nicaragua, including by mining Nicaraguan harbors. In reaction to this case, the United States revoked its consent to be subject to the ICJ's jurisdiction under the optional clause. Dept. of St. Letter and Statement Concerning the Termination of Acceptance of I.C.J. Compulsory Jurisdiction, Oct. 7, 1985, 24 Intl. Leg. Materials 1742 (1985). Hence, because of the principle of reciprocity, the United States now cannot invoke the ICJ's jurisdiction based on any other state's optional clause declaration.

The United States, however, still is bound to accept the ICJ's jurisdiction in cases filed by its treaty partners relating to the interpretation or application of many treaties, or the United States may itself pursue such cases, by virtue of compromissory clauses in those treaties. In 2003, for example, the ICJ decided a case in which jurisdiction was based on a compromissory clause in the bilateral 1955 U.S.-Iran Treaty of Amity, Economic Relations and Consular Rights. The case involved Iran's claim that the United States had bombed Iranian oil platforms in the Persian Gulf and U.S. counterclaims that Iranian mines had damaged U.S. shipping. Case Concerning Oil Platforms (Iran v. United States), 2003 I.C.J. 161. The United States may also agree to submit a particular dispute to the ICJ by a special agreement, as it did in the Gulf of Maine Case (Canada/United States), 1984 I.C.J. 246.

C. THE DISPUTE SETTLEMENT SYSTEM OF THE LAW OF THE SEA CONVENTION

From the beginning of the negotiations leading to the LOS Convention, several states (including the United States) insisted that effective means be provided for settling law of the sea disputes. See Louis

B. Sohn, U.S. Policy Toward the Settlement of Law of the Sea Disputes, 17 Va. J. Intl. L. 9 (1976); see generally A.O. Adede, The System for Settlement of Disputes Under the United Nations Convention on the Law of the Sea (1987). A strong system of dispute settlement could help reinforce Convention rules. In addition, in such a complex document, there would be some ambiguous compromises and conflicting provisions, requiring clarification and reconciliation through future decision making. Difficult negotiations led to an intricate system for the settlement of law of the sea disputes, which was spelled out in more than 100 articles scattered throughout the LOS Convention and several annexes.

The guiding principle is that the will of the parties must prevail and that the parties may by agreement select any dispute settlement method they wish. The LOS Convention recognizes that states will often settle their disputes informally. It also provides a system that, for most disputes, can lead to a binding third-party decision. With respect to nonseabed mining disputes, the LOS Convention provides for third-party tribunal jurisdiction "over any dispute concerning the interpretation or application of [the LOS] Convention." LOS Convention, Article 288(1). Jurisdiction also exists with respect to "any dispute concerning the interpretation or application of an international agreement related to the purposes of [the LOS] Convention" that is submitted "in accordance with the agreement." Id. at Article 288(2).

Unlike most other international instruments, the LOS Convention does not provide for a unitary system of dispute settlement. As different groups of states desired different procedures, it was agreed that a state may choose one of four main systems of dispute settlement: the International Court of Justice (ICJ), the new International Tribunal for the Law of the Sea (ITLOS), an international arbitral tribunal, or, for fisheries, marine environment, marine scientific research, or navigation disputes, a special technical arbitral tribunal. Id. at Article 287(1). If the parties to a dispute have not accepted the same procedure, they are obliged to submit it to arbitration (id. at Article 287(5)), and Annex VII to the Convention provides a foolproof method for selecting an arbitral tribunal. The Convention thus ultimately provides for obligatory third-party dispute settlement. Still, flexibility remains. Even after a dispute has arisen and has been submitted to a procedure provided for in the Convention, the parties may agree "at any time" to settle it by a different procedure. Id. at Article 280.

The scope of some LOS Convention provisions recognizing that parties to a law of the sea dispute may use alternate dispute settlement mechanisms has been tested in litigation. According to Article 281, if the parties to a dispute about the interpretation or application of the LOS Convention "have agreed to seek settlement of the dispute by a peaceful means of their own choice," the Convention's provisions for obligatory dispute settlement apply only: (a) where the means chosen by the parties have not led to a settlement, and (b) "where the agreement between the parties does not exclude any further procedure." Article 281 was at issue in the Southern Bluefin Tuna Case (Australia & New Zealand v. Japan), 23 Rep. Intl. Arb. Awards 1 (2000), in which Australia and New Zealand argued before an arbitral tribunal constituted under Article 287 and Annex VII of the LOS Convention that Japan's harvesting of tuna violated its Convention obligations to conserve and manage high seas fisheries. See Chapter 13. The tribunal, concluding that Australia's and New Zealand's claim presented a single dispute under both the LOS Convention and the 1993 Convention for the Conservation of Southern Bluefin Tuna, found that the parties had not settled their dispute by recourse to Article 16 of the latter treaty. Article 16, which provides that the parties have the responsibility to seek to resolve disputes by "peaceful means of their own choice," merely lists a range of dispute settlement options and does not ultimately mandate recourse to any one mechanism. Yet, invoking the last clause of Article 281, the tribunal also found that Article 16 of the 1993 Convention implicitly "exclude[d] any further procedure" under the LOS Convention and that the tribunal therefore lacked jurisdiction, thus ending the arbitration. The decision was controversial, because Article 16 does not expressly exclude the LOS Convention's dispute settlement provisions and because the tribunal's reasoning could erode the system of recourse to obligatory dispute settlement established in the LOS Convention. See Bernard H.

Oxman, Complementary Agreements and Compulsory Jurisdiction, 95 Am. J. Intl. L. 277 (2001).

Article 282 of the LOS Convention, which provides that parties may bypass the dispute settlement provisions of the Convention by agreeing in advance to use some other bilateral, regional, or general dispute settlement procedure entailing "a binding decision," was at issue in the MOX Plant Case (Ireland v. United Kingdom), 126 Intl. L. Rpts. 310 (2003). That case was an arbitration brought pursuant to Article 287 and Annex VII of the LOS Convention. Ireland alleged that the United Kingdom's commissioning and operation of a mixed oxide plant could release radioactive contaminants into the Irish Sea, violating the United Kingdom's LOS Convention obligations to protect the marine environment. The arbitral tribunal suspended its deliberations pending a ruling by the European Court of Justice concerning whether this dispute should have been pursued through the European legal system. In Case C–459/03 (European Commission v. Ireland), 2006 E.C.R. I–4635, ¶ 110, the European Court found that matters covered by the marine pollution provisions of the LOS Convention on which Ireland was relying in the MOX Plant case were "very largely regulated by" European Community law. The European Court concluded that "the autonomy of the Community legal system may be adversely affected" by Ireland's proceeding with the LOS Convention arbitration, id. at ¶ 154, and that Ireland had breached its European legal obligations by bringing the case to the arbitral tribunal without having informed and consulted competent Community institutions. According to the European Court, Article 282 of the LOS Convention preserves "the autonomy of the Community legal system," ensuring that "the resolution of disputes set out in the EC Treaty must in principle take precedence over that contained in Part XV of the [LOS] Convention." Id. at ¶¶ 124–125. See Nikolaos Lavranos, Protecting Its Exclusive Jurisdiction: The MOX Plant Judgment of the ECJ, 5 L. & Prac. Intl. Cts. & Tribs. 479 (2006). The arbitral tribunal constituted under Annex VII of the LOS Convention terminated its proceedings in June 2008, following a request from Ireland. Order No. 6, available at http://www.pca-cpa.org/. Yet another international tribunal also decided an issue related to the mixed oxide plant controversy: an arbitral tribunal constituted under the 1992 Convention for the Protection of the Marine Environment of the North–East Atlantic (OSPAR) denied Ireland's request for information under that treaty. Dispute Concerning Access to Information Under Article 9 of the OSPAR Convention (Ireland v. United Kingdom), 23 Rep. Intl. Arb. Awards 59 (2003).

Some treaties, rather than displacing the LOS Convention's dispute settlement mechanisms, instead incorporate them by reference. See LOS Convention, Article 288(2). This technique has been used, for example, with respect to disputes relating to the interpretation or application of the following treaties: the 1995 Fish Stocks Convention, Articles

30–32; the 2000 Convention on the Conservation
and Management of Highly Migratory Fish Stocks
in the Western and Central Pacific Ocean, Article
31; the 2001 Convention on the Conservation and
Management of Fishery Resources in the South
East Atlantic Ocean, Article 24(4); the 2001 UN-
ESCO Underwater Cultural Heritage Convention,
Article 25; and the 2004 Convention on Future
Multilateral Cooperation in North–East Atlantic
Fisheries, Article 18 bis (complemented by the
North East Atlantic Fisheries Commission Recommendation establishing procedures for the settlement of disputes). The United States is a party to
the first two of these conventions and thus, even
without accepting the LOS Convention, has agreed
to be bound by the Convention's dispute settlement system for certain fisheries and environmental disputes.

Where the parties to a dispute arising under the
LOS Convention have not settled their dispute informally, and where the parties have not displaced
the Convention's third-party dispute settlement
mechanisms, those mechanisms apply without any
exception to the vast majority of the provisions of
the Convention. In order to obtain general consensus on this part of the LOS Convention during the
Third United Nations Conference on the Law of the
Sea negotiations, however, three categories of disputes had to be subjected to different procedures.
First, some coastal states were not willing to accept
strict dispute settlement provisions with respect to
all disputes relating to the exercise by a coastal

state of its sovereign rights or jurisdiction in the exclusive economic zone (EEZ). It became necessary to subdivide these disputes into three groups. One group covers EEZ disputes relating to violations by either the coastal state or any other state of the provisions of the LOS Convention in regard to freedoms and rights of navigation, overflight, the laying of submarine cables and pipelines, or other internationally lawful uses of the sea, as well as disputes relating to violations by the coastal state of international rules and standards for the protection of the marine environment. Such disputes remain subject to the general system for the settlement of disputes. LOS Convention, Article 297(1). A second group of EEZ disputes relates to fisheries. Some EEZ fishery disputes will be completely excluded from the dispute settlement system due to the broad discretionary powers of the coastal state with respect to several aspects of coastal fisheries. Some other EEZ fishery disputes that involve the possibility of arbitrary actions of the coastal state will be subject to compulsory conciliation (i.e., resort to an international commission that can present a report on the facts and the law, which is not binding on the parties to the dispute but with which the parties would usually comply). Remaining disputes with regard to fisheries will continue to be subject to the general system of dispute settlement. Id. at Article 297(3). The third group of EEZ disputes concerns marine scientific research. This group is also subdivided into three subcategories, paralleling those relating to fishing. Id. at Article 297(2).

Second, while the disputes relating to the EEZ discussed above are automatically exempt from third-party dispute settlement procedures, another group of disputes may be excluded from such procedures if a party to the LOS Convention files a special optional declaration. The most complicated provisions relate to disputes concerning boundary delimitation or involving historic bays. Id. at Article 298(1)(a). Old boundary delimitation or historic bay disputes, i.e., those that arose before the entry into force of the LOS Convention, may be declared totally exempt from the LOS Convention's third-party dispute settlement procedures. Disputes arising after the entry into force of the LOS Convention will, however, at least be subject to compulsory conciliation similar to that used for fishery and scientific research disputes, although "mixed" disputes that necessarily involve the concurrent consideration of sea boundaries and of any unsettled dispute concerning sovereignty over a part of the mainland or over an island or group of islands are excluded from submission to compulsory conciliation. In addition, sea boundary disputes that have been finally settled by an arrangement between the parties, or that are to be settled in accordance with an agreement between them, also can be declared exempt from the LOS Convention's third-party dispute settlement procedures. Article 298 also establishes the possibility of a total exemption of disputes relating to two parallel activities: military activities (including military activities by government vessels and aircraft engaged in noncommercial service) and law enforcement activities by coastal states (if these activities are connected with those disputes involving fishing or marine scientific research that are themselves exempt from dispute settlement under Article 297(2) and (3)). Id. at Article 298(1)(b). Finally, in order to avoid discrepant decisions by different international authorities, disputes that are being dealt with by the Security Council of the United Nations may be exempted (by an optional declaration) from third-party dispute settlement under the LOS Convention, but they will become again subject to Convention procedures if the Security Council should cease to deal with the matter. Id. at Article 298(1)(c). Most states have thus far not chosen to opt out from applying the LOS Convention's dispute settlement procedures to the Article 298 categories of disputes. As of July 15, 2009, only twenty-six of the 159 parties to the LOS Convention had invoked any of the Article 298 opt-out provisions.

Third, most disputes relating to seabed mining are to be submitted to a special Seabed Disputes Chamber of the International Tribunal for the Law of the Sea in order to provide a uniform system of interpretation for the part of the Convention that establishes a seabed mining regime. Provisions relating to this Chamber are discussed in Section D and in Chapter 11, Section E.

The cost of access to international arbitration and adjudication has been of concern for developing states. International trust funds now exist, on which developing states may draw to facilitate recourse to tribunals. See Charles Claypoole, Access to International Justice: A Review of the Trust Funds Available for Law of the Sea–Related Disputes, 23 Intl. J. Marine & Coastal L. 77 (2008).

D. THE INTERNATIONAL TRIBUNAL FOR THE LAW OF THE SEA

The International Tribunal for the Law of the Sea (ITLOS), a court created by the LOS Convention, is located in Hamburg, Germany. See http://www.itlos.org. The ITLOS's twenty-one members, law of the sea experts from around the world, are elected by the parties to the LOS Convention for renewable nine-year terms. Unlike the International Court of Justice (ICJ), the ITLOS may hear cases involving the European Community, which is a party to the LOS Convention, as well as states. In addition, in limited circumstances described below, the ITLOS or its Seabed Disputes Chamber may also hear cases involving private parties. Despite these features, and despite the ITLOS's demonstrated efficiency and expertise, the ITLOS has had only fifteen cases between 1996, when its judges were first elected, and June 1, 2009. None of the cases involved private parties. The low number of cases may be explained in part by the fact that the ICJ and arbitral tribunals continue to hear law of the sea cases, in part by the fact that the options for private parties to initiate ITLOS cases are few, and in part by the general reluctance of states to submit interstate disputes to third-party tribunals.

The ITLOS has created several chambers, which parties to disputes may choose because of the cham-

bers' efficiencies or because of the particular expertise of the ITLOS judges comprising the chambers.
A Chamber of Summary Procedure can deal expeditiously with any case that could be submitted to the
full Tribunal. The ITLOS has also formed chambers
for fisheries disputes, marine environment disputes,
and maritime delimitation disputes. In addition,
parties to a dispute may request an ad hoc chamber.
Despite the flexibility for parties that chambers
could provide, as of June 1, 2009 only one case had
been submitted to a chamber at the request of
parties. Case Concerning Conservation and Sustainable Exploitation of Swordfish Stocks in the South-
eastern Pacific Ocean (Chile/European Commission), ITLOS Case No. 7, Order 2000/3 (2000).

The LOS Convention specifies that the Seabed
Disputes Chamber of the ITLOS will be the primary
third-party forum for hearing disputes relating to
seabed mining beyond the limits of national jurisdiction. LOS Convention, Article 187. This Chamber
is composed of eleven members chosen by the Tribunal from among its membership. Id. at Annex VI,
Article 35. The jurisdiction of the Seabed Disputes
Chamber extends not only to seabed mining disputes between parties to the LOS Convention, but
also to disputes between states and the International Seabed Authority (ISA). Furthermore, in contrac-
tual matters, the Chamber's jurisdiction extends to
disputes between the ISA and both state and private entities. Id. at Article 187. See Niels–J. See-
berg–Elverfeldt, The Settlement of Disputes in
Deep Seabed Mining (1998); John E. Noyes, The

International Tribunal for the Law of the Sea, 32 Cornell Intl. L.J. 109, 164–72 (1998). As of June 1, 2009, the Seabed Disputes Chamber had not yet heard any cases. For additional discussion of the Seabed Disputes Chamber, see Chapter 11, Section E.

The ITLOS may obtain jurisdiction in nonseabed mining cases in several ways. First, the ITLOS will have jurisdiction when all the states (or the European Community) that are parties to a dispute have selected the ITLOS in declarations made pursuant to Article 287 of the LOS Convention. As of June 1, 2009, twenty-four parties had named the ITLOS as a first choice among dispute settlement options. No cases have yet come to the ITLOS via this route.

Second, the ITLOS has "residual compulsory jurisdiction" with respect to provisional measures. LOS Convention, Article 290(5). The LOS Convention's negotiators recognized that states might need to have recourse to a forum that could quickly rule on provisional measures in urgent situations, involving not only the preservation of "the respective rights of the parties" but also the prevention of "serious harm to the marine environment." Id. at Article 290(1). Since it could take too long to constitute an arbitral tribunal to hear such requests, the ITLOS is available for these purposes, even if less than all the parties to a dispute have selected the ITLOS to hear their case. According to Article 290(5), the ITLOS may prescribe provisional measures "if it considers that *prima facie* the tribunal which is to be constituted" to hear the merits of a dispute, e.g., an arbitral tribunal, "would have jurisdiction and that the urgency of the situation so requires."

Article 290(5) has been an important source of cases for the ITLOS. The ITLOS has ordered provisional measures pursuant to Article 290(5) in the Southern Bluefin Tuna Cases (New Zealand v. Japan; Australia v. Japan), ITLOS Cases Nos. 3 & 4 (1999), the MOX Plant Case (Ireland v. United Kingdom), ITLOS Case No. 10 (2001), and the Case Concerning Land Reclamation by Singapore in and around the Straits of Johor (Malaysia v. Singapore), ITLOS Case No. 12 (2003). Orders of provisional measures are binding. For example, in the Southern Bluefin Tuna Cases the ITLOS found a prima facie basis for the jurisdiction of an arbitral tribunal to be constituted under the LOS Convention and, inter alia, ordered limits on "experimental fishing programs" and a resumption of negotiations concerning measures to conserve and manage southern bluefin tuna. As noted in Section C, the arbitral tribunal constituted to hear the merits of this case in fact found that it lacked jurisdiction under the LOS Convention, and it revoked the ITLOS's order of provisional measures as of the date of the arbitral tribunal's award. Nevertheless, the arbitral tribunal concluded that the ITLOS's order "had an impact: not merely in the suspension of Japan's unilateral experimental fishing program during the period that the Order was in force, but on the perspectives and actions of the Parties." Southern Bluefin Tuna Case (Australia & New Zealand v. Japan), 23 Rep.

Intl. Arb. Awards 1, ¶ 67 (2000). Several of the ITLOS's provisional measures have mandated reports or negotiations, in an effort to help the parties themselves find a solution to their disputes.

Third, the ITLOS also has residual compulsory jurisdiction in another type of proceeding, involving certain situations in which a coastal state has detained a foreign flag vessel or its crew. These situations are limited, including only detentions for certain fishing and pollution violations. See LOS Convention, Articles 73, 220, 226, 292. Detaining vessels for alleged violations of coastal state laws in such situations may cause owners tremendous financial hardship, and detaining crews may pose human rights concerns. Article 292 of the LOS Convention provides a mechanism whereby a flag state, or someone (such as a vessel owner) that the flag state has designated to act on its behalf, can obtain an order of prompt release of a vessel and crew on the posting of a reasonable bond or other financial security. The bond protects the coastal state's interest in having its laws enforced. A prompt release order is "without prejudice to the merits of a case before the appropriate domestic forum against the vessel, its owner or its crew," but addresses only the narrow question of release. Id. The ITLOS has found that the factors involved in determining what bond is reasonable "include the gravity of the alleged offences, the penalties imposed or imposable under laws of the detaining State, the value of the detained vessel and of the cargo seized, the amount of bond imposed by the detaining State and its form." Camouco Case (Panama v. France), ITLOS Case No. 5, ¶ 67 (2000). See Erik Franckx, "Reasonable Bond" in the Practice of the International Tribunal for the Law of the Sea, 32 Cal. W. Intl. L.J. 303 (2002). An Article 292 prompt release application is proper "not only where no bond is set" by the coastal state, "but also where ... the bond set by the detaining State is unreasonable." Hoshinmaru Case (Japan v. Russia), ITLOS Case No. 14, ¶ 65 (2007).

The ITLOS has considered several prompt release applications. In each case it has heard these applications and rendered judgment within twenty-nine days, in accordance with its rules. Rules of the Tribunal, Article 112, ITLOS/8 (2009), available at http://www.itlos.org/start2_en.html. The ITLOS ordered prompt release in the Camouco and Hoshinmaru cases just noted, and in the M/V Saiga Case (St. Vincent and the Grenadines v. Guinea), ITLOS Case No. 1 (1997), Monte Confurco Case (Seychelles v. France), ITLOS Case No. 6 (2000), Volga Case (Russia v. Australia), ITLOS Case No. 11 (2002), and Juno Trader Case (St. Vincent v. Guinea–Bissau), ITLOS Case No. 13 (2004). The ITLOS denied the application for prompt release in the Grand Prince Case (Belize v. France), ITLOS Case No. 8 (2001), finding that the detained vessel did not have the nationality of the state bringing the application. See Chapter 3, Section D. In the Tomimaru Case (Japan v. Russia), ITLOS Case No. 15 (2007), the ITLOS concluded that Japan's application was without object, since Russia's Supreme Court had already ruled on the merits and upheld a confiscation of the vessel. Significantly, however, in that case the ITLOS found that a national confiscation decision "should not be taken through proceedings inconsistent with international standards of due process of law" and that "a confiscation decided in unjustified haste would jeopardize the operation of article 292 of the [LOS] Convention." Id. at ¶ 76. For reviews of the prompt release mechanism, see Anne–Katrin Escher, Release of Vessels and Crews Before the International Tribunal for the Law of the Sea, 3 L. & Prac. Intl. Cts. & Tribs. 205–374, 411–507 (2004); Yoshifumi Tanaka, Prompt Release in the United Nations Convention on the Law of the Sea: Some Reflections on the ITLOS Jurisprudence, 51 Neth. Intl. L. Rev. 237 (2004).

Fourth, the ITLOS also may obtain jurisdiction when the parties to a dispute select the ITLOS via a special agreement. In the *Saiga* dispute, where the ITLOS had already heard a prompt release challenge and was familiar with many of the facts, the parties used a special agreement to authorize the ITLOS to consider provisional measures and hear the merits of their dispute. M/V Saiga (No. 2) Case (St. Vincent and the Grenadines v. Guinea), ITLOS Case No. 2, ¶¶ 41–43 (1999). The European Commission and Chile also finally jointly submitted to an ad hoc chamber of the ITLOS, via special agreement, a dispute related to the conservation of swordfish in the Pacific Ocean. Case Concerning Conservation and Sustainable Exploitation of Swordfish Stocks in the South-eastern Pacific

Ocean (Chile/European Commission), ITLOS Case
No. 7. See Marcos A. Orellana, The Swordfish Dispute between the EU and Chile at the ITLOS and
the WTO, 71 Nordic J. Intl. L. 55 (2002). For
discussion of the Swordfish Stocks case, see Chapter
13, Section C.3.

Fifth, the ITLOS may have jurisdiction not only
under the LOS Convention but also with respect to
"all matters specifically provided for in any other
agreement which confers jurisdiction on the Tribunal." LOS Convention, Annex VI, Article 21. The
1995 Fish Stocks Convention, which incorporates by
reference the dispute settlement provisions of the
LOS Convention, authorizes provisional measures
when states have been unable to agree on fishery
conservation and management measures, and the
ITLOS would be the likely forum to consider any
such provisional measures. See 1995 Fish Stocks
Convention, Articles 7(5)–(6), 16(2), 31–32. This
"any other agreement" basis for jurisdiction may
encompass agreements other than treaties between
states. Article 20 of the ITLOS Statute provides
that the ITLOS is open to entities other than states
parties in, inter alia, "any case submitted pursuant
to any other agreement conferring jurisdiction on
the Tribunal." See Rüdiger Wofrum, The Legislative History of Articles 20 and 21 of the Statute of
the International Tribunal for the Law of the Sea,
62 Rabels Zeitschrift für ausländisches und internationales Privatrecht 342 (1999).

The ITLOS may render advisory opinions in two
situations. Parties to an international agreement

related to the purposes of the LOS Convention could authorize the ITLOS to issue an advisory opinion on matters relating to that agreement. Rules of the Tribunal, Article 138, ITLOS/8 (2009), available at http://www.itlos.org/start2_en.html. In addition, the Seabed Disputes Chamber may render advisory opinions when requested by the Assembly or Council of the International Seabed Authority, in order to address "legal questions arising within the scope of their activities." LOS Convention, Article 191; see id. at Article 159(10). See also Chapter 11, Section E.

The ITLOS, which is only one of several forums available to hear law of the sea disputes, has in its few years of existence shown that it can act expeditiously and transparently. Its decisions have been well respected. Thomas Mensah, the first President of the ITLOS, commented:

> States [that], in their sovereign discretion, accept the jurisdiction of international judicial bodies will, in general, find it in their long term interests to comply with decisions of these bodies, even when the decisions are not favourable to them for one reason or another.... [T]he judgments and orders issued so far by the Tribunal have been fully complied with by the parties to whom they were addressed.

Thomas A. Mensah, The International Tribunal for the Law of the Sea: A Review of the First Five Years, in Globalism: People, Profits and Progress 106, 115 (2003). For analysis of the work of the

ITLOS and the dispute settlement system of the
LOS Convention, consult the Select Bibliography of
Settlement of Disputes Concerning the Law of the
Sea, available at http://www.itlos.org/start2_en.
html.

The ITLOS has also contributed significantly to
international law. Where the LOS Convention is
ambiguous, the ITLOS has fleshed out standards, as
with respect to the factors involved in determining
a "reasonable bond" in the prompt release context.
On other issues, it has reinforced existing LOS
Convention norms, as in its merits decision in the
M/V Saiga (No. 2) Case, discussed in Chapter 9,
Section B, where the ITLOS ruled against a coastal
state's attempts to extend its jurisdiction in the
exclusive economic zone beyond what the LOS Convention authorized. As a standing court whose
judges possess great legal expertise, the ITLOS can
help to settle disputes peacefully and contribute
rulings that respect and interpret the existing law
of the sea.

CHAPTER 16

THE FUTURE OF THE
LAW OF THE SEA

The law of the sea will change. New threats, such as climate change and collapsing fish stocks, demand legal attention. More intensive uses of the oceans and increased strains on ocean resources seem inevitable. These pressures have already led to much new law not anticipated a third of a century ago when the 1982 LOS Convention was being negotiated. See, for example, legal developments concerning the marine environment (Chapter 12), high seas fisheries (Chapter 13), and maritime terrorism (Chapter 14). New technologies will also prompt calls for new legal regimes. It is now possible to navigate unmanned vehicles at great depths, conduct marine scientific research by deploying automated devices able to steer their own drift, harvest marine genetic resources, produce energy from waves and offshore windmills, and recover underwater cultural heritage from vast ocean depths. See generally Bringing New Law to Ocean Waters (David D. Caron & Harry N. Scheiber eds., 2004).

One traditional tension in the law of the sea—that between the interests of coastal states and maritime powers—is likely to continue. At least in the foreseeable future, it seems probable that the law of the sea will retain the fundamental jurisdictional concepts of internal waters, the territorial sea, the contiguous zone, the continental shelf, the exclusive economic zone, and the Area. The law usually changes incrementally, building on past traditions, rather than radically. These jurisdictional concepts, along with other core compromises and principles embodied in the LOS Convention, emerged as the product of intensive work. Numerous treaties, state practice, and judicial and arbitral decisions have reinforced these concepts. They will not be lightly abandoned, particularly now that the LOS Convention has received widespread acceptance. The possibility of a complete enclosure of the oceans into "national lakes" appears remote. See Mark W. Zacher & James G. McConnell, Down to the Sea with Stakes, 21 Ocean Dev. & Intl. L. 71 (1990).

This said, some coastal states, concerned about security or environmental threats, have asserted increasing authority over activities in their coastal zones. See Chapters 8 (Section D.3), 12, and 14. International law experts have predicted that such assertions could well threaten the stability of navigation. See Craig H. Allen, Moderator's Report: Legal Experts' Workshop on the Future Global Legal Order, 60 Naval War College Rev. No. 4 (Autumn 2007) at 79, 88–91, 97. Private actors and flag states, seeking to exercise specific rights in coastal zones, will resist the expansion of coastal state jurisdiction. One significant rationale pushing the United States towards accepting the LOS Convention has been the Convention's role in ensuring navigational rights. See John E. Noyes, The United States, the Law of the Sea Convention, and Freedom of Navigation, 29 Suffolk Transnatl. L. Rev. 1 (2005). Should the United States decide to become a party to the LOS Convention, it will be well-positioned to help ensure that the Convention's guarantees, including its important provisions relating to navigational freedoms, are not undermined.

The expansion of coastal zones, and of the authority of coastal states within those zones, has not cured all the problems that such expansion was intended to cure. Threats to maritime security may not best be dealt with by relying on the exercise of coastal state sovereign authority over broad territorial seas, especially when many coastal states lack extensive maritime enforcement capacity. Rather, upholding navigational freedoms for military vessels in coastal zones and engaging in cooperative enforcement programs may better further the goal of maritime security. The "nationalization" of most living resources through the exclusive economic zone concept (see Chapter 9) has thus far not brought a long-term conservation and management solution for those resources, as many had initially hoped. Cooperative international measures to manage and conserve living resources that swim across international maritime boundaries will continue to be necessary, as will more effective national measures.

Indeed, even if one were to imagine, just as a thought experiment, that assertions of increased coastal state authority might some day lead to a "national lakes" division of the oceans, the world would still need an international law of the sea. Maritime boundaries would still need to be legally delimited. International law would remain essential for a host of other reasons too: as just noted, to manage and conserve vulnerable fish stocks that do not observe international maritime boundaries; to regulate the extraction of oil and mineral resources that overlap those boundaries; to regulate the vessels that cross those boundaries; to address cross-boundary pollution; and to facilitate countless other cooperative oceans endeavors.

The traditional picture of the law of the sea as involving tradeoffs between the interests of coastal states and maritime powers has been supplemented and in places essentially transformed by the evolution of global values. Influential actors emphasize the importance of sustainable development, an ecosystem-based approach to environmental issues, and the peaceful resolution of disputes. Some values have initially been articulated through nonbinding "soft law," which in turn influences public opinion, political agendas, and treaty negotiations. International law of the sea decision makers may also rely on global values, in order, for example, to fill gaps in treaty law.

Concern about the marine environment is likely to grow. Well-received twenty-first-century studies have depicted environmental crises facing the oceans and stressed the importance of an ecosystem-based approach. See Pew Oceans Commission,

America's Living Oceans: Charting a Course for Sea Change (2003), available at http://www.pewtrusts. org/. National oceans plans will likely increasingly emphasize the importance of ecosystem and sustainability values, as well as the need for continuing research, increased international coordination, and more public education about oceans issues. See Intergovernmental Oceanographic Commission, National Ocean Policy: The Basic Texts from Australia, Brazil, Canada, China, Colombia, Japan, Norway, Portugal, Russian Federation, United States of America (IOC Technical Series 75, 2007). See also An Integrated Maritime Policy for the European Union (the "Blue Book") (2007), available at http:// eur-lex.europa.eu/.

One continuing challenge will be to build solid regimes of treaty law—often dealing with specific regions or specific oceans topics—not only to give concrete expression to community values, but also to implement the law. International lawyers and government officials will increasingly seek to develop mechanisms to implement oceans law agreements, both regionally and globally. States, nongovernmental organizations, the United Nations, and specialized agencies and organs such as the Food and Agriculture Organization, the International Maritime Organization, and the United Nations Environment Programme are moving beyond the stages of norm creation and institution building. They now emphasize implementation and capacity building, to enable all states, and developing states in particular, to carry out their legal obligations.

Note, for example, initiatives at the United Nations involving training programs, trust funds, fellowships, advisory services, and other steps to implement existing law. See Oceans and the Law of the Sea: Report of the Secretary–General, UN Doc. A/61/63, ¶¶ 43–56, 276–278 (2006), and Addendum, UN Doc. A/61/63/Add.1, ¶¶ 177–201 (2006). Effective implementation of the international law of the sea also will mean an increased emphasis on compliance mechanisms. National enforcement of the international law of the sea will undoubtedly continue, but unilateral compliance mechanisms may be increasingly supplemented by regional ones, such as the port state memoranda of understanding used to combat the problem of substandard vessels (see Chapter 7, Section E). Whether formal international organizations will themselves be given more effective enforcement powers in the foreseeable future is debatable, but commentators have noted the benefits that could flow from such a development. See Louis B. Sohn, Managing the Law of the Sea: Ambassador Pardo's Forgotten Second Idea, 36 Colum. J. Transnatl. L. 285 (1997).

In all likelihood, conflicts among different international legal regimes will increase. Notions of comity, as well as negotiated solutions, will be employed to mediate such conflicts. Some law of the sea regimes could benefit significantly from improved coordination. For example, the various regional fisheries organizations (see Chapter 13) may work increasingly to mesh their standards and their enforcement and monitoring measures.

In addition, many law of the sea issues cannot be fully understood in isolation from other areas of international law, and this fact also poses challenges of regime coordination. The LOS Convention's strong environmental provisions have been supplemented both by soft law and other treaties—relating for example to biodiversity and sustainability—that were developed initially within the framework of international environmental law, without sole regard to the oceans. The law governing unregulated, unreported, and illegal fishing derives both from the law of the sea and from international trade law, which informs the actions port states may take with respect to offending fishing vessels. The law concerning marine genetic resources relates not only to the law of the sea but to international environmental law and international intellectual property law. The legal regime for Antarctica and the surrounding Southern Ocean differs in significant respects from the main body of the law of the sea. See Christopher C. Joyner, The Antarctic Treaty System and the Law of the Sea—Competing Regimes in the Southern Ocean?, 10 Intl. J. Marine & Coastal L. 301 (1995). Decision makers—treaty makers, judges and arbitrators, and those working for international and national institutions—will have to address an array of normative and jurisdictional overlaps. These overlaps signal the growing complexity and maturation of the international legal system.

One particularly important area of overlapping regimes may be human rights and the law of the sea. Legal responses to World War II reintroduced the individual as an actor in the international legal system, and the resulting international human rights law may intersect with oceans issues. Sailors sometimes face unsafe labor conditions, and individuals are still subjected to the slave trade and human trafficking. Refugees, passengers and crew members on board stateless vessels, and ocean miners with property claims all have rights. See Bernard H. Oxman, Human Rights and the United Nations Convention on the Law of the Sea, 36 Colum. J. Transnatl. L. 399 (1997). Indeed, the rights and responsibilities of actors in addition to states and individuals—including international organizations, nongovernmental organizations, "fishing entities" (e.g., Taiwan), and indigenous peoples—may well receive more attention in the future.

What mechanisms will be used to change the law of the sea? A Fourth United Nations Conference on the Law of the Sea is unlikely any time in the near future; states appear reluctant to open the door to formal renegotiation of the full range of traditional and new law of the sea issues, a development that would be likely with another general treaty-making conference. The LOS Convention contains elaborate mechanisms for amendments (see LOS Convention, Articles 155, 312–314; 1994 Part XI Implementation Agreement, Annex, § 4), but observers have questioned whether these mechanisms will ever be used. The Meetings of States Parties to the LOS Convention lack any general authority to modify it. See Stability and Change in the Law of the Sea: The

Role of the LOS Convention (Alex G. Oude Elferink ed., 2005). Much more probable vehicles for change are entirely new regional or global treaties that address specific oceans issues or, perhaps, additional agreements to "implement" the LOS Convention as discussed in Chapter 13, Section C. State practice and the practice of intergovernmental organizations will also continue significantly to shape the future of the law of the sea.

International law of the sea dispute settlement is likely to remain complex. No realistic prospects currently exist for one centralized, hierarchically organized dispute settlement system for this area of law. The dispute settlement system of the LOS Convention will also intersect with formal and informal mechanisms established under other regimes. This intersection could increase the risk of fragmented or inconsistent judgments. First, some tribunals faced with oceans-related cases may be authorized only to adjudicate specific subject matters, such as trade law issues. This restriction could hamper the ability of a limited-jurisdiction tribunal to address all the issues in a dispute. Second, different parties to a dispute may sometimes call on different international tribunals to decide the full case, or the same aspect of a case. Those tribunals may then develop abstention or other conflict-avoidance rules. As demonstrated by the MOX Plant judgment of the European Court of Justice (see Chapter 15, Section C), however, a regional economic organization may claim exclusive competence to settle, through its judicial organs, international law of the sea disputes between the member states of that organization. Should third-party courts and tribunals that are authorized to hear disputes under the LOS Convention defer too readily to dispute resolution mechanisms created by other treaties, the role of the LOS Convention as the central touchstone of analysis for law of the sea problems could diminish. Despite these pressures associated with intersecting regimes, we should expect that the judges of different international courts and tribunals operating under the LOS Convention and other global regimes typically will follow the same approach to treaty interpretation and draw on the jurisprudence of other courts. See Jonathan I. Charney, Third Party Dispute Settlement and International Law, 36 Colum. J. Transnatl. L. 65, 72–73 (1997); P. Chandrasekhara Rao, The International Tribunal for the Law of the Sea: An Evaluation, in 1 Liber Amicorum Judge Shigeru Oda 667, 677 (Nisuke Ando, Edward McWhinney & Rüdiger Wolfrum eds., 2002).

The modest caseload of many international courts and tribunals would increase significantly if their jurisdiction were modified to allow individuals to bring a range of law of the sea claims. Some international courts operating outside the law of the sea context hear cases involving individuals; the European Court of Human Rights (see http://www.echr. coe.int/echr), for example, handles over 10,000 such cases each year. The recognition that law of the sea issues may implicate individual rights could at some point increase pressure for changes in the jurisdiction of some international courts and tribunals that hear law of the sea cases.

Finally, in trying to divine the attitudes of national courts, as well as national agencies and legislatures, about the international law of the sea, one must analyze the often complex interplay of national and international law. In one possible future, national judges and decision makers will be aware of nondomestic perspectives, recognizing that the regulation and management of common spaces and scarce shared resources require respect for international law. This possibility may be a daunting one for countries that lean towards dualism with respect to the domestic implementation of international law, i.e., countries that as a rule require international law to be transformed into the national legal system before it can become operational there. Challenges exist even in so-called monist systems, where judges may directly apply international law. Those judges must be knowledgeable about the law of the sea, or misguided decisions may result. Effectively integrating international law into national legal systems through judicial, executive, and legislative means will remain one important way to implement the international law of the sea.

INDEX

References are to Pages

CLIMATE CHANGE
Baselines, effect on 132–133
Carbon sequestration, 390
Oceans, relationship with, 398

COASTAL STATE JURISDICTION
See also Boarding and Arrest of Ships and Crew; Continental
  Shelf; Exclusive Economic Zone; Internal Waters; Ma-
  rine Environment, Protection and Preservation of; Port
  State Jurisdiction; Territorial Sea
Jurisdiction over foreign vessels
  Contiguous zone, 236–239
  Exclusive economic zone, 415–417
  Internal waters and ports,189–202
    Enlarged port state jurisdiction, 202–206, 417–418
    Peace of port doctrine, 190–196
  Territorial sea, 225–227, 415–417
Jurisdiction to prescribe laws and regulations
  Artificial islands and installations, 292–297
  Cables and pipelines, 319
  Conservation and management of living resources, 261–266
  Exploitation and exploration of continental shelf resources,
    317–323
  Marine scientific research
    Continental shelf, 323–324
    Exclusive economic zone, 288–292

COLLISIONS AT SEA
Duty to render assistance, 37–42
Jurisdiction over, 71–77

COMMISSION ON THE LIMITS OF THE CONTINENTAL SHELF,
  310–317

COMMON HERITAGE PRINCIPLE
See also Deep Seabed
Deep seabed mineral resources, 336–338
Genetic resources, 361–364, 522
Hydrothermal vents, 361–364

CONCILIATION
See Settlement of Disputes

CONFLICTS
See Settlement of Disputes

†